D0301378

# Carolingian
# Essays

# Carolingian Essays

Andrew W. Mellon
Lectures in Early
Christian Studies

**edited by
Uta-Renate Blumenthal**

The Catholic University of America Press
Washington, D.C.

**Library of Congress Cataloging in Publication Data**
Main entry under title:

Carolingian essays.

Contents: Alcuin and the kingdom of heaven / Donald A. Bullough --
Carolingian Biblical studies / John J. Contreni -- Unity and diversity in
Carolingian canon law collections / Roger E. Reynolds -- [etc.]
1. Theology--Middle Ages, 600-1500--Addresses, essays, lectures. I.
Blumenthal, Uta-Renate, 1935-
BT26.C37   1983   230'.14   82-14562
ISBN 0-8132-0579-4

# Table of Contents

Introduction     vii

Alcuin and the Kingdom of Heaven: Liturgy, Theology,
and the Carolingian Age
*Donald A. Bullough*     1

Carolingian Biblical Studies
*John J. Contreni*     71

Unity and Diversity in Carolingian Canon Law
Collections: The Case of the *Collectio Hibernensis*
and Its Derivatives
*Roger E. Reynolds*     99

Pseudo-Dionysius, Gregory of Nyssa, and Maximus the
Confessor in the Works of John Scottus Eriugena
*Edouard Jeauneau*     137

The Problem of Speaking about God in John Scottus
Eriugena
*Dominic J. O'Meara*     151

Carolingian Baptismal Expositions: A Handlist of
Tracts and Manuscripts
*Susan A. Keefe*     169

List of Contributors     239

Index of Names     241

Index of Manuscripts     247

# Introduction

The majority of the essays which are published in this volume were first presented as Andrew W. Mellon Lectures in Early Christian Studies at the Catholic University of America. All of them illustrate various aspects and results of the Carolingian effort to revive learning in the Frankish empire from the time of Charlemagne (768–814) to Charles the Bald (840–877). It is well known that the period was a critical juncture in the history of the transmission and, of course, modification of the intellectual inheritance from Christian antiquity. Few would quarrel with the claim that it was primarily due to these Carolingian efforts that a shared religion and learned language came to provide intellectual bonds of the strongest kind throughout medieval Europe. These bonds endured and shaped society despite political, economic, and social upheavals.

The beginnings of the Frankish revival of studies — since the mid-nineteenth century often referred to as a renaissance — are so modest and often so obscure that the term "renaissance" can be misleading, although the imitation of even pagan antiquity was clearly evident in the period. But interest in pagan antiquity characterized only part of the educational effort of the Carolingians, and not the most important one. The study of pagan classical authors, not much in evidence before 800, was only incidental to the revival of the study of early Christianity, which was directed towards the elimination of ignorance and superstition among the Franks, who saw themselves as the chosen people of God ever since the baptism of Clovis in the early sixth century. Charlemagne was no dreamer who wished to surround himself with the intellectual splendors of Graeco-Roman antiquity for their own sake, but a practical politician and militarily successful ruler who was imbued with both piety and a deep love of learning. Einhard's deservedly famous description of

Charlemagne's studies bears repeating here, because it is a down-to-earth illustration of the revival of learning: "He [Charles] spoke easily and fluently . . . . He learnt Latin so well that he spoke it as fluently as his own tongue; but he understood Greek better than he could speak it . . . . The emperor spent much time and effort in studying rhetoric, dialectic and especially astrology. He applied himself to mathematics and traced the course of the stars with great attention and care. He also tried to learn to write. With this object in view he used to keep writing-tablets and notebooks under the pillows on his bed, so that he could try his hand at forming letters during his leisure moments; but although he tried very hard, he had begun too late in life and he made little progress."

Under these circumstances, a reference to late eighth-century Aachen as a "new Rome" or a "new Athens" is bound to raise eyebrows even as a poetical term, at least until one recalls the words of Alcuin in a letter of 799 to Charles. These words succinctly reveal the hopes of Charles and his court: "If many imitate your diligence and eagerness, a new Athens might arise in the Frankish empire at Aachen that will surpass all the wisdom of the Academy by its service on behalf of the Lord Jesus Christ. The old Athens shone only through the teaching of Plato and the seven liberal arts; the new Athens, however, enriched by the fullness of the Holy Spirit will surpass all the merits of worldly wisdom."

Historians sometimes deride Carolingian efforts as ineffectual, but such a judgment is an anachronistic distortion which conceals the essential fact that Charlemagne thought of the lack of education as a serious flaw in Frankish society. The steep decline in literary skill in Merovingian Gaul after the time of Gregory of Tours and Venantius Fortunatus is well known, Irish influence and a resurgence of interest in the religious life notwithstanding. Some of the monastic foundations of this period did indeed become enclaves of learning as well—Luxeuil and Corbie were no less influential than Bobbio and eventually St. Gall. Still, apart from a few exceptions (among them is the *Liber scintillarum*) the seventh century as a whole presents a discouraging picture as far as learning is concerned. Nor did matters take a turn for the better before the last two decades of the eighth century, despite the efforts of the Anglo-Saxon St. Boniface. No less a scholar than Paul Lehmann had to conclude that learning and scholarly activity were at their nadir until about 770.

It is not fashionable today to see history in the light of personality. Scholarly endeavors are rather directed towards a description of history from the perspective of the average man and his daily life. This approach has much to recommend it, but it would fail to do justice to a movement such as the Carolingian revival of study, not because the "man in the street" was not involved — at the very least, he was involved indirectly by means of sermon and liturgy, as Rosamond McKitterick has shown recently — but because the intensification of intellectual life in the Carolingian period owed so much to the personal concern of Charlemagne. As John Contreni points out in his essay, "Carolingian Biblical Studies," Charlemagne, his court, and his successors provided an essential ingredient to the revival of study that had been lacking formerly: the consistent support of public authority. Without this support, earlier attempts to reform the script, for instance, had failed to make much headway.

Charlemagne's *Admonitio generalis* of 789 and the epistle *De literis colendis* to Abbot Baugulf of Fulda (780–802), which was also circulated in slightly altered form to other ecclesiastics, are programmatic for the Carolingian effort to create a unified, spiritually harmonious and peaceful, Romano-Christian society that would be conscious of its roots in the age of the Church Fathers. The mandate to Baugulf and others to maintain schools to equip priests and monks for the pedagogical tasks detailed in the *Admonitio generalis* has as its premise the simple statement that "though it is better to do what is right than to know it, knowledge must precede action." Anybody who showed ability to learn and/or teach was to be taught in schools set up in bishoprics and monasteries, for Charles and his advisors had come "to fear lest, as skill in writing was less, wisdom to understand the Sacred Scriptures might be far less than it ought rightly to be . . . . Wherefore we exhort you . . . to vie in learning, so that you may prevail more easily and rightly in penetrating the mysteries of sacred literature . . . ." The schools mentioned in that particular mandate may have been schools exclusively for the clergy, but some indications survive that this was not a matter of principle. The plan of St. Gall, which envisions an internal as well as an external school, is one of these, and even if Notker's anecdotes contain no more than a kernel of truth, they show that there were schools where the elegant and arrogant sons of nobles rubbed shoulders with the diligent and dedicated poor. Charlemagne was surely too realistic as well as too knowledgeable to overvalue such episcopal and monastic schools, but as a realist he did not object to small beginnings. In the end, Charles's determination, support, and last but not least the example which he set with his court achieved a spiritual and intellectual regeneration that was remarkable. The extent of this revival is today — more than a thousand years later — probably most tangible in the manuscripts of the Carolingian period, tellingly demonstrated in several of these essays. Without the parchment treasures of Frankish cathedrals and monasteries, the links between barbarian Europe and the Mediterranean civilization of Greece and Rome would have become very fragile indeed. Carolingian *scriptoria*, and the interest in scholarship that was the reason for their existence, made the survival of this civilization possible when Spain had become part of the Islamic cultural sphere and the centers of Celtic Christianity, with their tradition of ascetic piety and classical learning, were devastated in the Viking invasions.

The papers which are here presented extend in range from the time of Charlemagne to that of his grandson, Charles the Bald. They deal with a variety of subjects: biblical studies, liturgy, philosophy/theology, and canon law — all areas in which Carolingian precedents were significant for later developments. They are still further evidence that textbook descriptions of the Carolingian efforts have to be revised. The strength of older, usually local, traditions and the harmonization of these strands with the Roman tradition which Charlemagne emphasized through the introduction of texts that were to be normative (like the Gregorian Sacramentary, the "authentic" *Regula sancti Benedicti*, or the canonical collection known as *Dionysio-Hadriana*) are very much in evidence in these essays. Centralization, therefore, did not necessarily imply the suppression of regional traditions, and the study of patristic texts did not mean that they were not simply summarized, simplified, and in general adapted to the needs of Frankish society.

UTA-RENATE BLUMENTHAL

# Alcuin and the Kingdom of Heaven:
## Liturgy, Theology, and the Carolingian Age
**Donald A. Bullough**

Writing in the summer of 800 to three fellow toilers in the cause of religious orthodoxy, Alcuin affirmed that it was (he believed) by divine dispensation that he had been called to service in the Frankish kingdom; and he added, a little defensively, that this was "as in my own country a certain very holy man endowed with the spirit of prophecy foretold to be the will of God."[1]

Even in an age more skeptical of prophetic visions and divine intervention, individuals who have apparently been denied a proper exercise of their talents in earlier life have not hesitated to see a belated opportunity as the fulfillment of destiny—just as they have not been averse to a retrospective adjustment of their own and others' past lives to make the pattern clearer or more artistic. The late Sir Winston Churchill did both. In an oft-quoted passage from his account of assuming office in May 1940 he declared: "I felt as if I were walking with destiny, and that all my past life had been a preparation for this hour and for this trial." Ten years previously, writing *My Early Life* to help recoup his financial losses

This is a revised version of an Andrew Mellon Lecture delivered at the Catholic University of America, Washington, D.C., on October 23, 1980. I am deeply grateful to Miss U.-R. Blumenthal who arranged the invitation and bore patiently with the delays in preparing the text for publication. The text incorporates material which was previously used for my Ford Lectures in the University of Oxford in Hilary Term, 1980. I gratefully acknowledge the financial help for visits to libraries given me at various times by the British Academy, the Carnegie Trust and the University of St. Andrews, without which my work on the manuscripts of Alcuin's works would have been impossible.

[1] MGH Epp. 4 (ed. Dümmler), no. 200, p. 332.

in the Great Crash, he claimed that he set sail from England to report the South African War "on October 11th [1899], the day of the expiry of the Boer ultimatum" and the firing of the first shots, when in fact he left — as he correctly recorded at the time — on the regular Saturday boat three days later. Alcuin's letter, like Churchill's claims, may nonetheless faithfully reflect a belief governing his actions at the time of writing.

Alcuin's first "biographer," an anonymous Ferrières monk writing not later than 829 but perhaps not much earlier than that year, was able to make extensive use of the reminiscences (collected over a number of years) of his *discipuli*, who in some cases were reporting what they had heard from the master himself.[2] The monk of Ferrières gives no special prominence to the rebuttal of Adoptionism, a question which will be discussed repeatedly in the course of this paper, for it is mentioned only once, in chapter ten (in the modern chapter divisions of the *Vita Alcuini*), which is concerned very largely with the synod of Aachen in ?799.[3] By contrast the *Vita* — unlike other early medieval *Lives* which offer considerable biographical detail, such as Jonas's *Vita Columbani* and Eddius's *Vita Wilfridi* — is convincingly detailed in its references to Alcuin's writings and generous, even lavish, in its account of his liturgical observances. Alcuin and liturgical practice shall concern us first, then. Almost every phase of the "biography" has its liturgical illustration: the Ascension Day antiphon associated with the dying Bede and wrongly credited to him as an original composition, although quoted in its standard ninth-century form and not in the slightly variant version of Cuthbert's *Epistola de obitu Bedae*;[4] Alcuin's observance as a little boy of the daytime "canonical hours" but very rare attendance at the night-hour which all *clerici* attended; the common observance of compline when he was an

---

[2] *Vita Alcuini*, ed. W. Arndt, MGH Scr. (in-fol.) 15/1:182–197. The "lost" Rheims MS used by Mabillon for his edition in fact exists as Rheims Bib. mun. MS 1395 (s. IX med., Rheims) fols. 89–113v. In my contribution to the XXa Settimana di Studio del Centro Italiano di Studi sull'alto Medioevo, 1972: *I problemi dell'Occidente nel secolo VIII* (Spoleto, 1973), pp. 577–580, I argued strongly for taking the *Vita* more seriously than has usually been the case as a documented "Biography" of a major Carolingian figure. I would now qualify the argument at some points, but I still hold to the basic approach I adopted in 1972.

[3] Ed. Arndt, p. 190f. The fullest and most recent discussion of the dating of the Synod, concluding for 799 (probably second half of May), is that of W. Heil, *Alkuinstudien*, 1 (Düsseldorf, 1970), especially pp. 20–54. But C. J. B. Gaskoin, *Alcuin: His Life and Work* (London, 1904; repr. New York, 1966), pp. 259–264 is still very much to the point.

[4] In *Bede's Ecclesiastical History of the English People*, ed. B. Colgrave and R. A. B. Mynors (Oxford, 1969), p. 582, with *O rex gloriose* where the standard later form was *O rex gloriae*. It is apparent nonetheless that a text of the *De obitu* was the *Vita*-author's source.

"adolescent" under Archbishop Egbert of York; Alcuin's insistence that his pupils should conduct themselves properly in public worship; the arrangement of what we call "votive masses" for ordinary weekdays and his own participation *levitice* (sc. as deacon) in a private mass on Sundays before the conventual mass, when abbot of St. Martin's, Tours; and the antiphon and verses which he recited at Vespers on his own deathbed.[5]

The prominence given to such matters is not merely a reflection of the personal liturgical and musical interests of the biographer's principal informant, Sigwulf, but of Alcuin's own interests — as we know from other sources. One of the most unexpected rephrasings of Bede's *Ecclesiastical History* in Alcuin's York poem is when the historian's

> confluebant ad audiendum verbum populi gaudentes

in the churches built by the Northumbrian king Oswald, becomes the poet's

> Christicolasque greges duxit devotus in illa
> Ut fierent domino laudes sine fine canentum.[6]

Some ten or more years after he had composed these lines, Alcuin was writing to Abbot Rado and the community of St. Vaast at Arras, for whom he had previously prepared an "improved" version of the Life of its founder. He had, he said, "(since your abbot's and your own precious affection requested it) composed verses for the *tituli* of your several churches and individual altars." The texts survive — twenty-seven separate inscriptions plus the dedicatory distich. The letter continues: "I have also taken some masses from *our* missal, for your use in the customary daily offices of the Church," which Alcuin then specifies. He concludes with the comment that "you may well have something like these already written in your sacramentaries and in daily use; however, lest I fail in the service of your love, I have written what we use and which I thought would prove helpful to you." A year or two later a similar list and letter accompanied "a little missal" (*cartula missalis*) compiled for the monks of Fulda in the hope that it would help them heal some of their internal differences.[7]

The Ferrières author of the *Vita* was not the only writer in the generation after Alcuin to be impressed by "Alcuin the liturgist." The deeply learned

---

[5]Caps. 4, 2, 5, 23, 24, 25.

[6]Bede, *Hist. eccl.*, 3.3 (ed. cit., p. 220); Alcuin, *The Bishops, Kings and Saints of York*, ed. P. Godman (Oxford, 1982), lines 282–283.

[7]MGH Epp. 4, no. 74; id., Poet. 1 (ed. Dümmler), pp. 308–312 (no. 88), with the more complete manuscript evidence reported by J. Lestocquoy in *Bull. de la Comm. départmentale des Monuments hist. du Pas-de-Calais*, n.s. 7 (1941), 54–59; id., Epp. 4, no. 250.

and technically accomplished Amalarius of Metz could not fail to be conscious of the criticisms that were directed against both his excessive allegorizing of the ceremonies of mass and office and his apparent innovations in the services of the Imperial Chapel and his cathedral churches; but he knew one compelling defense — that what he did was on the authority of Alcuin, "the most learned teacher of our whole country." The list of service books in the sacristy of the abbey of St.-Riquier in 831 includes three Gelasian mass books, nineteen Gregorian ones (the familiar and confusing terms making here their first formal appearance), and one

> Missalis Gregorianus et Gelasianus modernis temporibus ab
> Albino ordinatus.[8]

The picture produced by evidence extending over fifty years is full and clear: Alcuin is a liturgical enthusiast, an acknowledged expert and innovator.

Evidence for the forms of liturgical observance and worship in which Alcuin had been brought up at York, other than the retrospective indications of the *Vita*, is by contrast shadowy and uncertain. Even if we had direct knowledge of the shape of the liturgy introduced by the Romanizing Wilfrid and by John the Arch-chanter, when he was effectively "visiting professor" in Northumbria in 679/80, we would be unwise to assume that it was being maintained in every detail fifty, sixty, seventy years later; and indeed the much-quoted passage in Egbert's *Dialogue* which stresses the "Roman" origin of York's missal and antiphonary indicates, in my view, rather the contrary.[9] Nevertheless there is the complementary evidence, although still in a sense retrospective, of the liturgical citations in Alcuin's earliest florilegium, the strangely neglected and incompletely published *De laude Dei.*[10]

---

[8]*Amalarii episcopi opera liturgica omnia*, ed. J. M. Hanssens, 3, Studi e Testi 140 (Vatican City, 1950), pp. 94, 99; catalogue of 831 transmitted by Hariulf, *Chronique de l'abbaye de St.-Riquier* 3.3, ed. F. Lot (Paris, 1894), p. 93.

[9]Compare my comments in "Roman Books and Carolingian Renovatio," in *Renaissance and Renewal in Christian History*, ed. D. Baker, Studies in Church History 14 (Oxford, 1977), pp. 30-32.

[10]The presence of this florilegium in Bamberg, Stadtbibl., MS Misc. Patr. 17/B. II. 10 fols. 133-161ᵛ of s. X *ex* was first effectively made known by K. Strecker in his introduction to MGH Poet. 4, fasc. 2, pp. 452-454 who in id., pp. 943-962 published the *Miracula (et Hymnus) Nynie episcopi* which are its final section or — as I believe — were added to it. The title and "authorship" are provided by the incipit of the first of the four books: *Liber primus de laude Dei et de confessione orationibusque sanctorum collectus ab Alchonio* [sic] *levita*. The fullest analysis of the contents, with editions of certain portions including the *De antiphonario* (below) in its entirety, is that of Radu Constantinescu, "Alcuin et les 'Libelli precum' de l'époque carolingienne," *Revue de l'histoire de la spiritualité* 50 (1974), 17-56.

The most remarkable section is certainly the one *De antiphonario* — for it carries back the history of some "chants" a full century and provides a documentation, albeit highly selective, for the liturgy of a northern European church which is without parallel in the pre-Carolingian period. The extracts include a unique antiphon from the Christmas Eve or Christmas Day office which (it has been suggested) reflect Rome's anti-Monothelite stand in the time of Wilfrid and John. There are also two responsories from Vespers at the same season which are from a group quoted by Amalarius in an appendix to his *De ordine antiphonarii* as ones he had noted in "the old Roman antiphoner" although they were not sung in Francia.[11] The Nocturns at "cock-crow" (Matins) which are linked in the *Vita* with a vividly recalled episode in Alcuin's boyhood had long been part of the observance of every cathedral church. Compline, on the other hand, originated as a distinctively monastic service and may have remained such throughout the sixth and seventh centuries: one of the earliest records — indeed perhaps *the* earliest — of its celebration in a cathedral served by seculars would, if the *Vita*-author had been reliably informed, be at Egbert's York. Two or three of the extracts in the *De laude* further suggest that in Alcuin's lifetime the full canonical hours were celebrated there.[12]

When the young Sigwulf, Alcuin's future intimate companion, was sent to Rome and Metz in the 760s to study the ordering of services and "chant," he would certainly have returned with new texts and melodies. Notker of St. Gallen has a plausibly circumstantial account of the introduction into the Latin Office of a distinctive set of antiphons sung at Lauds on the Octave of the Epiphany: clerics accompanying a legation from Constantinople to the Frankish court, apparently in 802, had sung them in Greek and had so delighted Charles (who was listening in secret) that he insisted on their immediate translation into Latin while retaining — we are to infer — their original melodies. Liturgiologists and musicologists have

---

My debt to Father Constantinescu's partial edition and comments is very great, although I find myself often in disagreement with his interpretations. The existence of a second manuscript of the *De laude*, less the *Miracula Nynie*, Escorial MS b-IV-17 fols. 93–108, apparently written in southern France in the mid-ninth century, was brought to my attention by Mr. David Ganz (Oxford and St. Andrews, now Chapel Hill). A complete edition, based on both manuscripts, with commentary is in preparation.

[11]Constantinescu, pp. 42 (no. 32), 52–55; *Amalarii opera*, 3:108.

[12]*Vita Alcuini*, cc. 2, 5; P. Salmon, *L'Office divin au Moyen Age* (Paris, 1959), pp. 86ff., 205f.; Constantinescu, pp. 39 (no. 6), 43, 45, 46. Note that I regard the York cathedral community of which Alcuin was a member as one of clerks, not monks.

found good grounds for accepting Notker's words literally. There have, however, been skeptics; and I am firmly among them. Those who have argued for the truth of the story have unfortunately relied on an interpolated text of Notker, which alone names the first antiphon (*Veterem hominem*) and the achievement of "one [Latin] syllable to one note." The context and authentic wording of the passage in the *Gesta Karoli* make it difficult to regard it as a record of historical fact: it is rather an illustrative anecdote *ben trovato* — court clerics who are so clever that they can produce singable translations from the Greek without proper warning and before breakfast. The second antiphon in the set, *Te qui in spiritu et igne purificas humana contagia, Deum et redemptorem omnes glorificamus*, figures already in the *De laude* where there is no reason to suppose interpolation. The eighth-century Greek background of these antiphons — textually, less certainly musically — seems nonetheless established. They will therefore have been adopted in Rome in the middle years of the century and been transmitted from there to York, although whether directly or indirectly (as via Metz) and whether through the instrumentality of Sigwulf there is no means of knowing.[13]

The ten Rogation antiphons leading up to Ascension Day, which form a distinct group in the *De antiphonario* section of Alcuin's florilegium, belong to an earlier phase of Gallican influence: unlike most of the other texts here, the Northumbrian church's familiarity with them is independently recorded by Bede. (The antiphon for the Magnificat on Ascension Day, *O rex gloriae*, which Alcuin gives next is the one which Bede is recorded as singing on his deathbed.)[14] The language of a few of the extracts, seemingly without close parallels in later Frankish and English

---

[13] *Vita Alcuini*, c. 8; Notker, *Gesta Karoli Magni Imperatoris*, ed. H. F. Haefele, Scr. rer. Germ., n.s. 12 (Berlin, 1962), 2.7; J. Lemarié, "Les antiennes 'Veterem Hominem' du jour octave de l'Epiphanie et les antiennes d'origine grecque de l'Epiphanie," *Ephemerides liturgicae* 72 (1958), 3–38; O. Strunk, "The Latin Antiphons for the Octave of the Epiphany," Recueil des travaux de l'Institut d'Etudes Byzantines de Belgrade 8 (1964; Mélanges G. Ostrogorsky 2), pp. 417–426; Constantinescu, pp. 44 (no. 46 and note 104, with further bibliography), 52. Both Strunk, who expressed reservations, and Constantinescu who accepts the evidence of the *De laude* against Notker, failed to recognize the implications of Professor Haefele's major "correction" of Pertz's and Jaffé's text at this point.

[14] Constantinescu, pp. 47f., nos. 66–76 (where, however, no. 67 is properly the final clause of no. 66, Alcuin's wording being precisely that of the St. Denis antiphoner, BN MS lat. 17296 [s. XII]). See R. J. Hesbert, *Corpus antiphonalii officii,* 3 (Rome, 1968), no. 2237; Bede, *Hist. eccles.* 1.25, reporting the tradition that Augustine and his companions sang *Deprecamur te* (Constantinescu, no. 70) as they approached Canterbury — which can hardly be regarded as historical although editors and commentators have treated it as such; *Ep. de obitu Bedae* cit. (n. 4).

liturgical books, points uncertainly to Spain.[15] A distinctive section of the *De laude* brings together no less than ten "'O' Antiphons," i.e., those which provided the setting for the Magnificat at Vespers during the last days of Advent. Eight of the ten are reported by Amalarius, although in a different order, and figure also in the late ninth-century "Antiphonary of Compiègne." The ninth, *O Hierusalem civitas Dei summi*, is one of an additional group (sometimes called the "Monastic 'Os'")for which there has hitherto been no direct documentation earlier than the St. Gallen "Hartker Antiphonary" of ca. 1000, although (?Midland) English familiarity with it in the late ninth century or earlier is established by its having inspired the third of the vernacular "Advent lyrics." The tenth, *O, Joseph, quomodo credidisti quod antea expavisti*, etc., is particularly noteworthy. No such antiphon has been noted elsewhere; but its existence was postulated long ago to account for the very distinctive "Advent Lyric 7."[16] Alcuin's York and an unidentified English church somewhat later, it seems, were familiar with a set of antiphons which does not correspond exactly to that of any Continental book of Carolingian or post-Carolingian date.[17]

Perhaps the most remarkable, certainly the most puzzling group of texts in the *De antiphonario* is the final one of fourteen (out of a total of ninety-three) devoted to the Virgin Mary. Because Alcuin seems generally to have followed the order of the liturgical calendar, Father Constantinescu has supposed that it was derived in its entirety from the Office of the Feast of the Assumption (August 15).[18] The objections are obvious. None of Alcuin's passages occurs in precisely the same form in any known antiphonary and only two are partially paralleled (one, indeed, only in a single manuscript). One is loosely linked with the language of the Preface for the Mass of the Assumption; another, whose language is rather that of later Carolingian texts, would seem more at home

---

[15]Constantinescu, p. 38, n. 66 and passim, adopting from E. Bishop, *Liturgica historica* (Oxford, 1918), pp. 165–202 the notion of "Spanish symptoms." See further the Marian section considered below.

[16]Constantinescu, pp. 40f. (nos. 18–27); Amalarius, *De ord. ant.* 13, *Opera omnia*, ed. Hanssens, 3:44–49; J. J. Campbell, *The Advent Lyrics of the Exeter Book* (Princeton, N.J., 1959), pp. 8, 50, 85 (for Lyric 3 and its source); id., pp. 58–60, 91–93 (for Lyric 7, doubting an antiphonal source or inspiration).

[17]Another indication of the variable collections used by English and other churches in the eighth and ninth centuries is Lyric 10, whose source has been found in the so far unique antiphon with which Ivrea Bib. cap. 106 (s. XI) concludes the series: CAO 1, sec. 16, iii, no. 4012, with S. Tugwell in *Medium Aevum* 39 (1970), 34.

[18]Constantinescu, pp. 49–51.

in a litany. For the striking *benedicta imperatrix et gloriosa castitatis regina* I know of nothing strictly comparable until more than two centuries later. Moreover, after the first text in the group, *Porta facta coeli, virgo Maria facta est filia Dei,* the emphasis is on the ever-virginity of Mary and her motherhood of God. Father Constantinescu supposed a Spanish origin, or at least a Spanish background and inspiration, which is not implausible; but the hypothesis rests essentially on not very close parallels in writings attributed to Bishop Ildefonsus of Toledo which other scholars regard as ninth-century or Italian![19] The liturgical or other source of this section of the florilegium is, I believe, yet to be discovered; but its mere presence there points to a well-developed and largely unsuspected cult of the Virgin, with an unmistakable doctrinal basis, in the northern English church in which Alcuin spent his adolescence and early manhood. There is, indeed, one tiny piece of supporting evidence: Archbishop Eanbald II's succession in 796 was apparently not free from controversy; and when the pallium had been received from Rome, he chose as the day for his solemn confirmation in his office Friday, September 8 (797), the Nativity of the Blessed Virgin Mary.[20] If the texts were not drawn in their entirety from an imported book or books, they may indicate that the *cantores, lectores* or bishops of eighth-century York were more capable of composing syntactically sound and even elegant liturgical formulae than Mr. Hohler, for one, would allow.

Immediately preceding the extracts from the Antiphoner in the *De laude* Alcuin had transcribed a full text of the so-called "Niceno-Constantinopolitan" version of the Creed — that touchstone of orthodox belief since the Councils of Constantinople and Chalcedon, to which he

---

[19]CAO 1, sec. 106; *Missale Gothicum,* ed. H. M. Bannister (Henry Bradshaw Soc., 1917-1919), 1.30-31 where the opening words of the *collectio post nomina* seem to provide the only parallel to "vero virginali hospicio coelo" in Constantinescu, no. 83; *Tenth-Century Studies,* ed. D. Parsons (London and Chichester, 1975), pp. 35-36, 214; L. Scheffczyk, *Das Mariengeheimnis in Frömmigkeit u. Lehre der Karolingerzeit,* Erfurter Theologische Studien 5 (Leipzig, 1959), esp. pp. 33-35 (arguing that in the early Carolingian period "die Liturgie das gläubige Denken angeregt u. beeinflusst hat"), 152-155, 251-253.

[20]"Northern Annals" preserved in '*Symeonis monachi' historia regum,* ed. T. Arnold, *Symeonis opera omnia,* 2 (Rolls Series, 1885), p. 58: the two hexameter lines which "illustrate" the Feast are, however, probably additions by the tenth/eleventh-century Byrhtferth. The direction in which future search for the liturgical sources of the passages in the *De laude* should proceed is perhaps indicated by the texts analyzed in Dom B. Capelle's "La Messe Gallicane de l'Assomption: son rayonnement, ses sources," in *Miscellanea Mohlberg,* 2 (1949), pp. 33-59; Capelle, *Travaux liturgiques de doctrine et d'histoire,* 3 (Louvain, 1967), pp. 430-455, cf. idem, 276ff.

was to revert frequently in his polemics with the Adoptionists. Translated from the original Greek, it had at a surprisingly early date been adopted in Rome itself as the *symbolum* used at baptism, and as the summary of the essential articles of the faith used in the catechetical instruction of the young and the newly converted: the deacon Alcuin would therefore have rehearsed it frequently since the 760s. Its position in his florilegium, immediately after a *carmen Augustini*, which turns out to be the familiar *Gloria in excelsis* and is preceded by extracts from Augustine on the Trinity, offers at best qualified support to a now widely cherished belief; namely, that it was because Alcuin's York had sung the Creed in the Mass (after the Gospel), in imitation of previous Irish practice, that the Carolingian royal chapel began to do the same—and subsequently received papal approval for the novelty—in the last years of the century.[21]

Great weight was laid by Dom Capelle (who developed the theory) on the fact that Alcuin in his writings seems to quote the Creed in the precise version of the Irish "Stowe Missal," which is the earliest direct evidence of the practice of including it in the Mass anywhere in the West outside Spain. The differences between the *De laude* and the Stowe texts, although few and small, cannot however be ignored.[22] Nor can we base any argument on the presence of the *Gloria in excelsis*, here with the more usual title of *imnus angelicus*, also among the preliminary matter of the Stowe Missal. The late seventh-century Antiphonary of Bangor shows that at the period the Gloria was sung in Ireland (or in one part of Ireland) in the office, as in the East and parts of the West: it had been introduced

---

[21]Constantinescu, pp. 36–38. For the singing of the Creed and the part played by Alcuin see especially B. Capelle, "Alcuin et l'histoire du symbole de la messe," *Rech. de théologie ancienne et médiévale* 6 (1934), 249–260; id., "L'introduction au symbole à la messe," *Mélanges Joseph de Ghellinck* (Gembloux, 1951), pp. 1003–1027 = Capelle, *Travaux*, 3:60–81. Cf. L. Wallach, *Alcuin and Charlemagne* (Cornell University Press, 1959), pp. 152–154 who surprisingly supposes that the profession of faith in the letter to Elipand of Toledo, MGH Concilia 2, ed. A. Werminghoff, pp. 163–164 (which he convincingly attributes to Alcuin) was "the *Symbolum* used in the liturgy of the Mass at the royal collegiate (!) church at Aix-la-Chapelle" until 798, although it is manifestly not a liturgical Creed.

[22]Compare Constantinescu, pp. 36–38 with *The Stowe Missal*, ed. G. F. Warner, Henry Bradshaw Soc. 32 (1906), 2.8. The most noteworthy departures of the *De laude* text (Al.) from the Stowe text (S.)—not all in Constantinescu's apparatus, p. 37f.—are: *in unum dominum nostrum Iesum Christum* S., om. *nostrum* Al., om. *unum dominum nostrum* Alcuin, *Adv. Felicem* 1.9 (PL 101:134); *natum ex patre* S., *ex patre natum* Al. (but apparently always *natum ex patre* in Alcuin's later writings); *crucifixus autem* S., *crucifixus etiam* Al.; *passus et sepultus* S., *passus et sepultus est* Al.; *sanctam aecclesiam catholicam et apostolicam* S., *sanctam catholicam et apostolicam ecclesiam* Al.,; *unum babtismum* S., *unum baptisma* Al.: there are others.

into the Mass at Rome ca. 500, but for several centuries thereafter was to be sung by ordinary priests only on Easter Day and at their first mass after ordination. Alcuin's text in the *De laude* is significantly different from the two early Irish versions, although surprisingly close to that in a late hymnal.[23] It is still too commonly assumed (although not, any longer, by the best-qualified art historians and paleographers) that the normal direction of influence even in the late eighth century was from Ireland to northern England. Alcuin's and the Northern Annalist's contacts with "Mayo of the English" suggest one of the channels by which influence may often have run in the opposite direction.[24]

A continuing Irish strain in northern English piety — renourished from time to time by the travels of men and books — is however clearly evident in the collections of prayers and devotions, such as the "Book of Cerne" with its seventh/early eighth-century nucleus and subsequent accretions, of which the *De laude* is a more organized and personal variation. Edmund Bishop used them to point the contrast between the Celt who "by excess of words and sometimes by extravagance of form brings us easily and soon within the verge of unreality" and the Roman "who has the right sense, the right mind but leaves us cold as marble." The contrast may be accepted — provided we remember that both regarded their chosen forms of language as the most appropriate way of addressing their Maker personally and directly.[25]

[23] *Stowe Missal*, 2.4; *Antiphonary of Bangor*, ed. F. E. Warren, 2, Henry Bradshaw Soc. 10 (1895), pp. 31, 75ff.; L. Duchesne, *Christian Worship: Its Origin and Evolution*, 5th Engl. ed. (London, 1919), p. 166. The most substantial divergences of the *De laude* text from those in *S[towe]* and *B[angor]* are: *propter magnam gloriam tuam* for *pro* (so S.; *propter* in B.) *magnam mis(s)ericordiam tuam*; the omission of *sancte spiritus Dei, et omnes dicimus "Amen"*; and the final clauses *Quoniam tu solus sanctus, tu solus dominus, tu solus altissimus* (S., B.: *gloriosus*) *Ihesu Christe* (S., B. omit), etc. At all three points the *Lebar Brecc* (s. XIV) has a text identical with Alcuin's: see the convenient tabulation in *Antiphonary of Bangor*, 2:76ff.

[24] Compare N. K. Chadwick, "Bede, St. Colmán and the Irish Abbey of Mayo," in *Celt and Saxon*, ed. N. K. Chadwick (Cambridge, 1963), pp. 186–205. But for Bishop Ecgberht (d. 729) as a link between Ireland, Iona and the Northumbrian church see now A. A. M. Duncan's remarkable if occasionally over-ingenious analysis of the evidence, "Bede, Iona and the Picts," in *The Writing of History in the Middle Ages: Essays Presented to R. W. Southern*, ed. R. H. C. Davis and J. M. Wallace-Hadrill (Oxford, 1981), pp. 1–42, esp. pp. 20ff.

[25] *The Prayer Book of Aedeluald the Bishop, Commonly Called The Book of Cerne*, ed. A. B. Kuypers (Cambridge, 1902), of which pages 234–283 are E. Bishop's fundamental "Liturgical Note": Bishop, *Liturgica historica* (Oxford, 1918), pp. 384–391, the quotation from p. 385. See also K. Hughes, "Some Aspects of Irish Influence on Early English Private Prayer," *Studia Celtica* 5 (1970), 48–61.

The mingling of the two traditions can take unexpected forms, as we learn from the fragments of the only two calendars and sacramentaries whose Northumbrian origins, respectively in the second quarter and second half of the eighth century, are not in dispute. The former is the earliest with a feast of "S. Elijah," which points to Ireland (although Bede also included it in his martyrology) and has other distinctive features which reappear in later English liturgical manuscripts but are unknown elsewhere—notably, the Feast of St. Mark on 18 May. The later of the sacramentaries is the one per-sistently but wrongly associated with St. Boniface (the most recent attempt to defend the connection manages to transfer Nursling to Northumbria!). The affinities of the long-known fragments with parts of the sacramentary type that we (and presumably the St.-Riquier cataloguer) call "Gelasian"—the *sanctorale* of which seems likewise reflected in Bede's *Martyrology*—are generally acknowledged. Additional fragments discovered recently include a substantial portion of the canon of the Mass: characteristic formulae reveal it as essentially the pre-Gregorian (perhaps genuinely Gelasian) ver-sion of the canon, of which the Stowe Missal is a major testimony and with which indeed it shares some distinctive readings.[26]

---

[26](a) Munich, Hauptstaatsarchiv Raritäten-Selekt no. 108 (*Codices Latini antiquiores: A Paleographical Guide to Latin Manuscripts Prior to the Ninth Century,* ed. E. A. Lowe [Ox-ford, 1934-], 1236; hereafter cited as *CLA*): lost since 1945 but published with commentary by R. Bauerreiss, "Ein angelsächsisches Kalendarfragment . . . ," *Studien u. Mitteilungen O.S.B.* 51 (1933), 177–182, the text on 178–179; for *nt. sci. Helisei prophetae* at 14 June compare R. Kottje, *Studien zum Einfluss des alten Testamentes auf Recht u. Liturgie des frühen Mittelalters,* Bonner Hist. Forsch. 23, ed. 2 (Bonn, 1970); for Mark at 18 May, for which this is the earliest evidence and the "Metrical Calendar (al. Martyrology) of York," ed. Wilmart in *Revue bénédic-tine* 46 (1934), 66—which brings us very close to Alcuin—is the next earliest, cf. Bullough, "Roman Books," p. 32, note, and the references given there. (b) Berlin, Deutsche Staatsbibl. Lat. fol. 877 + Regensburg, Walderdorff Samml. (*CLA* 1052) + Regensburg, Bischöflichen Zen-tralbibl. Clm 1: the first two portions ed. by P. Siffrin in *Missale Francorum,* ed. L. Mohlberg et al. (Rome, 1957), pp. 79–83, the third by K. Gamber, *Sakramentarstudien,* Studia Patristica et Liturgica 7 (Regensburg, 1978), pp. 78–81.

For the affinities of the canon see Gamber, pp. 81–100 (broadly acceptable), for the ascription of Boniface's "Heimatkloster Nhutscelle" to Northumbria see id., p. 69 (manifestly unaccep-table). This is not the place to argue general problems of liturgical history. However, in the light of (i) the texts described under (a) and (b); (ii) the character of the *orationes matutinae et vesper-tinae* in the fragment London, BL Add. 37518 fols. 116–117 (*CLA* 176: but S. English of s. VIII[1] according to Bischoff); (iii) E. Bishop's declared conviction, after detailed analysis of the language of the prayers in the "Book of Cerne," that "As regards Roman material there is no suf-ficient ground for assuming that the writers used or knew any other book than *Gelas.* . . . the resemblances [being] distributed over *Gelas.* as a whole" (*Book of Cerne,* p. 283); (iv) Dom Quentin's demonstration that Bede's Martyrology, in its authentic form, was not influenced by the Kalendar *(Sanctorale)* of a Gregorian sacramentary (*Les Martyrologes historiques du Moyen*

For so many questions we would like to raise about York's liturgy in the eighth century, the *De laude* has no answers to offer. Its character, moreover, seems not to be compatible with inclusion of any truly independent composition by Alcuin himself. Apart, however, from being the earliest evidence of Alcuin's interest and skill in selecting from a wide range of reading and hearing, it throws some light on the way in which he treated nonbiblical materials to serve his clearly defined purpose: the petitions of saints, extracted from their *acta*, are adapted just enough to eliminate any reference to the supposed context in which they were first offered and to make them suitable for use by an ordinary sinner.[27] A similar technique had earlier been used — by whom and where are unknown, but possibly in Spain — to adapt texts which circulated in the early medieval West under the name of "Ephraem the Deacon" to create *orationes* which figure in a number of eighth- and ninth-century manuscripts, including the "Book of Cerne," sometimes with but often without an ascription to "sanctus Effrem(us) diaconus."[28]

The *Orationes sancti Effrem diaconi* which figure in the earliest Tours prayer book (now Troyes Bibl. munic. MS 1742) of ca. 805 and, without the initial prayer and the attribution to Ephraem, in later collections

---

*Age* [Paris, 1908], p. 684 et passim), it seems to me perverse to doubt that the sacramentaries used in English churches in the late seventh and for much of the eighth century were of a type close to although by no means identical with the "Gelasian" Sacramentary in Vat. Reg. Lat. 316 (for some of the qualification, cf. my "Roman Books," p. 31f. and add that the *disposition* of the prayers in BL Add. 37518 is not that of Reg. Lat. 316): and the admittedly eccentric view of C. Hohler (*Tenth-Century Studies*, p. 61) that the Vatican Gelasian "represent[s] an assemblage of Roman materials put together with a view to use in England in the seventh century" demands at least to be discussed, even if refuted.

[27]A particularly good example is the petition *Deus dilecti et benedicti filii tui Ihesu Christi Pater per quem tui agnitionem suscipimus*, with the rubric in the *De laude* MSS: *Policarpus de Historia ecclesiastica*, sc., from Rufinus, *Historia ecclesiastica* 4.33-34 (as Constantinescu, p. 24, was the first to recognize). For the later MS history of this prayer cf. n. 30.

[28]*Book of Cerne*, prayers 21, 24, 49, 50, with pp. xvii–xviii (Kuypers), 278–280 (Bishop). The best *mise au point* of the complicated history of the *Ephraemus latinus* is that of D. Hemmerdinger-Iliadou, with J. Kirchmeyer, in *Dictionnaire de spiritualité*, 4/1 (1960), cc. 815–819, although a proper listing of the MSS is still lacking. (London BL MS Harl. 3060, which Bishop cit. regarded as of particular importance, is a ?French MS of s. X²: but on the evidence of its other contents it may nonetheless be a direct copy of a "Visigothic" manuscript.) That Alcuin knew the Latin *corpus Ephraemi* is highly probable but not conclusively proved: the status or origin of the *sententia sancti Effrem* on the concluding fols. (77–77v.) of Angers Bibl. publ. MS 279 (W. France, ca. 2nd qu. s. IX) of which fols. 1–45 are Alcuin's two trinitarian works, is not clear.

whose contents derive directly or indirectly from Tours, are quite different—as is the *Oratio sancti Effrem diaconi* inc. *Domine Deus et Salvator meus, quare me dereliquisti?* which is already (without ascription) in the "Book of Cerne."[29] The Continental-manuscript contexts of prayers found earlier in Insular manuscripts—whether "Celtic" or "Roman" in Bishop's formulation—leave little doubt that in their wider dissemination Alcuin played a major part, with immeasurable and subtle effect on the hearts and minds of generations of readers.[30] They keep company with others that show Alcuin responding to new opportunities and new stimuli with *preces privatae* that earn him a distinctive place in a tradition which will lead through Anselm to Lancelot Andrews.

An exceptionally handsome Psalter written in the 780s, probably for a member of the Bavarian ducal family, was seemingly acquired by one of the Carolingian family that overthrew it and was subsequently used for devotional purposes in a nunnery, probably Notre-Dame, Soissons. Very early additions to the original manuscript are: the new Vulgate-text "Roman" series of *cantica*, for the organization of which Alcuin *may* have been responsible; a litany with nearly two hundred names and the earliest Carolingian *Laudes* which name Queen Fastrada who died in 794; and a rhythmical prayer for the well-being of a Rotruda who has been thought to be Charlemagne's daughter. Some years later a St. Amand scribe completed the manuscript with a small group of *preces*

[29]Troyes 1742 (W. Köhler, "Turonische Handschriften aus der Zeit Alkuins," *Mittelalterliche Handschriften: Festgabe . . . H. Degering* [Leipzig, 1926] pp. 172ff.): texts in A. Wilmart, *Precum libelli quattuor aevi Karolini* (Rome, 1940), pp. 14–17; later books without Tours-Troyes' initial prayer, inc. *Deus altissime qui solus sine peccato es*, and with some noteworthy variants: the Bavarian *Libellus precum* of ca. 820/30, Orléans Bib. mun. MS 184 (the source of Migne, PL 101:1383ff.: from Martène) pp. 302–306; the Tours *Libellus* of ca. 850, Paris BN lat. 13388 fols. 77v–79v (Wilmart, *Precum libelli*, pp. 140f.); the Beauvais Psalter, Florence Bib. Naz. Cod. Ashb. 54 fols. 147–148v (which I have not seen and rely for the details on H. Barré, *Prières anciennes de l'Occident à la Mère du Sauveur* [Paris, 1963], p. 12); Paris Bib. Nat. lat. MS 2731A fols. 61–63v, which Prof. Bischoff has recently credited to the Rheims-area scribe Framegaudus (s. IX *ex*); and elsewhere. *Domine Deus et Salvator meus: Book of Cerne* prayer 45; Orléans 184, p. 266 (PL 101:1386) and Paris BN lat. 1153 (*Officia per ferias*: St. Denis version) fol. 94 (PL 101:606) both with the title crediting it to *Effrem*.

[30]Note that an expanded version of the Polycarp prayer in the *De laude* occurs in the earliest MS of Alcuin's *libellus manualis*, Cologne Dombibl. cod. 106 (for which see below, n. 41 and p. 69) at fol. 71v: ed. Wilmart, *Precum libelli*, p. 59. According to Constantinescu, p. 25, it also occurs in the Bavarian *Libellus precum* (PL 101:1386), the St. Denis *Officia per ferias* (PL 101:555) and in BN lat. 13388: but I do not find it in any of these places.

*privatae.* The first, with the heading *Oratio sancta* and inc. *Dominator dominus omnipotens qui es trinitas una*, occurs almost simultaneously, with the title *Oratio sancti Gregorii papae*, in the Tours-Troyes prayer book and subsequently in other Tours-connected books. It proclaims its Irish origin, however, with (for example) its succession of petitions to Old Testament "saints" — Abel, Enoch, Noe, and so on — and indeed it is to be found, with the attribution to Pope Gregory, in both "the Book of Cerne" and the (slightly older?) "Book of Nunnaminster." The second prayer, given the heading *Oratio sancti Agustini episcopi* by the St. Amand writer, occurs subsequently in the mid-ninth-century St. Denis version of the pseudo-Alcuinian *Officia per ferias* (BN lat. 1153, the source of the edition copied by Migne).[31] Later in the ninth century another writer entered in two different places in the manuscript — the first under the representation of Christ on fol. 2v — the very distinctive prayer inc. *Domine Iesu Christe rex, virginum integritatis amator, mundo cor meum ab omnibus sagittis.* The same prayer text is found earlier (?820s/830s) in the south German "Fleury prayer book" now at Orléans (Bibl. Mun., MS 184). A variant text of the same prayer occurs in the Tours-Troyes collection written in the opening years of the ninth century, which in spite of its early date seems to me nonetheless the secondary or derived version. In no field except possibly that of historical annals is attribution to an individual on stylistic grounds more hazardous; but language, tone and manuscript context of the two versions argue powerfully for Alcuin as the composer, originally for a nun and perhaps

---

[31]The "Mondsee Psalter," Montpellier, Bibl. de la Fac. de Médecine MS 409 (*CLA* 795): many times described and extracts published, but most completely by F. Unterkircher, *Die Glossen des Psalters von Mondsee*, Spicilegium Friburgense 20 (Freiburg [Schweiz], 1974); a significantly revised codicological and paleographical description in B. Bischoff, *Die Südostdeutschen Schreibschulen u. Bibliotheken in der Karolingerzeit*, 2 (Wiesbaden, 1980), pp. 16–18. The original MS is defective after fol. 330$^v$, fols. 331–346 being substituted for the leaves removed sometime between 788 and 794 (the date for the *laudes* last edited by Unterkircher, p. 512f., therefore) and the prayers being added on the previously blank fols. 345–346 a few years later still. *Dominator dominus omnipotens*: Unterkircher, pp. 513f.; *Cerne*, pp. 103–106, with the variant readings of BL Harl. 2965 fols. 16$^v$–17 in the apparatus; Troyes Bib. mun. 1742 in Wilmart, *Precum libelli*, pp. 11–13, with the inc. *Dominator domine deus omnipotens*, which is also that of Orléans Bib. mun. MS 184, pp. 306–309; and in later collections. *Confiteor tibi domine omnia peccata*: Unterkircher, pp. 514f.; BN lat. 1153 fol. 42 (PL 101:553), with the title *confessio peccatorum post acceptam quietam*; and incompletely elsewhere.

even for a reluctant nun (from Charlemagne's own family or one of his enemies'?), presumably in the 790s.[32]

One prayer for which Alcuin's authorship is beyond reasonable doubt is the exceptionally long *Confessio* with which one section of the Troyes-Tours *libellus manualis* concludes. It figures again with unusual frequency in later prayer books or among the collections of prayers appended to Psalters: in the late ninth-century Angers Psalter and in the Charles the Bald Prayer Book at Munich it is described as "confessio quam Alchuinus composuit Carolo imperatori." The particular combination of private vices and public failings which are the subject of confession (with merciful lack of detail) and for which forgiveness is sought are certainly well suited to Charlemagne; and they remind us that at this level at least candor was not lacking in the relationships between the monarch and his intimates. The standing of the man for whom the *confessio pura* was composed is doubtless the reason why, unlike later adaptations, it contains no indication in its original form that it was to be said to a priest, however much this was in breach of Alcuin's confessional theory, which was the subject of widely circulated letters to the *pueri* of St. Martin's (before—in my view—he was their abbot) and to the monks of Gothia.[33] That Alcuin was prepared to subject himself to the régime he wished to impose on others is suggested by the wording of one of the two prayers recorded in the *Vita*, with its successive references to true

---

[32]Montpellier MS 409, fols. 2v and 331 (redated to IX[2] by Bischoff, op. cit. [n. 30], p. 18); Unterkircher, p. 52 and pl. I: with the readings *mundo cor meum, humilitatem et tranquillitatem patientiae pectori meo*. Orléans MS 184, p. 304, with the readings *munda cor meum, humilitatem et tranquillitatem* [*et* add. 2a manu] *pacientiam pectori meo*; cf. PL 101:1400. The Montpellier text is also that of BN lat. 13388 in Wilmart, *Precum libelli*, p. 140. Troyes MS 1742, fol. 62v: Wilmart, cit., p. 16, with the readings *muni cor nostrum, humilitatem patientiae* [sic] *pectori meo*. For Alcuin's notion of *patientia* (one of the four virtues additional to the cardinal ones) see his *De virtutibus et vitiis* cap. 9, which seems not to be substantially dependent on a preexisting text—unlike the immediately succeeding chapter *De humilitate*: PL 101:619–620.

[33]Troyes, bib. mun. MS 1742 fols. 69v–73: Wilmart, *Precum libelli*, pp. 21–24; then in Cologne Dombibl. MS 106 fols. 62–63, the principal variant readings in Wilmart, cit. *apparat*,; Orléans bib. mun. 184, pp. 329–330: for independent early evidence of authorship see Wilmart, *Rev. bénédictine* 34 (1922), 241, for other MSS, id., *Precum libelli*, p. 21, n. 4. The text in Angers bib. mun., MS 18 fols. 183v–185v (among prayers, some but not all of which are in earlier Tours-related books) has several notable variations from the printed text. Alcuin on Confession: MGH Epp. 4:194–198 (no. 131); id., 216–220 (no. 138), esp. the passages "Cur in secundo poenitentiae baptismate per confessionem humilitatis nostrae ab omnibus post primum baptisma peractis eadem divina miserante gratia sacerdotali similiter auxilio non debemus absolvi peccatis?"; "Si peccata sacerdotibus non sunt prodenda, quare in sacramentario reconciliationis orationes scriptae sunt?; Quomodo sacerdos reconciliet quem peccare non novit?" The main reason for thinking that the first letter was written *before* Alcuin went to St. Martin's as abbot,

confession, the performing of penance and subsequent remission of sins. Characteristically, the biographer asserts that this particular prayer arose out of an exchange between Alcuin and Benedict on the occasion of a visit by the latter.[34]

The *Vita*'s list of Alcuin's exegetical works likewise links most of them with the person or persons for whom and at whose request they had been written. This and the corresponding dedicatory prefaces were not merely exploiting a *topos*: Alcuin, like more than a few scholars in our own time, needed some pressing demand before he put into writing what he had taught and thought about over many years. When he sent his completed *Commentary on the Gospel according to St. John* (which was regarded as a difficult book) to Gisla and Rotruda, sister and daughter of Charlemagne, at Chelles at the beginning of 801 he declared:

> I confess that I had a desire to write this work about thirty
> years ago, but my pen did not stir as there was no one to
> arouse it.

If his memory was not playing him false, this was about the time when Liudger (the future bishop of Münster and abbot of Werden) and his fellow pupils at York were "imbibing *spiritalia dogmata*" from their master Alcuin. The *Vita*, indeed, has an improving story of the effect which a passage in St. John's Gospel had had on Alcuin at an earlier stage in his life, when he was reading, with *his* fellow pupils, to their master Ælbert. Both would have sought to communicate the Christian truths, the Catholic tradition which governed both belief and living, to their pupils in the same way: in a discursive oral comment on a select passage or passages of the Bible, using their own reading in the Fathers — and, where appropriate, pre-Christian didactic works — to extract the fullest possible range of meanings.[35]

---

and therefore in the period 793/4–796/7, is that he addresses himself to "sancti patres, doctores et ductores, ut ammoneatis discipulos *vestros* ut studiose discant." Note that the manuscript evidence for the dissemination of this text is considerably greater than Dümmler indicates: it figures not only in letter collections but also in all the copies or derivatives of the *libellus manualis* for Arno (below, n. 41).

[34] *Vita Alcuini*, c. 14: ed. cit., p. 192.

[35] *Vita Alcuini*, c. 21: ed. cit., pp. 194f.; MGH Epp. 4, no. 214, pp. 357f., which (unlike Alcuin's epp. nos. 195 and 213 and Gisla's and Rotruda's letter *to* him, exhorting him to complete the commentary [Epp. 4, no. 196, pp. 323–325]) does not accompany the Commentary in any MS but is preserved only by the twin St. Denis letter collections, BL Harl. 208 and BN nouv. acq. lat. 1096; Altfrid, *Vita Liudgeri prima*, c. 10: ed. Pertz, MGH Scr. 2:407, ed.

References by Alcuin to his own early reading of the Fathers (sc. at York) are scant but not without interest; unambiguous reflections of that reading in his later writings are hardly more numerous. One of the most revealing is a passage in his *De ratione animae* of 801 or later where Alcuin remarks:

> The blessed Augustine wrote a letter to blessed Jerome about the origin of the soul, wishing to know what that great scholar [*tantus doctor*] might declare on the subject [a notoriously difficult one]. If that book is available to you, read it . . . . Augustine presented, I believe [*ut arbitror*], some four opinions in that discussion and blessed Jerome replied to him in a very brief but most perceptive letter. I read the book in my homeland [*in patria*] but do not have it here, nor the letter written in reply to it.

There is no problem in the identification of the letters. They are ones exchanged between the two scholars in 415/16 which are transmitted together, but separately from any other letter by either Father, in at least one pre-Carolingian manuscript and are also included in a larger collection of letters in eighth/ninth-century manuscripts. Jerome's letter is, in fact, dismissive rather than perceptive; and it is clear from the passage quoted and the context in which it occurs that Alcuin remembered almost nothing of what either scholar had said.[36]

The *De laude* provides convincing evidence of familiarity with at least part of Augustine's *Confessions*, possibly in a manuscript of the family of the Bobbio manuscript Vat. lat. 5756, and with some sections of the

---

Diekamp (Münster i. Westf., 1881), p. 15; *Vita Alcuini,* c. 7: ed. cit., p. 188. For the expository and exegetical tradition to which Alcuin belonged, the most helpful accounts seem to me those of Miss B. Smalley, *The Study of the Bible in the Middle Ages,* 2nd ed. (Oxford, 1952; Notre Dame, Indiana, 1964), pp. 26–36 and P. Meyvaert in *Famulus Christi,* ed. G. Bonner (London, 1976), pp. 44–47, although neither writer is discussing Alcuin.

[36]PL 101:645; *Alcuin, 'De Ratione animae': A Text* . . . , ed. J. J. M. Curry (Ph.D. diss., Cornell University,1966), pp. 58–59. The letters are *Epistolae Augustini,* ed. Goldbacher, CSEL 44 (1904), nos. 166, 172 (*Epistolae Hieronymi,* ed. Hilberg, CSEL 56 [1918], nos. 131, 134). In early MSS this pair of letters is copied together, and with no other letters, in Milan Ambr. 0 210 sup. (*CLA* 358: N. Italy, s. VI) fols. 1–13, successively as part of a larger collection in Paris, BN lat. 12163 (s. IX), and as part of a similar collection with one other letter in between in Escorial & I.14 (*CLA* 1635: Spain s. VIII *ex*): in all three the "address" or title of Augustine's letter ends with the words *De origine animae.* The probability is strong that it was a MS of the first type that Alcuin had read in his York days. The list of Augustine's other works on the soul "qui necdum inventi sunt a nobis" is no less interesting.

*Soliloquia* and the *De Trinitate*. The presence in the "York poem's Library List" of *Victorinus* reminds us of the unexpected discovery that at the end of the century Alcuin—uniquely—had access to and made good use of a complete corpus of Marius Victorinus's writings on the Trinity, whose later manuscript transmission is in two entirely different collections. Moreover, to judge from the part played by Tours in the transmission of the Boethian trinitarian tractates, it is not unlikely that *Boethius* in the same line of the poem was intended to cover some or all of these.[37] More tenuous is the argument for supposing that Jerome's Commentary on Isaiah was known to Alcuin before he left York for Francia: Joseph "the Irishman," a onetime York pupil who followed his master to the Continent, declares in a prefatory letter that it is at Alcuin's command that he has produced a shortened version of the overlong Commentary to the benefit of potential readers; unfortunately we do not know exactly when or where he produced it.[38]

For one patristic commentary used by Alcuin in his last years, there is a possibility of direct access to the source of his knowledge, and of acquiring in the process a guidepost to the York scriptorium. The mid-eighth-century Durham Cathedral manuscript of Cassiodorus *On the Psalms*—best known for its two illustrations—is an abnormal text. It is considerably,

[37]Constantinescu, pp. 31f., listing the many short extracts from the *Confessions* bks. 1–7 in n. 44, where also the textual similarities with Vat. lat. 5756 are noted (but I am not entirely convinced). Note that the direct evidence pre-800 for the text of this work is limited to the Italian MS of s. VI, *CLA* 420 and the fragment also of s. VI, *CLA* 1640 and that the other two works of Augustine are *not* among those to which Bede can be shown to have had access at Wearmouth-Jarrow. Victorinus: *Versus Euboricensis ecclesiae*, ed. Godman (in *The Bishops . . . of York,* cit.), line 1548; P. Hadot, "Marius Victorinus et Alcuin," Archives d'hist. doctrinale et littéraire du Moyen Âge 21 (1954), pp. 5–19; also J. A. Jungmann, "Marius Victorinus in der karolingischen Gebetsliteratur," in *Kyriakon: Festschrift Johannes Quasten*, ed. P. Granfield and J. A. Jungmann, 2 (Münster i. Westf., 1970), pp. 691–697. Boethius: *Versus*, line 1548; M. Gibson in *Boethius*, ed. Gibson (Oxford, 1981), pp. 215f., rightly noting that Alcuin himself never seems to have drawn on the *opuscula sacra* but probably underrating the evidence for familiarity with at least part of the corpus in the circle of Alcuin's pupils at Tours in his lifetime (for this cf. the discussion below of Mr. J. Marenbon's account of the *Dicta de imagine Dei* [*De dignitate conditionis humanae*]).

[38]Dedicatory verses and epilogue: MGH Epp. 4:483–484. (The rest of the text is unpublished—understandably: five manuscript copies are known, of which only BN lat. 12154 preserves the letter-epilogue.) For Joseph's early career, which unfortunately gives no pointers to the date of his commentary, see: Altfrid, *Vita Liudgeri* capp. and 1.19, SS 2: 404, 409, ed. Diekamp, pp. 3, 23; MGH Epp. 3:615–616 of 788; id., 4:32–34; D. Schaller in *Medium Aevum Vivum: Festschrift W. Bulst*, ed. H. R. Jauss and D. Schaller (Heidelberg, 1960), pp. 34ff.

almost ruthlessly, abbreviated: since the normal method of abbreviation is the elimination of long passages in their entirety, the result is sometimes a text which has a degree of coherence and makes a kind of sense although very far from Cassiodorus's sense; but at other times the excisions produce a series of unconnected *obiter*. The Psalter text in the lemmata seems to be essentially Cassiodorus's *Psalterium Romanum* although occasionally modified, so that the subsequent commentary does not always fit![39] The abbreviated Preface of the Durham manuscript has a distinctive conclusion, found otherwise only in two late Psalters: this conveniently lists those Psalms that have a christological significance, foreshadowing the Two Natures in Christ, those that foretell the Passion, and finally "the seven Psalms of Penitence."[40]

The notion that certain of the Psalms had a penitential significance for the Christian reader is already to be found in Augustine; but the first commentator to single out psalms 6, 31, 37, 50, 101, 128 and 142 as being particularly appropriate was Cassiodorus, in the concluding remarks of his comment on each of them. The first person to comment on the *septem psalmi poenitentiae* as a group was Alcuin — as one section of a devotional handbook which was completed and first circulated before the end of 802. The first grouping of those same seven psalms *de penitentia* to form, with prayers, a distinctive private devotional exercise is in the

---

[39]Durham Cath. B II 33 (*CLA* 152), used intermittently (praef.; Pss. 1, 2, 3, 20, 21, 106) by M. Adriaen for his edition *Magni Aurelii Cassiodori expositio psalmorum*, 2 vols., Corpus christianorum 97, 98 (Louvain, 1958): essentially this is based on Paris BN lat. 12239–41 (*CLA* 638, 639, the first volume from an unidentified N. French house, the second and third being early examples of Chelles minuscule: see B. Bischoff, *Mittelalterliche Studien*, 1 [Stuttgart, 1966], pp. 21f.) [*Ger.*]. According to Dom Adriaen, p. xv, the psalter text quoted in the Durham MS [*D.*] "accomodatus est, non psalterio Gallicano ut saepe fit, sed Romano, ita ut non amplius concordet cum commentario." But neither his apparatus nor my collations of other sections justify this view: it seems rather that *D.* frequently preserves the Roman text which Cassiodorus used (cf. Adriaen, p. xix), or alters it slightly in accordance, presumably, with the version in current use in Northumbria — where *Ger.* and other Continental MSS naturally "gallicanize." Thus, at Ps. 3.6 *D.* has *quoniam Dominus suscepit me*, with Ro., as its text-lemma (line 105) and the commentary-lemma (lines 116–117), while *Ger.* has *quia* in the first place and *suscipiet* in the second, both with Ga. At Ps. 21.15 both *D.* and *Ger.* have *Sicut aqua effusa sunt et dispersa sunt ossa mea*: *effusa sunt* is Ro. against Ga.'s *effusus sum*, and Cassiodorus's omission of *omnia* or *universa* before *ossa* is confirmed by the commentary-lemma. At Ps. 31.5, *D.* has *iniustitias meas non operui* which is standard Ro. (against Ga.'s *iniustitiam meam non abscondi*), *Ger.* has *iniustitiam meam non operui*, which is supported by the commentary-lemma; both have *dixi pronuntiabo adversum me iniustitias meas* which is distinctively Ro. And similarly frequently.

[40]*D.* fols. 4v, 5: ed. Adriaen, CC 97:25 (apparatus)–26.

second part of the Tours-Troyes book of ca. 805 or even a little before, of which the first part is a text of his *De virtutibus et vitiis*. The earliest text in which the reciting of those psalms is declared to be of benefit "Si vis pro peccatis tuis poenitentiam agere" ("Et celerrime invenies clementiam Dei") is probably from Alcuin's pen, although the text or texts which follow it in ninth-century or later manuscripts are only intermittently Alcuinian.[41] Alcuin's direct and conscious dependence on Cassiodorus is not restricted to an acceptance of this novel categorization (and one of his rare attributed quotations in a letter). Alcuin's comments on the several verses of the Seven Penitential Psalms are mostly of between ten and thirty (printed) lines, extracted from two or three patristic commentaries. Where, however, they use Cassiodorus—not infrequently to provide the whole or greater part of Alcuin's text—it is the abbreviated text of the Durham manuscript, not the full text, which is their source. Particularly striking in this regard are the Alcuinian comments on Psalms 6.7 and 31.4. Cassiodorus's original comments have already been reduced in the Durham manuscript to a sequence of short sentences. Alcuin eliminates further clauses or sentences, at times to the point of unintelligibility or at least banality; and although he incorporated words of his own to give renewed point to the comment, as when he says of the *spina* in 31.4, "Quid est autem spina quae configitur, *nisi stimulus conscientiae peccatricis*?" he nowhere uses phraseology found only in the "complete Cassiodorus." In passages like these Alcuin shifts the focus of the commentary further from Cassiodorus's original dogmatic emphases—especially on Christology and the doctrine of grace—to his own moral-theological concern with the individual Christian's search for God.[42]

---

[41]Cassiodorus, *Expositio psalmorum*, ed. cit., 1, CC 97:78–79, 282–283, 353, 469–471; 2, CC 98:1190, 1280; Alcuin, *Expositio in psalmos paenitentiales*, PL 100:575–596, which together with the *Exp. in psal. cxviii* and the *Exp. in psal. graduales* (id., 598–638) are the central texts (with a copy of the much earlier letter to the *pueri* of St. Martin's on confession: above, n. 33) of the *manualis libellus* known from a letter copied in the final section of Vienna Nat. bibl. 808 (the 802 dating latterly defended by Bischoff, *Südostdeutsche Schreibschulen*, 2:135; cf. 270) to have been forwarded to Arno in (early?) 802 but of which the earliest of the ten variously incomplete copies is Cologne Dombibl. 106 (written ca. 809, at the Aachen Court?) and latest is the Admont MS (ex-no. 729) now Princeton Univ. MS Garrett 169, this part of s. XII *in*; Troyes Bibl. mun. MS 1742, fols. 75v–80: Wilmart, *Precum libelli*, pp. 27–30; the so-called *De psalmorum usu*, inc. *Si vis*, des. *gratiam perveneris*, PL 101:466–468, cf. J.-B. Molin in *Eph. liturg.* 90 (1976), 117–118; for the authorship see Wilmart in *Rev. bén.* 48 (1936), 262–265, Molin cit., pp. 116–123.

[42]Compare Cassiodorus, *Expositio* in Ps. 6.7, Ps. 31.4, ed. cit., 75f., 277: both drastically abbreviated in *D*. but retaining, in the second place, "spina est enim quae totum corpus

The late and incomparable Professor Lowe was never inclined to locate the scriptorium of the Durham Cassiodorus more precisely than "in a Northumbrian centre," a point unfortunately disregarded in the most recent extended discussion of the illustrated pages. He linked its majuscule script ("by several scribes of different habits") with "one of the hands" in a manuscript of Luke and John now at Cambridge, with a "composite" manuscript of the Sapiential Books (now London BL Egerton 1046) and—more tentatively—with the Berlin-Regensburg Gelasian Sacramentary Fragments. There is apparently no complete collation of the Cambridge Gospels but it seems to be agreed that their text is *not* that of the putative Neapolitan Gospel Book which was the exemplar of this part of *Amiatinus*, of the Lindisfarne Gospels and of the Stonyhurst St. John. A partial collation has been made of the Egerton manuscript, which shows significant differences from the text of the corresponding Old Testament books in *Amiatinus,* although still allowing it to be regarded as "Italo-Northumbrian." Finally, a fragment of the same abbreviated text of Cassiodorus's Psalm Commentary as in the Durham manuscript with a similar page layout and in a related but more careless hand has been recovered from a Werden binding; and Werden was a foundation of Alcuin's early pupil Liudger who was reputed to have taken with him from York *copia librorum.*[43] During the past half-century qualified paleographers have several times attributed surviving manuscripts

---

erigit atque recontinet"; Alcuin in PL 100:577. Note that if *configitur* correctly represents Alcuin's original text, it is the reading of Ga. not Ro. (*confringitur*) at this point but is already found in *D.*, against other MSS of Cassiodorus. For Cassiodorus's exegetical method in the *Expositio* (which, it is worth remembering, "is the only formal commentary on the entire Psalter surviving from the Patristic era") see especially R. Schlieben, *Cassiodors Psalmenexegese* (diss., Tübingen, 1970) which I unfortunately know only in the abbreviated version *Christliche Theologie u. Philologie in der Spätantike*, Arbeiten zur Kirchengesch. 46 (Berlin and New York, 1974): "die dogmatische u. die ethische Unterweisung der Ps." is here the subject of chap. III/2.

[43]*CLA* 152: cf. Lowe, "A Key to Bede's Scriptorium," *Scriptorium* 12 (1958), 185, n. 16 and R. N. Bailey, *The Durham Cassiodorus* (Jarrow Lecture, 1978); *CLA* 138; *CLA* 194a–b; *CLA* 1052 and above, n. 26; (Werden fragment) *CLA* (Suppl.) 1786. For the Gospel text in *CLA* 138 (Cambr. Univ. Libr. Kk.I.24 etc.) see *Novum Testamentum Latine*, ed. J. Wordsworth, H. J. White, 1 (Oxford, 1889), p. xxvii. The sample collation of *CLA* 194 (BL Egerton 1046) is my own: it suggests that the differences from Am. *may* be greater in Prov. than in Eccl.; and note that the significant variant readings in Eg. only intermittently recur in the lemmata of Alcuin's commentary *In Ecclesiasten*, PL 100:667–720, although the former favors (e.g.) the spelling *adoliscentia* which Alcuin later insisted—against the ancient grammarians—was the correct one. The *copia librorum* taken from York are noted in *Vita Liudgeri* c. 12: ed. Pertz, p. 408, ed. Diekamp, p. 19.

to York, only to have their views overtaken by even better-qualified paleographers. For one who makes no pretensions to be in either category, claiming for that city and church yet another group of manuscripts would seem to be the height of recklessness. But on the evidence cited we are surely brought very near to the books that Alcuin had at his disposal during his years as Ælbert's assistant and as *magister* at York.

Even cumulatively, this evidence does not give us any rounded picture of Alcuin's level of intellectual achievement at the time when he was invited to the Carolingian court. We are no better and perhaps not even as well informed about his early years there. His presence is, for example, completely ignored by Paul the Deacon in the several writings which are among the most important sources for the court circle and court learning before 786/7. Only a very few of Alcuin's letters, a group of figure poems and two or three other short verse compositions can be attributed with reasonable confidence to the years before 790—although there is convincing evidence for his intermittent involvement in the court's political activity, at least to the extent of helping to provide a biblical basis for the royal and episcopal correction of the conduct of clergy and laity.[44] It would therefore be a significant addition to our knowledge and understanding of both Alcuin and the court at this time if he was indeed the author—as at least one contemporary seems to have believed and has recently been powerfully argued—of a short but distinctive piece of speculative theology which later acquired a more distinguished but certainly illegitimate parentage.[45]

---

[44]Cf. K. Neff, *Die Gedichte des Paulus Diaconus*, Qu. u. Untersuch, zur lat. Phil. des M.as, 3/4 (Munich, 1908) and MGH Epp. 4:506–509, etc.; D. Schaller, as note 38 ad fin.; Scheibe, "Alcuin u. die *Admonitio Generalis*," *Deutsches Archiv* 14 (1958), 221–229. Scheibe's arguments are dismissed as "unconvincing" by R. McKitterick, *The Frankish Church and the Carolingian Reforms, 789–895* (London, 1977), p. 1, n. 2, but certainly wrongly. They are greatly strengthened by the quotations in non-standard-Vulgate form of, e.g., Exod. 23.8 (but partially conflated with Deut. 16.19) in *Adm. gen.* c. 63 and of Galatians 5.19–21 in id., c. 82: the latter recur in part (notably, the telling *possidebunt* for *consequentur*) in Alcuin's letter of ca. Aug. 793 to King Aethelred, Epp. 4:50, lines 11–14, the former in *ep.* 188, Epp. 4:315, lines 29–30 (*corda prudentium* in *Adm.*, *corda sapientum* in *ep.*, but *corda* is not standard in either of the OT passages). Was Alcuin recalling a liturgical lection in one or both places? Nor surprisingly, Galatians 5.16–24 is almost universal as a pericope, "the lectionary of Alcuin" indicating it for *ebdomada V post sancti Laurentii*: A. Wilmart, "Le Lectionnaire d'Alcuin," *Ephemerides liturgicae* 51 (1937), 136–197, here p. 160.

[45]J. Marenbon, *From the Circle of Alcuin to the School of Auxerre*, Cambridge Studies in Mediaeval Life and Thought, 3rd ser., vol. 15 (Cambridge, 1981), especially pp. 30–43,

The text *De imagine Dei,* a considerably expanded version of which figures in a number of later-medieval manuscripts under a similar title or as *De dignitate conditionis humanae,* expounds (or perhaps better, proceeds from) Genesis 1.26: "We have made man in our image and likeness." It is the superior worth (*dignitas*) of the human creature, created "consilio sancte Trinitatis et opere maiestatis divinae," that justifies the plural *faciamus*—thus following an exegetical tradition which goes back to the fourth-century Ambrose. Then, after the first of two or three passages which seem to be adaptations of Claudianus Mamertus, the author turns for inspiration and for part of his language to Augustine's *De Trinitate.* From this source he takes the parallel between the persons of the Trinity and the "intellect," "will" and "memory" which constitute the mind, only to remove it entirely from the context in which Augustine had proposed it. The author's discussion of "image" and "similitude" follows a similarly divergent course. His central argument is, in the words of Dr. Marenbon, that "Godlikeness lies within Man's potential, but must be achieved by individual effort. God has created Man in such a way that an individual man may possess the same moral virtues as his Creator, but may, through his misdeeds, lose any trace of such a resemblance to God."[46]

Within a very few years either side of 800 the shorter text *De imagine Dei* figures (although only once with that title) as a distinct entity or quoted extensively in the writings of others in a constellation of manuscripts written in widely separated parts of the empire. Without a rubric, it is the "bridging" item between a unique collection of philosophical texts and an equally distinctive collection of creeds and Psalter prefaces, both of them apparently originating at the Frankish court in the ?790s, in a book written for (Arch)bishop Leidrad of Lyons; again without a rubric, it is among the "school" texts—including *De ponderibus* but otherwise predominantly grammatical—written at more than one west German center but combined in a single volume at Lorsch

---

144–151. Since I concentrate on my points of disagreement with this major contribution to our understanding of Carolingian learning, it is important to emphasize that it was Mr. Marenbon's work (part of which he generously let me read in manuscript, in advance of publication) that showed me the inadequacy of my own treatment of both the *De imagine Dei* and the several *dicta* associated with it: what follows is a substantial expansion and rewriting of the lecture as delivered.

[46]Marenbon, pp. 158–161 (text), pp. 44–46, the quotation at p. 44. For the degree of dependence on Claudianus Mamertus see below, pp. 29–30.

in the early ninth century. It is the seventh of fifteen short texts (*dicta*) forming one part of a substantial collection of theological and pedagogic writings copied at Verona ca. 800/1 in which Alcuin figures prominently: the eighth *dicta* inc. *Iuste mihi videtur* credited in the rubric to his pupil Candidus, is the text incorporated in the *De imagine* to form the *De dignitate*. The *De imagine* is again copied in association with other writings of Alcuin and his circle in a mid-century Salzburg manuscript.[47] Some decades before this a cleric who latinizes his name as *Blancidius*, working in the Slav mission field and probably from Salzburg but possibly from Aquileia, included a long quotation in a moralizing letter to friends in Italy: the sole manuscript source is one of several books in the production of which Isenbert, a Bavarian who was for some time at Tours working closely with Alcuin's *discipuli*, is a collaborator if not the supervisor. About the same time Benedict of Aniane drew on the *De imagine* for the greater part of one of the "chapters" of the *Forma fidei de Trinitate* with which his *Munimenta verae fidei* begins. Earlier, Paulinus of Aquileia had used it rather unexpectedly as the starting point of his exhortation to a "lay ethic," sent ca. 795 to Count Eric of Friuli (d.799).[48] The earliest quotation of all, however, is in the now notorious *Libri Carolini*, as part of Book 1, chapter 7, where most of the middle sections follow immediately after a short passage introduced by the words *Ait enim beatus Ambrosius* and which is indeed from that writer's *De fide*. In the manuscript Vatican lat. 7207 this is an uncorrected passage, running across the end of one quire and the beginning of another, and therefore presumably of ca. 790/2.[49] The evidence is surely of dissemination from the royal court beginning in the early 790s, and subsequently also from Alcuin's Tours.

---

[47] Rome, Casa dei Padri Maristi, MS A. II.1, fols. 106v–107; *CLA* iv, 417, with bibliography of the older literature, the *terminus ante quem* almost certainly 814; Vat. MS Pal. Lat. 1719, fols. 46v–49: see B. Bischoff, *Lorsch im Spiegel seiner Handschriften* (Munich, 1974), p. 31, leaving the date of this non-Lorsch section open (cf. Marenbon, p. 42, n. 56); Munich Staatsbibl. clm. 6407, fols. 98–100v, written at Verona but taken almost immediately to Freising: *CLA* ix, 1282; Marenbon, chap. 2 passim, pp. 151–166, the Candidus *dicta* at pp. 161–163; Vienna Nat. bibl. cod. 458, fols. 175–77v: B. Bischoff, *Südostdeutsche Schreibschulen*, 2:82, 83, 155f., attributing it firmly to the Salzburg scriptorium, supervised by Baldo, in the (early) 830s (and not of s. X, as Marenbon, p. 149).

[48] MGH Epp. 4:484–490: for its MS source, Vienna Nat. bibl. cod. 966, and for Isenbert, see Bischoff, *Südostdeutsche Schreibschulen*, 1:232–233; Benedict of Aniane: *Munimenta fidei*, ed. J. Leclercq in Analecta monastica, ser.1 = Studia Anselmiana 20 (Rome, 1948), 27–66, with Marenbon, p. 37; Paulinus: PL 99:197ff., here 199a–200a.

[49] Ed. H. Bastgen, MGH Concilia 2, Suppl., pp. 22 (where at 1.35 the MS reading *Iam* should be restored to the text) –23, from Vat. lat. 7207 fols. 18v–19v — the end of qu. 3 and the beginning of qu. 4; for the significance of this see Ann Freeman, "Further Studies in the *Libri Carolini*," *Speculum* 40 (1965), 205–222.

On the basis of the same evidence it has been argued variously: that the author of the *Libri Carolini* was already familiar with the longer work *De dignitate conditionis humanae*, circulating in the late eighth century with a (false) attribution to Ambrose; that he had used a manuscript in which this passage—presumably excerpted from a longer work—had been copied immediately after a part of the *De fide* and had thereby been "attached" to Ambrose; and that we have to do with an original composition of the early Carolingian period.[50] On the first theory, Alcuin would have "lifted" the beginning and end of the text and claimed it for himself, or—perhaps more plausibly—used it in his teaching in such a way that others regarded him as its author: the middle section, inc. *Iuste mihi videtur*, would similarly have been annexed in the mid-790s by his *discipulus* Candidus, under whose name it occurs in an early tenth-century manuscript of Corbie, as well as the Verona manuscript. Dr. Marenbon will have none of this. He argues strongly and effectively for Alcuin's authorship, necessarily before 790, of the *De imagine Dei* as transmitted by the earliest manuscripts; and for Candidus's authorship in the next decade of the other *dicta* (singular!) which was conflated with it at a much later date, together with (most of) the other "Munich [sc. Verona manuscript] passages."[51]

The arguments against a pre-Carolingian origin and the early Carolingian division into two of the *De dignitate conditionis humanae* are certainly telling. There is no manuscript authority for the complete or conflate text before the early twelfth century; and an attribution to Ambrose is not found, apparently, before the mid-fifteenth century. In the period to ca. 1100 there are at least four manuscripts of the "Alcuin text" and five of the "Candidus text"; and the text of the former reads perfectly coherently. Finally, the argument from familiarity with Claudianus Mamertus's *De statu animae* shown supposedly by the *De imagine Dei* and certainly by others of the "Munich passages" may be even stronger than Dr. Marenbon claimed. It does *not* seem to be the case that Cassiodorus used Claudianus's work for his own *De anima*. The earliest evidence for post-fifth-century interest in it, therefore, is precisely in these *dicta* (plural!). The earliest extant copy of the *De statu animae* is in a

[50]H. Löwe, "Zur Gesch. Wizos," *Deutsches Archiv* 6 (1943), 369; L. Wallach, *Diplomatic Studies in Latin and Greek Documents from the Carolingian Age* (Cornell University Press, Ithaca and London, 1977), pp. 254–255; M. Mathon, *L'Anthropologie chrétienne en Occident de saint Augustin à Jean Scot Erigène* (Lille, 1964), 2:219; Marenbon, as next note.

[51]Marenbon, op. cit., pp. 36–38, 43 (Alcuin), 38–43 (Candidus); cf. 44–45.

manuscript written in northeastern France shortly after 800, which also contains Chalcidius's translation of the *Timaeus*—which again seems to point in the direction of the court library, subsequently dispersed.[52]

There are, nonetheless, serious difficulties in the attribution of the *De imagine Dei* to Alcuin. Scanty though the evidence is for his interests and activity during the first phase of his residence at court—from ca. 782 to early 790, interrupted by a visit to England in (probably) 786—it gives an entirely consistent picture, and one that is likewise consistent with the much fuller evidence for his subsequent development as a scholar and writer, of someone still essentially "a gatherer of other men's flowers" and littérateur reading Virgil and other poets and experimenting with verse forms himself. It does not absolutely exclude but it is difficult to reconcile with the composition of an original piece of theological writing.[53] The author of the *Vita Alcuini* does not include the work in his list of Alcuin's writings, which is very comprehensive if not absolutely complete.[54] The early manuscript evidence for Alcuin's authorship is minimal and the evidence of citation wholly negative. It can be argued that the substantial quotations in the *Libri Carolini*, the letter of "Blancidius" and Benedict of Aniane's *Munimenta fidei* are not credited to their author because it was then normal practice not to name *moderni* as distinct from *antiqui patres*. Alcuin himself, however, quoted Bede and Ælbert in his letters—but left unattributed his extensive quotation from Cassiodorus and other *patres* in his exegetical works; Amalarius (as we have seen) cited Alcuin in the context of liturgical practice; a little later, Gottschalk cited the authority of Alcuin on a grammatical (orthographic) point but also quoted at length from the *De fide Trinitatis libri tres*, apparently without acknowledgment.[55] Perhaps more to the point,

---

[52]The earliest "conflate" text is perhaps a MS not included in Dr. Marenbon's list, op. cit., pp. 149–151, namely Stuttgart Landesbibl. MS HB VII 48, fols. 55v–57v: S. Germany, s. XI/XII or XII¹. To the MSS of the "dicta Albini," nos. 1, 2, 3, 7 in that list, Göttingen, Univ. Bibl., MS Theol. 99, fols. 161v–162v of s. IX/X can apparently be added (Alcuin's name does not figure). The Claudianus-Chalcidius MS, Paris BN lat. 2164 (from Senlis Cathedral), is in a small, almost "capitular," script, which has long been dated to the eleventh century but which according to Prof. Bischoff (*Karl der Grosse, Lebenswerk u. Nachleben*, 2 [Düsseldorf, 1965], 48, 239) is that of a scriptorium in close touch with Charlemagne's court: almost certainly, therefore, the stemma proposed by A. Engelbrecht for his edition of the *De statu animae*, CSEL 11 (Vienna, 1885), p. xi, will have to be radically revised.

[53]Principal references in n. 44. For the visit to England, see the record of the legatine visit, MGH Epp. 4, no. 3, p. 28.

[54]*Vita Alcuini*, c. 21: ed. cit., pp. 194f.

[55]Gottschalk on Alcuin's insistence on the spelling *adoliscentia*: C. Lambot, *Oeuvres théologiques et grammaticales de Godescalc d'Orbais* (Louvain, 1945), pp. 388–389; unattributed

therefore, is the evidence of Benedict, writing within a few years of Alcuin's death or even within his lifetime. He had, he tells us, composed the *Forma fidei*, which constitutes almost half of the *Munimenta fidei*, at the insistence of Guarnarius who already knew by heart (!) Alcuin's *De fide Trinitatis* — "ac ideo id pro nichil habuit[t]" — and was perhaps acquainted with Gennadius's *De ecclesiasticis dogmatibus*. (The second half of the *Munimenta* is very largely taken up by complete texts of the *De fide Trinitatis*, followed by the *De Trinitate quaestiones XXVIII* and the *De animae ratione* — all correctly attributed to Alcuin — and of Gennadius's work, unattributed.) Its declared purpose is to bring the already informed reader to a truer understanding of his faith, "from things known to what is unknown, from creatures to the Creator"; and to this end the *Forma Fidei* has been lifted "de patrum orthodoxorum arcivis." It is in that part of the collection that the quotation from the *De imagine* occurs: specifically, in its eighth book where almost half of it follows immediately after substantial extracts from Augustine. If the author of the excerpted work was indeed a contemporary and friend, Benedict was remarkably ill informed or ingenuous.[56]

Two of the three manuscript copies written in or near to Alcuin's lifetime have no rubric with an author's name; in the Verona manuscript *dicta Albini* is written over an original *dicta alibi*. The context in which the *De imagine* and the "Candidus text" occur in the Salzburg manuscript can be used as an argument both for and against Alcuin's authorship of the first-named. Its rubric here (fol. 175) is simply *De imagine Dei*. The texts immediately preceding are Alcuin's three Psalm commentaries and the *Epistola ad pueros S. Martini,* sc. a truncated "Arno" *libellus manualis*. The Candidus text follows, with the rubric *Item de imagine Dei* (fol. 177v); this in turn is followed by (fol. 179) *Dictatus Paulini patriarchae,* i.e., Paulinus of Aquileia "on Baptism," and (fol. 186) by Alcuin's letter to the king on the proper methods of converting defeated Avars — by instruction, in the case of adults — with the (unique) rubric *Dictatus Albini magistri*. The compiler or the *magister* supervising the compilation and writing of this part of the manuscript, almost certainly

---

passages from the *De fide* in Gottschalk's *Excerpta de Trinitate*, id., pp. 108–130 passim, and in his *De Trinitate*, id., p. 245.

[56]Benedict, *Munimenta fidei*, ed. Leclercq (above, n. 48), pp. 47, 49, 55, 66 (Guarnerius and his feat of memory); id., pp. 64–65 (contents of BN lat. 2390 fols. 53v–85v); id., pp. 36–37.

Baldo, *may* have regarded an indication of the authorship of the first text *De imagine Dei* as superfluous because it continued a series of texts by Alcuin; but if so, it proves no more than that at Salzburg in mid-century he was believed to be the author; and logically this same argument must be extended (*item*) to the second or "Candidus" text. It may be, however, that Alcuin is credited with the authorship in a twelfth-century St. Denis manuscript now at Berlin, and at that date it is unlikely that the scribe had not found the statement in his exemplar.[57]

The very phrase *dignitas humanae conditionis* with which the comment on the Genesis lemma begins seems hardly Alcuinian. I do not find the concluding pair of words anywhere in the genuine writings, although without a concordance it is impossible to be sure. Even *dignitas* in the sense of "superior state" is unusual: when Alcuin wishes to express that notion he prefers the word *nobilitas*. It is the one he uses, for example, in his "Answer" to Sigwulf on this very passage of Genesis: "ut eius nobilitas ostenderetur"; it occurs repeatedly in the *De ratione animae* but notably in c. 3 (as in its opening line), where also phrases such as *nobilis a conditore creata* are to be found. The plural *dignitates* ("qualities" of the soul), on the other hand, is used repeatedly in the *De ratione* and in other writings of Alcuin, from at latest 795, and shares this usage with the *De imagine*. When the author of the *De imagine* wishes to refer to the quality of intelligence he uses the word *intellectus*; when Alcuin wishes to, he follows Augustine—in the *De Trinitate* and elsewhere (and it will be remembered that as late as 801 he had "never come upon" four of Augustine's works on the soul)—in using *intelligentia*.[58]

Dr. Marenbon has rightly stressed the significance of the revival of interest in Claudianus Mamertus amongst the circle of scholars at the court or with Alcuin at Tours in the 790s: the *De statu animae* gave them limited

---

[57]For clm. 6407, Pal. Lat. 1719 and Padri Maristi A. II. 1, see Marenbon, op. cit., p. 158. Frl. Dr. Eva Irblich has generously checked and amplified my notes on Vienna 458 (for the date and origin of which see note 47).

[58]*Nobilitas*: PL 100:520b; *De ratione* "3," PL 101:641a, ed. Curry p. 45; similarly *De rhetorica*, PL 101:643b, ed. W. S. Howell (Princeton University Press, 1941; repr. New York, 1965), p. 142: *animae nobilitas*, cf. PL 101:944a, Howell p. 146: *morum nobilitas* (from Cicero *De inventione* 2.53.159). Alcuin does, however, use *honoris dignitas* for "high rank, office of responsibility" in, e.g., *ep.* 44, MGH Epp. 4:90, to the archbishop of York (795), and *De vera philosophia*, PL 101:851c. *Dignitates: De imagine*, ed. Marenbon, p. 160; *De ratione* "5," PL 101:643b, ed. Curry, p. 52; but already in the "hortatory" letters of 795 or slightly earlier, MGH Epp. 4, nos. 38 et seq. *Intellectus, intelligentia*: compare *De imagine*, ed. Marenbon, pp. 159, 160 with *De ratione* "3," PL 101:641c, d. For an exceptional use of *intellectus* by Alcuin, see below, n. 65.

access to a range of Neoplatonic and even neo-Pythagorean concepts, albeit via a single intermediary.[59] It is not clear, however, that this is of much help in determining the date and authorship of the *De imagine* — or that, if it is, this points to Alcuin. The Verona manuscript *dicta* 12 (one of the two adopted unchanged by Benedict of Aniane to provide bridging passages between his *confessio* and the treatise on friendship in the first part of his *Munimenta fidei*) is an almost verbatim extract from Claudianus's third book, although with two changes of words and word order that produce a change of sense; *dicta* 2's concluding sentence combines phraseology taken from one chapter of the first book and two or more chapters of the third.[60] Of the three passages in the *De imagine* where the influence of Claudianus has been discerned, two are more or less free paraphrases and involve the reintegration of biblical texts which are merely echoed or quoted incompletely in their "source." The third passage, although more nearly a quotation, also forsakes some of Claudianus's distinctive language for its own; the immediately preceding sentence, with its (mis)quotation from Acts, has no parallel in the *De statu animae*.[61] The seemingly corresponding passages in Alcuin's *De animae ratione* are invariably closer to the language of the *De imagine* than to Claudianus:

---

[59]Marenbon, pp. 38, 43, 51-52 and Appendix 1, passim. For the place of Claudianus (*Opera*, ed. Engelbrecht: CSEL 11 [1885]) in the Neoplatonic tradition and his source(s), see P. Courcelle, *Les Lettres grecques en Occident de Macrobe à Cassiodore*, 2nd ed. (Paris, 1948), pp. 223-236. But E. L. Fortin, *Christianisme et culture philosophique au $V^e$ siècle: La querelle de l'âme humaine en Occident* (Paris, 1959), which I have not seen, may well modify Courcelle's conclusions.

[60]*Dicta* 12: Marenbon, p. 165; "*Munimenta Fidei*," ed. Leclercq, p. 53, with a copyist's error *Homo* for *Omne*: followed (p. 54) by *Quid est substantia* = *dicta* 13 (Marenbon, p. 165); Claudianus, *De statu animae* 3.3: ed. cit., p. 157. *Dicta* 2: Marenbon, p. 153, with which the editor compares *De statu animae* 1.14, ed. cit., p. 59. But "quo pacto corpus inI corporeo contemperari queat," etc. is hardly a source of "ita per haec corpori movendo ac regendo contemperavit," and does not account for the *dicta's* use in its final clause of Claudianus's very distinctive *inlocaliter* (Gk.ἀδιαστασία, Lat. *inlocalitas*: the adverb is not apparently found in any other writer), for which the source is presumably Bk. 3, esp. chaps. 1, 3-5 and — also for the preceding clause — 14.

[61]Marenbon, op. cit., p. 159 with n. 9, p. 161 with n. 14: the corresponding passages in Claudianus are ed. Engelbrecht, p. 118 (where the quotation from Matt. 22.37 omits the concluding "et ex tota mente tua" — *ex* for Vulg. *in* being characteristic of one or more branches of the tradition, including Amiatinus and the earliest Tours Bibles — although the opening word was almost certainly, as in the *De imagine, Diligis* [not -*es*] which is the reading of BN lat. 2164 and of two tenth-century MSS), and id., p. 85 (where Ps. 48.13 [and not as Marenbon, cit.] is simply echoed in the words "intellexisset . . . inspientibus . . . comparata iumentis"); Marenbon, p. 159 with n. 5 (= ed. Engelbrecht, p. 155), Acts 17.28 "In ipso enim vivimus et movemur et sumus" being quoted in the *De imagine* as "In eo vivimus et movemus et sumus."

the one which at first sight seems closest of all, but with some phrases interpolated directly from the *De statu*, proves to be a long passage which Alcuin has copied with only two changes from Lactantius's *De opificio Dei*! and apparent echoes of Claudianus elsewhere in the *De animae ratione* are probably to be accounted for in some other way.[62] As a final contribution to the question of authorship, the reintegrated Psalm text in the *De imagine* could have been taken from either the Gallican or the Roman version (Augustine had quoted the same verse in a related passage of the *De Trinitate*, but in his own "African" version); a second quotation, however, is categorically Gallican: and Alcuin's Psalter was certainly Roman.[63]

These negative arguments, it may be claimed, are not decisively against Alcuin's authorship of the *De imagine Dei*: differences in language and approach in texts written more than ten years apart for different purposes are not unusual; and the points in common between the earlier work and the *De animae ratione* and other works of Alcuin's years at Tours are as numerous or as significant as the differences. Unfortunately the very features which one would expect to show the greater constancy, such as biblical citation, vocabulary and use of conjunctions and particles, are the ones where the differences are most marked: they are the less to be expected in a man who, having emerged as a writer late in life — he was already about 50 when he is supposed to have written the *De imagine Dei* — thereafter regularly quoted both himself and the texts with which he had acquired an everyday familiarity at York. If noncontextual evidence can be adduced in favor of Alcuin as the author, I might still be persuaded! But on present evidence it is far more probable that the *De imagine Dei* was a late fifth/sixth-century work (of Gallic origin?) which, with others similarly neglected for centuries, resurfaced at the Carolingian court in the 780s — like, in fact, the *De decem categoriis*, "edited" by Alcuin with a dedicatory verse preface, the Paul-Seneca correspondence, also with Alcuin's verse preface, and other works with which Alcuin had nothing to

---

[62]Cf. Marenbon, op. cit., p. 159 n. 7, p. 160 nn. 10, 11, 13, p. 159 n. 14. Alcuin, *De animae ratione* 8, PL 101:643a, ed. Curry, p. 51: "Nec etiam aliquis potest . . . impatiens habeat" is *De opificio Dei* 16.9.10, ed. M. Perrin, Sources Chrétiennes 213 (Paris, 1974), pp. 194, 196. Perrin's Commentary volume, Sources Chrét. 214:387–389 demonstrates the dependence of these passages on the tradition of Platonic and Neoplatonic ideas. I have not found quotations from Lactantius elsewhere in Alcuin's or his contemporaries' writings: but not surprisingly there are at least two early ninth-century MSS of both *De opificio* and *Institutiones*.

[63]Ps. 48.13 (Marenbon, p. 161); Ps. 92.1 (ibid.): "Dominus regnavit decore indutus [est]," which in Ro. is "Dominus regnavit decorem induit."

do.[64] Much of the thinking of the *De imagine Dei* would have had an obvious appeal to a man whose love of praising God was already matched by a belief in another kind of love, in the power open to man to pray for grace so as to be released from the consequences of sin. It was one that might well have figured in his teaching during his last years at the Frankish court, although this is not absolutely proved: it is not certain that Candidus was with him at that time, and the earliest echoes or quotations of the *De imagine* in Alcuin's authentic works are in his writings against Adoptionism when he was already at Tours.[65]

The earliest quotation of all is, as has already been noted, in the *Libri Carolini* — to continue with the accepted but post-medieval title — where it is used to support the countering of one of the propositions of the Greek Council of Nicaea (act. 6, t. 1).[66] It has therefore played a part in the lively debate, which has latterly shown signs of developing into a gladiatorial contest, over the composition and authorship of the work, "the most substantial and most original piece of theological writing of the Early Carolingian period." Was it essentially the work of Theodulf, future bishop of Orleans, although substantially revised and corrected at the first "fair-copy" stage (represented by the now unfortunately incomplete MS Vat. lat. 7207), possibly after debate and criticism, as Miss Ann Freeman (latterly sustained by Mr. Paul Meyvaert) argues? or was it throughout the work of Alcuin, as Professor Wallach maintains? To take up any position in the debate at this stage is to risk being dubbed "unscholarly" or dismissed from the circle of *amici*; and like Alcuin I would regard the latter as the greater loss. It is, however, impossible to stand aside: if Alcuin played the principal or indeed any part in the drafting or revision of the *Libri*, they provide us with a major body of evidence for his reading, scholarly methods and theological outlook in a phase of his life when these are otherwise largely undocumented.[67]

---

[64]See L. Minio-Paluello, *Aristoteles latinus*, 1:1–5: *Categoriae vel Praedicamenta* (Brussels, 1961), pp. lxxvii–xcvi, 133–175, but especially pp. lxxxvi–xci; *Epistolae Senecae ad Paulum et Pauli ad Senecam (quae vocantur)*, ed. C. W. Barlow, Papers and Monographs of the American Academy in Rome 10 (1938), especially pp. 94–104; and many of the works in the "Court library list" in Berlin, Staatsbibl. Diez B. 66.

[65]Below, pp. 53, 57 and nn. 120, 129. The one substantial quotation is in *De virtutibus et vitiis*, chap. 3, PL 101:615d, where *toto intellectu* is unchanged! —an interesting addition to Wallach's fundamental analysis of the sources of this work in *Alcuin and Charlemagne*, chap. 12.

[66]Above, p. 24 and n. 49.

[67]The major contributions to this debate, which provide full references to the older literature are: Ann Freeman, "Theodulf of Orléans and the *Libri Carolini*," *Speculum* 32

Any attempt to claim for Alcuin the overall authorship of the *Libri* in their complete version (known only from Paris, Bibl. de l'Arsénal 663, a Rheims manuscript of the mid-ninth century) has to face the awkward fact that they are, unlike most works of *eruditio* of the period, internally and externally dated—namely, to the years 790 (probably mid-) to 793, less certainly to the shorter period late 790–792; and Alcuin was away from the court in northern England for all or the greater part of 790–93! If he was engaged, when the Northumbrian political situation permitted, in preparing the Frankish reply to Nicaea II's pronouncements on images, the absence of any reference (even oblique) to the subject in his letters of these years, or indeed in any letters, is remarkable.[68] The character of the mutilated first fair copy requires us to suppose (with Mr. Wallach) that not only had Alcuin traveled to Northumbria with a boxload of often unusual books but with four scribes who had all learnt the court-type minuscule created in the early 780s (still, probably, the writing style of a very few) and thoughtfully introduced "Visigothic" spellings to

---

(1957), 663–705; L. Wallach, *Alcuin and Charlemagne*, pp. 169–177; A. Freeman, "Further Studies in the *Libri Carolini*," *Speculum* 40 (1965), 203–289; ibid., "Further Studies in the *Libri Carolini*, III: The Marginal Notes in Vat. Lat. 7207," *Speculum* 46 (1971), 597–612; Wallach, *Diplomatic Studies in Latin and Greek Documents from the Carolingian Age* (Cornell U.P., Ithaca and London, 1977), pts. 2 and 3 (bringing together a number of studies previously published elsewhere: see p. 377 of the bibliography); P. Meyvaert, "The Authorship of the *Libri Carolini*: Observations Prompted by a Recent Book," *Rev. bénédictine* 89 (1979), 29–57. Of the several "outside" commentaries or attempts to umpire the dispute, I note only E. Dahlhaus-Berg, *Nova Antiquitas et Antiqua Novitas*, Kölner Hist. Abh. 23 (Cologne and Vienna, 1975), pp. 169–216.

[68]The (first) Preface's *ante triennium* (ed. Bastgen, p. 3) is clearly crucial, whether or not "the prefaces to all four books were composed together at one time, after the rest of the LC had been completed" (so Meyvaert, p. 41): it is effectively supported by *Liber Pontificalis*, ed. L. Duchesne, 1 (Paris, 1886), p. 512 (*Vita Hadriani* 88 *fin.*) which marks a sharp break in this *vita*, and by the opening section of Hadrian's reply to the Frankish so-called *Capitulare*, MGH Epp. 5:3f. The period of Alcuin's absence in England is established by his letters, Epp. 4, nos. 6 and 7, 8–10 (arrival in 790), 16 seq. (presence during Lent and probably until Easter 793; departure before June 8th): some "undated" letters probably belong to the years 790/93. The only firm *terminus ante quem* is, of course, *Capitulare Francofurtense*, c. 2: MGH Conc. 2/1 (ed. Werminghoff), p. 165 (c. 2). Accepting Miss Freeman's view of the marginal (Tironian) notes as preserving the king's personal indications of approval of the final text of LC (as against Wallach's belief that they are the work of a scribe who "was in all probability familiar with Cassiodorus's *notae* and the symbols that accompany his *Expositio Psalmorum*"! see *Diplomatic Studies*, pp. 272–286), there is still the problem of when and where the text of LC was read to him: in Bavaria, where he was—when not fighting further east—during 792 and much of 793? (in which case, were the LC compiled and/or "fair-copied" there? which may not be irrelevant to future consideration of the style of the decorative initials) on the way back north, at the end of 793? or at Frankfurt itself?

ensure that, 1100 years later, Miss Freeman would reach the wrong conclusion. Unless we are gravely misled by the evidence of other manuscripts whose association with him is indisputable, both Alcuin and his amanuenses wrote (as we should expect) Insular minuscule.[69] Determined to disprove Miss Freeman's contention that the distinctive form of many of the biblical citations shows the pervasive influence of Visigothic liturgical texts — antiphons, verses, etc. — Mr. Wallach usually fails to ask the one "right" question, namely: if Alcuin quotes in his authentic writings an exactly comparable text to one in the *Libri Carolini*, in what form does he quote it? Thus he laboriously lists and analyzes, with a false page reference and a misquotation, the antiphon and verses which, according to the *Vita*, Alcuin recited at Vespers as he lay dying; but as none of them is quoted in the *Libri Carolini*, they give no support to Mr. Wallach's principal hypothesis. He cannot fairly be criticized for not taking account of the evidence of Alcuin's florilegium *De laude Dei* — given its final form (it will be recalled) probably at the very time that Alcuin is supposed to have been composing the *Libri* against the Greek concept of images. But a comparison between the section *De antiphonario* and the plausibly liturgical citations or reminiscences in the *Libri Carolini* shows no single point of identity; nor do the earlier sections of the florilegium or any other of Alcuin's authentic writings show familiarity with biblical texts in Old Latin versions (other than liturgical *cantica*), either directly or through "a catena of patristic *testimonia*" as Mr. Wallach's alternative hypothesis demands.[70] I content myself with two specific examples. Mr. Wallach has countered Miss Freeman's view that an abbreviated quotation from the Epistle to the Hebrews is based on a text in the Visigothic Antiphonary with evidence that it *could* be Frankish: had he compared other and equally distinctive quotations from the same Epistle with

---

[69]Prof. Wallach does indeed question whether Vat. Lat. 7207 is the work of scribes trained in Charlemagne's "court scriptorium" and, moreover, whether words attributed to Prof. B. Bischoff are to be understood in that sense; *Diplomatic Studies*, pp. 188f. To a query from me on this point, Prof. Bischoff replied (first orally and subsequently in a letter) that his view was and is that in so far as purely paleographical considerations — ductus, letter forms, etc. — can provide an answer, the writers of the manuscript are certainly "Court scribes." For Alcuin's hand see especially Bischoff, "Aus Alkuins Erdentagen," *Mittelalterliche Studien*, 2 (Stuttgart, 1967), pp. 17–19 and pl. I. The two eleventh-century English manuscripts of Alcuin's letters, BL Cott. Vesp. A xiv and Cott. Tib. A xv, can be shown to derive at least in part from a manuscript in Insular script: but this archetype need not be earlier than the mid-ninth century.

[70]*Diplomatic Studies*, pp. 219f., 223ff., 248ff. and passim. For the *De laude*, cf. above, pp. 4ff.

parallel quotations in Alcuin's letters and in his *Commentary on Hebrews*, he would have found that the "peculiar" readings in both are never those of the *Libri Carolini*. He allows that a quotation from Deuteronomy 32 *may* be, in his own words, "an 'indirect Spanish symptom'" since this is an Old Latin canticle version; unfortunately, it is the very verse which Alcuin quotes in a letter of 798, also in a pre-Vulgate version but in that of the (different) Roman and English canticle, with *aget iudicium* in place of the Spanish (and *Libri Carolini*'s) *reddam ultionem*.[71]

Nevertheless Alcuin was asked to comment, while still in England in 792, and did so in an *epistola* which he took with him when he returned to Francia in the late spring or early summer of 793. This is the categorical statement of a Northumbrian (probably York) Annalist. It cannot be brushed aside on the grounds of the late *manuscript* tradition of the annal or by citing it from the derived versions of still later English chronicler-historians or simply because it is inconvenient. Although it is transmitted only as part of a "historical compilation" by Byrhtferth of Ramsey round about the year 1000, context and content leave no room for doubt that the "792" entry was composed and written down as near to the event as eighth-century annals usually were.[72] There is, indeed, no other time when a northern English chronicler is likely to have had both the knowledge and the occasion to document the distinctive position achieved by the deacon and former York *magister* Alcuin during his seven or eight years at the Frankish royal court.

---

[71]Hebrews: Wallach, *Diplomatic Studies*, pp. 236–238, obscuring the fact that is the combination of "Sancti [qui] per fidem vicerunt . . . , adepti sunt repromissiones, extinxerunt impetum ignis . . ." that links LC with the Antiphonary of Leon, against both the Antiphonary of Compiègne ("Omnes sancti . . . sunt promissiones, obturaverunt ora leonum") and the Vulgate text of Heb. 11.33–34 ("Qui per fidem devicerunt . . . repromissiones, obturaverunt ora leonum, extinxerunt impetum ignis"): cf. *Diplomatic Studies*, pp. 238–239 on Isaiah 60.20 in LC and the Antiphonary of Leon, and Mr. Meyvaert's pointed comment in *Rev. bén.* 89:34, n. 1; note further that while Alcuin several times quotes Heb. 11.6 and 12.6 in his letters, he seems never to quote either 11.13 or 11.33–34. Deuteronomy: Wallach, *Diplomatic Studies*, p. 238, with which compare Epp. 4:206 (line 31); for this Vulg. reading in the "Roman" canticle as sung in England, see H. Schneider, *Die Altlateinischen Biblischen Cantica*, Texte u. Arbeiten 1 (Beuron, 1938), pp. 29–30, 46ff. with the Vespasian Psalter fol. 149v (facsimile in Early English Manuscripts in Facsimile, 14 [1967]).

[72]Pseudo-Symeon, *Historia regum*, ad an. 792 in *Symeonis monachi opera omnia*, ed. T. Arnold, 2 (Rolls Series, 1885), pp. 53–54 (of which Roger of Wendover, quoted by Wallach, op. cit., p. 13 n., after von den Steinen, is an unreliable derivative): for Byrhtferth's editorial activity see the fundamental study by M. Lapidge, "Byrhtferth of Ramsey and the Early Sections of the *Historia Regum* Attributed to Symeon of Durham," *Anglo-Saxon England* 10 (1981), 97–122. The (near-)contemporaneity of the Northumbrian Annals is certainly not disproved by the recording of Continental events under the wrong year: the Annalist's account

The letter, whatever form it took,[73] is lost and no reference to it has been identified in Alcuin's later writings. Is there anything in the final version of the *Libri Carolini* which might be derived from it? Miss Ann Freeman's analysis excludes any serious possibility that the "editorial" corrections in the Vatican manuscript owe anything to Alcuin's intervention (although a niggling doubt remains about the *confessio fidei* — the Pelagian version of the Credo! — which begins Book 3, over a massive erasure);[74] and the evidence of vocabulary, style and citation amply favors the view that the (original) author of Books 1–3 is also the author of Book 4, which is missing from the Vatican manuscript. On unity of authorship Mr. Wallach, who once believed that Alcuin had edited someone else's text but now rejects all "editorial" intervention after discussion, is in full agreement.[75] Although all the force of *auctoritas* is therefore against me, I still believe the answer to my question is "yes."

---

of the death of Pope Hadrian and the placing above the tomb of a gold-lettered epitaph commissioned by the Frankish king or of the treasures made available to the Franks by the defeat of the Avars, entered respectively under 794 and 795 instead of 795 and 796, are clearly based on some good written source — letters from Alcuin or someone else from York resident at the court? — and were presumably added subsequently to annals which had originally only recorded Northumbrian events. There is an interesting semantic problem in the language of the 792 Annal, which may have some bearing on the argument whether the assertion in Charlemagne's letter to the Spanish bishops in 794 (MGH Concilia 2:159; cf. 160) that "necnon et de Brittanniae partibus aliquos ecclesiasticae disciplinae viros convocavimus" is evidence of the presence of other "Britons" than Alcuin at Frankfurt: *contra*, Wallach, *Alcuin and Charlemagne*, pp. 165ff.; but defended by J. M. Wallace-Hadrill, *Early Germanic Kingship in England and on the Continent* (Oxford, 1971), p. 118. According to the Annalist, Alcuin "epistolam . . . illam . . . sum eodem libro [sc. synodali] *et persona* episcoporum ac principum nostrorum regi Francorum attulit." The reading *et* is supported by both manuscripts of the *Historia post Bedam*; and although the construction is highly unusual, it can hardly mean anything other than "(and) in the name of" the Northumbrian bishops and nobles. The implication seems to be that although the Northumbrian church had been canvassed for its opinion, it was only through Alcuin that it was conveyed to Frankfurt.

[73]I hazard the guess that the lost letter was not a sustained, properly argued answer to the central points raised by "the image-worshippers" but rather one that dealt discursively with several points that particularly interested or excited Alcuin, along the lines of his *epist.* nos. 143, 145, 163, etc. For the possibility of a more specific link between LC and Alcuin's *epist.* no. 163, see below, n. 79.

[74]See on this Freeman in *Speculum* 40:216. The LC text of the Creed is repeated exactly (e.g., with the omission of *asserimus*, wrongly introduced by Bastgen in his edition: cit., p. 107, 1.36) and with a henceforward standard attribution to St. Jerome (!) among the prefatory material of the court "Dagulf Psalter," written ca. 794/5, Vienna Nat. bibl. MS lat. 1861 fol. 9v and in the court-derived Leidrad MS, Rome, Casa dei Padri Maristi MS A. II. 1, fol. 100.

[75]Wallach, *Diplomatic Studies*, pp. 200–201, 293f., etc. Cf. *Alcuin and Charlemagne*, p. 174: "I believe that Alcuin is not the author, but rather the final editor of the treatise, the larger part of which was probably drawn up for Charlemagne by another theologian."

The view put forward fifty years ago by von den Steinen,[76] on the basis of Pope Hadrian's reply to the (lost) preliminary version he had been sent (the *Capitulare*), seems to me clearly correct—namely, that the chapter "That the synod can in no way be equated with the first Council of Nicaea" (Bk. 4, chap. 13) was originally thought of as the one with which the treatise would end, except perhaps for the *conclusio* which its overall form demands. Recently, Father Sieben has argued—in some of the most illuminating pages of his remarkable study of the development of the conciliar idea in the early church—that two earlier chapters in Book 3 (chaps. 11, 12) enunciate a radically new concept of what makes a council "universal": the notions of both "horizontal" and "vertical" assent to the council's decrees are retained; but the former is to be based on the adherence of a multiplicity or majority of churches (*plures consentientes*) and not merely of a select few patriarchal churches, while the latter is not satisfied by an indiscriminate accumulation of testimonies but only by finding support in texts whose authority and relevance have been previously established (*probatio*).[77] These are the necessary precondition of the biblical-typological and numerological, as well as the historical, arguments in Book 4, chapter 13.[78] Chapters 14 to 27 or 28—the latter the *conclusio* of the completed version—are therefore in some sense a supplement to the work as originally envisaged, reinforcing some of the earlier "arguments against the Greeks" and introducing a few new ones.

Outstanding among the latter are those constituting chapter 23, answering the supposed proposition of the Fathers at Nicaea that "what is held dear is adored and its converse." The one philosophical text used by the compiler or author of the earlier books is the *De categoriis decem*. Here, however, the demonstration of falsity is supported by substantial extracts from Boethius's *In Aristotelis periermenias* ed. prior and Apuleius's *Periermenias*, together constituting a uniquely early and well-marshalled application of propositional logic to theological questions.[79] The two texts are found in association

[76]W. von den Steinen, "Entstehungsgesch. der Libri Carolini," *Quellen u. Forschungen aus italienischen Archiven u. Bibliotheken* 21 (1929/30), 1-93, here especially 42, 46, 48f.; followed by Dahlhaus-Berg, *Nova Antiquitas et Antiqua Novitas*, pp. 207ff.

[77]H. J. Sieben, *Die Konzilsidee der Alten Kirche*, Konziliengeschichte, ed. W. Brandmüller (Paderborn-Munich, etc., 1979), here especially pp. 324-334. I am indebted to Mr. Paul Meyvaert for directing me to this work in the course of one of our many discussions of the problems of *Libri Carolini* and of Alcuin's intellectual development.

[78]Compare Dahlhaus-Berg, pp. 207-209.

[79]Wallach, *Diplomatic Studies*, pp. 69-77; Rome, Casa dei Padri Maristi, MS A. II. 1, *CLA* iv, 417 (cf. pp. 23f. above, and Marenbon, *From the Circle of Alcuin*, p. 52). For the court connections of the collection of Creeds that forms the penultimate section of the Leidrad MS, see below.

in the court "logical corpus" copied for Leidrad of Lyons. This chapter of the *Libri Carolini* has clear and specific links with both the *De grammatica* and *De dialectica* of Alcuin (written, in my view, ca. 795–797 but based on his teaching over many years) and with a letter of ca. 798/9 in which he answers linguistic and metaphysical problems raised by his favorite pupil Candidus on behalf of the king.[80] The syllogistic method is used again in the group of short writings on theological problems which have recently been characterized as emanating "from the circle of Alcuin" in the last years of the eighth century and have plausibly been attributed to Candidus.[81] The absence of anything comparable in Theodulf's authentic works, at any phase of his life, is not necessarily significant. Verse compositions bulk large in the corpus; the principal prose works are a treatise on baptism, a set of homilies and his episcopal synodal decrees, plus the collection of patristic excerpts (concluding with the poet Prudentius) *De processione spiritus sancti*.[82] There are, nonetheless, several points at which an author familiar with and sympathetic to Late Antique "philosophy" could have made use of its methods or language without incongruity. In fact, Theodulf's verse *praefatio Bibliothecae*, sc. "of the Bible," suggests very strongly that his concept of the scope and function of *dialectica* was notably different from Alcuin's and his pupils'.[83] If congruence (or lack of it) with an author's other works is evidence of authorship, the case for regarding Alcuin's letter from England as the basis of this particular section of *Libri Carolini* is surely compelling.[84]

The same may be said of the final chapter or *conclusio* (chap. 28). Father Sieben has argued convincingly that no new synodal theory is proposed here, as in 3.11 and 12. Rather, ignoring what its title declares to be the subject of the chapter, it plays on the word *universalis* to the following

---

[80]Wallach, op. cit., especially pp. 69, 75: but the claim on p. 69 that "LC. II 31 shows the indirect influence of the *Categoriae decem* through the intermediary of Alcuin's *Dialectica*" is obviously to be rejected; MGH Epp. 4:263 (*ep*. 163).

[81]Marenbon, *From the Circle of Alcuin*, chap. 2, esp. pp. 53ff., texts on pp. 158, 164f.

[82]D. Schaller, "Philologische Untersuchungen zu den Gedichten Theodulfs von Orléans," *Deutsches Archiv* 18 (1962), 13–91; Dahlhaus-Berg, *Nova Antiquitas et Antiqua Novitas* (cit., n. 67), esp. chap. 2.

[83]Ed. Dümmler in: MGH Poet. 1:532–538; better, ed. H. Quentin in: *Biblia Sacra iuxta Latinam Vulgatam versionem*, 1 (Rome, 1926), pp. 52–60; fullest list of MSS by Schaller, cit., table after p. 16. Sources and interpretation of the *Praefatio*: Dahlhaus-Berg, pp. 77–89, on vv. 61–66.

[84]Mr. Meyvaert seems to me—for once—to be guilty of special pleading when he argues (*Rev. bén*. 89:51) that Theodulf *might* have been able to consult a text of "Apuleius" at Fleury.

effect: although an ecclesiastical assembly may seem ecumenical because its membership is universal, it loses that status when it departs from universal, i.e., traditional, Catholic doctrine; whereas a gathering of only two or three provinces might be "universal" because it does not depart "ab universorum fide et traditione."[85] Some modest additions can be made to Professor Wallach's lexicographic and linguistic arguments for Alcuin's involvement, including the distinctive *conventicula*—used in a similarly pejorative sense in a letter to the archbishop of Canterbury, and rather differently in the record of the English legatine visitation of 786.[86] Moreover, the unexpected adaptation of the familiar Gospel text Matthew 18.20—instead of its direct quotation, as in the documents drawn up by Alcuin at Frankfurt for sending to the Spanish Adoptionists—to a distinctive "Cum ergo duarum et trium provinciarum praesules in unum conveniunt" provides a striking and suggestive link with the almost certainly genuine penultimate chapter of the *acta* of the Roman Council of 679, decreeing the local combatting of heresy: as the Council which had heard and upheld Bishop Wilfrid's appeal, a copy was almost certainly available at York before a falsified version became a weapon in Canterbury's assertion of its primacy.[87]

If these are indeed Alcuin's principal contributions to the *Libri Carolini*, they are modest enough. But they are entirely in line with his formation and attitudes hitherto—the born teacher's or professional adviser's interest in correct method, on an issue in which he is not intellectually fully

---

[85]Sieben, *Konzilsidee*, pp. 334ff.

[86]See Wallach, *Alcuin and Charlemagne*, pp. 175f., and add MGH Epp. 4:448, 21 (l. 30).

[87]W. Levison, "Die Akten der römischen Synode von 679," in *Aus Rheinischer u. Fränkischer Frühzeit* (Düsseldorf, 1948), pp. 267-294, text at pp. 288-293. Compare:

| acta c. 11 (p. 292f.) | LC 4.28 (ed. Bastgen, p. 227.) |
|---|---|
| saluberrima doctrina sacrorum canonum quam et pontificalium decretorum statuimus . . . non inveniant nec disseminent sua scismata vel errores, dum falce piae doctrinae, praesule praedicante, . . . et in multorum praesulum cum suo archiepiscopo convenientium concilio . . . sicut ubi duo vel tres congregati in nomine Domini . . . multo magis, ubi plures unianimiter ad confitendum *etc* | Cum ergo duarum et trium provinciarum praesules in unum conveniunt, si antiquorum canonum institutione muniti aliquid praedicationis aut dogmatis statuunt, quod tamen ab antiquorum Patrum dogmatibus non discrepat, catholicum est quod faciunt, et fortasse dici potest universale, quoniam, quamvis non sit ab universi orbis praesulibus actum *etc* |

Indeed, passages in the letter to Elipand and the synodal letter prepared at Frankfurt, of which Alcuin's authorship seems certain (see n. 88) are even closer to *acta* cit.: see most conveniently Wallach, *Alcuin and Charlemagne*, p. 175.

engaged; or rather, is engaged only in that he shares with the principal author a rejection of doctrinal *novitates* and of the notions of political and ecclesiastical authority by which they were being sustained. Alone, they could never have justified the Frankish king's extraordinary request, and the acceptance of it by the members of the synod, that they should accept him "in suo consortio sive in orationibus, eo quod esset vir in ecclesiasticis doctrinis eruditus" — the admission of a deacon and *magister* into the company of episcopal *doctores!*[88] The case must have rested principally on his drafting of two anti-Adoptionist documents, a letter in Charles's name to Archbishop Elipand of Toledo and a "synodal letter" in the name of the assembled bishops to their brethren in Spain.[89]

The view maintained by Spanish bishops who were seeking to overturn more bizarre heresies in the early 780s, that Christ was the truly-begotten Son of God in respect of his Divine Nature but adoptive Son of God in his human nature, seems already to have come to the notice of the Frankish court and of Alcuin by 788/9; and one of the two main proponents, Bishop Felix of Urgel, acknowledged his errors at Regensburg and Rome, while Alcuin was in Northumbria, in 792.[90] The heresy may have worried Alcuin more than most of the bishops to whose *consortium* he was admitted in 794 — for it conflicted with propositions that he had evidently read and found sympathetic in Augustine's *De Trinitate* while still at York and then in the simpler *De imagine Dei*. To deny that in his humanity as well as in his divinity Christ was begotten of God would make it more difficult to sustain the view that godlikeness lies within

---

[88]MGH Conc. 2/1:171 (c. 56). This unusual—unique?—episcopal honoring of a man who had not been advanced beyond deacon's orders has attracted surprisingly little comment, perhaps because there has been a tendency to ante-date (and thereby to exaggerate) Alcuin's influence on "matters of church and state": compare the minor part allocated to Alcuin in the record of the English legatine councils in 786, MGH Epp. 4:28. He was, however, clearly far more influential when he returned to Northumbria in 790. *Consortium*, which occurs in a number of different contexts in Carolingian capitularies and synodal decrees (but *consortium episcoporum* seemingly only in the Carolingian-period *Vita Eusebii Vercellensis*, ed. Ughelli, *Italia Sacra*, 4/2:756c), is here being used in its basic meaning of "fellowship" in the fullest sense.

[89]Wallach, *Alcuin and Charlemagne*, pp. 169ff.

[90]I regard *Admonitio generalis* c. 82 (MGH Capit. 1:62): "quia scimus temporibus novissimis pseudodoctores esse venturos" etc., as a specific reference to the spread of the Adoptionist heresy; and cf. Epp. 4:117 (no. 74): "sunt tempora periculosa, ut apostoli praedixerunt, quia multi pseudodoctores surgent, novas introducentes sectas." The essential references for the (ill-documented) Regensburg synod in 792 are in Böhmer-Mühlbacher, *Regesta imperii*, 1, 2nd ed. (1908), 317b, 318a: there is possibly additional indirect evidence for the names of some of the participants.

man's potential, even though individuals have through their sinfulness marred their image-likeness to God. If Alcuin, as one suspects, never fully grasped (like most of us!) the psychology of Augustine's notion of a human selfhood composed of will, intelligence and memory (forming one substance), he was to proclaim subsequently his awareness of the in-separability of the Divine Trinity from that triad of the soul.[91]

Alcuin evidently assumed that the several statements sent from the Frankfurt synod to the dissentient Spaniards had disposed of their heresy once and for all. In 795 he was still hoping to return to his beloved York and end his days there; and only in 796 did he accept that this would not happen.[92] His main preoccupations in those years were ones which had their origins in his four decades of learning and teaching at York: the linked responsibilities of the education of *adolescentes*, the effective communication of *evangelica veritas* and everyday pastoral guidance, all adapted to the needs and capacity of the recipients. This is abundantly clear in the prefatory letter of what is (if we reject Alcuin's authorship of the *De imagine Dei*) his first written work of exegesis, namely — to use the title found in the earliest, Corbie, manuscript — *Questiones in Genesim ad litteram* [thus associating it with the more elaborate work of Augustine's] *per interrogationes et responsiones Albini magistri*. The in-terrogator, his pupil and companion Sigwulf, is worried about quite other problems than how man is "made in the image of God." Alcuin duly obliges with concise answers "maxime historicae et simplici respon-sione," there being other and more difficult questions which would re-quire a very different treatment. If the answers he gives are not always those found in the "weighty volumes" he uses, this is because they were not tackling questions put quite in the way that Sigwulf does. Moreover, even when Alcuin uses sentences or phrases taken from earlier authors — principally but hardly exclusively Augustine — without change or with minor changes to expound his Genesis text, the context in which they occur and the adaptations (however slight) commonly have the ef-fect of altering the sense of the source commentary.[93]

---

[91]Marenbon, *From the Circle of Alcuin*, pp. 44ff., but applying his comments to the *De animae ratione* and other genuine works of Alcuin (as argued above, pp. 29–31).

[92]MGH Epp. 4:87–89 (no. 43), 90, 92; ibid., 147, 169.

[93]Prefatory letter in Epp. 4, no. 80, full text of the *Questiones* in PL 100:516–566. The ti-tle quoted is that in Düsseldorf (ex-Stadtbibl., now Heinrich Heine-Institut) cod. B.3 (*CLA* viii, 1183) fol. 25: written in "a-b script," seemingly in a community of nuns in the vicinity of Corbie; the text is apparently that of Alcuin's "second edition" of ca. 798. For the title of

Giving a definitive written form to aspects of his teaching for the lasting guidance of those already grounded in the faith was not Alcuin's only preoccupation in his final years at the court. The recent rapid success of Carolingian arms in the southeast, a decade after the painfully achieved victory over the Saxons, had brought to the fore major problems of pastoral theology, and possibly drawn attention to the continuing consequences of "liturgical disarray."[94] During Alcuin's time at York the ceremony and sacrament of baptism, whatever the scope and character of the cathedral's responsibilities in the matter, will almost invariably have been bestowed on infants whose sponsors answered for their beliefs.[95] Frankish conquest had re-created the adult catechumenate. The unique copy of the "Old Gelasian" sacramentary made at Chelles in the middle (or third quarter) of the century preserved the greater part of the ancient Lenten-season services that were a preparation for adult baptism; its text of this Easter Eve service, however, includes interpolations referring to the baptism of *infantes*, without giving the formula used at the font. "Frankish Gelasian" sacramentaries adapt their received texts to the needs of infant baptism in various ways, and at least two provide the formula hitherto lacking — *Baptizo te in nomine Patris*, etc.[96] The *Hadrianum*,

---

Augustine's work in early Carolingian MSS see, e.g., Paris BN lat. 1804 (S. France, s. IX *in*) fol. 37: *Beati Augustini in Genesim ad litteram quaestionum libri duodecim. De principio Genesis*; similarly, Berlin Phillips 1651 (Rose no. 24) (court of Louis the Pious/E. France?, ca. 810–830) fol. 3. Later MSS of Alcuin's work usually call it simply *Quaestiones* (*Albini*) *in Genesim* or something similar. For Alcuin's sources cf. Katherine O'Brien O'Keefe in *Sacris Erudiri* 18 (1978/9), 463–483.

[94] The one good English-language account of the baptismal rites in the early Carolingian period is G. Ellard, *Master Alcuin, Liturgist* (Chicago, 1956), chap. 4, although I disagree with him on a number of points of detail. Dahlhaus-Berg, pp. 92–98, is helpful and has additional references. See also T. C. Akeley, *Christian Initiation in Spain c. 300–1000* (London, 1967), esp. pt. 2.

[95] The English legatine synod of 786, c. 2 (MGH Epp. 4:21) is specific on the responsibilities of sponsors at infant baptisms, as are several subsequent Carolingian conciliar decrees. The requirement that "baptismus secundum canonica statuta exerceatur et non alio tempore nisi pro magna necessitate" refers to the (revived?) Roman practice of baptism only on Easter Eve or exceptionally at Pentecost: see M. Andrieu, *Les Ordines Romani du Haut Moyen Age*, 2 (Louvain, 1948), pp. 380–447, esp. 382f., 400ff.; id., 3 (1951), pp. 79f.; Akeley, *Christian Initiation,* pp. 162ff. By analogy with Rome and with cathedral churches in Francia in the eighth century it is likely that in Alcuin's lifetime the only font in York was at the cathedral and that some infants were brought in from country districts: but surprisingly I do not find any reference to baptismal responsibilities in Alcuin's letters to York clergy. For the creed used in these ceremonies, see below.

[96] "Old Gelasian": Vat. MS Reg. Lat. 316, *CLA* i, 105, vi, [p.] xxii; ed. H. A. Wilson (Oxford, 1894), pp. 34–60 (1.26–36), 78–88 (1.42–44), with Andrieu, op. cit., 2:380ff. "Frankish [*al.*

the "Gregorian" Papal mass book sent to the Frankish court in the late 780s, was singularly unhelpful; and an already old Roman *ordo*, which may have reached Francia earlier, introduced other elements of confusion.[97]

Alcuin's position on the central pastoral-theological problem is unambiguous. His notion both of the human personality and of "true faith" made any repetition of the coercion practiced on the Saxons unacceptable. Writing to the king to congratulate him on the decisive defeat of the Avars, he emphasizes the urgent necessity of sending properly qualified missionary clergy. Matthew's words "Go, teach all nations, baptizing them in the name of the Father and of the Son and of the Holy Ghost" are glossed with a telling passage from St. Jerome's Commentary: "First, they teach all peoples; and *when these have been taught*, they are dipped in water." Instruction is to take account of age, and for the person who has reached maturity the framework is supposedly found in Augustine's *De cathecizandis rudibus*, which had, of course, been composed to meet very different circumstances: in fact, Alcuin simply lists four groups of dogmatic topics, to be treated successively, beginning (unexpectedly but not uncharacteristically) with "the immortality of the soul." When very shortly afterwards Bishop Arno of Salzburg, in whose mission area the newly annexed territories were, asked him for something "on preaching to the pagans," Alcuin — pressed for time — sent him a copy of his letter to the king, which duly figures in a later Salzburg manuscript with the rubric *Dictatus Albini magistri*.[98] A promise to write to Arno in the future at greater length was, however, kept. Here Alcuin emphasized again the importance of conversion by proper instruction and the working of the Holy Spirit *in anima per fidem* before baptism in water; but he devoted very much more of the letter to symbolism and the "mysteries" of the baptismal ceremonies than to the techniques of evangelization. Its importance in the eyes of its recipient is nonetheless suggested by its being copied onto the opening leaves of the earliest

---

Eighth-century] Gelasians": Paris, BN lat. 12048 (*CLA* v, 618), *Liber Sacramentorum Gellonensis*, ed. A. Dumas (CC 1593; Turnhout, 1981), p. 100 (no. 707); Karlsruhe *Aug.* CXII (*CLA* viii, 1081), *Das Palimpsestsakramentar im Codex Augiensis CXII*, ed. A. Dold and A. Baumstark, Texte u. Arbeiten 12 (1925), p. 26. For the formula in "Gallican" books and the significance of the *Gellone* texts see especially Andrieu, *Ordines*, 3:89f.

[97]*Le Sacramentaire grégorien*, ed. J. Deshusses (Fribourg [Switz.], 1971), p. 188: but cf. p. 336, an early addition for sickroom baptism; Andrieu's Ordo 11, *Ordines*, 2:380–447 (noting especially the observations at 407–408) and its adaptation in Ordo 15 (Frankish, 3rd quarter of eighth century), *Ordines*, 3:45–125, especially 110–112, 116–120.

[98]MGH Epp. 4, nos. 112, 110: for the Salzburg MS of the latter see above, pp. 27f.

manuscript of any of Alcuin's letters (and other works), written apparently at Arno's northern abbey of St. Amand in the latter part of 798 or the early months of 799 but very quickly taken to Salzburg.[99]

The greatly extended use of "the sacred ceremonial of baptism" for adult converts, accompanied probably by a continuing uncertainty as to its precise forms, prompted Alcuin to produce succinct accounts of the significance of its necessary component elements. He may well have begun by preparing a florilegium of relevant older texts: one such, under a title that begins "Of the office of baptism and its mystical senses," is transmitted by three ninth-century manuscripts, all apparently from the lower Loire and all containing other works of Alcuin's. Prominent among the excerpts are ones from the early sixth-century letter of the Roman deacon John to Senarius of Ravenna (preserved uniquely and not quite complete in a mid-ninth-century manuscript), answering a query about the three Lenten "scrutinies" and other features of the baptismal liturgy in terms of an adult catechumenate, although Senarius had specifically raised it in relation to *infantes*.[100] Adapted, shortened or amplified they provide a substantial part of the framework of Alcuin's brief exposition of the baptismal ceremonies in a letter to his onetime pupil Oduin—written, apparently, sometime in 798—and as one section of the long letter to "the monks of Gothia."[101] The several allegorical explanations, notably lacking in the excesses of later commentators, seem to be substantially Alcuin's own (at least, I have failed to identify any direct sources); and one is particularly telling. John the Deacon had said that the triple immersion in the water at baptism was obviously right: "nam qui in trinitatis nomine baptizandus accedit, ipsam utique trinitatem debet demersione signare et illius se agnoscere beneficiis debitorem *qui tertio die resurrexit a*

---

[99]MGH Epp. 4, no. 113, where, however, the reading of Vienna Nationalbibl. cod. 795 *Praesagum nomen tibi* must be restored to the beginning of the letter (to give a properly Alcuinian hexameter); full facsimile of the MS ed. F. Unterkircher, *Alkuin-Briefe u. andere Traktate*, Codices Selecti 20 (Graz, 1969): for the makeup, origin and scribes of the MS see now the remarkable analysis by Bischoff, *Südostdeutsche Schreibschulen*, 2:115–119.

[100]Florilegium: A. Wilmart, *Analecta Reginensia*, Studi e Testi 59 (Vatican City, 1933), pp. 153–156, 157–170 (text); John the Deacon's letter: id., 156–157, 170–179 (text).

[101]MGH Epp. 4:202f. (no. 134), 214f. (no. 137). The Oduin letter initially circulated as part of a *libellus*, consisting of a "second edition" of the *Quaestiones in Genesim* and four letter-treatises and evidently compiled under Alcuin's personal supervision ca. 798 (as a "Lenten-book" or Easter gift for his friends?), which is best represented by Paris BN lat. 13373, Munich clm. 14727 and Munich clm. 14760. The earliest evidence for the *libellus* is the copying of three of the letters (but not the Oduin letter) as a distinct group in Vienna 795 fols. 150v–155.

*mortuis.*" Alcuin, by contrast, says of the triple immersion that "recte
*homo qui ad imaginem sanctae Trinitatis conditus est* per invocationem
sanctae Trinitatis ad eandem renovatur imaginem et . . . tertio elevatus
de fonte per gratiam resurgat ad vitam."[102]

Alcuin's exposition clearly met a widefelt need. In the form of the complete letter to Oduin or increasingly commonly with the omission of everything before "Primo paganus caticumenus fit" and with some such title as
*Ratio de sacro baptismati*, it was copied down to the twelfth century in
books intended for library or schoolroom and for sacristy or choir.[103]
Whether Alcuin or someone under his direct inspiration subsequently combined parts of both the letter to the king and the letter to Oduin with
passages from the Fathers to form a more elaborate "missionary handbook"
(or a section of one) with a more limited circulation is debatable.

A probably Mondsee manuscript of the 820s opens with just such a
text, entitled *Ordo de catecizandis rudibus vel quid sunt singula quae
geruntur in sacramento baptismatis.* The same work with omissions and
other slight changes occurs in a Freising manuscript of about the same
date and (copied from it) in another Freising manuscript of the late ninth
century. A greatly expanded version, with additions from – among other
works – Augustine's *De catecizandis rudibus* and Alcuin's own *De fide
sanctae Trinitatis*, is to be found in a onetime Fécamp manuscript now at
Rouen, from which it has recently been edited by M. J.-P. Bouhot. On
the assumption that the Freising version is the "original" one, it was attributed by its first editor to Arno and more recently – in respect of its
opening section (before the extracts from Nicetas of Remesiana) at
least – to Bishop Hitto of Freising. A link with Charlemagne's "questionnaire" to a number of his bishops in 812 about their teaching of the baptismal ceremonies which itself appears to be based on Alcuin's letters on
the subject has been suggested and denied. Already in 1937, however,
Professor Heinz Löwe argued (in a study apparently ignored by all subsequent commentators) that the Freising text was Alcuin's own and
perhaps earlier than the Oduin letter, with which it nonetheless has some

---

[102]Wilmart, *Analecta Reginensia*, p. 174, cf. p. 161 (florilegium); Epp. 4:202, 214.

[103]I have noted nine such manuscript texts additional to those listed by Dümmler, and
there are doubtless others. According to J.-P. Bouhot in *Revue des études augustiniennes*
24 (1978), 280–282, *Primo paganus* is an older text which Alcuin merely copied into his two
letters: but this notion is difficult to reconcile both with the links between Alcuin's
phraseology and the florilegium extracts from John the Deacon and with the change of
wording quoted in the text.

passages in common.[104] The consequential proposition, however, that the Mondsee text was an expansion of Alcuin's original version, by someone who inserted additional passages both from that letter and from Nicetas's *Instructio*, is not easy to accept: a reverse relationship between the two seems far more plausible. The novel theory of M. Bouhot that the long Fécamp version is the original one, the work of a cleric in the circle of Arno who took as his starting point the copy of Alcuin's letter to the king and developed from it a comprehensive guide to the preparation for admission into the Church of adult converts based on patristic authors and Alcuin himself, presents other difficulties. A thorough reexamination of all relevant texts may point the way to a definitive solution. Meanwhile, all that can be claimed with confidence is that a presumably south German *Ordo de cathecizandis rudibus*, compiled to help those working in the Avar mission field, and constructed on the principle that true faith could only be professed by those who had been guided to a proper understanding of its tenets, owed its inspiration and some of its wording to Alcuin.[105]

[104]MSS: Vienna, Nat. Bibl. cod. 1370, newly dated and localized by Bischoff, *Südostdeutsche Schreibschulen*, 2:11, 24; Munich, clm. 6325, 6324 (Bischoff, op. cit., 1:107, 2:222); Rouen, Bib. mun. MS 469 (A.214). Editions: (from clm. 6325, fols. 134v–140v) A. R. Burn, in *Zeitschrift für Kirchengeschichte* 25 (1904), 148–154; (id., fols. 134v–136 only) R. McKitterick, *The Frankish Church and the Carolingian Reforms*, p. 213; (from clm. 6325, 6324 with some use of the other two MSS) H. Löwe, *Die Karolingische Reichsgründung und der Südosten,* Forsch. z. Kirchen- und Geistesgesch. 13 (Stuttgart, 1937), pp. 171–177; (Rouen 469) J.-P. Bouhot, "Alcuin et le 'De cathecizandis rudibus,'" *Recherches augustiniennes* 15 (1980), 204–230. Authorship and connection with inquiry of 812: Burn, l.c. (*for* the connection; Arno the author), McKitterick, op. cit., pp. 211f. (*against* the connection; Hitto the author: but this depends on assumptions about clm. 6325 and Vienna 1370 which are in large part incorrect); Löwe, op. cit., pp. 177–181, cf. pp. 93ff. The best text of the questionnaire is in *Amalarii opera*, ed. Hanssens, 1:235f.; a good summary account of its sources and the answers, with references to previous literature, is in Dahlhaus-Berg, pp. 99–105, to which add now Bouhot, art. cit., pp. 197–200.

[105]Bouhot, pp. 194–200, 230–238. Bouhot seems to me clearly right when, remarking on the omission from the Freising text of some rubrics and development of the arguments under each head which are in the Mondsee text, he concludes that on the basis of the Munich MSS "il serait très difficile – et dans la pratique impossible – de reconstituer le texte transmis par le manuscrit de Vienne" (p. 197). His notion, however, that a ?Salzburg cleric in 812 answered the questions posed in the imperial letter by omitting almost everything in an existing "long" *Ordo* that was not relevant to them, while retaining *its* sequence and departing from that of the questionnaire; and that subsequently another cleric abbreviated it further, often to the point of unintelligibility but skillfully omitting (mostly) passages from Nicetas that may have been identified as such and passages from Alcuin's letters that certainly weren't, is extraordinarily difficult to believe.

The creed quoted at length in the Fécamp and Mondsee texts of the *Ordo* which we know as "the Apostles' Creed," in its eighth-century (*textus receptus*) version, is of little help in this connection. It is unlikely but not excluded that Alcuin had that particular creed in mind when he wrote in his letter to Oduin: "Deinde *symboli apostolici* traditur ei fides." The baptismal *symbolum* used at York in his lifetime was almost certainly the long and difficult "Niceno-Constantinopolitan" creed which he had copied into his florilegium, as it undoubtedly was in contemporary Rome. The "profession of faith" included in the letter written in Charles's name to the heretical Spanish bishops in 794 is a mosaic, in which that same creed is a major but not the only substantial element.[106] Alcuin held to the view over many years that all the essential articles of the Christian faith were to be found in the credal statements of the Fathers and he implies that the age of composing such statements was already long past; but he never asserted as categorically as his friend Paulinus of Aquileia that the Niceno-Constantinopolitan creed was a unique touchstone and *fundamentum fidei.*[107]

The Frankish court's familiarity with the "new" Apostles' Creed, in a context which implies that it was already established as a feature of the offices sung in the Chapel, is however shown by its inclusion in the final section of the "Degulf Psalter" (Vienna, Nat. Bibl. MS lat. 1861), written for presentation to the Pope in, probably, 794–795. The particular combination of the nine "Roman" canticles, all in a Vulgate (as distinct from

[106]"Apostles' Creed" in the S. German *ordo*: ed. Bouhot, p. 219f. The tests for this eighth-century revision of the "Old Roman" creed (for the origins of which see Kelly, *Early Christian Creeds*, pp. 397-420) are particularly: *qui conceptus est de Spiritu sancto, natus ex Maria virgine* in place of *Natus est de Spiritu sancto et Maria virgine; passus* before *sub Pontio Pilato*; and the addition of *et vitam aeternam*: Kelly, pp. 369f., lists eight other differences. Evidence for knowledge of the "Old Roman" version in England is provided by London BL Roy. 2 A xx (*CLA* ii, ed. 2, 215) fol. 12, of which there is a "diplomatic" edition in Kuypers, *Book of Cerne*, p. 205; and perhaps by Oxford, Bodl. Laud. gr. 35 (*CLA* ii, ed. 2, 251) fol. 226v, an addition to the original MS in eighth-century uncial although perhaps not English uncial. Niceno-Constantinopolitan Creed in the baptismal ceremonies: Gelasian Sacr., ed. Wilson, pp. 53-55 (1.35), *Lib. sacr. Gellonensis*, ed. Dumas, pp. 68-70, nos. 544-548, with J. N. D. Kelly, *Early Christian Creeds*, 3rd ed. (London, 1972), pp. 346-348; for the "York" text of this creed, see above. Profession of faith: MGH Conc. 2:163-164, convincingly analyzed by Wallach, *Alcuin and Charlemagne*, pp. 152-154, but wrongly supposing it to have been used in the Aachen Chapel "liturgy of the mass."

[107]Synod of Friuli, 796/7: MGH Conc. 2:180ff., 187; of Alcuin's exuberant praise for the text produced by Paulinus (including *filioque*) for general circulation in the Frankish dominions, Epp. 4, no. 139.

an Old Latin) biblical version, with the *Te Deum, Gloria* and Creeds which figures here for the first time, has been credited to Alcuin: at this date and for that destination his involvement does not seem very likely, although certainly not to be ruled out entirely.[108] More plausible, but still unproven, is the attribution to Alcuin of the collection of creeds which likewise makes its first appearance in the preliminary matter of the Psalter. It was well suited as an instrument for battering (Alcuin's own metaphor) the maintainers of false belief; and both the court and Tours have a documented place in its subsequent diffusion, with subtractions from and additions to the original five.[109]

[108]Fullest description of the texts in Vienna 1861 (*CLA* x, 1504) fols. 146–150v in R. Beer, *Monumenta palaeographica Vindobonensia*, 1 (Leipzig, 1910), pp. 32f. (I am grateful to Frl. Eva Irblich for enabling me to study this marvelous and precious manuscript for as many hours as I wished under difficult conditions for the library.) I think it unlikely that Alcuin, who had been brought up with the Roman Psalter and the Roman *cantica*, would have thought a Gallican Psalter with a new liturgical supplement with revised texts of the established *cantica* an appropriate text to send to the pope, as supposed by J. Mearns, *The Canticles of the Christian Church Eastern and Western in Early and Medieval Times* (Cambridge, 1914), p. 62. That it established itself quickly as a standard feature of Psalters — and therefore of the Office — in Francia is demonstrated by Mearns, pp. 63ff. and Schneider, *Altlat. Bibl. Cantica*, p. 53 (see also F. Wormald, *The Utrecht Psalter* [Utrecht, 1953], p. 13). Both Amalarius and Hrabanus Maurus quote it as the normal *cantica* series (the second-named observing that it is not used in Rome itself) without connecting it with Alcuin: Schneider, p. 54, with references. I have little doubt that it was created for and first sung in the royal chapel, whose head was now (Arch)bishop Hildebald of Cologne (for whose active interest in its services see the references collected by J. Fleckenstein, *Die Hofkapelle der deutschen Könige*, 1: *Grundlegung. Die karolingische Hofkapelle*, Schriften der MGH 16/1 [Stuttgart, 1959], p. 50). It may be relevant that in Vienna 1861 a second — anonymous — scribe takes over from Dagulf precisely where the text of the supplement begins (fol. 146: the second leaf of a quire).

[109]Vienna 1861, fols. 5–10, the complete collection subsequently in Rome, Casa dei Padri Maristi, MS A. II 1 fols. 107–110 (followed in both by the pompous paraphrase of the Lord's Prayer, inc. *Siderio genitor residens*) and in Brussels, Bibl. royale, MS 8654–72 of s. IX *in* (Bischoff; not s. X as in the Brussels *Catalogue*), fols. 108–111: the latter is an unusual version of the miscellaneous "handbook" for clerics, favored by ecclesiastics who were or had been in close touch with the court. Partial collections, in association with other creeds, are in the final section of Benedict of Aniane's *Munimenta fidei*, BN lat. 2390, fols. 94v–102v, and in Karlsruhe cod. Aug. XVIII fols. 13v–63v. The main argument for crediting Alcuin with the compiling of the basic five-creed collection, although hardly a conclusive one, is that Insular symbols and Insular symptoms occur in the text of the *Expositio fidei catholicae sancti Hieronimi* (recte *Pelagii*) in both the Vienna and the Marist MSS, and at different places (and also in the isolated text of the same creed in Vatican MS Lat. 650 fols. 37v–38v). If he were responsible, then it is ironical that the *Fides sancti Ambrosii* including *Patrem et filium et spiritum sanctum confitemur* should figure in all five collections: for it is now generally accepted that this creed (of which the earliest MS appears to be the mid-eighth-century Milan, Bibl. Ambr., cod. I, 101 sup., fols. 73v, 75: ed. E. S. Buchanan in *Journ. Theol. Studies* 8 [1907], p. 542) is Priscillianist!

A similar degree of uncertainty prevails over the form of words which Alcuin favored or was accustomed to for baptism at the font. The view that he was responsible for the adoption of the distinctive *Et ego te baptizo,* etc., rather than the *Baptizo te,* etc., of the "Frankish Gelasians" and of the *Hadrianum's* prayer set for the baptism of the sick, depends entirely on the appearance of the first of these forms in the "Gregorian Supplement." If, as is now widely accepted, the author of the latter was Benedict of Aniane and not Alcuin, the occurrence of the *Et ego* formula in non-Gregorianized Spanish books acquires a new significance; and it becomes more probable that *Baptizo te* was the form with which Alcuin was familiar.[110] His insistence on the accompanying threefold immersion, on the other hand, is unambiguous and indeed obsessive. Pope Gregory I and no doubt many after him regarded a single or a triple immersion with indifference, as pertaining to practice and not faith. To Alcuin, who found grounds for denying Gregory's authority on this point, the triple immersion was both a type of the Trinity and a visible manifestation of the workings of Divine Grace. Rejection of the alternative "single immersion" which was normally practiced in Spain, and of the perhaps more truly aberrant triple repetition of the entire baptismal formula, became inextricably linked with the task of overthrowing once and for all the "false teaching" of the Adoptionists.[111]

---

[110]The key texts are: *Sacr. Gellon.,* ed. Dumas, no. 707 (p. 100); *Das Palimpsestsakramentar im Cod. Aug. CXII,* ed. Dold and Baumstark (n. 95), p. 26—the editors somewhat ante-dating the MS; *Ordo* 15, c. 74 (the initial words, however, omitted in the MSS), *Ordo* 28, c. 75; ed. Andrieu, *Ordines Romani,* 3:112, 407 (for the dates of these texts see the editor's introductions); *Le Sacramentaire grégorien,* ed. J. Deshusses, 1 (Fribourg en Suisse, 1971), no. 982 (p. 336), cf. Suppl. no. 1085 (p. 378). For Alcuin's supposed authorship of the latter, compare Ellard, *Master Alcuin,* chap. 4, especially pp. 71ff., with the views of Deshusses, considered below, pp. 66f. Akeley, *Christian Initiation in Spain,* pp. 176f., 191ff., cf. 212, noted "the absolute unanimity" of the (late) *libri ordinum,* "decidedly unlike in some respects, . . . that the baptismal sentence begins *et ego,*" and the hints in pre-711 Spanish writers that it may already have been in use in their time: but he was understandably reluctant to assert categorically its Visigothic-Spanish origin.

[111]The hardening of Alcuin's attitude can be followed from Epp. 4, no. 113 (p. 165) through id., no. 134 (p. 202) = no. 137 (p. 214) to id., no. 137 (212) and no. 139 (p. 221): see further Andrieu, *Ordines,* 3:87ff. (unfortunately with out-of-date references and wrong dates), Ellard, *Master Alcuin,* pp. 74ff. and (for the Spanish background, the single immersion being originally anti-Arian) Akeley, *Christian Initiation,* passim, noting (pp. 177, 191) that neither Spanish liturgical texts nor the polemic of the Adoptionists ever specify the number of immersions customary in their churches. Pope Gregory's certainly authentic letter—cf. Alcuin in Epp. 4, no. 137 (p. 215)—is in his *Registrum* Lib. 1, no. 41, ed. Hartmann, MGH Epp. 1:57: but there is a branch of the MS tradition in which it is lacking and Alcuin's *epistolaris liber* was presumably of this kind.

The tone of Alcuin's surviving correspondence from 795/6, in conjunction with the evidence of his other activities, is — I have argued — good evidence that he thought that the issue had been settled by the statements, largely his, sent from Frankfurt to the Spanish clergy. Such confidence, too many years spent dealing with generally respectful adolescent pupils and (more recently) lecturing the rulers of three kingdoms on their conduct, probably explain why, having learnt shortly after his arrival at Tours in 796/7 that the heresy was far from dead, Alcuin addressed himself in the terms he did to Felix of Urgel and his powerful supporter Elipand of Toledo.

The letter to the first-named is preserved only in the later pages of the St. Amand–Salzburg manuscript of 798/99, a copy having presumably been sent to Arno for the edification of the archbishop and his clergy, one of whom subsequently provided the "title" *Epistola Albini ad Felicem hereticum.*[112] Alcuin was here writing *litterae exhortatoriae,* but of a special kind: "It is with great love and humility that I have written. . . . As the love of many waxes cold at the end of the world, what can insignificant men like us do better than follow the teaching of the Apostles and the Gospels? . . . All the world bears witness that we proclaim Christ the true son of God." In spite of his complaints about Tours's deficiencies compared with beloved York, Alcuin had found there books that were very germane to his purpose of facing doctrinal falsehood with truth: notably, a recent copy of the Latin *acta* of the Council of Ephesus in 431.[113] After a perhaps quick but intelligent reading — suggesting long experience of "gutting" substantial texts — he set an amanuensis to copying out passages he had indicated, in some cases with his autograph marginal note. Alcuin was thus provided with a florilegium (at second hand) of

[112]Epp. 4, no. 23; Vienna 795 fols. 179–183v: for the writers of these leaves see now Bischoff, *Südostdeutsche Schreibschulen,* 2:117. Bischoff had earlier proposed the redating of the letter to 797: "Aus Alkuins Erdentagen" [1962], *Mittelalterliche Studien,* 2 (Stuttgart, 1967), here pp. 16f.; see further W. Heil, *Alkuinstudien,* 1 (cit. above, n. 3), pp. 14–17 — making it one of the starting points for a remarkable reexamination of the chronology of the Adoptionist dispute, with important consequences for the history of these years.

[113]L. Ott, "Das Konzil von Ephesus (431) in der Theologie der Frühscholastik," in *Theologie in Geschichte und Gegenwart: Michael Schmaus zum 60. Geburtstag,* ed. J. Auer and H. Volk (Munich, 1957), pp. 289f.; Bischoff, "Aus Alkuins Erdentagen," pp. 14ff. and pl. 1; G. B. Blumenshine, ed., *Liber Alcuini contra haeresim Felicis,* Studi e Testi 285 (Vatican, 1980), especially chap. 3 and pp. 105–109. The full text of the Latin *acta* of the Council of Ephesus in the Tours MS, BN lat. 1572 is in E. Schwartz, *Acta conciliorum oecumenicorum,* 1, 3 (Berlin-Leipzig, 1929).

Athanasius, Cyril and other definers and defenders of trinitarian orthodoxy: the fifteen or so that were quoted in the letter to Felix were
evidently only part of a larger collection which eventually included
material from a much wider range of patristic authors. Somewhat later —
towards the end of 797 or even early in 798 — Alcuin sent to Elipand what
was in effect a mini-treatise rather than a letter: it is to be noted that it was
not included in any of the letter collections made by his friends or pupils
but is transmitted only as part of a dossier on Adoptionism in two ninth-
century manuscripts which seem to have as a common source a collection
long kept at the Frankish court. Citing only passages in the New Testament and Psalter in support, Alcuin argues that the idea that Christ was
*adoptivus* can only be maintained by those who have a wrong notion of
baptism (especially Christ's) and are not as familiar as they ought to be
with either the Gospels or the *doctores*.[114]

Before the end of March 798, however, Alcuin's expanded florilegium
had provided him with substantial sections of a *Libellus* "against the
heresy of Felix," apparently intended from the start for a wider reader-
ship than the heretics alone. The opening sentences suggest that Alcuin
was in danger of letting metaphor run away with him. The notion that
true Christian teachers are the medicine of the soul is an old one, used by
Alcuin in (for example) the poem with which he had concluded a letter to
Canterbury at the time of the sack of Lindisfarne in 793: now it is expanded into an analogy between what — as he has learnt from "secular
histories" — medical men have done in plague conditions and what he is
seeking to do. Of the sixty-six pages that follow (in the unique extant
manuscript), all but about sixteen are taken up with patristic *testimonia*.
It does not seem to have impressed its first readers very much. Alcuin
sent it first to the king "nec in libelli nomen exploratum sed in scedulis
dispersum": it was returned without any serious examination by
Charles's other advisers. Presumably for this reason Alcuin then "published" it, by sending copies to a bishop who was making his own collection
of testimonies — probably but not certainly Theodulf of Orléans — and

---

[114]Epp. 4, no. 166, redated by Heil, *Alkuinstudien*, pp. 11–12, 58 n. 326. The MSS are
Rheims, Bib. mun. cod. 385 (a Hincmar MS) which was "lost" at the time of Dümmler's
edition, fols. 95v–101, and Paris BN lat. 5577 of s. IX *ex.* fols. 20–27; Vat. Reg. lat. 69 is a
copy of the second-named (unless it is a twin, as Wilmart thought), Paris BN lat. 2386 is
*perhaps* a copy of the Rheims MS. An earlier and in some respects better witness to the first
part of the ?court dossier (corresponding to Rheims 385, fols. 61–95) is in one of Baturich
of Regensburg's MSS, Munich clm. 14468, fols. 30v–88, of 821.

to "the monks of Gothia," without the dedication to the king which a later letter suggests had been Alcuin's original intention.[115] It would nonetheless be a mistake to dismiss the treatise as a work of no apologetic or intellectual interest. Equally, it would be a mistake to claim too much for it. The predominance of (acknowledged) quotation is evidence first and foremost of Alcuin's assiduity, a skill in garnering — to use his own already quoted metaphor — "other men's flowers" and a respect for the *auctores*: *novitas* must always be suspect.[116] Paulinus of Aquileia's "Three Books against Bishop Felix of Urgel" is in that sense more original and more closely argued.[117] The patristic citations from

[115]Best edition by Blumenshine, cit., pp. 55–99, from the Lorsch MS, Vat. pal. lat. 290. Compare with c. 1 (Blumenshine, p. 55), Epp. 4, no. 17, p. 48. Note that when Alcuin wrote to the king in early February 798 (Epp. 4, no. 143), the main intellectual preoccupation of both men seems to have been why Septuagesima, etc., were so called: Isanbert, apparently a S. German pupil of Alcuin's in his Tours days, regarded his letter and the king's further comments (Epp. 4, no. 144) as sufficiently important to include them in a distinctive collection of Alcuin and Alcuin-related texts, now Vienna 966 (at fols. 24v–27). The reference to the sending of the unbound MS of the work against Felix is a merely incidental feature of a letter which is principally concerned with the problems of the *saltus lunae*, Epp. 4, no. 145, p. 243, and which in the early ninth-century Tours collection, Troyes, Bib. mun. MS 1165, fol. 22v, has the lemma *Item ad domnum regem responsio contra quasdam obiectiones*. The evidence that copies of the libellus were sent in the early summer of 798 to Theodulf and to the monks of Gothia comes from Epp. 4, no. 160, of that date, and id., no. 205 of early summer 799 (the chronology established by Heil, *Alkuinstudien*, pp. 24ff., 27, 67, 70), p. 340, second paragraph. Neither letter is included in any of the letter collections and *ep.* 160 is extremely defective in its unique MS source. After *an* [ . . . ] *tite* in the title Delisle believed that he could read the upper parts of the name *Teotulfo*, now completely destroyed! but Heil ("Der Adoptionismus, Alkuin und Spanien," in *Karl der Grosse, Lebenswerk und Nachleben*, 2, ed. B. Bischoff [Düsseldorf, 1965], p. 106) is very skeptical. It is unfortunate that this is the very text commonly cited as the earliest evidence of Theodulf's promotion to the see of Orléans. The choice of a bishop with whom Alcuin was in touch at this time through Benedict of Aniane seems, however, to lie between Theodulf and Leidrad. (On the other hand, Heil is clearly right in saying [*Alkuinstudien*, p. 67, n. 353] that the editorial *distulimus* at p. 259, 1. 18 must be replaced by a future tense.) Alcuin's letter to Beatus of Liébana, uniquely preserved in a tenth-century Spanish manuscript (best ed. by W. Levison, *England and the Continent in the Eighth Century* [Oxford, 1946], pp. 318–323) which not surprisingly is entirely devoted to Felix's heresy and his own attempts to counter it, must also be dated to the spring or summer of 798.

[116]C. J. Gaskoin, *Alcuin: His Life and Works* (London, 1904; reprinted New York, 1966), pp. 139–158 is still the only good English-language account of Alcuin's critiques of Adoptionism. Heil, "Adoptionismus," pp. 134ff., *Alkuinstudien*, pp. 55ff. offers an independent view of his doctrinal position in the light of more than a century of German historical theology. I have not attempted to do more than complement these accounts with particular reference to the development of Alcuin's thought. For his attitude to *novitas* see Epp. 4, no. 23, p. 61 (lines 17–19), *Contra haeresim Felicis*, ed. Blumenshine, p. 78 (lines 2–4: c. 41).

[117]Paulinus, *Contra Felicem libri III*, PL 99:343–468, dedicatory letter to Charlemagne re-edited by Dümmler, Epp. 4:523–525 (from Paris, BN lat. 2846); A. Wilmart, "L'ordre des parties dans le traité de Paulin d'Aquilée contre Felix d'Urgel," *Journ. Theol. Studies* 39

the Acts of the Council of Ephesus, however, offered a new generation of
Western theologians a modest-sized but certainly useful sourcebook of early
Greek Christology; and if they read it, like other Latins both earlier and
later, in the light of Pope Leo I's (and Chalcedon's) "in two natures," they
were encouraged to do so by the substantial quotations from the Pope's
Christmas, and some other, sermons with which Alcuin supported his position.[118] Alcuin can hardly be said to have abandoned Augustine in his
defense of what he believed to be the orthodox doctrine of Christ's Sonship.
He acquires further weapons for his armory not from the great *De Trinitate*,
which has little that is germane to his present purpose (and indeed may be
felt to overstress the human nature of the Divine Christ), but from the *Enchiridion* and above all from the *Tractatus in Iohannem*, which he may only
recently have read in its entirety and which he quotes more frequently than
any other text; for this has as its focus the Incarnate Christ, the relationship
of whose Divine and human natures is willed by God.[119] The personal element is not limited to the choice of texts for citation. Addressing Felix

---

(1938), 22–37, where the confused order of the text in the Paris MS and the edition is corrected
from Vat. Reg. 192, fols. 1–101 (N. Fr., s. IX[1] and not North Italian, as Wilmart). Heil would
redate Paulinus's work to 799, because his revision of the chronology of Alcuin's letters and the
events they describe require him to treat Epp. 4, no. 208, p. 346, in which Alcuin acclaims it
highly ("ita ut nihil his addi de quaestionibus, nuper habitis inter nos et partes Feliciana, opus
esse arbitrabar"), as the final section of a letter consisting of Dümmler's nos. 179, 184, 208 which
he dates August 799: *Alkuinstudien*, pp. 40–45, 49, 70f. But since Paulinus's dedicatory letter
draws attention to the fact that his work was completed in a year with 366 days, a 799 dating is
categorically excluded. Without prejudice to Heil's other revisions, *ep.* no. 208 must still be
regarded as a separate letter (*perhaps* defective at the beginning) of the summer of 800: for some
of the implications see below, pp. 58ff. and n. 135.

[118]Unfortunately, Dr. Blumenshine has identified Alcuin's quotations only with the corresponding passages in Migne's reprint (PL 54), overlooking Dom A. Chavasse's magnificent
new edition, *Sancti Leonis magni Romani pontificis tractatus septem et nonaginta* (CC 138,
138A; Turnhout, 1973). Chavasse demonstrates conclusively that Alcuin's source was a MS of
"l'homéliaire du type S," represented *inter alia* by the incomplete Troyes, Bib. Mun. cod. 853 and
the earliest MSS of the "Alan of Farfa" and "Egino" homiliaries, which incorporates "the second
collection" of Leo's sermons: ed. cit., pp. xlvi–lix (description and analysis of the homiliary
MSS), pp. clxii–clxiii (identification of Alcuin's citations). Chavasse also shows that the unidentified "Augustine" quotation (*recte* Petrus Chrysologus), *Contra haeresim* c. 13, ed. Blumenshine, p. 61, and the whole of c. 46, pp. 81f., which combines passages from more than one
source, are taken from the same homiliary: ed. cit., p. clxii.

[119]See the list of citations in Blumenshine, p. 106. In fact Alcuin does not make use of
Augustine's comments on the opening verses of John's Gospel either here or (more surprisingly)
in his *Commentaria in Iohannem*. The first tractate quoted by him is tr. 7, on Ioh. 1.34–51.
Augustine had almost certainly preached the first 54 of the *In Iohannis evangelium Tractatus
CXXIV* (Corpus Christianorum 36: introd. by R. Willems; Turnhout, 1954) in – probably – 413,
while he was completing his great *De Trinitate*, although preparation may have begun much

directly at approximately midpoint in the treatise, Alcuin begins with an appeal to the implications of man's *anima rationalis*, in words that tellingly link now-familiar passages in the *De imagine Dei* and the *De ratione animae*: "anima rationalis quae in te est et totum corpus tuum vivificat, vegetat et movet. . . ."[120] There is the firm stand taken on Mary's motherhood of God: she is *Dei genetrix*—an originally literary expression which became a theological "term of art" in the Latin versions of the Council of Ephesus. Even the passage which worried Hauck because it seemed to be invoking God's almighty power to account for the mystery of Christ's birth to Mary can be put to Alcuin's credit: it is the complement of a man whose theology was rooted in prayer to "authorities'" demonstration of the truth of the Two Natures which require that He be born in that way.[121]

When Alcuin's *libellus* reached the Aachen Court, its resident scholars may already have been in possession of the elaborate restatement that Felix had prepared of his position and sent there, rather than to Alcuin—perhaps as a deliberate insult.[122] Only when it was passed to him did Alcuin discover that he had seriously misjudged his opponents. A letter was ready for dispatch to the king, with Alcuin's answers to some of the problems that were currently preoccupying him—the progression of the sun through the zodiac, the length of the solar year and related numerological problems. To this he added a postscript which can (and, I

---

earlier; the remainder were written subsequently. A. E. Schönbach, "Uber einige Evangelienkommentare des Mittelalters,"*Sitzungsber. Ph.-Hist. Kl., Akademie Wien* 164 (1903), 43ff., argues that the *libellum excerptionis in Iohannis evangelium* which Alcuin wanted Beornred of Sens, who was making a copy, or Richbod of Trier to send to him, Epp. 4, no. 49, p. 93, was Alcuin's own collection of extracts from Augustine and that its compilation goes back to Alcuin's years in York: the first hypothesis is possible but cf. p. 62, the second is in my view unlikely.

[120]Ed. Blumenshine, p. 74, c. 36. Compare *De imagine Dei* (ed. Marenbon, p. 159): "sic anima in suo corpore ubique tota viget, vivificans eum [al. illud] movens et gubernans"; and *De ratione animae*, ed. Curry, p. 54 (c. 6): "anima est spiritus intellectualis rationalis semper in motu semper vivens bonae malaeque voluntatis capax" (although recall that Alcuin was here making use of Isidore, *De differentiis*, 2.27.30).

[121]*Contra haeresim Felicis*, ed. Blumenshine, p. 55, c. 2, cf. p. 64, c. 20 (a quotation from Gregory of Nazianzus, in the version of the Latin *acta*); id., p. 82, c. 48, which comes at the end of a succession of testimonies to Christ's being born of Mary as "true God and true man." For the origins of the *Dei genetrix* formula and for its importance in the Adoptionist controversy, particularly but not exclusively to the orthodox side, see Scheffczyk, *Mariengeheimnis*, cit., pp. 100f., 58–99.

[122]For the chronology of these exchanges, Heil *Alkuinstudien*, pp. 25ff., 57 is fundamental. Felix's text is lost and is known only from Alcuin's and Paulinus's replies to it.

54 DONALD A. BULLOUGH

believe, should) be understood as despairing or hysterical or both: the in-
credible heresies he had found in Felix's text could be answered only if he
had the help of others; and Charles had to act vigorously if his dominions were not to be ravaged by this impiety.[123] Shortly afterwards, having received a letter sent by the king from his camp in northeast Saxony,
Alcuin wrote again. He answered further "astronomical" queries, not
without asperity because he felt that some of his earlier views had been
misrepresented in the transmission; but he slipped in an appreciative
reference to his being given the opportunity of answering the subverter
Felix, with the double request that copies of the treatise be sent to others
of whose scholarship and orthodoxy he approved and that he be given
time for his own reply.[124]

It proved a major undertaking, even with his collection of texts (his
*fiches* or card index) at hand and the collaboration of his *pueri* — his
graduate seminar as it were! — and simultaneously he continued to
answer questions from the court and elsewhere and to compile *libelli* on
quite different topics. In consequence, although a draft for "editorial
criticism" had gone to the king and been returned in the early part of 799
(a year earlier, that is, than Dümmler supposed when dating the letters in

---

[123]Epp. 4, no. 148, pp. 237–241 (original letter), 241 (postscript). I infer that the
sentences introduced by the words "Nuper mihi venit libellus" are an addition to an already
complete letter, not from the fact that in Vat. MS Reg. Lat. 226 fol. 4 this paragraph is
omitted (the collection which the letter introduces is deliberately planned as the first part of an
astronomical/computistic handbook; and the exceptionally early copy in Lucca Bib. Com.
MS 490 breaks off earlier) but (i) from the characteristic rhythmic-prose coda " . . . conser-
vare dignetur, desiderantissime David" which now precedes *Nuper*, etc.; (ii) because in London,
Lambeth Palace Library, MS 218, pt. iii — English, s. X²; but clearly derived (perhaps through a
single intermediary) from the early Tours collection which is most completely preserved in
Troyes 1165 — at fol. 156 the words "Nuper . . . libellus" are written in two lines of decorative
capitals, to form a distinct heading. I would have expected to find Alcuin's several answers
to computistic problems, inc. *Sol igitur primo anno post bissextum . . . , Si vis scire
quomodo adcrescant singulis anni diebus . . .* and *Et si scire vis, quantum cotidie crescat . . .*
circulating independently in ninth-century manuscripts: even with the help of David E.
Thompson, *A Partial Transcription of Vatican Reginensis 309 with Commentary* (M. Litt.
thesis, University of St. Andrews, 1978) as well as the standard collections of incipits, I
have failed to do so. But the text of Alcuin's letter from "Sol igitur" to " . . . multum valent
tales rationes [*sic*]" is copied in its entirety into Milan, Bibl. Ambr., H. 150 inf. (from Bobbio but of French origin, ?810): that this is the correct relationship of the two seems to be
established by the just-quoted concluding words, which are the precise reading of Vat. Reg.
226; by the immediately preceding "quod sexta aetate venit filius Dei humanum genus
reparare ad pristinam dignitatem conditionis suae"; and by the section inc. *Solebat magister
mihi saepius dicere.*

[124]Epp. 4, no. 149, pp. 242–245. The lemma in Troyes 1165, fol. 7v, is *Item ad domnum
regem de Martis stella et quibusdam questionibus.*

his great edition), the "publishable" version was long delayed: it was still not ready when Felix was brought before the Frankish king at Aachen in May or June of that year, and Alcuin paid a last visit to the court to engage — for the first and only time — in verbal dispute with him.[125] The definitive text of the "Seven Books against Felix of Urgel," completed in the aftermath of the conciliar debate, is only slightly less impressive as a contribution to theological argument than the *Libri Carolini:* it is, even at its most derivative, the work of "a mind clear and resolved in its purpose." It is not so clear that Alcuin accuses Felix and his supporters of being Nestorians; but he certainly believes that the heresy of Adoptionism leads to the same result — Christ becoming two persons, because Son of God in two ways. He also says in one place that Felix has fallen into the error of Pelagius, which is unconsciously ironical since the so-called "Faith of St. Jerome" in the early Carolingian credal collections is now universally accepted as Pelagius's. His opponent's own doctrinal restatement, known only from the extracts quoted here, is answered point by point. To this end Alcuin expounds texts drawn from both Old and New Testaments which contradict Felix, with the help of a wide range of patristic testimonies: the use made of Origen, who had himself departed from the true faith, is justified in the dedicatory preface by reference to Jerome. A degree of tightness is given to the argument by a modest use of the methods (but not the language) of "dialectic."[126]

Very occasionally Alcuin transcends the limits of inherited thought and learning. In the first part of the difficult but clearly important Book 2, chapter 12, he demonstrates the absurdity of making Christ twice "Son of God"; and he then endeavors to explain what is involved in God's assumption of the flesh, which distinguishes Him from those who become "sons of God" by adoption through grace. If Alcuin had said, with the Symbol of the 11th Council of Toledo (which he almost certainly

---

[125]Accepting, that is, the chronology proposed by Heil, *Alkuinstudien*, conveniently tabulated pp. 67–70, involving (*inter alia*) the antedating of Epp. 4, nos. 202, 203, 204.

[126]Text: PL 101:128, 127–230; prefatory letter also, Epp. 4, no. 203 (pp. 336–337). Interpretation: in addition to Gaskoin, cit., and Heil, "Adoptionismus," see Heil, *Alkuinstudien*, pp. 58ff. *Antecessor tuus Pelagius (licet aliis verbis):* 3.3, ed. cit., c. 164. Origen: cf. Epp. 4:337 and the quotation from *Hom. V in Isaiam*, ed. cit., c. 152d, etc.; although *Comm. in ep. ad Rom.* is already quoted in the *Liber contra haeresim Felicis*, 54, ed. Blumenshine, p. 86. "Dialectic": cf. 1.13, ed. cit., c. 139 (where indeed it is said that "alia substantia est Dei Patris, de qua essentialiter natus est Dei Filius"); 2.12, ed. cit., cc. 155–156. But at the same time Alcuin is highly critical of the Adoptionists' attempt to penetrate the divine mysteries by *ratio humana* alone: see the passages collected by Wallach, *Alcuin and Charlemagne*, pp. 151f.

knew), that in that assumption "Deus enim Verbum *non accepit* personam hominis sed naturam," he would have been on safe ground; instead he declares that "persona *perit* hominis, non natura"! This startling proposition, which I do not find elsewhere, hardly leads naturally to the wholly orthodox conclusion that although deified the flesh of Christ remains human within divinity, so that the man in perfect obedience to God is perfect man. Perhaps Alcuin spontaneously used unorthodox language because of the need to insist that Christ was *not less human* than man who had been made in the image of God—man who (as he believed) has the potential for godlikeness if he wills himself to seek God and whose qualities come from God, the goodness of Whom derives from Himself alone.[127]

Alcuin is most clearly innovatory in his treatment of Mary as the Mother of God and of her relationship both with fallen man and with the Incarnate Word: here he takes up the doctrines implicit in the Marian liturgical passages included in his *De laude* and indicates the path which orthodox theology was generally to follow in the next three or four centuries.[128] The binding authority of the Council of Ephesus's *Dei genetrix* is reaffirmed, the impossibility of reconciling this with the notion of a Christ who only "post nativitatem adoptatus est in Filium Dei" is again insisted on and "testimony" cited; but in two places in the Sixth Book, Alcuin considers the qualities that were proper to the Mother of God. Biblical evidence is found for her noble, indeed royal, ancestry and the therefore purely metaphorical significance of *ancilla (Dei)* is argued in contradistinction to Felix's views. In a striking passage taken from but slightly adapting the mid-fifth-century Arnobius the Younger (not previously used by Alcuin), he links the wool dyed with imperial purple which she spins at the Annunciation with her worthiness to bear the

---

[127]PL 101:156; J. Madoz, *Le Symbole du XI^e Concile de Tolède*, Spicilegium sacrum Lovaniense, Et. et Docs. 19 (Louvain, 1938), p. 23: for the source—Fulgentius—see id., pp. 84f. Cf. Gaskoin, op. cit., pp. 157f., Heil, "Adoptionismus," pp. 152f. Gaskoin compares Alcuin's proposition with the citation from Paschasius (*recte* Faustus of Riez, *De Spiritu sancto*) in the letter composed by Alcuin in the name of the Frankish bishops at Frankfurt in 794, MGH Conc. 2/1:150: but "quia persona personam consumere potest" is very far from being the same notion. Alcuin's familiarity with the Toledan symbol only a year or two later is clear from the *De fide sanctae Trinitatis* 1.14, PL 101:22 (from Madoz, cit., p. 18); and Wallach makes it the source of at least two phrases in the Frankfurt *professio fidei*, Conc. 2/1:163f., although the precise wording "in forma Dei aequalis Patri, in forma servi minor Patre" is noticeably closer to Augustine, *De Trinitate* 1.7, ed. W. J. Mountain, Fr. Glorie, CC 50 (Turnhout, 1968), pp. 43–44, than to the corresponding passage in the symbol, Madoz, *Symbole*, p. 24.

[128]Scheffczyk, *Mariengeheimnis*, pp. 87ff.; cf. pp. 24ff., 58ff., and passim.

Ruler of Heaven. The whiteness of the wool is also the symbol of her perfect purity, both before and after conception: the *maledictio* which Eve brought to man is now superseded by the *benedictio* of the second mother of mankind, the Virgin Mary. Even the concepts and language of the *De imagine Dei* can be brought to bear on the mystery of the birth of Him who is "Man in all things true, God in all things perfect." Just as the first man "de terra virgine sanctae Trinitatis consilio formatus est dicente Domino: Faciamus," etc., so the second Adam is wrought from the earth of a virginal womb (!) by the operation of that same Trinity. At the beginning of the final book similarly, Alcuin abandons the traditional simple formulation of the Old Roman Creed—"qui natus est de Spiritu sancto et Maria virgine"—for a phraseology comparable with but more elaborate than the one recently adopted by the reviser who gave the Universal Church its "Apostles' Creed": "ex divina sancti Spiritus *operatione* et gloriosa beatae Virginis *castitate* conceptus est et natus."[129] The notion of *castitas* as a dynamic element in the Motherhood of God is a striking departure from its established passive role among the Christian virtues—the avoidance of sexual sinning—familiar to Alcuin from its (occasional) appearance in liturgical texts or "private" prayers and from the pseudo-Augustinian sermon which is the main source of his *De virtutibus et vitiis*, chapter 18: *De castitate*.[130] It had no future as such; but it foreshadows the increasing ninth-century preoccupation with Mary's *virginitas in partu* and its physical-real nature.[131] A liturgical—or prayer-based—theology is giving way to a more biblical and "learned" theology. Exceptionally, Alcuin himself had no doubts about the merits of his "Seven Books." As soon as they had received royal approval, a copy was sent to Benedict of Aniane and Leidrad of Lyons who had been commissioned to supress the heresy in southwest France.[132]

[129]*Adv. Felicem* 1.13, ed. cit., 138c, 2.20, ed. cit., 162b–c, with Scheffczyk, p. 88; id., 6.1 and (especially) 9, ed. cit., 201–202, 210–212; and compare with the passage quoted in the text (from 211b) Marenbon, p. 158: "consilio sancte Trinitatis . . . creatus sit [al. est] homo"; 7.2, ed. cit., 213c.

[130]Pseudo-Augustine, *Sermo* 291, in PL 39:2296–2297, the source of PL 101:626–627; *casta, castissima* in (e.g.) prayers in the *Book of Cerne*, ed. Kuypers, pp. 154, 155 (*oratio Alchfridi*) but the substantive seemingly only in the "antiphon" in Alcuin's *De laude* (Constantinescu, p. 50, no. 84): "Vere benedicta imperatrix et gloriosa castitatis regina, quae cum honore virginitatis gaudium patris habes," and in "private prayers" perhaps not until the eleventh-century Oxford, Bodl. Lib., MS d'Orville 45, fol. 37v. For pre-Carolingian and Carolingian notions of Mary's "perpetual virginity" and its implications, see Scheffczyk, *Mariengeheimnis*, chap. 4, who has, however, been misled by the attribution to Ildefonsus of Toledo and to Ambrosius Autpertus of sermons that are of other—sometimes much later—dates: see H. Barré, "Le sermon 'Exhortatur' . . . ," *Rev. bén.* 67 (1957), 10–33; id., *Prières anciennes*, pp. 108f. and passim; *Ambrosii Autperti opera*, ed. R. Weber, CC cont. med. 27B (Turnhout, 1979), pp. 885ff.

[131]Scheffczyk, pp. 202–237.

[132]Epp. 4, no. 207, p. 345: accepting the interpretation and redating to 799 (Jun. 26) proposed by Heil, *Alkuinstudien*, pp. 23ff., 44f., 70.

Alcuin may well have believed that he had written the definitive refutation of Adoptionism. If so, he was again quickly disillusioned. Probably in the late summer of 799 he received an offensively worded but carefully documented reply from Elipand, written before the Aachen disputation, together (it seems) with a copy of a letter previously sent by the writer to Felix. Alcuin was deeply upset by the accusation that his own position was a diminution of Christ's humanity; but except when he was actually challenging Elipand's interpretation of his authorities he had little new to say. There are signs, however, that he had been forced to think a little more deeply about what Nestorius had in fact believed and maintained. In the First Book he rephrased his definition of the Virgin's Motherhood of the God-Man to underline the inseparability of the two natures; and the apologetic treatise on these Natures which constitutes the Third and Fourth Books is evidence of a greater maturity of theological thought.[133] This time the king was simply bypassed: an unbound copy went straight to the two legates to assist them in their worsting of the heretics (if Heil's chronology is accepted, nearly a year earlier than Frobenius and Dümmler supposed).[134] More encouragingly, Felix and the priest with him (who "was worse than his master") had meanwhile confirmed their abjuration of heresy while in Leidrad's care. Either the two earlier treatises had carried greater conviction than the exchanges between the protagonists would lead us to expect; or, as one may suspect, Felix's personal encounter with Alcuin accomplished what no refutation and counterrefutation could achieve. When Leidrad brought Felix to St. Martin's on his way to or from the south next year, Alcuin found him all sweetness and light, the old hatred gone! His conversion was not perhaps total or final: Agobard of Lyons later discovered evidence to the contrary; and Elipand was unrepentant. If Adoptionism had ever been a social and political problem for the Frankish ruler, and not primarily an intellectual

---

[133]Elipand: *Epistola ad Albinum*, ed. Dümmler from Paris BN lat. 2388, Epp. 4, no. 182, ed. J. Gil from Rheims, Bibl. mun., MS 385, Corpus scriptorum Muzarabicorum 1 (Madrid, 1973), pp. 96–109; *Ad Felicem nuper conversum*, ed. Dümmler, Epp. 4, no. 183, ed. Gil, Corpus 1:109–111; cf. Heil, *Alkuinstudien*, p. 37; Scheffczyk, *Mariengeheimnis*, pp. 67ff., Heil, "Adoptionismus," pp. 122ff. Alcuin: *Adversum Elipandum libri IV* (of which I have been able to locate only 4 MSS), PL 101:243–300, esp. 250b, 271ff.; cf. Scheffczyk, pp. 91f., Heil, *Alkuinstudien*, pp. 61ff.

[134]Epp. 4, nos. 200–201 (redated by Heil, *Alkuinstudien*, pp. 47ff., 71, suggesting at p. 49 that *ep.* no. 200 is properly the dedicatory letter: cf. PL 101:243), and especially pp. 331, 334: "iubeatis ligare et involvere et in modum unius corporis conponere has quaterniones, ne forte sparsi rapte dispergantur per manus legentium vel forsitan invidentium nomini meo."

one, it rapidly ceased to be one in the months either side of the expedition to Rome and the imperial coronation.[135]

Alcuin was free to devote himself to other matters. By 801 he was engaged in the compiling of devotional *libelli*, on the supervising of the first of the Tours Bibles, in the composition of his moral treatise *De virtutibus et vitiis*. Most notably, between (?late) 799 and circa March 801 he completed a long-envisaged Commentary on St. John's Gospel, in which the Evangelist "without doubt was particularly concerned to make manifest the divinity of our Lord Jesus Christ, being equal to the Father." It is the only one of Alcuin's exegetical works whose stages of composition are documented in his letters, and it is the only one which has been the subject of detailed analysis in the present century; but many unresolved problems remain.[136]

At the beginning of Lent 800 the royal nuns of Chelles, Gisla and Rotruda, received from Alcuin a commentary on John, chapters 13–21 — the account of the Passion — with apologies for not having been able to treat the whole Gospel because of his "editorial" work on the Bible.[137] It is drawn overwhelmingly from Augustine's *Tractatus in Iohannis evangelium*, supplemented occasionally by passages from homilies of Gregory or of Bede, and with no obvious attempt to normalize the lemmata in line with the Tours Bibles. Except in the "homiletic" sections, the commentary sticks very closely to the Gospel text. Like his main source, Alcuin shows little interest in etymologies; unlike that same source, he ignores textual problems

---

[135]Epp. 4, no. 207, redated by Heil, *Alkuinstudien*, pp. 23–47 passim, 70 to June 26 *799*; id., no. 208. This cannot be the final part of another letter of 799 (above, n. 117), and Leidrad's reported arrival at St. Martin's with Felix (p. 346) must be the visit anticipated in id., no. 165, if this is rightly *post*-dated to Jan./Feb. 800 (Heil, cit., pp. 46, 71): the copy of the letter in Vienna 795 is on a leaf of the ternio (fols. 192–197) constituting the first addition to the original MS of 798/99, which makes this possible. An unpublished text in the Corbie MS of the beginning of the ninth century, Berlin-Dahlem, Preuss. Kulturbesitz Handschr. Abt., cod. Hamilton 132, fols. 248v–251v has the title *Epistola contra hereticos qui carnem humanam cum qua Christus in celum post resurrectionem ascendit, separant de divinitate et eandem carnem non credunt ubique esse sicut et divinam*: it declares that this new heresy has arisen when the heresy of the Adoptionists "est refutata, maxime quoque a christianissimo adque a Deo electissimo imperatore nostro Karolo funditus est delata."

[136]Text: PL 100:758–1001, prefatory letters better in MGH Epp. 4:323–325 (no. 196), 354–357 (no. 213). Discussion: A. E. Schönbach, "Über einige Evangelienkommentare des Mittelalters," *Sitzungsberichte der Wiener Akademie, Ph.-Hist. Kl.* 146 (1902–1903), 43–67; cf. 34–42: also Heil, "Adoptionismus," in *Karl der Grosse*, 2:146, and B. Fischer in id., 158f.

[137]Epp. 4:322f., no. 195: for the date see Fischer cit. (last note). The prefatory letter is retained before Bk. 5 in a number of MSS of the complete work: the latest I have noticed is in the twelfth-century Clairvaux MS, Troyes Bibl. mun. 441, at fols. 138–138v.

and—generally—conflict of opinion. The common thread in what is retained and what is added is that Christ was betrayed and died that all men (and women) might be saved, if through grace they aspire always to a greater Christlikeness in their own lives. Alcuin's method and the consequent adaptation of his exemplars is well illustrated by his treatment of Christ's journey to Calvary and His crucifixion between two thieves: the *alia solutio* of the problem of the "hour" at which this happened is entirely omitted, as is Augustine's antithetical (and theatrical) account of how "piety" and "impiousness" will view what is taking place. Conversely, Augustine's unwillingness to tackle in this context the great mysteries of the empty tomb (John 20.5-10) opens the way for an extended allegorizing exposition of these verses, based on two homilies of Gregory but with linking passages which are at least partly Alcuin's own.[138]

This Passion-narrative commentary enjoyed a limited circulation on its own, although seemingly with a defective conclusion.[139] Prompted by Gisla and Rotruda, who complained that Augustine's treatment of the Fourth Gospel was both too big and too difficult, Alcuin was, however, soon at work on the earlier chapters—difficult for anyone, he observed. By the time the news of the imperial coronation reached him he had a text ready to be sent to Chelles. The royal recipients were to arrange for the making of a fair copy of the two installments of his Commentary, introducing a division into Books and chapters, and return it to the author.[140] What thus became Books 1-5 of a seven-book Commentary is in great part—from the concluding passages of Book 2, chapter 5 to the end of Book 5—exactly comparable in approach, technique and sources to Books 6 and 7. But in spite of the statement in Alcuin's prefatory letter of the paramount authority of Augustine, the *Tractatus* are not used until his tr. 12, chapters 12, 13, commenting on John 3.17-21, with their emphasis on man's coming to truth and light by acknowledging his sinfulness to God. By contrast, the preceding one-and-a-half books are taken almost exclusively from Bede's Homilies, with a single passage inserted from Pope Gregory, as are several passages in the preface.[141]

---

[138]Compare PL 100:980-981 with *Tractatus* 117.1-3 (CC 36:651-653); PL 100:987-989 with *Tr.* 120.8-9 (CC 36:663f.). For the nonstandardization of the biblical quotations see Fischer in *Karl der Grosse*, 2:174.

[139]An example is Basel, Universitätsbibl., Cod. 0 II 28, fols. 1-66v, of the first or second quarter of the ninth century: from St. Maximin, Trier but probably written somewhere else on the left bank of the Rhine. For the defective ending see Epp. 4:358 with Schönbach, p. 52.

[140]Epp. 4:357f. (no. 214: preserved only in the twin St. Denis letter collection MSS).

[141]Epp. 4:357 (no. 213); PL 100:783-784, CC 36:127-129; PL 100:743-783, Epp. 4:354-356. For the text of Bede's homilies from which Alcuin's extracts are taken (nos. 1.2; 1.8; 1.15-17, 2.18; et al.) see *Bedae opera*, 3: *Opera homiletica*, ed. D. Hurst, CC 122 (Turnhout, 1955).

Schönbach, indeed, thought that he could show that Alcuin had originally composed a rather different version of the opening books in which passages from Augustine — eliminated during revision — were combined with the (lengthier) extracts from Bede, and with a distinctive preface which in the definitive version was replaced by the letters exchanged between Gisla and her niece and Alcuin: a unique copy of this putative "first edition" of Books 1–5 is in a St. Gallen manuscript (Stiftsbibl. 258) of the third quarter of the ninth century.[142] Alcuin's familiarity with earlier parts of Augustine's *Tractatus* is established by his use of them in the *Liber contra haeresim Felicis*; but Schönbach's theory is hardly acceptable. The insertion of extracts from one writer into longer and complete extracts from another, with a consequent overlap of treatment or contradiction or both, is quite uncharacteristic of Alcuin's exegetical works, although common enough in his contemporaries or near-contemporaries. His prefaces normally take the form of a dedicatory letter, indicating at varying length his purpose and something of his method, or of a group of verses or even a combination of the two: he shows less interest than, say, Bede in the author of the text on which he is commenting or in the circumstances of its composition.[143] The St. Gallen Preface's declared intention of considering first the life of the Evangelist and thereafter "de loco et tempore, causa quoque scribendi nos pauca disseremus" — both the scheme of inquiry proposed and the precise wording of its final clause — point unmistakably in the direction of Ireland; so, a little less clearly, do the apocryphal and other texts used to supplement the quotations from Alcuin quoting Bede. Some Insular feature in the main text and the intervention of an Irish corrector make it most likely that the whole work originated in Continental-Irish circles in the middle decades of the ninth century.[144]

---

[142]Schönbach, pp. 54–66. A fuller paleographical description of the MS is A. Bruckner, *Scriptoria Medii Aevi Helvetica*, 3 (Geneva, 1938), p. 88.

[143]For the use of *Tractatus* 7 and 8 see *Liber contra haeresim Felicis*, ed. Blumenshine, p. 106. Alcuin's treatment of Bede's much longer *In Cantica canticorum expositio* (PL 91:1065–1236), with some material introduced from Gregory, for his own *Compendium in Canticum canticorum* (PL 100:639–664) is briefly discussed by F. Ohly, *Hohelied-Studien*, Schr. der Wissenschaftl. Gesellschaft . . . Universität Frankfurt am Main (Wiesbaden, 1958), pp. 70–72. Letter prefaces: *Interrogationes et responsiones in Genesin*, Epp. 4, no. 80; *Comm. in Iohannem*, final version, as n. 135; verse preface: *In Canticum canticorum* , MGH Poet. 1:299 (no. 78), inc. *Hunc cecinit Salomon*; combined preface *In Ecclesiasten*, Epp. 4, no. 251 (pp. 406–407: verses inc. *Flumina qui metuat*).

[144]Compare with the preface, ed. Schönbach, pp. 57f., Bischoff, "Wendepunkte in der Gesch. der lateinischen Exegese," in *Mittelalterliche Studien*, 1:217f. For the apocryphal

Alcuin's use of Bede and not Augustine for his exposition of the early chapters of the Fourth Gospel is not difficult to account for. The latter's approach and language would obviously have been unhelpful to Alcuin's intended readers. Augustine's treatment of the opening words (preached to a fifth-century North African congregation) answered none of the questions that they are likely to have asked. When he reached verse 18: "Unigenitus Filius qui est in sinu Patris, ipse enarravit," he had nothing, in this context, to say on *Unigenitus*. Bede's Homilies on the other hand were, like Alcuin's interests and sympathies, Christ-centered—His co-eternity with the Father, His Incarnation, His coming to save fallen man, the calling of the first Apostles: characteristically, in this last instance, Augustine expounds only *Messias, latine unctus*, which Bede largely ignores ("*Messias* Hebraco sermone *Christus* dicitur Graeco, Latine autem *unctus* interpretatur") to concentrate on the Apostles and the ways in which Christ reveals himself to the world. Alcuin, as has been rightly said, "revered Bede," whose work he had been abbreviating and making accessible to a wider audience at least since the time he used the *Ecclesiastical History* as the basis of the poem on his native York.[145] It seems to me not impossible that "the collection of extracts" on the Fourth Gospel to which he had referred in 795 was compiled from Bede, Gregory, etc., rather than from Augustine: in view of the short time available to Alcuin for the completion of his Commentary, it would obviously have been good sense to incorporate such a collection more or less as a whole in the definitive version of a Commentary intended to reveal, like the Gospel itself, "the Divinity of our Lord Jesus Christ, equal to the Father."[146]

---

texts used, see Schönbach, pp. 59ff., although this can now be supplemented and corrected; Irish familiarity with Augustine's *Tractatus* is demonstrated by the short commentary in Milan, Ambr. cod. F. 60 sup., fols., 50–54 (privately printed *Pro manuscripto*, Steenbrugge, 1961) and by the text edited from Vienna Nat. bibl. lat. 997 by J. F. Kelly, *Scriptores Hiberniae minores*, CC 108C (Turnhout, 1974), pp. 105–131.

[145]Compare *Tractatus* 1 (in Ioh. 1.1–5), ed. cit., pp. 1–11 and *Tractatus* 3.17, ed. cit., pp. 27–28 with Bede, hom. 1.8 and 1.2, ed. cit., pp. 52–59 and 11f., from which PL 100:743–746, 752–753; also *Tractatus* 7.13, ed. cit., p. 74 with Bede hom. 1.16, ed. cit., pp. 114–116: but the corresponding section in Alcuin's Commentary (PL 100:760–761) is not from Bede's homily and I have so far failed to identify the source (a clue should be given by the opening words: "In fide non est ordo: ubicunque fidelis est anima," etc.). Alcuin's "reverence for Bede" has been finely expounded by Peter Godman, with particular reference to the *versus* "The Bishops, Kings and Saints of York," in his introduction to a critical edition and translation of that poem (Oxford Medieval Texts, 1982), pp. lxxv–lxxxviii.

[146]Above, pp. 52f. and n. 119.

Alcuin was now free to concentrate on the composition of a last major theological work, while others were preparing collections of his letters. The (*Sermo*) *De fide sanctae Trinitatis et de incarnatione Christi: libri tres* was ready for presentation to the emperor in the autumn of 802. In his dedicatory letter Alcuin sees it as in some ways the counterpart to and an expression of the unique authority which Charles has gained in this world—a political power held up by the defense of Christian truth: specifically, it will vindicate Augustine's conviction that the *dialecticae disciplinae rationes* have a proper and necessary place in any exposition of the doctrine of the Trinity.[147] Perhaps for the first time in his theological or exegetical writings, Alcuin transcends his sources. Augustine's *De Trinitate* is drawn on but handled with considerable freedom, not least to reduce the text to a more acceptable scale. Passages from his own earlier works are adapted and rewritten and incorporated in a sustained argument. The Marian sections of the anti-Adoptionist treatises are expanded and refined. One of the most remarkable features of the *De fide*—a work of old age—is the intermittent but extensive use of the trinitarian writings of the mid-fourth-century Marius Victorinus, whose speculative theology is of great power but also of extraordinary difficulty, because of its attempt to defend and explain the Nicene definition of the Trinity in terms of a particular brand of Neoplatonic metaphysics. Marius's hymns are similarly a major source for the hymnic invocation of the Trinity which is the first of two or three appendices to Alcuin's text, although with the metaphysics left out.[148] Inevitably Victorinus's ideas are not fully integrated into the Carolingian writer's treatment of the central problems of the Christian faith; but few others in the Middle Ages even made the attempt. The *De fide* is the most substantial and effective work of its kind for many centuries. Gottschalk, no mean judge of doctrinal exposition, used it extensively. A very early Bavarian copy may well have been owned by a layman (or -woman), who added a text of the Lord's Prayer in the vernacular, before it was gifted to St. Emmeram's at Regensburg. In the late thirteenth century a well-educated priest in southern Austria,

[147]PL 101:11–58, best edition of the prefatory letter (which concludes with verses) Epp. 4, no. 257 (pp. 414–416). For a brief but telling judgment see Heil, "Adoptionismus," pp. 147f. The only adequate account of the work in English is Gaskoin, pp. 159–163. Alcuin uses the word *sermo* in his preface: but I have not noted it as part of the title in any surviving manuscript (there are nearly 100).

[148]Alcuin's use of Victorinus was first clearly demonstrated by P. Hadot, "Marius Victorinus et Alcuin," *Archives d'histoire doctrinale* 29 (1954), 5–19. Victorinus's trinitarian

apparently ignorant of Abelard and finding Aquinas too difficult, included a full text in a solid trinitarian handbook. Interest in it was resuscitated — if, indeed, it had ever been moribund — in the immediately pre-Reformation decades: apparently because of its presence in a (late-medieval?) manuscript of a standard homiliary for which an early printer rightly foresaw a steady demand, it was first printed with that homiliary in 1493 and reprinted in the many subsequent editions during the next century.[149]

In all this there seems no place for what has come to be regarded in the present century as Alcuin's most substantial and most enduring contribution to the Western Church, and even the reason why he had been invited to the Frankish royal court; namely, the compiling of a substantial Supplement to the inadequate "Gregorian Sacramentary" sent from Rome by Pope Hadrian, which (it is supposed) had been expected to provide Francia with a standard or "authentic" mass book.[150] Liturgical texts played a part, albeit not a very large one, in the exchanges between the main protagonists in the Adoptionist controversy. In support of their own position, the Spanish bishops quoted texts from the liturgy of Toledo, with its roll of distinguished and orthodox incumbents, already in the letter to their Frankish brethren; and the bishops assembled at Frankfurt replied in kind, with quotations from the Sacramentary — credited to the correct day — to demonstrate that "noster vero Gregorius, pontifex Romanae sedis et clarissimus toto orbe doctor, in suis orationibus semper eum unigenitum nominare non dubitavit." The texts may well have been

---

writings have been re-edited by P. Henry and P. Hadot as CSEL 83 (Vienna, 1971), where it is noted (intro., p. x) that "Alcuinus integrum corpus operum theologicorum Victorini cognovisse videtur," after which the MS tradition is a divided one. For the hymn and its sources see J. A. Jungmann in *Kyriakon: Festschrift J. Quasten*, ed. P. Granfield and J. A. Jungmann, 2 (Münster i. Westf., 1970), pp. 691–697.

[149]C. Lambot, *Oeuvres de Godescalc*, cit., pp. 108–129 and passim; Munich clm. 14510 pt. ii (fols. 76–186), with Bischoff, *Südostdeutsche Schreibschulen*, 1:250f. and *Frühmittelalterliche Studien* 5 (1971), 123: the Lord's Prayer is on fol. 78, after the preface; Graz, Universitätsbibl. MS 724; Basel (Nicholas Kessler) edition of *Homeliarium doctorum*, 1493 (and not, as has been generally supposed, for the first time in the 1506 edition).

[150]Ellard, *Master Alcuin*, chaps. 6, 7; E. Bourque, *Étude sur les Sacramentaires romains*, 2/2, Studi di Antichità cristiana 25 (Vatican City, 1958), esp. pp. 147-250: a warning note, however, already in the review of Ellard by C. Hohler, *Journ. Eccl. Hist.* 8/2 (1957), 222-226. The standard edition of both *Hadrianum* and the Supplement is J. Deshusses, *Le Sacramentaire grégorien*, 1, Spicilegium Friburgense 16 (Fribourg en Suisse, 1971).

chosen by Alcuin from the court *Hadrianum*.[151] Defending *unigenitus* against Felix in 799, Alcuin draws his attention to the mass prayers of the Roman Church (although without reference to Gregory) "which we are accustomed to sing": two — shortened — are among those quoted at Frankfurt, the others are new and correctly cited. Elipand's sharply worded letter to Alcuin has a substantial section of *testimonia* from the Toledo liturgy, partly overlapping with the earlier letter of his fellow bishops and partly new. Alcuin's reply quotes four *orationes in celebratione et oraculis missarum* "which blessed Gregory composed." Three are the first three Frankfurt texts; the fourth is quite different, and although also cited from the mass set for the Feast of the Exaltation of the Holy Cross, is not to be found in the standard collect or any other prayer for that day. Until recently it was known otherwise only as the opening prayer of the votive mass of the Holy Cross in many later "Gregorian Sacramentaries." However, in the recently discovered "Sacramentary of Trent," written ca. 825 probably in that vicinity, the collect for the feast on 14 September is the one which Alcuin quotes.[152] The most plausible theory about the complex textual history of this book is that its immediate exemplar was a Salzburg sacramentary the nucleus of which was a *Gregorianum* independent of and earlier than the book sent by Hadrian to the Frankish king. If this is correct, it indicates that Alcuin at Tours was using a mass book very different from that with which he had been familiar when young, but one that was not exactly of the form of the court *authenticum*.[153]

Both these versions of the Roman (stational) mass book were startlingly deficient as a norm for usage in ordinary Frankish churches; and bishops,

[151]MGH Conc. 2/1:113; id., 145–146. The Spanish bishops' texts and the Masses from which they are said to be taken, like Elipand's similar citations some six years later, do not always correspond with the later *Liber Mozarabicus sacramentorum*, as its editor M. Férotin, Monumenta ecclesiae liturgica 6 (Paris, 1912), noted in listing Elipand's (but not the bishops') liturgical citations, id., pp. xxx–xxxii. The texts quoted from the Frankish side are exactly those of the *Hadrianum*: for Alcuin's probable responsibility for this reply see above.

[152]PL 101:227; Epp. 4, no. 182, p. 305, Gil, Corpus, p. 102; PL 101:266f.; "Sacramentary of Trent" text in Deshusses, *Sacramentaire grégorien*, p. 711, no. 368*.

[153]MS Trento, Castel de Buon Consiglio, s.n., most recently described from a paleographical and codicological standpoint by Bischoff, *Südostdeutsche Schreibschulen*, 2:183. For its contents and place in the history of the Gregorian Sacramentary see esp. Deshusses in *Revue bénédictine* 78 (1968), 261–282, id. in *Rev. bén.* 80 (1970), 213–237 but esp. 224ff.; id., *Sacramentaire grégorien*, pp. 7f., 709–715; and the references in n. 154. For the colophon, see also my comments in Studies in Church History 14, ed. D. Baker, Ecclesiastical History Soc. (Oxford, 1977), pp. 45f.

abbots and *cantores* had either to continue using their old books simultaneously or to extract from them those mass sets and other prayers which they found indispensable for the proper celebration of the liturgical calendar, with minor editorial modifications. What set Alcuin apart from most of the others who undertook this task was his experience in the composition or adaptation of *orationes peculiares*. He now extended this to the composing of a small number of new masses to serve devotional needs, as he explained in the letters sent to St. Vaast and Fulda.[154] The thirteen masses indicated there are clearly discernible in a whole range of ninth-century sacramentaries that come from all parts of the empire *except* France south of the Loire. The first is almost always a *missa de sancta Trinitate*, followed by one for the remission of sins, with others "of the Holy Cross," "of the Virgin Mary," etc., and—with some exceptions—one *honore omnium sanctorum*. The first and last are quite unknown before Alcuin referred to them, unless that for "All Saints" had previously been offered at York. A number of the "votive masses" which often accompany these and have a similar structure and use similar language must—Dom Deshusses has argued—have the same origin: composition by Alcuin at Tours. Moreover, we may even have (in two manuscripts from Rheims) a short preface he wrote to accompany one or more of his *cartulae missales*.[155]

The great Supplement, introduced by the preface *Hucusque*, has to be detached from Alcuin. A claim that it is incompatible with what we know of his preoccupations and editorial techniques during his years at the court and at Tours would be going too far: Alcuin's evident ability even in his sixties to adapt to new liturgical forms and practices or to respond under pressure to the evident need for a fuller statement of *evangelica veritas* than he had initially believed to be necessary would suggest that such a major undertaking was *not* beyond his capacity. But the evidence of the

---

[154]Epp. 4, nos. 250, 296: a convenient analysis of both in Ellard, op. cit., pp. 146–150: but his account of the Masses to which the letters refer has been almost completely superseded by the studies cit. next note.

[155]H. Barré, J. Deshusses, "À la recherche du Missel d'Alcuin," *Ephemerides liturgicae* 82 (1968), 17–42; Deshusses, "Les messes d'Alcuin," *Archiv f. Liturgiewissenschaft* 14 (1972), 7–41, the text *Catholica est fide* edited from Rheims Bibl. mun. MS 213, fol. 6; id., 214, fol. 4v; id., "Les anciens sacramentaires de Tours," *Rev. bén.* 89 (1979), 281–302. Deshusses is in no doubt that Alcuin composed the standard mass sets for All Saints while on the Continent, while expressing himself a little less categorically about the alternative mass set *Exaudi domine famulos* which is so far known only from BN lat. 9430 fols. 208–209 and Tours Bibl. mun. MS 184, fols. 266v–267: see *Rev. bén.* 80 (1970), 227f.; id., 89:294f.

letters, of the *Vita* and of his pupils with liturgical interests is that his contributions in this field, although noteworthy, were of a more spasmodic, more incidental kind. Moreover, whether or not we accept the now widely held view that the Supplement is attributable to Benedict of Aniane or his immediate circle, the language and approach of the *Hucusque* preface point to another milieu, and a more authoritarian attitude to *religio Christiana* (in the sense of outward observance) than is characteristic of Alcuin in the late eighth century.[156]

Alcuin's last guidebook to the ascent to the Kingdom of Heaven was in a notably different form, and fittingly brings together the several strands of his preoccupations, teaching and writing over several decades. A letter in the final section of the second Arno collection begins by recalling that Adelbert, a member of Alcuin's community temporarily at Salzburg, had come with a request that he should compose a letter "on confession and penitence" for the *iuvenes* there. Alcuin's reply was that he had sent or was sending a copy of what he had written on the subject long ago for the sons of St. Martin, which he was sure would do – to which he added that Adelbert should come back to get a copy of the new book on the Trinity to take to Arno. From the concluding letter in the collection, it is apparent that shortly afterwards he had second thoughts, perhaps because he was working on the second part of his handbook for Count Wido. Alcuin now advises Arno that he has asked his friend and pupil Fridugis to deliver to him – and let him not be allowed to forget to hand it over because of his other preoccupations! – a much more comprehensive *manualis libellus*. (He would have sent other books he had been preparing but Fridugis had to leave too soon for these to be ready.)[157]

The contents are listed in the letter: short expositions of the Seven Penitential Psalms, of Ps. 118, of the fifteen Gradual Psalms; the *parvum psalterium* composed by Bede, "of sweet-sounding verses that praise God and petition him"; Bede's hymn on the Six Days of Creation, etc.; the letter on confession for youngsters; an old hymn on the Gradual

---

[156]Text: Deshusses, *Sacr. grég.*, pp. 351-605; authorship: Deshusses in *Archiv f. Liturgiewissenschaft* 9/1 (1965), 48-71, id., *Sacr. grég.*, pp. 64ff. The doubts of Klaus Gamber, latterly in *Sakramentarstudien*, Studia Patristica et Liturgica 7 (Regensburg, 1978), pp. 102-105 where he also argues (pp. 110-119) for an origin at Lérins (!) before the year 800, are not widely shared.

[157]MGH Epp. 4, no. 258, preserved only in Vienna Nat. Bibl. cod. 808 and its Salzburg copy of 854-859, Munich clm. 14743: for the two MSS see Bischoff, *Südostdeutsche Schreibschulen*, 2:135, 160f. and passim; Epp. 4, no. 259 (for the scribe see Bischoff, p. 135).

Psalms; finally, "other prayers" and Bede's hymn *elegiaco metro con-positum* on queen Æthildrytha.[158] The book sent to Arno does not survive. The oldest copy (perhaps more accurately, version) is a manuscript now at Cologne which was the cooperative effort of a large number of scribes a few years after Alcuin's death. It begins with a letter to Arno which is found only here and in other versions of the same collection, and which must be regarded as a preface specially composed after the rest of the collection had been put together: almost every line of the verses with which it concludes echoes some earlier poem. It is followed by a contents page which in the Cologne copy and two others opens with the words "In huius codicilli corpore" but elsewhere with the more normal "In hoc corpore."[159] It is of no great moment that even the first surviving version has the items in a different order from that in the letter to Arno: the first copies probably reached the recipients in unbound *quaterniones* whose sequence could easily be changed. It is unfortunately not clear whether the Tours scriptorium itself made multiple copies or whether it retained an exemplar which others borrowed to make their own versions: there are weighty arguments for both processes. The later copies are all in varying degrees less complete, although all have *expositiones in psalmos* and the letter on confession, and most have the "old hymn," the beautiful and probably Irish *Ad Dominum clamaveram*.

---

[158]The texts in question are: (i) PL 100:575-596; (ii) id., 597-620; id., 619-658; (iii) ostensibly the *collectio Psalterii Bedae*, ed. J. Fraipont, in *Bedae opera*, 4: *Opera rhythmica*, CC 122:452-470, but the only actual example in this group of *manuales libelli*, viz., Cologne Dombibl. cod. 106, fols. 65-71, has a number of substantial differences from the editorial text, some of which bring it closer to the *parvum psalterium* of the *De laude* (in the Bamberg MS at ff. 137-139); (iv) ed. Fraipont, pp. 407-411; (v) Epp. 4, no. 131 (cf. above, nn. 33 and 41); (vi) *Analecta hymnica*, ed. C. Blume, 51 (Leipzig, 1908), pp. 293-294 (no. 223); (vii) *alias orationes*: cf. above, pp. 13-15 passim; (viii) Bede, *Historia ecclesiastica* 4.20, ed. Colgrave and Mynors (Oxford, 1969), pp. 396-400.

[159]Cologne, Dombibl. cod. 106 has several times been described, although never completely satisfactorily or accurately: the best is L. W. Jones in *Speculum* 4 (1929), 27-61, corrected and amplified in id., *The Script of Cologne from Hildebald to Hermann*, Mediaeval Academy of America (Cambridge, Mass., 1932), cf. Wilmart, *Precum libelli*, pp. 5f., 49-59. The Werden litany is an addition after Liudger's death in 809: and I suggest that the most likely circumstance in which scribes of very different backgrounds and training (as revealed in their scripts) collectively wrote a book of this nature is a great assembly at Aachen, not improbably that of 809. The "contents page" is headed "In huius codicelli corpore continentur" in Rheims, Bibl. mun. MS 438 (s. IX, first/second quarter; St. Amand) at fol. 44 and Ivrea Bibl. Capit. MS 30 (s. IX; N. It.) at fol. 6; it is headed "In hoc codice continentur" in Munich clm. 14447 (ca. 820/30; Salzburg) at fol. 8v and in Karlsruhe *Aug.* CXXXV at fol. 136. The terminology and usage are older but Tours seems to have played a major part in their dissemination in the ninth century.

Only the Cologne version, however, included Bede on Creation, three verses of which had already been among the extracts in the *De laude Dei,* and the Bedan "little Psalter," variants of which are a feature of other devotional collections linked with Tours but post-Alcuin in date of compilation.[160] Yet none of them seriously misrepresents the essential character and purpose of the *enchiridion, id est manualem librum:* as the prefatory letter puts it, the soul must necessarily benefit from deep knowledge of and rumination on the Psalms with their elaborate number symbolism, while the perfection of studies has a very special relationship with one number — "seven." The manual was to be read as an extended meditation on mysteries which are only partially revealed even to those who have understood the full significance of the seven pillars on which Wisdom's dwelling-place is built — which, like Salvation itself, "requires fuller explanation."

The anonymous biographer of Alcuin knew of two contemporary visions, from both sides of the Alps, of his being received into the Kingdom of Heaven immediately after his death.[161] It is not for the historian to test the validity of such reports, nor to know whether Alcuin's defense of the faith against the "execrable heresy of Adoptionism" was placed above all his other achievements, as he would apparently have wished. The historian of his earthly pilgrimage can see without difficulty some of the threads that link his activities as liturgist, exegete and theologian at the different phases of his life and in responding to new challenges: he is also entitled to discern a common purpose in Alcuin's striving towards a spiritual goal. In 800 or in 804 Alcuin might have said with greater truth that in this world he had found and followed "the royal road, deviating neither to right nor to left." His most enduring achievement is surely that, to an extent unmeasurable by the historian, to whom the deeper recesses of the individual soul, enhanced by the worship of God Incarnate in Christ, are forever barred, he had pointed out that road to others. For the rest of the Middle Ages and even beyond, Western Christians who were unfamiliar with his name and life prayed to God or thought about God in language that, however firmly rooted in a scriptural and patristic tradition, had been given a wider currency and accessibility through Alcuin and his works.

---

[160]See now esp. J. -B. Molin, "Les Manuscrits de la 'Deprecatio Gelasii': usage privé des Psaumes et dévotion aux litanies," *Ephemerides liturgicae* 90 (1976), 113–148.

[161]*Vita Alcuini,* cc. 26, 27: ed. Arndt, MGH Scr. 15/1:196.

# Carolingian Biblical Studies

## John J. Contreni

Observers of the Carolingian period have not come to a consensus in their attempts to characterize the impetus behind the labors that so stimulated thought and learning in Francia and the Empire during the eighth and ninth centuries.[1] For the first critics and still for many today, the accomplishments of the Carolingians coming after what seems to have been a slough of despond between the patristic age and the Carolingians, the period is best defined as a renaissance. Others recoil from a word that has been overused by medievalists and thus drained of meaning, a word that focuses on a narrow group of scholars, and one, too, that smacks of classicism. More recently, and more accurately, the notion of religious reform and renewal have come to be regarded as the mainspring of Carolingian intellectual life. It is not my purpose here to enter into what some dismiss as a semantic quarrel or to sew together the disparate theses into a cloak of new design. Disagreement is healthy. The different schools of thought, each with its own perspective, have enriched our understanding by emphasizing the different varieties of the Carolingian experience.

Acknowledging the different paths Carolingians pursued does not mean, however, that we cannot make general statements about their quest. What strikes me as typical of intellectual life from about 750 to 900 is its

Research for and writing of this essay were greatly facilitated by the tenure of a fellowship in the Center for Humanistic Studies at Purdue University. I wish also to acknowledge the unfailing help of the staff of the Interlibrary Loan Office, Purdue University Libraries.
[1]See the bibliography gathered in John J. Contreni, "Inharmonious Harmony: Education in the Carolingian World," *Annals of Scholarship: Metastudies of the Humanities and Social Sciences* 1 (1980), 81–83 [81–96].

programmatic and very self-conscious nature. The Carolingian dynasts and their clerical advisers were not intellectual innovators. They certainly would disown any such label. The significance of Carolingian efforts lay in another direction. Carolingian leaders promoted and Carolingian scholars executed the organization and dissemination of what had, by their time, become an accepted body of knowledge and attitude toward learning. Within this general framework, differences of talent, temperament, resources, and generations produced different results. Variety, inconsistency, and even contradiction abounded in an intellectual landscape where truth, unity, and unanimity were the desired harvests.[2] The tensions built into all phases of the Carolingian experiment, from polity to theology, constituted the most important legacy the Carolingians left for the future history of Western European civilization.

Carolingian education and biblical studies were not immune from the disparity between ideal and practice. On the one hand, by the ninth century the liberal arts program had been set as the basic educational program of the schools. A canon of "school-authors" had also been proposed as the textbooks for Carolingian youth. In reality, the program was problematical. What was the origin of the arts? How are they to be defined? Which are the liberal? Which the mechanical? Questions of detail and practical exigencies led to uneven emphases among the constituents of the program. Grammar was the art supreme. Some were especially keen for dialectic. The more practical study of chant, *computus*, and notarial skills served the majority.[3]

The arts were not, of course, studied for themselves. They provided students, some of whom would later become masters in their own right, with the tools they would need to plumb the mysteries of the Bible. Study of the arts was a propaedeutic to higher study. The arts were the pillars

---

[2]Ibid., pp. 84–91. See also Marta Cristiani, *Dall'unanimitas all'universitas da Alcuino a Giovanni Eriugena: Lineamenti ideologici e terminologia politica della cultura del secolo IX*, Istituto storico italiano per il Medio Evo, Studi storici, fascs. 100–102 (Rome, 1978).

[3]See Wesley Stevens, "Walahfrid Strabo—A Student at Fulda," *Canadian Historical Association, Historical Papers* (1971), 13–20; idem, "Compotistica et astronomica in the Fulda School," in *Saints, Scholars, and Heroes: Studies in Medieval Culture in Honour of Charles W. Jones*, Margot H. King and Wesley M. Stevens, eds., 2 vols. (Collegeville, Minnesota, 1979), 2:49 [27–63]; Günter Glauche, *Schullektüre im Mittelalter: Entstehung und Wandlungen des Lektürekanons bis 1200 nach den Quellen dargestellt*, Münchener Beiträge zur Mediavistik und Renaissance-Forschung 5 (Munich, 1970); John J. Contreni, *The Cathedral School of Laon from 850–930: Its Manuscripts and Masters*, Münchener Beiträge zur Mediavistik und Renaissance-Forschung 29 (Munich, 1978); idem, "John Scottus, Martin Hiberniensis, The Liberal Arts, and Teaching," in press; and, Pierre Riché, *Les écoles et l'enseignement dans l'Occident chrétien de la fin du Ve siècle au milieu du XIe siècle* (Paris, 1979), pp. 221–280.

which supported the temple of Wisdom—they were essential to the edifice of Christian learning. One did not dally at the pillars, however, but went beyond them to the study of the Bible.[4]

These last words bring to mind, of course, Beryl Smalley's famous book, *The Study of the Bible in the Middle Ages*, the second edition of which is now thirty years old.[5] Smalley provided medievalists with both a bold and brilliant synthesis of manuscript research and the work of other scholars. The chapters on the Carolingians were admittedly sketchy, but it would be pedantic to carp at the nine pages Smalley devoted to the eighth and ninth centuries, especially since, despite the passage of years, they remain fundamentally sound.[6] I do want to mention her book, however, in order to underscore a difference between the approach to the study of the Bible typified by Smalley and the one followed here. Smalley and others have chosen to follow the "high road" in their investigations of biblical studies. The main emphasis has been on exegesis and the theological speculations embedded in the commentaries of the eighth- and ninth-century masters. The Carolingian commentators are a stage in

---

[4]The image is Alcuin's. See his *De grammatica*, MPL 101:760, and Marie-Thérèse d'Alverny's "La Sagesse et ses sept filles: Recherches sur les allégories de la Philosophie et des arts libéraux du IXe au XIIe siècle," in *Mélanges dediés à la memoire de Félix Grat*, 2 vols. (Paris, 1946-1949), 1:245–278.

[5]New York, 1952.

[6]*The Study of the Bible in the Middle Ages* does, however, need to be read alongside Henri de Lubac's *Exégèse médiévale: Les quatre sens de l'Écriture*, 2 vols. in 4 (Paris, 1959-1964), a book which on many points directly confronts Smalley. Among general works, C. Spicq's *Esquisse d'une histoire de l'exégèse latine au moyen age*, Bibliothèque thomiste 26 (Paris, 1944), pp. 9–60, is still useful although inaccurate on some matters of detail. M. L. W. Laistner, *Thought and Letters in Western Europe, A.D. 500 to 900*, 2nd ed. (London and Ithaca, 1957), pp. 298–306, though brief is sensible and based on the author's detailed studies of individual Carolingian commentators. See below, notes 42, 46, and 79. Robert E. McNally, *The Bible in the Early Middle Ages*, Woodstock Papers: Occasional Essays for Theology, no. 4 (Westminster, Maryland, 1959) provides a good, general sketch with a handy listing of the medieval biblical commentaries. *La Bibbia nell'alto Medioevo*, Settimane di studio del Centro italiano di studi sull'alto Medioevo 10 (Spoleto, 1963) offers a rich collection of fundamental essays. *The Cambridge History of the Bible*, 2: *The West from the Fathers to the Reformation*, G. W. H. Lampe, ed. (Cambridge, 1969) has a good bibliography but is generally uneven. Chapter VI-2, "The Exposition and Exegesis of Scripture from Gregory the Great to St. Bernard" by Jean Leclercq, is particularly disappointing. *The Bible and Medieval Culture*, W. Lourdaux and D. Verhelst, eds., Mediaevalia Lovaniensis, series 1, Studia 7 (Leuven, 1979) has nothing on the Carolingian period. Pierre Riché's excellent study, "Divina pagina, ratio et auctoritas dans la théologie carolingienne," in *Nascita dell'Europa ed Europa carolingia: Un'equazione da verificare, Spoleto, 19–25 aprile 1979*, Settimane di studio del Centro italiano di studi sull'alto medioevo 27 (Spoleto, 1981), pp. 719–758, came to my attention while this essay was in press.

the long, unfolding continuum of biblical criticism. My interest is focused on biblical studies as part of the educational process. Specifically, the road I have chosen to follow heads ultimately to an understanding of the goals, methods, and tools of biblical studies in the Carolingian context. Such an investigation of the process of biblical education is inherently worthwhile. It may also enable us to appreciate better the work of Carolingian masters, who, with an exception or two, have generally been passed over as second-rate compilers.[7]

The Carolingians were not the first in the post-patristic world to propose a plan of studies leading to improved understanding of the divine pages. One thinks immediately of Cassiodorus and of his overture to Pope Agapitus to establish a school for sacred studies in Rome and of his *Institutes of Divine and Secular Learning* which had to suffice for the ill-starred school.[8] One also remembers Isidore of Seville's treatment of the subject in the *Origines* and elsewhere in his works.[9] Bede, in addition to commenting on various books of the Bible, produced handbooks such as the *De schematibus et tropis* to facilitate biblical studies.[10] The ideals, commentaries, and manuals of these masters would be enormously influential to later generations of masters and students throughout Europe. However, I think that it is fair to say that in their own time, the programs of Cassiodorus, of Isidore, and of Bede bore limited fruit despite historians' talk of Ostrogothic, Isidorian, and Northumbrian renaissances. The missing ingredient was the consistent support of public authority. That is what is new about studies, particularly biblical studies, in the Carolingian realms. Public authority, which was so busy dealing with military affairs, heresy, the political structure, dynastic

---

[7]Paschasius Radbertus and John Scottus are the general exceptions although Leclercq, "The Exposition and Exegesis of Scripture," p. 187, opts for curious reasons for Alcuin and Rabanus Maurus. For the general view of Carolingian exegetical activity, see, *inter multa*, ibid.; Smalley, *Study of the Bible*, pp. 37–38, and Riché, *Écoles et enseignement*, p. 284 (see below, note 78).

[8]*Cassiodori Senatoris Institutiones Edited from the MSS.*, R. A. B. Mynors, ed. (Oxford, 1937), preface (p. 3, 1–13). See also Pierre Riché, *Education and Culture in the Barbarian West from the Sixth through the Eighth Century*, trans. John J. Contreni (Columbia, South Carolina, 1976, 1978), pp. 132–135.

[9]*Isidori Hispalensis episcopi Etymologiarum sive Originum libri xx*, W. M. Lindsay, ed., 2 vols. (Oxford, 1911), VI, i–iv. See also *Clavis patrum latinorum, editio altera*, Eligius Dekkers and Aemilius Gaar, eds., Sacris Eruditi 3 (1961), nos. 1190–1197.

[10]See M. H. King, ed., *Bedae Venerabilis opera*, pars I: *Opera didascalica*, Corpus christianorum, Series latina, 123A (Turnhout, 1975), pp. 142–171, and *Clavis*, nos. 1344–1366, 2333. See also *Famulus Christi: Essays in Commemoration of the Thirteenth Centenary of the Birth of the Venerable Bede*, Gerald Bonner, ed. (London, 1976), especially Paul Meyvaert's contribution, "Bede the Scholar," pp. 40–69.

concerns, the running of the estates, the minting of coins, the reform of monasticism, also took under its wing education.

What is so admirable about Carolingian legislation is not that it was original, but that it was clearly stated and consistently applied. The earliest monuments of the Carolingian program were announced in the famous and oft-quoted *Admonitio generalis* and the *Epistola de litteris colendis.*[11] These documents ordained that students be taught the basics — reading, chant, shorthand, *computus*, and grammar — and that especial attention be directed to the copying and study of the Scriptures. All monasteries and cathedrals were invited to follow these prescriptions. One suspects that the royal will was felt heaviest in the "public" schools, that is, in the schools whose support and direction came under royal jurisdiction. What Charlemagne and his court began, his sons and grandsons continued. A whole series of royal legislation touching on education issued from the courts of the ninth century. Biblical studies were implicit in all the legislation. Some of it, such as the canons of the Roman councils of 826 and 853 and of the Council of Savonnières of 859, referred explicitly to the study of the Bible.[12] Moreover, by the second quarter of the ninth century, the bishops and abbots of Francia began to take the initiative and issued prescriptions for their own jurisdictions.[13] By 819 Rabanus Maurus had put together a handbook for the training of clergy, an entire section of which was dedicated to outlining a program of biblical studies.[14] Around 885-886, Notker of Saint Gall wrote

[11]MGH Legum Sectio II: *Capitularia regum Francorum*, 1 (Hanover, 1883), pp. 52-62 (no. 22) and 78-79 (no. 29). See Pierre Riché, *Education and Culture*, pp. 497-498, and *Écoles et enseignement*, pp. 65-75, for the background and development of Charlemagne's educational policy. See also Luitpold Wallach, "Charlemagne's *De litteris colendis* and Alcuin," in his *Alcuin and Charlemagne: Studies in Carolingian History and Literature*, revised and amended reprint (New York and London, 1968), pp. 198-226.

[12]See MGH Concilia I-2:581 (cap. 34), and *Sacrorum conciliorum nova et amplissima collectio*, J. D. Mansi, ed., 53 vols. (Florence and Venice, 1759-1798; repr. Graz, 1960), 14:1008 (cap. 34). See also Riché, *Écoles et enseignement*, pp. 76-79, and, especially, Thomas F. X. Noble, "The Place in Papal History of the Roman Synod of 826," *Church History* 45 (1976), p. 10 [1-16] and p. 4 of the appendix [1-5].

[13]Rosamond McKitterick, *The Frankish Church and the Carolingian Reforms, 789-895*, Royal Historical Society: Studies in History (London, 1977), in a fundamental work, studied the ninth-century diffusion of the Carolingian decrees and capitularies and the thirty-four extant episcopal statutes they inspired. See especially pp. 1-79.

[14]*Rabani Mauri de institutione clericorum libri tres*, Alois Knöpfler, ed., Veröffentlichungen aus dem Kirchenhistorischen Seminar München 5 (Munich, 1900), bk. 3 (= MPL 107:377b-420a). For Rabanus and his fellow Carolingian commentators, the best general guide is now Franz Brunhölzl, *Geschichte der lateinischen Literatur des Mittelalters*, 1: *Von Cassiodor*

what amounts to a confident bibliographic essay surveying the best guides to the study of the Bible.[15]

Legislation and guidebooks alone were not sufficient. Personnel and material resources—in the case of biblical studies, books—had also to be marshalled. The recruitment and patronage of scholars, especially foreign-born ones, to Francia is a well-known feature of the Carolingian program. I shall not linger on that topic here except to note that whatever the originality of the foreign contribution to Carolingian intellectual life in general and to biblical studies in particular that originality seems confined to the first Anglo-Saxons, Italians, Visigoths, and Irishmen who found support and encouragement at Charlemagne's table. Within a generation, their contributions, whose novelty and distinctiveness have been more assumed than clearly defined, had been assimilated into a Carolingian, European cultural life. When Charlemagne's grandson, Charles the Bald, patronized John Scottus, an Irishman, he maintained a master of enormous talent and fresh inspiration, but a master nonetheless who fits more comfortably the rubric "Carolingian" than "Hiberno-Latin."[16]

Studies, particularly biblical studies, require books as well as masters. Charlemagne requisitioned books from Rome to be recopied for the lecterns of Francia's royal, episcopal, and monastic libraries.[17] Individuals, from the

---

bis zum Ausklang der karolingischen Erneuerung (Munich, 1975) which, unlike Max Manitius, Geschichte der lateinischen Literatur des Mittelalters, 1: Von Justinian bis zur Mitte des zehnten Jahrhunderts (Munich, 1911; repr. 1965), surveys both theological and exegetical literature. Manitius remains useful for manuscript references and older bibliography as well as for his analysis.

[15]De illustribus viris qui ex intentione sacras scripturas exponebant, aut ex occasione quasdam sententias divinae auctoritatis explanabant, in Das Formelbuch des Bischofs Salomo III von Konstanz aus dem neunten Jahrhundert, Ernst Dümmler, ed. (Leipzig, 1857), pp. 64–78; also, MPL 131:993–1004. Manitius, Geschichte, p. 358, called this work "das erste kritische Handbuch der lateinischen Patristik."

[16]John Scottus's script was Insular, his Latin employed a few "Hibernisms," and he occasionally used Old Irish words in his teaching. See John J. Contreni, "The Biblical Glosses of Haimo of Auxerre and John Scottus Eriugena," Speculum 51 (1976), 411–434, and Ludwig Bieler, "Remarks on Eriugena's Original Latin Prose," in The Mind of Eriugena: Papers of a Colloquium, Dublin, 14–18 July 1970, John J. O'Meara and Ludwig Bieler, eds., (Dublin, 1973), pp. 140–146. But save for a few nautical images that Édouard Jeauneau has isolated in his writings (see Jean Scot: Homélie sur le prologue de Jean, Sources chrétiennes 151 [Paris, 1969], pp. 12–14), there is nothing patently Irish in Eriugena's work. See also, John J. Contreni, "The Irish 'Colony' at Laon during the Time of John Scottus," in Jean Scot Érigène et l'histoire de la Philosophie, René Roques, ed., Colloques internationaux du Centre National de la Recherche Scientifique 561 (Paris, 1977), p. 67 [59–67].

[17]See Paul Lehmann, "Erzbischof Hildebald und die Dombibliothek von Köln," in Erforschung des Mittelalters: Ausgewählte Abhandlungen und Aufsätze, 5 vols. (Stuttgart, 1959-1962), 2:140

learned Hincmar of Reims to the more humble Martinus Hiberniensis, constantly sought to augment their libraries with texts that would aid their study of the Bible.[18] Charles the Bald turned his court into a center for the translation and dissemination of Greek texts, particularly of the Greek Fathers whose work would open new interpretive doors to Carolingian masters.[19] Of course, the book par excellence, the *bibliotheca*, the *sacra scriptura*, the *divina historia* did not go neglected by Carolingians. The Carolingian period is one of great significance for the history of the Latin Bible. Charlemagne, emulating his father, Pepin, who sponsored a corrected version of the lectionary, often expressed his desire for an error-free biblical text: free, that is, from grammatical and orthographical errors. It once was thought that he confided the task of producing a standard edition of the Bible to Alcuin and that the Alcuinian Bible became the official Bible of the Carolingian Empire.[20]

Alcuin, among his many other scholarly accomplishments, did indeed prepare a biblical text for his master, but it goes beyond the evidence to see in his work a "revision" of the text or an official Bible. Alcuin corrected errors and made stylistic improvements, but did not broach editorial questions. Nor was Alcuin alone in his concern for an improved, error-free biblical text. Others responded to the wishes of the court. At least four other biblical texts from the late eighth and early ninth century have been identified.[21] If the Alcuinian Bible did predominate, its

---

[139-144], and Bernhard Bischoff, "Die Kölner Nonnenhandschriften und das Skriptorium von Chelles," in *Mittelalterliche Studien*: *Ausgewählte Aufsätze zur Schriftkunde und Literaturgeschichte*, 3 vols. (Stuttgart, 1966-1967, 1981) 1:18 [16-34].

[18]See Contreni, *Cathedral School of Laon*, p. 39, for Martin's tally of Jerome commentaries either in or missing from his collection; and *Loup de Ferrières*: *Correspondance*, Léon Levillain, ed., 2 vols. (Paris, 1924-1935), 2:146 (no. 108) for Lupus's loan of Bede's *Collectio ex opusculis sancti Augustini in epistulas Pauli Apostoli* to the archbishop of Reims.

[19]Édouard Jeauneau, "Jean Scot Érigène et le grec," *Archivum Latinitatis Medii Aevi* (*Bulletin du Cange*) 41 (1979), 12-23 [5-50].

[20]See Bonifatius Fischer, *Die Alkuin-Bibel*, Aus der Geschichte der lateinischen Bibel 1 (Freiburg-im-Breisgau, 1957) *contra* F. L. Ganshof, "La revision de la Bible par Alcuin," *Bibliothèque d'Humanisme et Renaissance* 9 (1947), 7-20 (English translation by Janet Sondheimer in F. L. Ganshof, *The Carolingians and the Frankish Monarchy*: Studies in Carolingian History [Ithaca and New York, 1971], pp. 28-40).

[21]See Bonifatius Fischer, "Bibelausgaben des frühen Mittelalters," in *La Bibbia nell'alto Medioevo*, pp. 586-597 [519-600], and idem, "Bibeltext und Bibelreform unter Karl dem Grossen," in *Karl der Grosse*: *Lebenswerk und Nachleben*, Wolfgang Braunfels et al., eds., 5 vols. (Düsseldorf, 1965-1968), 2:156-216.

favor owed more to the activity of the scriptorium at Tours under
Alcuin's successors than to any royal directive. The Tours scribes flooded
the market, so to speak, with Bibles based largely on Alcuin's work.[22]
Still, they did not drive out their "rivals." In addition, later ninth- and
tenth-century Bibles combined texts from earlier Bibles to produce new
textual traditions.

Much detailed work remains to be undertaken before we can understand fully the Carolingian history of the biblical text. One conclusion
has already emerged from the work of the few, hardy scholars who have
braved the thicket of Carolingian biblical studies. From the point of view
of scholarship, the most important Bible is that of Bishop Theodulf of
Orléans, the Visigothic émigré to Francia, accomplished and sometimes
mordant poet, politician, episcopal administrator, and author of the
*Libri Carolini*.[23] Theodulf's Bible, of which only six complete or partial
copies survive, is a work of true critical editorial scholarship. No two of
them textually are precisely identical. At each stage in the development
and refinement of the text, Theodulf consulted other textual traditions,
alerting readers with marginal annotations to the sources of variants very
much as a modern editor uses an *apparatus criticus*. In Theodulfian
Bibles, minuscule *s* preceding an alternate reading stood for a Spanish
source; *a* for Alcuin's Bible; Roman numeral *ii* for a reading common to
both Alcuin and the Spanish tradition; *h* for a reading based on the
Hebrew; and, *al* for "other." The compact format of the Theodulfian
Bibles enhanced their utility. Anyone coming to one of Theodulf's
pandects from an Alcuinian Bible will notice the different format immediately. The Tours product of the post-Alcuinian period is a sump-
tuous book, both large and ornate. At 33 cm. by 24 cm., Theodulfian
Bibles are half again smaller. Complete copies contain fewer folios, approximately 320 to the 420 of the Tours Bibles. Even the script is on a
smaller scale; some would even say that it is microscopic.[24]

---

[22]See Fischer, *Die Alkuin-Bibel*, pp. 13–14, for a chronological roster of Tours Bibles.

[23]See Brunhölzl, *Geschichte*, pp. 288–289; Elisabeth Dahlhaus-Berg, *Nova Antiquitas et
Antiqua Novitas: Typologische Exegese und isidorianisches Geschichtsbild bei Theodulf von
Orleans*, Kölner Historische Abhandlungen 23 (Cologne and Vienna, 1975); Paul Meyvaert,
"The Authorship of the Libri Carolini: Observations Prompted by a Recent Book," *Revue
bénédictine* 89 (1979), 29–57; and Thomas F. X. Noble, "Some Observations of the Deposi-
tion of Archbishop Theodulf of Orleans in 817," *Journal of the Rocky Mountain Medieval
and Renaissance Association* 2 (1981), 29–40.

[24]See Dahlhaus-Berg, *Nova Antiquitas*, pp. 39–76; and Fischer, "Bibelausgaben," pp.
593–596, for these details and comparisons.

The impression that Theodulf's Bibles were organized more for utility and study rather than for display and gift-giving[25] is strengthened by examining the *Hilfsmittel* Theodulf included in his Bibles. The last twenty-five folios of the complete Bibles are dedicated to four supplementary texts. Isidore of Seville's *Chronica minora* from the *Origines* (5.39), a précis of world history down through the six ages to the seventh century A.D., provided the reader not only with an outline of unfolding biblical history, but also with a sense of comparative historical chronology. The second book of the *Instructiones* of Eucherius of Lyon follows the *Chronica minora*.[26] Eucherius explained Hebrew proper names, difficult words, peoples, places, rivers, holy days, vestments, animals and birds, weights and measures, and Greek names one would encounter in the Scriptures. Two pseudonymous works complete Theodulf's selection of extrabiblical texts. Pseudo-Melito's *Clavis* provided symbolic and allegorical explanations of biblical vocabulary in contrast to the factual emphasis in Eucherius's work.[27] An abbreviated version of the *Liber de divinis scripturis* of Pseudo-Augustine with its moral explanations of selected biblical passages completed Theodulf's biblical appendices.[28] As Elisabeth Dahlhaus-Berg has pointed out, these four works exemplify the threefold method of biblical exegesis — the historical, the allegorical, and the tropological.[29] They also attest to a keen pedagogical sense on Theodulf's part.

Most Carolingian biblical exegesis, in fact, was inspired precisely by pedagogical concerns, not by a desire to advance the cause of scholarship nor by any impulse to push on to new exegetical frontiers. It was the desire to teach, to introduce the Bible to the educated layman or laywoman, to the busy ecclesiastical administrator, and to the beginning

---

[25]This is not to say that the Theodulfian Bibles are artless. They have long attracted the attention of art historians. Fischer, *Die Alkuin-Bibel*, p. 8, called them "elegant": "Hier ist schon etwa 800–814 das vorweggenommen, was die Schreibschule von Tours erst ab 830 erreichen wird: die einbändige Bibel als Gesamtkunstwerk aus einem Guss."

[26]*Sancti Eucherii Lugdunensis opera omnia*, Carolus Wotke, ed., CSEL 31 (Vienna, 1894), pp. 140–161.

[27]Joannes Baptista Card. Pitra, *Analecta sacra Spicilegio solesmensi parata*, 2: *Patres antenicaeni* (Paris, 1884), pp. 6–127.

[28]F. Weihrich, ed., CSEL 12 (Vienna, 1887), pp. 287–700. Weihrich printed the Theodulfian excerpts at the bottom of the pages in his edition. Ann Freeman, "Further Studies in the Libri Carolini," *Speculum* 40 (1965), 263 [203–289], has remarked that Theodulf's work on the *Clavis* deserves further investigation. A study of the principle of selection governing Theodulf's version of the *Liber de divinis scripturae* would also be worthwhile.

[29]*Nova Antiquitas*, pp. 86–87.

student that mattered most. This is a truism, no doubt,[30] but I think it important to stress the influence of the audience in shaping biblical studies. Carolingian scholars worked within a particular cultural context that conditioned their work. Comparison is fundamental to historical analysis. As we compare, however, we must keep in mind that the context of the Fathers or of the university theologians was not that which tempered biblical studies in the eighth and ninth centuries. To understand how the Bible was taught in the Carolingian world, we must seek to discover the context that animated Carolingian masters when they commented on the Bible. Fortunately, such a task is made easier for us by the commentators themselves. Many of them in the prefaces or dedications of their works revealed the sources of their inspiration as well as the methodology and goals of their works. Several common themes emerge from the prefatory letters.[31]

First of all, it is quite obvious that personal attitudes and material conditions affected biblical studies. The disclaimers masters voiced about their own inadequacy and smallness as they faced the task of biblical explanation seem disingenuous and formulaic. But, for the believer who attempts to fathom a text convinced that it has proceeded from the mouth

---

[30]A truism, that is, more for the patristic and early medieval than for the scholastic and high-scholastic periods by which time biblical studies had become highly professionalized and arcane to the beginner and certainly to the laity. The best minds spoke to and wrote for each other and advanced students.

[31]I realize that studying the prefaces of the Carolingian commentaries might not be entirely satisfactory on several accounts. First, there are a whole series of commentaries either without prefaces or whose prefaces have not been published. One thinks of Sedulius Scottus's biblical *collectanea* and Haimo of Auxerre's many commentaries. In both cases the actual substance of their commentaries leaves me with no doubt that had they written prefaces, they would have expressed more or less the same sentiments and reflected the same motivations as their colleagues. (One cannot be so confident, of course, about John Scottus's fragmentary, acephalic commentary on John.) Secondly, one might object that the prefaces cannot be trusted, that their sometimes grandiose, sometimes obsequious prose achieved rhetorical effect at the price of veracity. Dungal of Pavia certainly took Claudius of Turin to task for statements Claudius made in his prefaces (see MGH Epp. 4:596, note 4; 599, note 1; 607, note 1). Thirdly, one might also object that the Carolingians in their prefaces repeated clichés taken over from the Fathers. I have considered all these problems and have concluded that they do not compromise our attempt to understand the motivations, intentions, and conditions of Carolingian biblical studies. A cliché or commonplace, even if often repeated, is not meaningless. Furthermore, I am convinced that on the whole Carolingian masters wrote for the reasons they stated and accomplished what they reported in their prefaces. What is needed more than anything, of course, is a fresh look at the Carolingian biblical commentaries that would combine the industry and source criticism of M. L. W. Laistner (see notes 6, 42, 46, 79) with the intellectual sensitivity of Paul Meyvaert (see note 10).

of the Almighty God, intellectual humility is the only possible attitude.[32] Attempting to explain the divine law for Claudius of Turin was akin to trying to touch the heavens with one's hand.[33] There was always the fear that something wrong might be written, that the Fathers might be misrepresented. Readers were asked to correct anything objectionable they found in a commentary and to improve the work if they could.[34] Some commentators, following the example of Bede, identified the sources of their excerpts by inscribing the initials of the appropriate Father in the apposite margins. This technique served to guarantee the integrity of the Carolingian master's work, to identify his contributions as distinct from those of the Fathers, and to warn the reader or teacher that any dissonances in the commentary were only apparent since the excerpts were taken out of context from different works and different Fathers.[35] These kinds of comments and strategies are so persistent that we automatically

---

[32]Rabanus Maurus, *De clericorum institutione*, 3.2 (ed. Knöpfler, p. 191; MPL 107:379b-c): "Fundamentum autem, status et perfectio prudentiae, scientia est sanctarum scripturarum; quae ab illa incommutabili aeternaque sapientia profluens, quae ex ore altissimi prodiit, primogenita scilicet ante omnem creaturam spiritus sancti distributionibus, per vasa scripturae lumen indeficiens, quasi per laternas orbi lucet universo, ac si quid aliud est, quod sapientiae nomine rite censeri possit, ab uno eodemque sapientiae fonte derivatum, ad eius respectat originem." Claudius of Turin to Abbot Dructeramnus, preface, commentary on Genesis, MGH Epp. 4:590, 8-11: "Non solum credimus, sed etiam videmus et tenemus fidelem Dominum in verbis suis et sanctum in omnibus operibus suis, qui dignatus est eclesiae suae promittere per Esaiam, quod repleretur terra eius scientia sicut aquas maris operantes. Quod factum est post evangelicas et apostolicas scripturas, quando plura ne innumerabilia opuscula aedita sunt a sanctis patribus, ortodoxis fidei eclesiae defensoribus. Post quos omnes ego indignus et ultimus. . . ."

[33]Letter to Abbot Theodemirus accompanying his *Liber informationum litterae et spiritus super Leviticum*, MGH Epp. 4:602, 31-33: "Et sicut difficile est quemquam manu posse caelum tangere, ita difficile est omnia sacramenta legis divinae, sicut tu precipis, explanare."

[34]Claudius of Turin, ibid., p. 603, 31-35: "En, carissime frater, sicut potui, respondi quibusdam inquisitionibus tuis: pro qua re obnixe deprecor, ut si quid de his rebus, unde me interrogas, si quid invenisti melius vel deinceps invenire potueris, gratissimum habebimus, si nos feceris nosse, quia ego magis amo discere quam docere." See also the letter which accompanied Claudius's response to Theodemirus's questions on the book of Kings, ibid., p. 607, 37-p. 608, 6. Rabanus Maurus, in the letter to Archbishop Otgarius of Mainz which accompanied the commentary on Ecclesiasticus, wrote (MGH Epp. 5:428, 1-5): "De caetero quoque moneo lectorem, si eius prudentiae alicubi in hoc opere nostro vel sensus displiceat vel oratio sordescat, non nos temerario iudicio cito reprehendat, sed magis infirmitati et ignorantiae veniam tribuat, sciatque loca ibi esse difficilia et diversis enigmatibus valde obscura, unde debet ignoscere labori nostro, aut, si quid melius potuerit invenire, nos in eius sententiam paratos sciat transire." Rabanus made much the same request of Bishop Freculphus of Lisieux when he sent his commentary on Genesis to him. See ibid., p. 394, 8-13.

[35]Claudius of Turin noted in the preface to his comments on Genesis, MGH Epp. 4:592, 14-17: "Et ne ab aliquibus praesumptor et temerarius diiudicarer, quod ab alieno armario

cast them off as commonplace. Common they may be, but I read them as the sincere self-doubts of scholars in pursuit of biblical wisdom, wisdom which, as Rabanus Maurus knew, was the source of all wisdom that illuminated the universe, but which, when misinterpreted, as Florus of Lyons pointed out, became instead the source of all evil.[36] There is another, more immediate side to this litany of exculpation. The definition

---

sumpserim tela, uniuscuiusque doctoris nomen cum suis characteribus, sicut et beatus fecit presbiter Beda subter in paginis adnotavi." Theodemirus asked him to continue the practice in his Leviticus commentary, but Claudius noted that Bede only listed his authorities in two of his works, the commentaries on Luke and Mark. More tellingly, he admitted (ibid., p. 603, 9–11): "Quod ego ideo omisi facere, quia sententias quorundam, quas adnotaveram prius sub nomine aliorum, diligentius perquirens, aliorum eas esse repperi postea." Freculphus of Lisieux requested that Rabanus Maurus note his sources in the margins of the commentaries he commissioned: ibid., p. 392, 15–24. Rabanus did so in the commentaries on Matthew (ibid., p. 389, 35–38, where Bede is cited); Genesis (ibid., p. 394, 1–4); Numbers (p. 398, 14–18); Kings (ibid., pp. 402, 33–403, 10); the Pauline Epistles (ibid., pp. 429, 25–430, 5); and Ezechiel (ibid., p. 477, 21–37). Apparently, Rabanus's diligence in listing his sources drew some criticism. He felt called upon in the prefatory letter to the Ezechiel commentary to defend himself (11.24–29): "Quid enim peccavi in hoc . . . oportunis locis simul cum nota nominum eorum in opusculis meis interposueram? Magis enim mihi videbatur salubre esse, ut humilitatem servans sanctorum patrum doctrinis inniterer, quam per arrogantiam, quasi propriam laudem quaerendo, mea indecenter proferrem." Angelomus of Luxeuil, probably Rabanus's critic, wrote in the preface to his commentary on the Canticle of Canticles, that the system popularized by Rabanus did not fit his style of composition (ibid., p. 627, 5–10): "Sed sciendum vero, quia ut moris est quorundam scriptorum, non in pagella e regione singulorum doctorum viritim litteris insignitis assignaverimus nomina omnia, sed ex eorum dictis profecto expositorum nonnulla compaginare ex multimodis, breviter recidendo videlicet demptis superfluis, multimoda, nonnulla vero ex prolixioribus sensum eorum sequentes coniungere decerpendo, aliqua nostra interpolando augmentare censuimus longiora." Paschasius Radbertus followed the example of Bede and Rabanus in his commentary on Matthew. See MGH Epp. 6:141, 26–28.

[36]See above, note 32, and Florus of Lyons, *Libellus de tenenda immobiliter veritate*, MPL 121:1083c–1084c: "Exortum est magis dolendum ac lugendum malum, ut videlicet, contempta veritate scripturarum sacrarum, calcata auctoritate beatissimorum atque orthodoxorum patrum, per quos ecclesia dei aedificatur et illustratur, praesumant aliqui etiam de rebus praecipue ad fidem pertinentibus ex proprii sensus temeraria praesumptione quae apertissime contraria sunt divinae veritati, et ipse docere, et aliis tenenda statuere atque conscribere." Florus probably had John Scottus in mind. See André Wilmart, "Une lettre sans adresse écrite vers le milieu du IXe siècle," *Revue bénédictine* 42 (1930), 149–162. Rabanus Maurus, *Commentarius in Eziechelem*, MGH Epp. 5:477, 38–40: "Illi enim, qui laudem quaerunt et ab hominibus videri appetunt, dictent vel scribant quicquid voluerint, et laudatores suos atque adolatores, undecumque possint, sibi adquirant." Walahfrid Strabo worried that his précis of Rabanus's commentary on Exodus would deform the master's teaching, ibid., p. 516, 4–8: "Quorum ego ultimus Strabus ipsam . . . notavi, humiliter lectorem deposcens, ut si quid extra lineam rectitudinis in illa positum invenerit, non magistro imputet, sed meae tarditatis ignaviae, misericorditer tamen mihi compassus veniam tribuat postulanti."

and institutionalization of an official culture by the Carolingians inevitably circumscribed digressions or, at least, got authors who strayed from what had been defined as true and right into trouble. Claudius of Turin, Gottschalk of Orbais, John Scottus, all found themselves on the wrong side of the interpretive line at one point or another.

This general intellectual precondition was complemented by another personal factor. Many of the Carolingian commentators were very busy people in positions of high spiritual and administrative responsibility. Serving as bishop or abbot, living the life of the Rule, attending court, fulfilling political functions left scant opportunity for perusing texts, reflection, and writing. Scholarly work, undertaken on demand, was at best squeezed into a busy routine. Claudius of Turin portrayed himself studying and writing while on the alert for Saracens — by night holding a sword, by day books and a quill.[37] From what we know of their lives as administrators, correspondents, friends of the court, and authors of non-exegetical works, these complaints about limited time for writing ring true.

What strains belief is that a Claudius, an Alcuin, a Rabanus Maurus, or a Haimo of Auxerre produced as much as they did, especially in light of the less than ideal working conditions with which they had to contend. We are so used to reconstructing libraries and to extolling book production during the Carolingian period that we sometimes fail to remember that it was indeed a rare library that could provide the scholar with all the texts needed. Hincmar of Reims and Martinus Hiberniensis were not the

---

[37]Preface to the commentary on Corinthians, MGH Epp. 4:601, 19-22: "Post medium veris procedendo armatus pergameno pariter cum arma ferens, pergo ad excubias maritimas cum timore excubando adversus Agarenos et Mauros; nocte tenens gladium et die libros et calamum, implere conans ceptum desiderium." That the see of Turin was no sinecure is reflected in the preface to the commentary on Josue, ibid., p. 609, 15-16: "Propter nimiam pressuram atque angustiam et diras infestationes perversorum hominum iniquorum, qui me nimis [minis ed.] conturbant . . . ." On the same theme, see ibid., p. 602, 21-25. Work on Matthew, Ephesians, Phillipians, and Galatians was slowed by poor eyesight and episcopal duties. See ibid., pp. 595, 13-18, 596, 24-25, and 598, 35-40. In his letter to Abbot Dructeramnus accompanying the Galatians commentary, Claudius noted (p. 597, 5-7) that he had many excerpts in hand, but needed time and health to complete the job. Alcuin listed as two of the reasons he was unworthy to respond to Sigvulfus's questions on Genesis the following (ibid., p. 122, 23-24): "Maxime nobis, qui saeculi occupationibus distrahimur et diversis itenerum molestiis fatigamur." Rabanus Maurus's specific complaints about his health, episcopal and monastic duties, and political involvement can be found at MGH Epp. 5:393, 27-30, 296, 19-21, 431, 6-7, 441, 35-37. As one busy man to another, he described for King Louis the German in glowing terms the leisure of those who have time to read, meditate, and write as they wish. Ibid., p. 468, 11-15.

only scholars whose libraries were deficient.[38] Rabanus Maurus envied the library Hilduin of Saint-Denis had at his disposal at the palace where he served as archchaplain.[39] Bishop Humbertus of Würzburg could boast about the wide range of patristic authors in his library, but Freculphus of Lisieux did not have a complete Bible, much less commentaries on particular biblical books.[40] Christian of Stablo had heard of Bede's commentary on Luke, but could not lay hands on a copy of it.[41] Angelomus of Luxeuil's library lacked a complete patristic commentary on Kings.[42] Alcuin's work on Genesis was partially affected by his inability to bring all the necessary books along with him.[43] Paschasius Radbertus consulted a galaxy of sources for his Matthew commentary, but admitted that he could not find Fortunatianus and Victorinus.[44]

The expectations of the masters' patrons were as important an influence on the shape of Carolingian biblical studies as were books. The great majority of eighth- and ninth-century biblical commentaries were

[38]See above, note 18.

[39]Preface to the commentary on Kings, MGH Epp. 5:402, 15-16: ". . . quid vobis, qui divites estis in omnibus, in omni scientia et omni doctrina, et apud quem librorum maxima copia est." Rabanus noted the poverty of his library at Fulda "qui nec multos libros habent nec diversorum auctorum codices." See the preface to the commentary on Daniel, ibid., p. 468, 1. See also p. 393, 21-23. The commentary on Matthew, however, was written from Fulda for the "lector pauperculus, qui copiam librorum non habet." Ibid., p. 388, 28.

[40]Humbertus, letter to Rabanus Maurus, MGH Epp. 5:440, 21-24: "Non tamen propterea ista posco, quasi desint nobis istius operis scriptores; habemus namque Origenem, Victorinum, Ambrosium, Hieronimum, Cassianum, Isidorum, Augustinum, Fulgentium atque pontificem insignem eloquentissimumque Gregorium et ceteros patres, quorum nomina non necesse tibi credimus enumerari." Freculphus, ibid., p. 392, 28-31, anticipating that Rabanus might suggest that he prepare his own commentary on the Pentateuch, forewarned that he could not do so "quoniam nulla nobis librorum copia, ut haec facere possimus, subpeditat; etiamsi parvitas obtunsi sensus nostri vigeret; dum in episcopio nostrae parvitati commisso, nec ipsos novi veterisque testamenti canonicos repperi libros, multo minus horum expositiones."

[41]Preface to the commentary on Matthew, MGH Epp. 6:178, 17-19. "In Luca quoque audio post sanctum Ambrosium eumdem Bedam manum misisse, sed non potui invenire adhuc in tota eius expositione, nisi quasdam eius homelias."

[42]Preface to his commentary on Kings, MGH Epp. 5:622, 33-36: "Igitur cum a quampluribus fratribus et etiam a nonnullis prudentibus et nobilibus viris rogarer, ut secundum sollertiam doctorum et traditionem magistri viri disertissimi aliquod opusculum in volumine Regum digererem, eo quod a nullo doctorum per omnia expositum apud nos haberetur antiquorum . . . . " Ernst Dümmler,, who edited this letter for the MGH, misinterpreted the last phrase. See M. L. W. Laistner, "Some Early Medieval Commentaries on the Old Testament," Harvard Theological Review 46 (1953), 29-30.

[43]Letter to Sigvulfus, MGH Epp. 4:122, 24-25: "Et quia pondera librorum nobiscum portari nequeunt . . . ."

[44]MGH Epp. 6:140, 35-36: "Licet Fortunatianum et Victurinum in eo opuscula edidisse dicatur, quos necdum invenire potuimus."

not produced as disinterested works of theological speculation. They were made to the order of patrons, patrons who in most instances stated very explicitly what they hoped to obtain from the master. The emperors, kings, queens, archbishops, bishops, abbots, nuns, priests, and occasional laymen and laywomen who commissioned biblical expositions comprised an audience with very definite preferences. If we poll them, a pattern will begin to emerge.

Foremost among the desiderata was that the commentary be based on the Fathers, not one Father usually, but as many as possible. Patristic *florilegia* or *collectanea* such as those of Eugippius, Paterius, Latchen, and Defensor of Ligugé had a long history before the Carolingian period.[45] Wicbod's *Quaestiones in Octateuchum*, an early Carolingian representative of the genre compiled for Charlemagne, is typical.[46] Wicbod built his master-student dialogue on the sure foundation provided by the works of Augustine, Gregory, Jerome, Ambrose, Hilary, Isidore, Eucherius, and Junilius. Readers wanted the Fathers and masters were sure to provide them. *Feci sicut mandasti*. This phrase or its equivalent occurs frequently in the prefaces of the commentaries.[47]

Carolingian esteem for and extensive use of the works of the Fathers does not mean that Carolingian masters were uninspired hacks. In the first place, their attitude toward the biblical text and to the tradition and authority they believed inherent in patristic scholarship put any thought of going beyond the Fathers out of consideration. A later race of pygmies, perched on the shoulders of the patristic giants, might claim that it could see farther. It sufficed for the Carolingians to serve not as

[45]Eugippius, *Excerpta ex operibus sancti Augustini*; Paterius, *Liber testimoniorum veteris testamenti ex opusculis sancti Gregorii*; Latchen, *Ecloga de Moralibus Iob quae Gregorius fecit*; Defensor of Ligugé, *Liber scintillarum*. For these, see *Clavis*, nos. 676, 1718, 1716, 1302. For the Carolingian florilegia, see now, Rosamond McKitterick, *The Frankish Church and the Carolingian Reforms*, pp. 154–183.

[46]MGH PAC 1:95–97; MPL 96, 1105–1168 (=MPL 93:233–285); MPL 93:285–456; 95–97. For Wicbod, see Wilhelm Levison, *England and the Continent in the Eighth Century* (Oxford, 1946), pp. 107, 128–129; M. L. W. Laistner, "Antiochene Exegesis in Western Europe during the Middle Ages," *Harvard Theological Review* 40 (1947), 30–31; and Bernhard Bischoff, "Wendepunkte in der Geschichte der lateinischen Exegese im Frühmittelalter," *Mittelalterliche Studien,* 1:249. For the use to which his work was put in a ninth-century school, see Contreni, *The Cathedral School of Laon*, pp. 37–48, 40, 68, 96, 102, 112–113, 144, 157.

[47]See Alcuin, MGH Epp. 4:122, 21; 200, 7–8; 389, 14; Josephus Scottus, ibid., p. 483, 24–25; Claudius of Turin, ibid., pp. 594, 3–5; 596, 25; 601, 30; 603, 28; 607, 37; Rabanus Maurus, ibid., 5:394, 1; 395, 31; 396, 36; 398, 8–9; 399, 33; 424, 24; 441, 27; 462, 32; 465, 28; 476, 35; Prudentius of Troyes, MPL 115:1449c.

successors, but as imitators and disciples of the Fathers.[48] Secondly, we must remember that the charge to combine the Fathers in one volume editorially and intellectually was a real challenge — one the commentators acknowledged and embraced eagerly. There was nothing mechanical about their work. Choices had to be made, especially since readers demanded brevity along with their Fathers.[49] Busy prelates, such as Bishop Humbertus of Würzburg, the one who already had all the Fathers in his library, wanted a succinct guide to the Heptateuch. Remembering Isidore of Seville, he remarked pointedly to Rabanus Maurus that wordiness and obscurity make for tedious reading.[50] Where models were unavailable, the Carolingian master was quite prepared to make his own contributions. Rabanus Maurus had only heard of a commentary on Wisdom by Bellator, but did not have it at hand. Beyond that, he knew only a few relevant sermons by Augustine and Ambrose and thus had to go it largely on his own.[51] He also trusted to his own ingenuity, fortified by divine

[48]Rabanus Maurus, letter-preface to Emperor Lothair accompanying the commentary on Ezechiel, MGH Epp. 5:476, 43–477, 4: "Feci enim non quasi successor papae Gregorii et predicator plebis Dei . . . sed quasi imitator et discipulus, non solum ipsius memorati papae, sed et aliorum sanctorum doctorum vestigia sequendo."

[49]See Alcuin, MGH Epp. 4:407, 8–9; Claudius of Turin, ibid., pp. 598, 15–16, 607, 30–31; Rabanus Maurus, ibid., 5:430, 30–33, 468, 19; MPL 112:654c: "Ego vero praedicationem de singulis arripiens compendiose eam explicare adnitar: moris siquidem nostri est, ut non absolute prologorum narrationem quando sufficienter sensus veritatis in paucis poterit explicari." Sometimes brevity had to be sacrificed for utility as Rabanus explained in the preface to the commentary on Ezechiel, MGH Epp. 5:477, 8–15. Claudius of Turin wrote that the sense of the heavenly mysteries in Matthew could not be related or explained in a few words and prayed "ut non vos [Abbot Justus] terreat prolixa exposito nec voluminis magnitudo." See ibid., 4:595, 1–7. Josephus Scottus knew the dangers involved in the process of abbreviating: "Si quis autem haec quasi breviora et ob id obscuriora dispiciat — sepius enim brevitatem comitatur obscuritas — ad fontem, unde haec hausimus, erecto cervice currat." See ibid., p. 483, 30–33. For Walahfrid Strabo's reservations, see above, note 36. See also the remark in the preface to the commentary on Paralipomenon, MGH Epp. 5:423, 27–29: "Non enim longos florentesque tractatus, in quibus plausibilis ludit oratio, sed commentarios in divinas historias scribere decrevi, quorum officium est preterire manifesta, obscura disserere."

[50]After assuring Rabanus that it was not for want of books (see above, note 40) that he asked Rabanus to comment on the Heptateuch for him, the bishop wrote, MGH Epp. 5:440, 24–30: "Qui in tantum tuae sunt industriae cogniti, ut veraciter illorum linguam vestrum dicere possim sermonem, ut quod illi mira pulchritudine ac nimia longitudine sermonis proferebant, tu eorum vestigia sagaciter prudenterque sequendo, commatico mellifluoque conprehendas sermone. 'Brevi enim expositione succincta,' ut ait Isidorus doctor egregius, 'non faciunt de prolixitate fastidium; prolixa ergo et occulta tedet oratio, brevis et aperta delectat.'" See Isidore of Seville, *Quaestiones in vetus testamentum, praefatio,* 3 (MPL 83:207c–208b).

[51]Letter-preface to Archbishop Otgarius of Mainz, MGH Epp. 5:426, 10–15: "Verum cur ego ad exponendum hunc librum laborem adsumpserim, hec causa fuit, quia nullius antea super totum librum expositionem inveni, licet presbiter praedictus Bellator octo libros in eo se fecisse, ut predixi, commemoret. Sed haec hactenus ad nos non pervenerunt. Ego autem hoc opus

grace, to comment on Deuteronomy.[52] Christian of Stablo promised his brothers that he would attempt a commentary on Luke if he could not find the one by Bede that he had heard about.[53] Paschasius Radbertus, in the absence of an earlier commentary on Lamentations, wrote his own.[54]

Even when the many works of the many Fathers provided a sufficient base for a commentary, the Carolingian master still had to face critical editorial problems. What to do if the Fathers were silent on this or that point, not out of ignorance, Rabanus Maurus remarked, but because of preoccupation with other concerns?[55] Claudius of Turin's response was not typical. He was able to answer some of the questions on the book of Kings Abbot Theodemirus of Psalmody sent him, but hesitated to discuss others since he could not find earlier commentaries and would not presume to teach what he did not understand.[56] Others were not so reluctant. According to Florus of Lyon, some trusted to their own judgment and ran roughshod over the Fathers.[57] Certainly there was danger here, but masters the mettle of Rabanus Maurus, Angelomus of Luxeuil, and even Claudius of Turin on occasion accepted the perils, aided as they thought by the divine grace which opens the mouth of the mute and causes infants to speak.[58]

---

meum tribus libellis perstrinxi, quatenus aliquantam intellegentiam in mysteriis predicti libri avido lectori darem, ceterum perfectiora perfectioribus reservans."

[52]Letter-preface to Freculphus of Lisieux, ibid., p. 399, 11–15: "Sed quia in hunc librum cuiuspiam explanationem proprie non inveni, necesse habui, ut perspectis anteriorum librorum expositionibus, inde ad huius libri enodandas questiones adsumerem facultatem. Hec autem quae noviter ibi a legislatore inserta repperi, divina gratia largiente, pro modulo nostri ingenioli, quantulumcumque explanare curavi."

[53]MGH Epp. 6:178, 19–20: "Si vero nec invenero et vestrum omnium cohortatio adfuerit, et in hoc quoque laborare temptabo, si tamen gratum vobis fore speravero."

[54]See his letter to Odilmannus, MGH Epp. 6:136, 30–34.

[55]MGH Epp. 5:398, 11–13: "Ubi quoque minus elucidatum eorum sententiis vel pretermissum, non pro eorum ignorantia, sed forte pro occupatione . . . ."

[56]MGH Epp. 4:608, 33–38: "Quedam vero remanent indiscussae, quia nec in antiquis translationibus aliquid exinde translatum repperi nec in maiorum nostrorum opusculis aliquid expositum legi. Et haec me ignorare fateor, quia nec quidpiam me aliquid exinde legisse reminiscor. Et ideo de imperitia non erubesco, quia de lectione non doceor. Haec de periculo formido, quia, quae non intellego docere non presumo."

[57]See above, note 36.

[58]Rabanus Maurus completed the phrase cited in note 55 above with the following explanation: ". . . aliqua repperi, caelesti gratia confidens, quae aperit os mutum et linguas infantium facit esse disertas [Sap. 10.21], temptavi pleraque iuxta eorum sensus vestigia inserere, non tamen latenter, ne forte pro fraude furti arguerer, sed manifeste ea agnominis mei prenotatione depinxi, sicut et in aliis opusculis nostris iam me fecisse recordor, ut sciret lector, qua securitate patrum dicta legere posset quantaque cautela nostra rimari deberet." See MGH Epp. 5:398, 13–18. Claudius of Turin appealed to the same verse from Wisdom

This gathering of many sources, the choosing from within and among them, the arranging, paraphrasing, supplementing, the creation of a new synthesis takes, as Paul Meyvaert has noted apropos of Bede, a kind of genius to do well.[59] Carolingians such as Theodulf wrestling with various biblical texts or the commentators searching out the authorities showed a real zest for the task. They also appreciated the judgmental and creative nature of the process. Alcuin in his commentary on Ecclesiastes drew from all the Fathers, but expressed a preference for Jerome.[60] Claudius of Turin was just as discriminating. He followed Augustine in his commentary on Matthew because, he explained, just as the tongue speaks more than the other organs of the head, so too Augustine is preeminent among biblical expositors.[61] Rabanus Maurus favored Hesyschius on Leviticus and Josephus on Paralipomenon while Angelomus thought Gregory the Great the best guide to the Canticle of Canticles.[62]

This kind of favoritism, tempered undoubtedly by personal preferences and library resources, was exceptional. The goal was to harmonize all the Fathers. The image of the *medicus*, used by both Alcuin and Angelomus, was a particularly apt one. The *medici* gather herbs and medicines from many sources to confect a medicament that would restore health to the user.[63] Balance, as Angelomus noted, was important. Too much of one

---

for the same purpose in his preface to his comments on Ephesians and Phillippians. Ibid., 4:598, 8–9. See also for Claudius, ibid., pp. 596, 28–597, 4. Rabanus frequently acknowledged that he supplemented the Fathers (ibid., 5:394, 4–7; 395, 31–34; 399, 14; 400, 31–32; 403, 1–6; 423, 24–27; 442, 3–6; 468, 18; 477, 6–7). For the commentary on the Pauline epistles, however, he noted: "Nec ex meo sensu in hoc opere plura protuli, sicut in aliis opusculis meis feci, credens sobrio lectori sufficere quod in patrum sententiis editum repererit." See ibid., p. 430, 5–7. For Angelomus of Luxeuil, see ibid., pp. 621, 37–622, 4; 623, 26–27; 626, 34; 627, 14.

[59]"Bede the Scholar," p. 62.

[60]MGH Epp. 4:407, 8–9.

[61]He explained that his work was taken "ex tractatibus doctorum et maiorum nostrorum, qui nos in studio huius operis sicut scientia ita et tempore praecesserunt, id est Origenis, Hilarii, Ambrosii, Hieronimi, Agustini, Rufini, Iohannis, Fulgentii, Leonis, Maximi, Gregorii et Bedae. Sed sicut in arce capitis inter omnia membra lingua plus membris omnibus sonat, ita in exponendo evangelium inter hos omnes est beatissimus Agustinus." See MGH Epp. 4:594, 10–15. Claudius included another appreciation of Augustine in the preface to the commentary on Romans; see ibid., p. 599, 8–20.

[62]See MGH Epp. 5:396, 23–24; 423, 33–35; 626, 35–36. For the commentary on Kings and Paralipomenon, Rabanus also consulted a contemporary Jew "in legis scientia non ignobiliter eruditi." See ibid., p. 403, 6–7; 423, 34.

[63]Alcuin, letter-preface to the commentary on John, MGH Epp. 4:356, 39–357, 5: "Solent namque medici ex multorum speciebus pigmentorum in salutem poscentis quoddam medicamenti conponere genus, nec se ipsos fateri praesumunt creatores herbarum vel aliarum

ingredient would overwhelm the others. Too little would diminish the potency of the whole.[64] Some of what the Fathers wrote was superfluous, some rather sketchy in spots. Angelomus compared his sources to the pipes of an organ. All are of different lengths, but in the hands of a skilled musician, they can be made to emit a pleasing melody.[65] Paschasius Radbertus referred to Cicero's telling of the story of the painter Zeuxis who, wishing to paint a portrait of Helen, chose the five prettiest girls from Croton as models. From each he selected only the most beautiful feature since no individual girl was perfectly beautiful. In like wise, the commentator must select what is most appropriate from each Father.[66] As with the physician, musician, or painter, the work of the commentator called for choice and skill. Dissonance and contradiction, always possible when the opinions of the Fathers are taken out of context and juxtaposed one with the other, stemmed, of course, not from the Fathers, but from inattentive readers unaware or neglectful of the commentator's procedures.[67]

---

specierum, ex quarum conpositione salus efficitur egrotantium, sed ministros esse in colligendo et in unum pigmentaria manu conficiendo corpus. Sic etiam, sic forsan meae devotionis labor aliquid vestrae caritati proficere valet. Nec ex uno quolibet paternae possessionis prato mihi flores colligendos esse censeo, sed multorum patrum." Claudius of Turin resorted to a less flattering image to describe his use of sources in his Ephesians and Phillippians commentary: ". . . non tam ex maiorum tractatibus quam ex diversorum tractatum sententiis, veluti mendicus non habens propriam segetem, sed post terga metentium ex aliorum messem congregat sibi victum, ne hiemis tempore fame periclitetur: ita et ego ex aliorum dictis has brevi stilo comprehendi epistolas." Ibid., p. 598, 12–16.

[64]Letter-preface to Emperor Lothair accompanying the commentary on the Canticle of Canticles, MGH Epp. 5:627, 26–30: "Unde iam tandem supplex exoro decus augustale aeque et eos quibus fortassis legere contigerit, ut quod ego more medicorum ac pigmentariorium, qui ut diversa unguenta et antidota temperatim possint componere, bilanciis statere aeque ponderare satagunt, ut una alteram non superabundet, nec de aliis minus utilia derelinquant, sed aequa lance sua componant . . . ."

[65]Ibid., 14–18: "Scimus namque, scimus, quod concentu organi fistulae aeris aliae longiores sunt, aliae breviores, sed uno flatu follibus amministrato et docta manu imperante digitisque attrectando unam, cum sint diversae fistulae, armoniam velut salpix, tubarum voces atque concentum dulci cantilena melos afflando attonitis auribus suaviter reddunt."

[66]Prologue to his commentary on Matthew, MGH Epp. 6:141, 2–20. Paschasius introduced his image with this phrase, "Nec ideo profecto compilator veterum appellandus . . . ." The story of Zeuxis occurs in Cicero's *De inventione* 2.1–3.

[67]Rabanus Maurus, letter-preface to the commentary on the Pauline epistles, MGH Epp. 5:429, 30–430, 3: "Sunt enim eorum sensus in aliquibus concordantes, in aliquibus vero discrepantes. Unde necessarium reor, ut intentus auditor per lectorem primum recitata singulorum auctorum nomina ante scripta sua audiat, quatenus sciant, quid in lectione apostolica unusquisque senserit, sicque in mentem suam plurima coacervans possit de singulis iudicare, quid sibi utile sit inde sumere."

In addition to requesting a brief commentary grounded in the Fathers on a particular portion of the Bible, Carolingian readers frequently stipulated the kind of commentary they had in mind. Emperor Lothair requested a literal commentary on Genesis, a spiritual commentary on Jeremiah, and an anagogic commentary on Ezechiel.[68] Freculphus of Lisieux preferred a spiritual commentary on the Pentateuch.[69] Some friends urged Rabanus Maurus to prepare a commentary both historical and allegorical on Macchabees.[70] Theodemirus of Psalmody requested historical, allegorical, and tropological comments on the difficult questions he posed on the book of Kings.[71]

These patrons were the scholars and are not typical of all those who were expected to study the Bible. The image of the Gospel preached to fishermen before it was preached to philosophers was still an effective one in the ninth century.[72] The letter Gisela and Rodtruda wrote to Alcuin soliciting a commentary on John illustrates perfectly this second, more rudimentary level of biblical study. The women, daughter and sister of Charlemagne, in an artful letter which betrays their self-proclaimed intellectual limitations, said that they consulted Saint Augustine for help in understanding John's gospel, but that the Father's writings, obscure in many places and laden with circumlocutions, were beyond them. It was enough for them to sip the sweet water of a brook, not to plunge into the depths of the deepest rivers.[73] Gisela and Rodtruda asked Alcuin to remember Jerome's relationship with Roman matrons and how the Father deigned to answer their prayers, even to the point of dedicating works to

---

[68]Letter to Rabanus Maurus, MGH Epp. 5:475, 31–39.

[69]Letter to Rabanus Maurus, MGH Epp. 5:392, 15–18: "Eo itaque modo opus hoc conpendiosum fieri flagitamus, ut primum sensus littere, ac deinde spiritalis intellegentia accurate succisa prolixitate pandatur, et singulorum nomina auctorum, in fronte notentur pagellae, ex quibus presentes decerpseritis sententias."

[70]Ibid., p. 470, 4–5.

[71]Ibid., 4:605, 28–31.

[72]Berengaudus of Ferrières, *Expositio super septem visiones libri Apocalypsis,* MPL 17:969c–970a: "Ita et indoctis hominibus plus proficit divina scriptura mediocriter prolata quam si philosophico aut poetico sermone proferatur: sciantque dominum nostrum Jesum Christum sacramenta doctrinae suae non primo philosophis, sed piscatoribus tradidisse, ut per piscatores veniret ad philosophos."

[73]MGH Epp. 4:324, 25–27: "Habemus siquidem clarissimi doctoris Augustini homeliatico sermone explanationes in eundem evangelistam, sed quibusdam in locis multo obscuriores maiorique circumlocutione decoratas, quam nostrae parvitatis ingeniolo intrare valeat. Sufficit vero nostrae devotioni de rivulis dulcissimae aquae potare, non profundissimis gurgitum fluminibus nostras inmittere carinas." The same image was used by Josephus Scottus, ibid., p. 483, 38–484, 1, and by Angelomus of Luxeuil, ibid., 5:620, 11–14.

them and corresponding with them from far Bethlehem. They pointed out that the Loire was no Tyrrhenian Sea and that it was easier for a messenger to cover the distance from Tours to Paris than it was from Bethlehem to Rome.[74] Given the context of their letter and their relationship with Alcuin, the women's clever *exemplum* was quite apropos. Their sense of geography was, of course, unerring. But there is a fundamental discrepancy in their comparison. The world of Jerome and his Roman matrons was not that of Alcuin and his royal nuns. The Roman women, unlike their Frankish sisters, probably would have understood what Augustine had to say about John's gospel. The cultural gulf which separated the Mediterranean world of the patristic period from that of Carolingian Francia was immense.

Biblical study based on the Fathers alone would never succeed for the majority of Carolingian students. Masters had to intervene to edit out of the Fathers whatever was considered unessential and to simplify the language. *Plane stylo* was the goal.[75] Rabanus Maurus omitted references to the Septuagint in his Ezechiel commentary and excised the philological discussions from Jerome's commentary on Isaiah in order to avoid contention and to simplify the narratives.[76] Josephus Scottus shortened Jerome's commentary on Isaiah at the request of Alcuin and in

---

[74]Ibid., 4:324, 36-325, 3: "Memento clarissimum in sancta ecclesia divinae scripturae doctorem, beatissimum siquidem Hieronimum, nobilium nullatenus spernere feminarum preces, sed plurima illarum nominibus in propheticas obscuritates dedicasse opuscula; saepiusque de Bethleem castello, Christi dei nostri nativitate consecrato, ad Romanas arces epistolares iisdem petentibus volare cartulas, nec terrarum longinquitate vel procellosis Adriatici maris fluctibus territum, quin minus sanctarum virginum petitionibus adnueret. Minore vadosum Ligeri flumen quam Tyrreni maris latitudo periculo navigatur. Et multo facilius cartarum portitor tuarum de Turonis Parisiacam civitatem, quam illius de Bethleem Romam, pervenire poterit."

[75]Alcuin, letter-preface to the commentary on John, ibid., p. 357, 13: ". . . cautissimo plane stilo praevidens . . . ." Rabanus Maurus, letter-preface to Louis the Pious accompanying the commentary on Paralipomenon, ibid., 5:423, 27-29: "Non enim longos florentesque tractatus, in quibus plausibilis ludit oratio, sed commentarios in divinas historias scribere decrevi, quorum officium est preterire manifesta, obscura disserere." See also Claudius of Turin's prefatory letter to his commentary on Genesis, ibid., 4:592, 17-18: "Sed [eius] opusculum quibusdam in locis operosum est, et non ab omnibus eum intelligibilem arbitror." Following Augustine, *De doctrina christiana* 4.11.26, Claudius remarked (ibid., 33-34): "In lectione enim divina non est amanda verba, sed veritas."

[76]Letter-preface to Emperor Lothair, ibid., 5:477, 14-16: "Septuaginta vero editionem in plerisque locis omisi, ubi eam videlicet ponere non necessarium arbitrabar." Ibid., p. 502, 11-16: ". . . aliquantis ex eo sententiis omissis, propter interpretum varietatem et diversitatem linguarum, que ab ipso doctore in eodem opere multis in locis inserta repperi, ea tantummodo, que ad sobrium sensum et ad mysticum intellectum pertinere et utile esse minus doctis lectoribus estimavi, inde excerpsi, interponens in quibusdam locis dicta sancti Gregorii papae atque sententias nobilissimi doctoris Augustini, necnon et aliorum patrum sententias."

the process "left out Jerome's discussion of variant Greek readings, that is, his citations of the Septuagint, Symmachus, Aquila, and Theodotion."[77] In cases such as these, the question of originality is a moot one.[78] Josephus and Rabanus succeeded in providing their readers with the essential Jerome, devoid of the scholarly apparatus that would have been meaningless and intimidating to all but the most highly trained.

Christian of Stablo, who taught some sixty years after Josephus Scottus, would have approved the earlier master's pedagogical technique. The readers of Christian's commentary on Matthew had not been able to grasp that gospel after going through it twice.[79] Reading Jerome's commentary would not help either. Christian observed that the inhabitants of a province are best addressed by someone who speaks the language of that province. In order to understand Jerome on Matthew, Christian's readers would need a commentary on Jerome. Christian thus felt justified in offering his readers a simple, historical commentary rather than "irrationally" introducing them to the spiritual sense of Matthew. Christian's commentary, in fact, reads like the school texts students read as introductions to classical authors. *Tempus, locus,* and *persona* are first discussed.[80] Christian pointed out that all the liberal arts could be

---

[77]Joseph F. Kelly, "The Originality of Josephus Scottus' Commentary on Isaiah," *Manuscripta* 24 (1980), 180 [176–180]. Josephus Scottus, letter-preface to Alcuin, MGH Epp. 4:483, 25–28: "Ita enim mihi precipiebas, ut in cunctis pernecessarium tantum sensum et Hebraice veritatis tramitem sequens tam LXX quam aliorum interpretum et tractorum incerta et confusa declinarem vestigia."

[78]See the title to the fine study cited in the previous note and Pierre Riché's concluding remarks on Carolingian biblical studies in his *Écoles et enseignement*, p. 284: ". . . les exégètes du Haut Moyen Age n'ont pas produit d'oeuvres originales . . . . L'histoire de la théologie médiévale de type scholastique commence véritablement au XIe siècle."

[79]*Expositio in Matthaeum evangelistam, prologus,* MGH Epp. 6:177, 23–24, 178, 4–7: "Nam quia perspexi iuvenibus vestris post expositum bis textum evangelii Mathei oblivioni habere, statui apud me ipsam expositionem eo tenore literis mandari, quo coram vobis verbis digessi. Et si aliquis requirit, quare post beatum Hieronimum hoc ausus fuerim agere, respondeo, quia perspexi beatum Hieronimum multa verba quasi levia praeterisse et parvulis sensu difficilia reddidise. Idcirco quod mihi aliquando difficile visum fuit facile volentibus scire reddidi. Et usus loquendi melius intelligitur de his, qui de eadem provincia sunt, quam aliquid depravate usi. Habet enim unaquaeque provincia morem proprium loquendi, quem alia non habet, et ideo suavius auditur . . . . Studui autem plus historicum sensum sequi quam spiritalem, quia inrationabile mihi videtur spiritalem intellegentiam in libro aliquo quaerere, et historicum penitus ignorare, cum historica fundamentum omnis intellegentiae sit et ipsa primitus quaerenda et amplexanda, et sine ipsa perfecte ad aliam non possit transiri." See M. L. W. Laistner, "A Ninth-Century Commentator on the Gospel According to Matthew," *Harvard Theological Review* 20 (1927), 129–149.

[80]MPL 106:1264b: "In omnium principiis librorum tria quaerenda sunt, tempus, locus, persona. Similiter de isto evangelio haec tria tenenda sunt." For the Irish use of this approach to biblical studies, see Bernhard Bischoff, "Wendepunkte," pp. 217–218.

found in the Scriptures. He was not above using a homey agricultural example to explain the order of the Gospels in Greek manuscripts: Euphemius, a Greek, told him that Matthew and John came first because as a good farmer knows, the strongest oxen are hitched to the yoke first.[81]

The commentaries that I have discussed were complex affairs that taxed their authors. Some of the masters possessed more of the necessary genius to carry out their tasks than did others. Most commentators did succeed in fulfilling the wishes of their readers and delighted in their accomplishment: Here you have, they said in one form or another, a useful guide, a manual or enchiridion, collected from the many works of the Fathers, and gathered into one volume, suitably organized and brief, so that you might quickly find what you seek.[82]

Now, while these commentaries are important and merit further, detailed study, they are only the tip of the iceberg. Their diffusion in Carolingian times was, I believe, relatively limited. Rabanus Maurus had a difficult time providing his friends with copies of his works.[83] Contemporary

---

[81]MPL 106:1266a: "Interrogavi enim Euphemium Graecum cur hoc ita esset. Dixit mihi in similitudinem boni agricolae, qui quos fortiores habet boves primo iungit."

[82]Rabanus Maurus, letter-preface accompanying the commentary on Leviticus, MGH Epp. 5:396, 28–33: "Sed tua diligentia, hoc responso non contenta, precipiebat ut ex prefati viri opere necnon et ex aliorum patrum scriptis, qui in eundem librum non per ordinem, sed viritim quasdam sententias exposuerunt, in unum colligerem, ut in promptu haberes, quid unusquisque eorum inde senserit. Feci sicut mandasti et ex confuso sententiarum ordine quendam ordinem digestionis variorum doctorum sententias alternando atque commiscendo composui." See also in Rabanus's other prefaces, ibid., pp. 395, 31–34; 402, 23–31; 423, 22–27; 429, 13–20; 430, 24–33; 466, 5–15; 467, 35–468, 10; 470, 1–8. The same sentiment is expressed in the preface to the penitential he prepared for Archbishop Otgarius of Mainz: ibid., p. 462, 30–35. See also Alcuin, ibid., 4:389, 13–18, and Angelomus of Luxeuil, ibid., 5:623, 26–39; 626, 32–627, 4.

[83]Three passages in Rabanus's letters illustrate how fitful, limited, and slow the dissemination (one cannot say "publication") of scholarly work was in the ninth century: letter to Bishop Fridurichus of Utrecht (ibid., 5:400, 36–39): "Ante annos ergo aliquot tractatum in evangelium Mathei, quem rogante bonae memoriae Haistulfo archiepiscopo confeceram, tibi ad rescribendum accommodavi. Sed quia illum necdum recipere potui, remunerationis vice presens opus transmisi, ut saltim hoc beneficio ammonitus, remittas foenus quod acceperas"; letter to Bishop Humbertus of Würzburg (ibid., p. 441, 29–33): "Priorum vero librorum commentarios, hoc est Pentateuchi Moysi, quos petente sancto viro Freculfo, non sine labore edidi, iam sibi ad rescribendum transmisi; quos cum recepero, exemplar eorum tibi scriptum destinabo. Iesu Nave vero expositionem bonae memoriae Friduricho, Traiectensis aecclesiae episcopo, nuper transmisi. Hoc similiter, ut mihi redditum fuerit, si Dei voluntas est, tibi committere curabo"; letter to Bishop Samuel of Worms (ibid., p. 430, 34–37): "Accipite ergo foenus vobis commissum et per scriptores strenuos iubete illud citius in membrana excipere, ut, si quid vobis utilitatis possit inde conferri, in promptu habeatis; et nobis quod nostrum est otius restituatis, ne aliis optatum cibum edentibus nostri apostolicorum dapium inedia diutius ieiuni remaneant."

library lists rarely mention these commentaries.[84] The commentaries reflect the conditions of Carolingian biblical study but were not the mainstays of it. To deepen our understanding of biblical studies, we must consider other texts, particularly the fruits of Hiberno-Latin exegesis.

There were those in the eighth and ninth centuries who expressed misgivings about the contribution Irishmen made to Carolingian scholarship.[85] In more recent years, there has been a tendency to retreat from earlier hyperbole and to view Irish masters not as unique, but as one component of the early medieval intellectual and cultural scene.[86] For my part, I have no trouble defining most surviving eighth- and ninth-century Irish biblical scholarship as Carolingian. Almost all of what does survive was copied and used in Carolingian centers by Irishmen and non-Irishmen alike. Furthermore, whatever was characteristic about Irish scholarship in its first encounters with the Carolingian world — that is, when Alcuin and Theodulf questioned it — soon was absorbed into the Carolingian amalgam. Not only John Scottus, but Sedulius Scottus and Martin Hiberniensis, despite different talents and interests, seem thoroughly Carolingian to me.

Still, by virtue of its quantity and its quality the Irish contribution to Carolingian biblical studies merits separate treatment. A little more than twenty-five years ago, Bernhard Bischoff gave us our first panoramic view of the extent of Irish biblical scholarship in his important

---

[84]See, for example, Maieul Cappuyns, "Les 'Bibli Vulfadi' et Jean Scot Érigène," *Recherches de théologie ancienne et médiévale* 33 (1966), 137–139 (a library collection which, with the exception of an important collection of works by Wulfad's friend, John Scottus, contains no ninth-century author); Pierre Riché, "Les bibliothèques de trois aristocrates laics carolingiens," *Le Moyen Age* 69 (1963), 87–104; Frederick M. Carey, "The Scriptorium of Reims during the Archbishopric of Hincmar (845–882 A.D.)," in Leslie Webber Jones, ed., *Classical and Mediaeval Studies in Honor of Edward Kennard Rand* (New York, 1938), pp. 41–60; Contreni, *Cathedral School of Laon,* pp. 76–77. Among the scores of commentators Notker of Saint Gall listed in his *De illustribus viris* (see note 15 above) only Alcuin and Rabanus Maurus represent the Carolingian period. By the tenth century, Carolingian commentaries began to crowd patristic and early medieval commentaries for space on library shelves. See Germain Morin, "Le catalogue des manuscrits de Gorze," *Revue bénédictine* (1905), 1–14.

[85]See James F. Kenney, *The Sources for the Early History of Ireland: Ecclesiastical (An Introduction and Guide)*, rev. ed., Ludwig Bieler (New York, 1966), nos. 340 (i), 342, 343, 385; and, Bernhard Bischoff, "Theodulf und der Ire Cadac-Andreas," *Mittelalterliche Studien* 2:19–25.

[86]See Edmondo Coccia, "La cultura irlandese precarolingia: Miracolo o mito?" *Studi medievali,* ser. 3, 8 (1967), 257–420; Clare Stancliffe, "Early 'Irish' Biblical Exegesis," *Studia patristica* 12 (1975), 361–370; Michael Lapidge, "The Authorship of the Adonic Verses *Ad Fidolium* Attributed to Columbanus," *Studi medievali,* ser. 3, 18 (1977), 249–314.

"Wendepunkte in der Geschichte der lateinischen Exegese im Frühmittelalter."[87] The catalogue of exegetical works he appended to his study listing 39 separate works—many of which appear in more than one form—and more than a hundred new manuscript witnesses to them[88] documents beyond a doubt that Irish exegesis worked into the very fabric of Carolingian biblical studies. However, it is important to note that Irish exegesis did not influence higher biblical criticism. In fact, one of the turning points in biblical exegesis Bischoff had in mind occurred when Carolingian expositors such as Christian of Stablo and Paschasius Radbertus turned away from Irish explanations.[89] But, what offended them and Theodulf had greater appeal at a more introductory level. The quantity of surviving Irish exegesis is explained by its quality.

The biblical musings, some would say contortions, of Irish masters are suffused with a concern for detail, number, places, persons, events, customs, lists, languages, and the first times someone or something is mentioned. All of this was fitted often onto a schematic, almost scholastic, question-and-answer framework. Irish familiarity with biblical apocrypha enabled them to embellish their glosses on the canonical books with "new" and unusual bits of information generally unavailable to their Continental colleagues. Finally, the compilatory vogue, which meant so much to the Carolingians, is everywhere evident in Hiberno-Latin exegesis where it found its fullest expression in the anonymous encyclopedic compilation Bischoff has dubbed the *Bibelwerk*.[90] Undoubtedly the product of Irish schools, the *Bibelwerk*, which extends over the entire Bible, found welcome reception on the Continent. All the manuscripts are Continental. Only one of them is copied in Irish script.

One does not have to search hard for the reasons behind the widespread diffusion of these Hiberno-Latin works in the Carolingian world. They were popular because they answered admirably the needs of students of the caliber of Gisela and Rodtruda or of the students of Josephus Scottus, Angelomus of Luxeuil, or the students for whom Walahfrid Strabo's epitome of Rabanus Maurus's commentaries on Leviticus and Exodus

---

[87]See above, note 46. An English translation by Colm O'Grady is available in Martin McNamara, ed., *Biblical Studies: The Medieval Irish Contribution*, Proceedings of the Irish Biblical Association 1 (Dublin, 1976), pp. 74–160.

[88]"New," that is, not already reported in Kenney's *Sources for the Early History of Ireland* or in the volumes of Friedrich Stegmüller's *Repertorium Biblicum Medii Aevi*, 11 vols. (Madrid, 1950–1980), which had appeared before the publication of Bischoff's catalogue.

[89]"Wendepunkte," pp. 227–229. For Theodulf, see Bischoff's study cited above, note 85.

[90]"Wendepunkte," pp. 222, 231–236.

were destined. Although Irish concern for nitpicking detail seems excessive and pedantic to modern readers, it sufficed that for the little, as Gisela and Rodtruda noted, only a little was necessary.[91] One had to drink the milk of the historical and literal before one could quaff the heady wine of the anagogical interpretation.[92]

Carolingian masters, of course, did not depend on the Irish exegetes alone for the tools they used to explicate the Bible to their young charges. There was a whole body of patristic and medieval texts, such as the ones Theodulf appended to his Bibles, that circulated and were indispensable for the beginner.[93] Even more rudimentary were the glossaries which proliferated during the Carolingian period. Glossaries helped the beginner to read. In turn, the Bible, particularly the Book of Psalms, served as the primer for the beginning reader of the early Middle Ages.[94] Glossaries are often anonymous affairs. Detailed source-criticism by generations of scholars has succeeded in revealing some of the process of compilation that went into glossary making. The "Abrogans" and "Abavus" glossaries, so named after their first entries, were widely used.[95] So was the so-called "Rz" glossary, which eschewed an alphabetical order to follow the biblical text book by book. The "Rz" glosses, which occasionally employed Old High German words, were copied widely. Haimo of Auxerre knew one variety of them which he used in his teaching and in his own exegetical works.[96] Jerome's biblical prefaces, peppered as they are with abstruse terms and Greek words, prompted their own series of glosses, thus confirming Christian of Stablo's observation that Jerome's comments sometimes required their own commentary.[97]

---

[91] MGH Epp. 4:324, 29-30: "Scis enim optime parvis parva sufficere, nec ad mensam magnatorum pauperum turbam accedere posse." Bischoff, commenting on the Carolingian reaction to Irish exegetical literature, noted ("Wendepunkte," p. 229), "es war die Rückkehr zu einer schlichteren, weniger spitzfindigen und weniger pedantischen Art der Auslegung."

[92] See the preface to the *Allegoriae in universam sacram scripturam*, MPL 112:849a-b, attributed to Garnier of Rochefort.

[93] See Riché, *Écoles et enseignement*, pp. 280-284.

[94] Ibid., pp. 223-224.

[95] See Georg Goetz's "Glossographie" in Pauly-Wissowa's *Real-Encyclopädie* (Stuttgart, 1910), 7:1433-1466, as well as the introductory and prefatory material in Wallace M. Lindsay, *Glossaria latina*, 5 vols. (Paris, 1926-1931), and Georg Goetz, *Corpus glossariorum latinorum*, 7 vols. (Leipzig, 1888-1923), especially pp. 217-227, "De glossariis novi et veteris Testamenti," in the first volume.

[96] See Elias Steinmeyer, "Untersuchungen über die Bibelglossare: Rz und sein Einflussbereich," in Elias Steinmeyer and Eduard Sievers, *Die althochdeutsche Glossen*, 5 vols. (Berlin, 1879-1922), 5:108-407; Bischoff, "Wendepunkte," pp. 207-209; and Contreni, "The Biblical Glosses of Haimo of Auxerre and John Scottus Eriugena," pp. 418-420.

[97] See Contreni, "Biblical Glosses," p. 417, and p. 92, above, for Christian of Stablo.

Even the great John Scottus taught from biblical glosses.[98] The interest of his almost 700 glosses does not derive solely from their association with one of the most prominent of Carolingian intellectual figures. The glosses exemplify some of the basic themes of Carolingian biblical studies that have been the subject of this paper. Some of them are bilingual, combining Latin with occasional Old Irish words.[99] They are predominantly concerned with the minutiae of biblical history—the place and personal names, Hebrew weights and measures, vestments, jewelry, animals, stones, plants—rather than, as we might suspect with John Scottus, allegorical and theological discussions. Their concern with these details points in the direction of the Hiberno-Latin tendencies mentioned above. They also point in the direction of chapter ten of the third book of Rabanus Maurus's *De clericorum institutione* in which just this kind of biblical study is recommended.[100] There is a third interesting feature evident in the glosses. The text from which the biblical words derive was of Spanish, perhaps even Theodulfian inspiration. The glosses thus bear witness to the still fluid biblical textual tradition of mid-ninth-century Francia.

The students who began their study of the Bible with these simple glosses were heirs to at least a half century's concentration on biblical studies. It is a pity that we know less about the actual methods of instruction than we do about the texts that supported it.[101] In the case of the glosses associated with John Scottus, one can imagine a master and students reading the Bible and pausing for explanations of unusual words. In one manuscript, the master has copied the lemma words into the margin so that they could easily be found. The commentaries reflect two possible teaching methods. The straightforward exposition by the master could be read either to or by students. Some of the Carolingian commentaries were first presented orally in the *schola* before they were given more

---

[98]See Contreni, "Biblical Glosses," pp. 411–434. With the collaboration of Pádraig O'Neill I am preparing an edition of these glosses.

[99]The Rz glosses interspersed Old High German words among their Latin definitions. Rabanus Maurus, following Augustine, *De doctrina christiana* 4.9, specifically recommended the use of the vernacular in scriptural studies. See *De institutione clericorum* 3.30 (ed. Knöpfler, p. 249; MPL 107:408a-b): "Quamvis in bonis doctoribus tanta docendi cura sit vel esse debeat, ut verbum, quod nimis obscurum sit vel ambiguum, latinum esse non possit, vulgi autem more sic dicatur, ut ambiguitas obscuritasque vitetur, non sic dicatur, ut a doctis, sed potius ut ab indoctis dici solet."

[100]*De institutione clericorum* 3.10 (ed. Knöpfler, pp. 204–206; MPL 107:386a-d) = Augustine, *De doctrina christiana* 2.16.

[101]Pierre Riché has discussed what little evidence survives. See *Écoles et enseignement*, pp. 214–220, and, for a slightly earlier period, *Education and Culture*, pp. 458–477.

permanent form.[102] Another approach to biblical instruction was enormously popular. The question-and-answer dialogues used in all disciplines were also applied to biblical studies. Wicbod's *Quaestiones in Octateuchum*, Alcuin's *Interrogationes et responsiones in Genesim*, and Haimo of Auxerre's *Scolia quaestionum* all employed this format.[103] We should not deduce from the widespread use of this pedagogical strategy that a dialectical, Socratic method of study was encouraged. The master and disciple question-and-answer sessions were more like catechism recitations. The student was expected to know the appropriate answer, not to arrive at a solution to the problem posed by a process of critical analysis. For the Carolingian student and master alike, biblical study, indeed all study, was a religious experience, not an intellectual one.[104] The students were the soil, the masters the planters and waterers, God was the grower.[105]

[102]See Claudius of Turin's letter-preface to his commentary on Corinthians, MGH Epp. 4:601, 30-34, and that of Christian of Stablo to his commentary on Matthew, ibid., 6:177.

[103]For Wicbod, see above, note 46. For Alcuin's *Interrogationes*, see MPL 100:515-566, and Brunhölzl, *Geschichte*, pp. 274-275. Haimo's *Scolia*, collected by his disciple Heiric of Auxerre and superbly edited by Riccardo Quadri, *I Collectanea di Eirico di Auxerre*, Spicilegium Friburgense 11 (Friburg, 1966), has yet to be exploited fruitfully by historians. For a good introduction to the genre, see Gustave Bardy, "La littérature des *quaestiones et responsiones* sur l'Écriture sainte," *Revue biblique* 41 (1932), 210-236, 341-369.

[104]I am making a distinction here between what I see to be a fundamental difference between medieval and modern inquiry. For medieval scholars and certainly for the Carolingian masters who have been the subject of this essay, successful inquiry could not be considered apart from the deity and divine grace. Medieval pedagogy and scholarship also aimed at the spiritual growth of its participants. Modern intellectual inquiry is not only more secular and critical, it is also less willing to make the claims for its truth that medieval religious inquiry did.

[105]See Claudius of Turin's use of this verse from 1 Corinthians 3.7, in his letter to Abbot Theodemirus of Psalmody, MGH Epp. 4:608, 12-15.

# Unity and Diversity in Carolingian Canon Law Collections:
## The Case of the *Collectio Hibernensis* and Its Derivatives

**Roger E. Reynolds**

It is now conventional textbook wisdom that when the early Carolingian rulers, Pepin, Charlemagne, and Louis the Pious, went about trying to consolidate the Frankish realm, they attempted in matters religious and intellectual to impose a form of unity through the use of Roman texts. In the area of liturgical reform Charlemagne is said to have attempted to put down the "anarchy" of local Gallican uses of the eighth century by asking from Pope Hadrian a "pure" copy of the Roman *Gregorian Sacramentary*. This sacramentary was then placed in the scriptorium at Aachen and scribes from throughout the realm are said to have come to make copies from it. A similar procedure is said to have been used in monastic reform. A "pure" copy of the *Regula sancti Benedicti* was brought from Monte Cassino to Aachen and perhaps used there as a model for visiting scribes to copy. And finally, in matters of ecclesiastical law Charlemagne is said to have requested and received from Pope Hadrian a copy of the ancient *Collectio Dionysiana,* which was then copied and diffused throughout the Carolingian realm.

During the past two decades this neat textbook description of early Carolingian attempts to impose unity through "Romanity" has begun to fray at the edges. It has been shown that while there were indeed successful attempts at reform through the introduction of Roman books, there was immediate and very substantial modification of these texts and that local and regional traditions continued to flourish throughout the late eighth and ninth centuries. For example, Raymund Kottje in a brilliant article in 1965 showed on the basis of extant manuscripts that in southern France and northern Italy of the late eighth and early ninth century the ancient canonical *Concordia Cresconii* and the newly compiled Lyonese *Collectio Dacheriana* were at least as popular as the *Collectio Dionysio-Hadriana*.[1] Hubert Mordek a few years later demonstrated that the popularity of the Gallican *Collectio Vetus Gallica* continued even as Charlemagne was "imposing" the *Collectio Dionysio-Hadriana* and that a manuscript of this competing Gallican collection was even made for Charlemagne's court library, presumably to supplement the Roman collection.[2] More recently Susan Keefe has shown that in the initiatory rite of baptism, old Gallican and Milanese traditions quickly infiltrated the newly imported Roman ceremonies.[3] And finally, in matters penitential Kottje has demonstrated that the celebrated "Roman" penitential book of Halitgar of Cambrai is filled with traditional Frankish texts.[4] In short, the Carolingian ideal of Roman unity was often deflected in matters canonical and liturgical by texts and practices traditional in the Frankish realm.

In the scholarship of the past twenty years another element in the Carolingian mixture of Roman and non-Roman traditions has received perhaps less recognition than it deserves — the Irish. The role of the Irish in Carolingian culture and religious life has, of course, long been recognized and studied intensively. And in one area of canon law — penitential discipline and its texts — scholars eagerly await the studies promised by Kottje's "Bussbücher-Forschung."[5] Nonetheless, there has been insufficient examination of the influence that the major Irish collection of canon law, the *Collectio Hibernensis*, had in the Carolingian period.

---

[1]Raymund Kottje, "Einheit und Vielfalt des kirchlichen Lebens in der Karolingerzeit," *Zeitschrift für Kirchengeschichte* 76 (1965), 336–341.

[2]Hubert Mordek, *Kirchenrecht und Reform im Frankenreich: Die Collectio Vetus Gallica, die älteste systematische Kanonessammlung des fränkischen Gallien: Studien und Edition,* Beiträge zur Geschichte und Quellenkunde des Mittelalters 1 (Berlin–New York, 1975), p. 282.

[3]Susan Ann Keefe, "Baptismal Instruction in the Carolingian Period: The MS Evidence" (Diss., Toronto, 1981).

[4]Raymund Kottje, *Die Bussbücher Halitgars von Cambrai und des Hrabanus Maurus: ihre Überlieferung und ihre Quellen,* Beiträge zur Geschichte und Quellenkunde des Mittelalters 8 (Berlin–New York, 1980), pp. 185–190.

[5]See Raymund Kottje, "Die frühmittelalterlichen kontinentalen Bussbücher: Bericht über ein Forschungsvorhaben an der Universität Augsburg [nunc Bonn]," *Bulletin of Medieval Canon Law,* n.s. 7 (1977), 108–111.

This has been due in part to the fact that the great nineteenth-century study by Paul Fournier, "De l'influence de la collection irlandaise sur la formation des collections canoniques,"[6] appeared to be definitive and in part because scholars have waited to base new studies on the edition of the *Collectio Hibernensis* promised by Professor Sheehy.[7] But even while awaiting the new edition, several advances make it possible to give further precision to Fournier's work and to go beyond it, especially for the Carolingian period. One of these advances has come in the identification of further ninth-century manuscripts by Mordek and in Professor Bischoff's dating and locating of these and many codices known to Fournier.[8] Moreover, a number of texts that appear in the *Collectio Hibernensis* and its derivatives have been edited or studied in more detail. Hence, without claiming to be exhaustive, it would seem appropriate in a volume on the Carolingian period in which Irish scholarship plays a prominent role to bring this new material together to emphasize that the Carolingian canonistic complex contained not only Roman and Frankish elements, but a strong Irish component in the *Collectio Hibernensis* and its derivatives.

That there continued to be an Irish canonistic component in an age when the Roman was dominant is surprising for several reasons. First, the types of canons and authorities in the *Collectio Hibernensis* were clearly unlike those in the Roman and Gallican collections and were, therefore, subject to suspicion. There were the expected conciliar and papal canons, but many books of the *Hibernensis* contained substantial amounts of biblical material and snippets from the Fathers. Often these were, as Fournier says, "plutôt destinés à poser des principes qu'à réglementer en termes rigoureux l'action des divers organes de la société ecclésiastique."[9] Such texts had occasionally accompanied non-Irish collections to add authority to papal and conciliar texts,[10] but never were as many genuine and suspect texts used or as liberally sprinkled through the collections. Second, while there was no denying that the Irish were among the foremost scholars and missionaries of the Carolingian age, elements of their ecclesiastical discipline were suspect—the

---

[6]Paul Fournier, "De l'influence de la collection irlandaise sur la formation des collections canoniques," *Nouvelle revue historique de droit français et étranger* 23 (1899), 27–78 [in this article the pagination is taken from the 'extrait' of Fournier's study].

[7]See Mordek, *Kirchenrecht,* p. 259.

[8]See especially Mordek, *Kirchenrecht,* pp. 255–259.

[9]Fournier, "De l'influence," p. 48.

[10]See Roger E. Reynolds, "Basil and the Early Medieval Latin Canonical Collections," in *Basil of Caesarea: Christian, Humanist, Ascetic: A Sixteen-Hundredth Anniversary Symposium,* ed. P. J. Fedwick (Toronto, 1981), p. 513.

wandering, unusual notions about the relationship of abbots and bishops, and the like. Hence, the canon law collection epitomizing this discipline would be suspect. Most important, however, Irish penitential discipline was vigorously attacked in the Carolingian period, and the books that contained this discipline, the penitentials, were condemned by several early ninth-century councils.[11] It might seem surprising that the attacks on the penitentials should also have touched the *Collectio Hibernensis*, until it is recalled that the *Hibernensis* itself had Irish penitential texts within it[12] and that the penitentials were often contained in the same manuscripts as the *Hibernensis*.[13] Hence, the attacks on the Insular, especially the Irish, penitentials also very probably cast a pall over the canonical *Collectio Hibernensis*.

It has been well documented that the Carolingian condemnation of the Insular penitentials was only partially successful and that as useful instruments of ecclesiastical discipline they continued to be copied and modified for centuries.[14] So it was in the ninth century with the *Collectio Hibernensis*. The canons themselves might have lacked the authority of those in the Roman collections the Carolingians promoted, but they dealt with a multitude of matters untouched by the Roman, and, just as important, they were systematically arranged.[15] To trace the continuation of the *Hibernensis* in the ninth century let us look at it in its own and its derivative forms under the following headings: (1) complete, partial, and fragmentary manuscript exemplars; (2) abridgments; (3) collections dependent on *Hibernensis* canons; (4) isolated extracts from the *Hibernensis*; (5) the *Collectio Sangermanensis* and its supplement; and (6) Carolingian *liturgica*.

## 1. Complete, Partial, and Fragmentary Manuscript Exemplars of the *Collectio Hibernensis*

Until the new edition of the *Hibernensis* by Professor Sheehy appears, we shall not know exactly what the contents of the various recensions of

---

[11]See Cyrille Vogel, *Les "libri paenitentiales,"* Typologie des sources du moyen âge occidental 27 (Turnhout, 1978), pp. 39f.

[12]See e.g., the critical apparatus in *The Irish Penitentials,* ed. Ludwig Bieler and D. A. Binchy, Scriptores latini Hiberniae 5 (Dublin, 1963), pp. 54–58.

[13]Bieler-Binchy, *The Irish Penitentials*, pp. 16–24.

[14]See Vogel, *"Libri paenitentiales,"* passim.

[15]See Allen J. Frantzen, "The Significance of the Frankish Penitentials," *Journal of Ecclesiastical History* 30 (1979), 411.

the collection were, but traditionally they have been divided into an A or shorter, and a B or longer version of the text. Both versions continued to be copied into the late tenth century and are represented relatively complete in three manuscripts of the first half of the ninth century. Form A is found in Orléans, Bibl. de la Ville 221 (193) (s. IXin., Brittany) and St. Gall SB 243 (s. $IX^1$, St. Gall); and Form B is found in Oxford, Bodl. Hatton 42 (s. $IX^{1-med.}$, Brittany).[16] Since these manuscripts date to a time precisely when both Roman and Frankish collections were dominating all others, one wonders why they were copied at all. But the places of origin provide us with the clue. The manuscripts were written in areas with significant Celtic traditions or populations, St. Gall and Brittany.

St. Gall, of course, had grown out of the Irish mission of St. Columbanus, and although in the late eighth and early ninth century a multitude of canonistic texts could be found there,[17] it was widely known as having been a Continental foyer for Insular texts. Brittany, too, had an established Celtic tradition, and it was in part due to the Celtic population there that the Carolingian rulers had difficulty exercising their authority. In his study of the diffusion of the manuscripts of the *Collectio Dionysio-Hadriana* Kottje pointed out that it was in southern and western France and in northern Italy with their indigenous collections that the *Collectio Dionysio-Hadriana* had its most modest diffusion in the first half of the ninth century.[18] And although Mordek's results have modified this view in part,[19] it still appears to be the case that the *Dionysio-Hadriana* made the least headway in areas with their own canonistic traditions and collections, such as the *Concordia Cresconii* and *Collectio Dacheriana*. Hence, it is not surprising to find that the *Hibernensis* was copied in the early ninth century in a region with its own Celtic canonistic tradition, Brittany. And indeed, Irish influence is seen in the Breton Orléans manuscript in the text that precedes the *Collectio Hibernensis*, the *Virtutes quas Dominus dominica die fecit,*[20] a tract that the late Professor McNally attributed to the Irish.[21] Moreover, it may be significant that a later

---

[16]Mordek, *Kirchenrecht*, pp. 256f.

[17]See Raymund Kottje, "Kirchenrechtliche Interessen im Bodenseeraum vom 9. bis 12. Jahrhundert," in Johanne Autenrieth and Raymund Kottje, *Kirchenrechtliche Texte im Bodenseegebiet,* Vorträge und Forschungen, Sonderbd. 18, Konstanzer Arbeitskreis für mittelalterliche Geschichte (Sigmaringen, 1975), pp. 32–36.

[18]Kottje, "Einheit und Vielfalt," p. 337.

[19]See Mordek, *Kirchenrecht*, pp. 243–249.

[20]P. 21.

[21]Robert E. McNally, "Dies Dominica: Two Hiberno-Latin Texts," *Mediaeval Studies* 22 (1960), 355–361; and Scriptores Hiberniae minores 1, Corpus christianorum, Ser. lat. 108B (Turnhout, 1973), pp. 181–186.

manuscript of the A Form of the *Hibernensis*, Paris BN Lat. 3182 (s. X$^2$), was written in Brittany. This later manuscript, however, contains also the *Collectio Vetus Gallica* and *Collectio Dionysio-Hadriana*,[22] suggesting a gradual penetration of Roman and Frankish collections into areas hitherto under Celtic domination.

In the origins of the partial and fragmentary forms of the *Hibernensis* written in the late eighth and early ninth century the influence of Irish centers of culture can again be seen. The fragment of Form B in Karlsruhe, Bad. LB Aug. XVIII, fols. 75r–90v (s. IXin.), was written on the island of Reichenau, renowned for the number of Irish texts copied there.[23] Futher, two of the three manuscripts copied with extracts containing the first half of the *Hibernensis* to L. 38, c. 18, originated in areas with heavy Irish influence: Cambrai, Bibl. mun. 679 (619) (between 763 and 790, northeast France, Peronne?) and Cologne, DB 210 (Darmst. 2178) (s. VIII$^2$, northeast France).[24] It is interesting, too, that Tours, Bibl. mun. 556, a manuscript of the *Hibernensis* with the same configuration of contents as that in the Cambrai and Cologne manuscripts, was written in the last quarter of the ninth century at Marmoutier near Tours, where, according to Kottje,[25] there was an obvious and significant lacuna in the production of manuscripts of the *Collectio Dionysio-Hadriana*.

Beyond these partial manuscripts of the *Hibernensis* there exist two fragments of codices that Mordek speculates may contain the collection with clear indicia of Irish origins. The fragment in Trier, SB 137/50, fols. 48r–61v, was written in the second half of the eighth century either in Ireland itself or on the Continent in an Irish center,[26] and Munich, Clm 29410/2, was written at the turn of the eighth century on the Continent in an Irish hand.[27]

## 2. Abridgments of the *Collectio Hibernensis*

Inasmuch as the *Hibernensis* could be found in the late eighth century in a variety of complete recensions and in versions containing only portions of the

[22]Mordek, *Kirchenrecht*, pp. 153, 244.

[23]See, e.g., Roger E. Reynolds, *The Ordinals of Christ from their Origins to the Twelfth Century,* Beiträge zur Geschichte und Quellenkunde des Mittelalters 7 (Berlin–New York, 1978), pp. 69–71.

[24]Mordek, *Kirchenrecht*, p. 257. Also see below, pp. 110, 127.

[25]Kottje, "Einheit und Vielfalt," p. 337.

[26]Mordek, *Kirchenrecht*, p. 257.

[27]Mordek, *Kirchenrecht*, p. 257; and cf. Bernhard Bischoff, *Die südostdeutschen Schreibschulen und Bibliotheken in der Karolingerzeit, 2: Die vorwiegend österreichischen Diözesen* (Wiesbaden, 1980), p. 291. In this fragment there is at least a part of the *Collectio Hibernensis,* L. 1, c. 18.

complete text, it is not surprising that collections were quickly compiled in which selected canons were extracted in full or partial versions. There exist seven manuscripts with such abridgments of the *Hibernensis*, five of which were written in the late eighth or early ninth century in areas or specific localities with long Insular traditions.

(a)   The Abridgment of Cambridge, Corpus Christi College 279

The latest of the abridgments was written in the latter half of the ninth century in the vicinity of Tours, which, as was mentioned, conspicuously lacks extant manuscript witnesses to the *Collectio Dionysio-Hadriana*. The Celtic connection of this abridgment lies in the fact that it was a copy, according to Allen Frantzen,[28] of a Breton manuscript. Although the canons drawn from the *Hibernensis* number only eighty,[29] it is significant that many of them are drawn from the early chapters on the ecclesiastical hierarchy and that many collections dependent on the *Hibernensis* would also borrow these texts.[30]

(b)   The Abridgment of Würzburg, UB M.p.th.q.31, fols. 1–41

A second manuscript with an abridgment of the *Hibernensis* was written in part by an Anglo-Saxon scribe at the turn of the eighth century, probably in Germany. It contains not only a peculiar section devoted almost exclusively to an abridgment of the *Hibernensis*, but also a second mixed collection, to be dealt with later, in which fragments that may be from, or inspired by, the *Hibernensis* appear.[31] In the first part of the manuscript is a vast florilegium of some 603 texts attributed to the fathers, Augustine, Jerome, Gregory, Ambrose, and Gregory Nazianzus, most of which come from the *Hibernensis*. The structure of the collection is unusual in that the books, beginning with L. 21 of the *Hibernensis*, are assigned *Hibernensis* titles after which there generally follow two or three rubrics again drawn from the *Hibernensis*, followed by the mélange of patristic texts. The sequence of books, however, does not follow the major recensions of the *Hibernensis* but often leaps from late to early books and back again. Most of the books from LL. 2–67 of the *Hibernensis* are represented in the Würzburg abridgment.

---

[28]Frantzen, "Frankish Penitentials," p. 419, n. 73.
[29]Fournier, "De l'influence," p. 5.
[30]See Reynolds, *Ordinals of Christ*, p. 62, n. 39; and below, p. 114.
[31]Fols. 52–59, on which see below, p. 110.

(c)    The *Collection in 250 Chapters*

Three manuscripts with what is known as the *Collection in 250 Chapters* based on the *Hibernensis* were written in southeast Germany. Two are now in Munich, Clm 4592 (s. IX2/4, prov. Benediktbeuren) and Clm 6434, fols. 41r–75r (s. VIIIex., Freising), and one is in Vienna, ÖNB 522 (s. IX2/3, Salzburg).[32] The canons in this collection are drawn from the *Hibernensis* beginning at L. 20. Although the three manuscripts are all now from southeastern German centers with long traditions of Irish texts, the version of the *Collectio Hibernensis* in them is like that found in northern French recensions of the widely diffused *Collectio Vetus Gallica*.[33] Of special interest is the Vienna manuscript, written in the second third of the ninth century in Salzburg and annotated by Magister Baldo.[34] Not only was this scholar interested in the Roman canonical collections there,[35] but he was also involved in the glossing and supplementing of the Insular canonistic texts written in this center which had as recently as the late eighth century had the Irishman Virgil for its abbot-bishop and John the Anglo-Saxon for bishop.[36] The Vienna manuscript, like its counterpart in Munich, Clm 4592, is also significant for the diffusion of the *Hibernensis* in that a second collection in them, the so-called *Collection in 400 Chapters,* has canons drawn from the *Hibernensis*.[37] Further, in the Vienna manuscript, fols. 1v–2v, there is a short Hiberno-Latin introduction to the Gospels.[38]

(d)    The *Sangermanensis* Abridgment

Related to the *Collection in 250 Chapters* is another abridgment of the *Hibernensis* in Paris, BN Lat. 12444, fols. 75v–96v and 105r–136v.[39] Again canons are drawn from the *Hibernensis* beginning with a form

---

[32]Roger E. Reynolds, "Canon Law Collections in Early Ninth-Century Salzburg," in *Proceedings of the Fifth International Congress of Medieval Canon Law, Salamanca, 21–25 September 1976,* ed. S. Kuttner and K. Pennington, Monumenta iuris canonici, Ser. C, Subsidia 6 (Vatican, 1980), p. 32; and Mordek, *Kirchenrecht,* p. 258.

[33]Mordek, *Kirchenrecht,* p. 52.

[34]Bischoff, *Schreibschulen,* 2:159f.

[35]Reynolds, "Canon Law Collections," p. 25.

[36]Reynolds, "Canon Law Collections," p. 19.

[37]See below.

[38]Bernhard Bischoff, "An Hiberno-Latin Introduction to the Gospels," *Thought: A Review of Culture and Idea* 54 [n. 214, Robert E. McNally Memorial Issue] (1979), 234.

[39]Fols. 97r–104v originally followed fol. 29v.

of the introduction and L. 19,[40] but due to the mutilated state of the manuscript, we can no longer tell how far they continued. Several aspects of this manuscript are interesting as they touch on its probable place of origin, Fleury, and the use and diffusion of the *Hibernensis* and Irish texts there. As has been noted, the region around Fleury seems to have produced few manuscript exemplars of the *Collectio Dionysio-Hadriana*, suggesting that other traditions were more popular.[41] That the Irish tradition was one of these is seen in our Paris manuscript, which contains not only the *Hibernensis* abridgment, but also the *Collectio Sangermanensis*, one of the most celebrated derivatives of the *Hibernensis*.[42] Moreover, we know that Irish liturgical and paracanonical texts had made their way from southeastern Germany, especially Salzburg, to Fleury because Orléans, Bibl. de la Ville 184, written in the early ninth century in the vicinity of Salzburg, with its "Alcuinian" prayers,[43] Bavarian litany, and copy of "Virgil's" *Liber de numeris,*[44] had been taken at least by the tenth century to Fleury.[45]

(e) The Abridgment of London, BL Royal 5.E.XIII

At least two ninth-century manuscripts of the *Hibernensis* written on the Continent made their way to Worcester, Oxford, Bodl. Lib. Hatton 42 and Cambridge Corpus Christi College 279.[46] And in fact, Worcester seems to have been a center where Irish texts were used well into the twelfth century.[47] Hence, it is not surprising to find another ninth-century abridgment of the *Hibernensis* in a codex whose provenance is Worcester, London, BL Royal 5.E.XIII. The manuscript is a vast florilegium of texts, and on folios 52r–68v under a title "Incipiunt pauca fundamenta de sinodali libri" there is a text into which extracts from the *Hibernensis* have been woven. They are taken from L. 1 and following of the *Hibernensis* and are arranged in the sequence of the *Hibernensis*.

---

[40]Although sections drawn from or resembling L. 1, cc. 14–16 (on which cf. below, p. 109, n. 53) and L. 2, cc. 5–25, have been inserted into and after L. 37 on fols. 117r–v and 119r–121r.

[41]Kottje, "Einheit und Vielfalt," p. 337.

[42]See below, pp. 119–124.

[43]Cf. PL 101:1383–1416, and Aimé-Georges Martimort, *La Documentation liturgique de dom Edmond Martène: Étude codicologique,* Studi e Testi 279 (Vatican, 1978), p. 508, nr. 1131.

[44]Cf. Reynolds, *Ordinals of Christ,* p. 67, n. 58.

[45]Bischoff, *Schreibschulen,* 2:36.

[46]Mordek, *Kirchenrecht,* pp. 257f.

[47]Reynolds, *Ordinals of Christ,* p. 123, n. 30.

Included among the texts on the ecclesiastical hierarchy are an Ordinal of
Christ and the *De officiis vii graduum*, two pieces that had an extraordinary diffusion thanks to the *Hibernensis*.[48]

### 3. Collections Dependent on *Hibernensis* Canons

Had the canons of the *Hibernensis* been contained only in the collection
itself or in abridgments, their impact might have been much less in the
Carolingian period than it actually was. Entire collections or abridgments
could easily have been identified and suppressed, but insofar as many
canons of the *Hibernensis* proved to be valuable supplements to other
canon law collections, they lost their association with the suspect Irish collection and became useful parts of widely accepted canonical compilations. In this section some of these collections with their *Hibernensis*
canons will be treated. It should be noted, however, that one of the most
conspicuous of these is lacking here, the *Collectio Sangermanensis*, which
because of its importance as a bridge between canonistic and liturgico-
didactic collections will be treated later.

(a)   The *Collectio Vetus Gallica*

One of the earliest Frankish collections to use sections from the
*Hibernensis* was the first major systematic collection of the Gallican
church, the *Collectio Vetus Gallica*. In its earliest recension no texts from
the *Hibernensis* were used, but when the *Vetus Gallica* reached Corbie it
seemed appropriate to add monastic canons from Insular sources including the *Hibernensis* and the so-called *Penitentiale Discipulus
Umbrensium*. These canons were added, it seems, in several layers and derived from a text of the *Hibernensis* something like that in Vienna, ÖNB
522 and Munich, Clm 4592.[49] Within the body of the *Vetus Gallica* in
many manuscripts, canons from the *Hibernensis*, LL. 39 and 42, were appro-
priately added to the books dealing with monasticism.[50] But many of these
same canons were also inserted at less appropriate places in the ninth-century
manuscripts Oxford, Bodl. Bodl. 572 (s. IX[1], northern France)[51] and Paris,
BN Lat. 10588, fol. 73v (IX[1], southern France, Burgundy?).[52]

[48]Reynolds, *Ordinals of Christ*, p. 75.
[49]Mordek, *Kirchenrecht*, p. 52.
[50]Mordek, *Kirchenrecht*, pp. 535–538.
[51]Mordek, *Kirchenrecht*, p. 98, n. 3.
[52]Mordek, *Kirchenrecht*, p. 237.

Another layer from the *Hibernensis* was also added to conclude several southern French manuscripts of the *Vetus Gallica*, Berlin, DSB Phill. 1763 (s. IXin., France, rather southerly) and Albi, Bibl. Roch. 38bis (s. IXca. med., southern French). In these instances the *Hibernensis*, L. 1, c. 16a (the famous text attributed to the emperor Constantine granting judicial immunity to the clergy)[53] was attached to the Sylvestrian accusatorial canon that established the sequence of clerical accusations.[54] This same combination of texts from the *Hibernensis* and the Sylvestrian accusatorial canon was also used in a number of eighth- and ninth-century manuscripts as a preface to all the canons of the *Vetus Gallica*: Brussels, Bibl. Roy. 8654–72 (s. VIII/IX, prov. St. Bertin); Einsiedeln, SB 205 (s. IX2/4, Switzerland); St. Gall, SB 675 (s. IX[1], perhaps Bavaria); and Vienna, ÖNB 2171 (s. IX3/4, southwest Germany).[55] To place this "Constantinian" quotation as an introduction to the *Vetus Gallica* is something like the use of the same text (but deriving from the original, not the *Hibernensis*) in the Vatican manuscript of the Salzburg *Collection in Two Books*, Vatican, Reg. Lat. 407 (s. IX3/4, vicinity of St. Gall) as a prologue to L. 1.[56] Much later in the thirteenth century the *Hibernensis* text would also be used as an introduction to the *Collectio Dionysio-Hadriana* in Barcelona, Archivo de la Corona de Aragón, Ripoll 105.[57]

(b)   The *Collection of Bonneval*

From the *Collectio Vetus Gallica* many texts passed to the first *Collection of Bonneval*, compiled sometime between 816 and the mid-ninth century and found in the unique codex, Paris, BN Lat. 3859 (s. IXm.–3/4, "Gallien"). Here again, canons from the *Hibernensis*, LL. 39 and 42, on the monastic life were borrowed from the *Vetus Gallica*.[58]

---

[53]To use the "Constantinian" text as an addendum to the collection is not far removed from the *Collection in 250 Chapters*, noted above, which concluded with a longer version of this text not found in the *Hibernensis* (Vienna, ÖNB 522, fol. 113v). It should be noted that a "longer" version of this canon, but truncated with "expectate iudicium rel." is in Paris, BN Lat. 12444, fol. 117r-v, on which see above n. 40.

[54]See Reynolds, *Ordinals of Christ*, p. 30.

[55]Mordek, *Kirchenrecht*, pp. 274f., 277, 291, 299.

[56]Fol. 5r. On this manuscript see R. E. Reynolds, "The Pseudo-Augustinian 'Sermo de conscientia' and the Related Canonical 'Dicta sancti Gregorii papae,'"*Revue bénédictine* 81 (1971), 313.

[57]Mordek, *Kirchenrecht*, p. 245.

[58]Mordek, *Kirchenrecht*, p. 535; and "Die Rechtssammlungen der Handschrift von Bonneval—ein Werk der karolingischen Reform," *Deutsches Archiv* 24 (1968), 373f., 384, 417f.

(c)   The *Collection of 450 Chapters* of Cologne, DB 210

It was noted in connection with fragments of the *Hibernensis* that one group of manuscripts breaks off with texts ending at L. 38, c. 18. Among this group was Cologne, DB 210 (Darmst. 2178). But this manuscript is not so much a "pure" example of a partial manuscript of the *Hibernensis* as a dependent collection. Not only has the traditional division of the *Hibernensis* texts into books and chapters been broken down, but many of the *Hibernensis* canons themselves have been reduced and many non-*Hibernensis* texts have been added. These additions include a host of canons from Greek, African, and Gallican councils, including Epaon, Clermont, and Orléans V, and several papal decrees.[59]

(d)   The Collection of Würzburg, UB M.p.th.q.31, fols. 52–59

It has already been seen that the collection in this Würzburg manuscript was preceded by an abridgment of the *Hibernensis* (fols. 1–41).[60] Between this abridgment and our collection on fols. 52–59 there was inserted a partial manuscript of the *Collectio Vetus Gallica* written at almost the same time in western Germany in a scriptorium under Irish influence. In the collection on fols. 52–59 there is a mélange of canons, papal documents, patristic fragments, and even works attributed to Boniface, one of which had wide circulation in southeastern Germany under the title *Dicta sancti Gregorii papae*.[61] According to Fournier, who followed Nürnberger's description of this collection, there are canons drawn from the *Hibernensis*, LL. 1, 11, 17, and 21, but in many instances they have readings differing from those Wasserschleben gives. Hence, until the new edition of the *Hibernensis* appears, it may be more prudent to say that these canons of the Würzburg collection were inspired by rather than drawn from the *Hibernensis*.

(e)   The *Collection in 400 Chapters*

The manuscripts Munich, Clm 4592 and Vienna, ÖNB 522, which as we have seen contained the abridgment of the *Collectio Hibernensis* called the *Collection in 250 Chapters*, also were the vehicle for another collection in

---

[59]See the description of this collection by Hermann Wasserschleben, *Die irische Kanonensammlung*, 2nd ed. (Leipzig, 1885), xxv.

[60]See above, p. 105.

[61]See Reynolds, "'Sermo de conscientia,'" pp. 310–317; and "Canon Law Collections," p. 23, n. 46.

400 chapters. This collection, compiled at the earliest in the late eighth or early ninth century, seems to have had a much wider diffusion in the Carolingian realms than did the Irish *Collection in 250 Chapters* and is found in manuscripts whose origins were far removed from southeastern Germany with its Irish connections: Paris, BN Lat. 2316 (s. IX2/4, southern France) and Metz, Bibl. mun. 236, fols. 143–206 (s. VIII/IX, perhaps Rhenan: destroyed during World War II).[62]

The material in the *Collection in 400 Chapters* is an unusual mix, almost as strange as the *Collectio Hibernensis* itself. There are first long passages from the Bible showing the parallels between Old and New Testament texts. In this material Fournier pointed out possible extracts from the *Hibernensis,*[63] but in many cases it is possible that they were taken from Scripture itself or other florilegia in which the Old and New Testament texts were juxtaposed. Then, there are large numbers of Insular and Frankish penitential texts such as the *Penitential of Theodore, Penitential of Martène*, and the like.[64] Together with this "suspect" material are found canons which were clearly drawn from the *Collectio Hibernensis,* such as those from L. 46, *De ratione matrimonii,*[65] which as will be seen had an extraordinary diffusion in manuscripts and canon law collections from the ninth century on.[66] Finally, there is material in the *Collection in 400 Chapters* that would have been perfectly acceptable in a Frankish milieu, extracts from the *Collectio Vetus Gallica.*[67] It is interesting, as Mordek has shown, that the *Collection in 400 Chapters* in the early ninth-century manuscript, Paris, BN Lat. 2316, contains a fragment of the *Vetus Gallica* in a form related to that in Würzburg, UB M.p.th.q.31, fols. 42–51, which was written in the late eighth or early ninth century in a scriptorium with Irish influence.[68] Moreover, in this same Paris manuscript there is a large extract from the *Collectio Dionysio-Hadriana*. This codex of the *Collection in 400 Chapters* is, therefore, striking evidence that the Carolingians did not hesitate to combine the officially sanctioned *Collectio Dionysio-Hadriana* with Frankish and suspect Insular texts.

---

[62]Mordek, *Kirchenrecht*, pp. 162, 262, and 283f.
[63]Fournier, "De l'influence," p. 15.
[64]See especially, Vienna, ÖNB 522, fols. 144r–149r.
[65]Vienna, ÖNB 522, fol. 148v.
[66]See below, pp. 115f.
[67]Mordek, *Kirchenrecht*, pp. 162–164.
[68]Mordek, *Kirchenrecht,* p. 301.

(f)  The *Collection of Laon*

One of the most intriguing collections compiled before the middle of the ninth century is the collection which goes under the names of the *Collection of St. Petersbourg* or the *Collection of Laon*, but which might better be called the *Collection of Cambrai* because both of its extant manuscript witnesses were perhaps written there: Laon, Bibl. mun. 201 (ca. s. IXm., Cambrai?) and Leningrad, Publ. Bibl. Q.v.II.5 (s. IX4/4, Cambrai?).[69] This collection was written with Carolingian reform ideology in mind since its first canon is entitled, "De eo quod secundum ordinem Romanum facere debemus."[70] But it nonetheless has many of the same characteristics as the *Collectio Hibernensis* and its derivative, the *Collectio Sangermanensis,*[71] except one, systematization. The *Collectio of Laon* contains extracts from the Fathers, conciliar and papal canons drawn from the *Collectio Dionysio-Hadriana*, penitential material, didactic pieces on the sacraments, and even liturgical formularies.[72] Also, like the *Collection in 400 Chapters* it contains canons drawn from the *Collectio Vetus Gallica.*[73] The canons from the *Hibernensis* derive primarily from L. 14 and following.[74] Since, as has often been pointed out,[75] there was a copy of the *Hibernensis* at Cambrai in the late eighth century, it might be expected that these canons of the *Collection of Laon* depend on it. But, alas, there are canons taken from books of the *Hibernensis* beyond those found in L. 38 of the Cambrai manuscript of the *Hibernensis*. Moreover, it has been by no means proven that the *Collection of Laon* was compiled at Cambrai.[76]

(g)  The *Penitential of Martène*

In both the *Collection in 400 Chapters* and the *Collection of Laon* we have seen the combination of canons from the "acceptable" Frankish

---

[69]Mordek, *Kirchenrecht*, p. 164. nn. 312f.

[70]See Paul Fournier, "Notices sur trois collections canoniques inédites de l'époque carolingienne," *Revue des sciences religieuses* 6 (1926), 219.

[71]See below, pp. 119–124.

[72]See Michel Andrieu, *Les Ordines Romani du Haut Moyen Âge*, 1, *Les manuscrits* (Louvain, 1931), pp. 349f.

[73]Laon, Bibl. mun. 201, fol. 90r.

[74]Fournier, "Notices," p. 223.

[75]See, e.g., Fournier, "Notices," p. 229, and John J. Contreni, *The Cathedral School of Laon from 850 to 930, Its Manuscripts and Masters,* Münchener Beiträge zur Mediävistik und Renaissance-Forschung 29 (Munich, 1978), p. 82.

[76]See Mordek, *Kirchenrecht*, p. 165, n. 315.

*Collectio Vetus Gallica*, penitential material, and the *Hibernensis*. The same is true with the penitential named after its ancient editor, Dom Edmond Martène.[77] This Frankish penitential has been dated by its modern editor, Walther von Hörmann, to between 802 and 813,[78] but it may have been compiled later since the manuscript in which it is found, Florence, Bibl. Med.-Laur. Ashburnham 82 (32) [Cat. 29], was written in western France during approximately the third quarter of the ninth century.[79] The manuscript itself was in Fleury and then Orléans until the depredations of G. Libri,[80] when a portion of what is now Orléans, Bibl. de la Ville 116 (94) was removed, ultimately to be transferred to Florence. The codex as a whole is an extraordinary one, containing among other items prayers like those of the Salzburg, then Fleury manuscript, Orléans, Bibl. de la Ville 184,[81] the Mass commentary *Dominus vobiscum*[82] like the one attributed to Alcuin in the Salzburg manuscript Budapest, Ors. Széch. Kön. 316,[83] several Carolingian expositions on baptism and the Creed,[84] a unique Ordinal of Christ,[85] and extracts from the *Collectio Hibernensis* derivative, the *Collectio Sangermanensis*.[86]

In his study of the *Penitentiale Martenianum* Mordek has shown that substantial sections are based upon the *Collectio Vetus Gallica*,[87] but even more important he has shown that many of the canons that von Hörmann attributed to the *Vetus Gallica* were probably based on the *Collection in 400 Chapters* or a collection underlying both it and the *Penitentiale Martenianum*. But beyond this there are clear borrowings from the *Hibernensis*, LL. 15–18 and 45–47.[88] It is especially interesting to see that these latter canons are drawn from the celebrated book in the *Hibernensis* on matrimony

---

[77]See Vogel, *"Libri paenitentiales,"* p. 78.

[78]Walther von Hörmann, "Bussbücherstudien," *Zeitschrift der Savigny-Stiftung für Rechtsgeschichte, Kan. Abt.* 1 (1911), 195–250; 2 (1912), 111–181; 3 (1913), 413–492; 4 (1914), 358–483.

[79]Mordek, *Kirchenrecht*, p. 200, n. 525.

[80]On Libri's depredations, see Roger E. Reynolds, "An Unexpected Manuscript Fragment of the Ninth-Century Canonical Collection in Two Books," *Bulletin of Medieval Canon Law*, n.s. 8 (1978), 35–38.

[81]See above, p. 107.

[82]*Amalarii episcopi opera liturgica omnia,* ed. J. M. Hanssens, 1, Studi e Testi 138 (Vatican, 1948), pp. 284–338.

[83]See Reynolds, "Canon Law Collections," p. 31, n. 106.

[84]These are currently being studied by Dr. Keefe.

[85]See below, p. 130.

[86]See below, p. 122.

[87]Mordek, *Kirchenrecht*, pp. 199–201.

[88]Fournier, "De l'influence," p. 17.

and, as one might expect in a penitential, from the books in the *Hibernensis* entitled *De questionibus mulierum* and *De penitentia*.

## 4. Isolated Extracts from the *Collectio Hibernensis*

Despite the fact that such canonical collections as the *Dionysio-Hadriana* and the *Vetus Gallica* with their "authentic" papal and conciliar canons received the approval of the Carolingian rulers, the usefulness of the *Hibernensis* did not diminish because many of its texts—especially patristic and Scriptural ones—were lacking in these "official" collections. But just as important, several sections of the *Hibernensis* dealt with matters inadequately covered in the Roman and Frankish collections. Hence, these sections were often reproduced and used as isolated extracts in manuscripts or were added to canonical collections of Roman, Frankish, or Hibernian types and even to florilegial collections and biblical exegetical texts.

(a)   Extracts on the Ecclesiastical Hierarchy

The early books of the *Hibernensis* contain a long line of definitions of the clerical grades based largely on Isidore's work and its derivatives, and these nicely supplemented the strictly legal material of the papal and conciliar canons. These texts were often used in such abridgments as those of Cambridge, Corpus Christi College 279,[89] but they were also abstracted from the *Hibernensis* and used in a variety of canonical, liturgical, and florilegial manuscripts. In the last section of this paper we will look at some of these extracts as they were modified and placed in Carolingian *liturgica*, but here several direct borrowings from the *Hibernensis* canons on sacred orders should be mentioned.

In L. 8 of the *Hibernensis* there are two valuable epitomes of the origins and duties of the clerics. The first, called an Ordinal of Christ, lists the grades which Christ is thought to have fulfilled in his life and is of a type called the Hiberno-Hispanic Hierarchical because the two lower grades of exorcist and lector are listed according to a sequence used in Isidore's work.[90] The second epitome in L. 8 is the little tract entitled *De distantia graduum*, which entered pontifical manuscripts of the tenth and eleventh centuries under the title *De officiis septem graduum*.[91] By

[89]See above, p. 105.

[90]Reynolds, *Ordinals of Christ,* pp. 34, 61–63.

[91]See Roger E. Reynolds, "The *De officiis vii graduum*: Its Origins and Early Medieval Development," *Mediaeval Studies* 34 (1972), 113–151.

the ninth century both of these texts on the ecclesiastical hierarchy in L. 8 had been used in the canonical *Collectio Sangermanensis*, Paris, BN Lat. 12444, and in the florilegial tract in London, BL Roy. 5.E.XIII.[92] Slightly later in the tenth century they would also appear in modified forms in the canonical manuscript, Vesoul, Bibl. mun. 73, with its snippets of the *Collectio Sangermanensis.*[93]

(b)   Extracts on Matrimony from the *Collectio Hibernensis*, L. 46

In many of the abridgments and derivatives of the *Hibernensis* some of the most frequently reproduced texts were from L. 46 entitled *De ratione matrimonii*. Extracts from this book were reproduced in a variety of canon law collections and manuscripts well into the high Middle Ages, but of particular interest here is their wide diffusion in Carolingian manuscripts. Maassen, Fournier, and Mordek have all presented substantial lists of isolated texts with the whole or partial text of L. 46, and several more exemplars can be added to these with dates and places of origin. What is also of special interest is the connection of many of the earliest manuscripts of this text with southeastern Germany, particularly Salzburg with its long tradition of texts based on the *Hibernensis*. Among the early manuscripts from Salzburg or southeast Germany with texts from L. 46 are Vienna, ÖNB 424 (s. IX2/4, Salzburg),[94] the *Mondsee Pastorale*, Vienna, ÖNB 1370 (s. IX1/4, Mondsee) with its rich collection of Salzburg texts,[95] and Munich, Clm 6242 (s. IX1/3, Freising) and 6245, fol. 59v (s. IX/X, Freising).[96] Related to the early Salzburg manuscripts are slightly later codices that contain the addenda to the Salzburg *Collection in Two Books*, Vatican, Reg. Lat. 407,[97] and Pal. Lat. 973 (s. IX2/2, northeastern France).[98] More distantly related to these manuscripts is Vatican, Reg. Lat. 421,[99] with its extract from the *Hibernensis*, L. 46, and the tract popular in Salzburg and southeast Germany,

[92]Reynolds, *"De officiis vii graduum,"* pp. 131f.; and *Ordinals of Christ*, pp. 74f.

[93]Reynolds, *Ordinals of Christ*, pp. 74f., n. 21.

[94]Fol. 7r. Reynolds, "Canon Law Collections," p. 27, n. 70; and Bischoff, *Schreibschulen,* 2:145f.

[95]Fol. 90r. Reynolds, "Canon Law Collections," pp. 26f.

[96]Mordek, *Kirchenrecht,* p. 259.

[97]Fols. 74v–75r.

[98]Fol. 39r–v.

[99]Fol. 22v. Professor Bischoff has kindly written me that this section of the MS, once belonging to St. Gall, SB 899, is from St. Gall, s. 2-3/3 IX.

*De observatione iiii temporum.* [100] Slightly outside the orbit of southeast German and Salzburg influence is the Bodensee manuscript, Freiburg, UB 8 (s. IX$^2$) with its excerpt from L. 46 of the *Hibernensis.* [101] By the middle of the ninth century a section from L. 46 had found its way into manuscripts of the Pseudo-Isidorian forgeries: the Pseudo-Isidorian *Benedictus Levita,* [102] and the manuscript, Paris, BN Lat. 1557, [103] which Bernard Merlette suspects may originally have been part of the famous Laon Pseudo-Isidore manuscript, Paris, BN Lat. 9629, glossed by Hincmar of Laon. [104]

(c)  Salzburg Fragments

Two late eighth- and early ninth-century products of Salzburg, both containing fragments of the *Collectio Hibernensis* not hitherto noted in canonistic studies, have recently been brought to light. One of these is in Wolfenbüttel, Herz.-Aug. Bibl. 579 (Helmst. 532) (s. IX2/4, Salzburg), which contains a vast miscellany of texts including canonistic fragments also found in the Salzburg *Collection in Two Books,* [105] an Ordinal of Christ, [106] and a group of patristic and canonistic texts. Worked into these have been snippets drawn from the *Collectio Hibernensis*, L. 27. [107]

The other item, in a manuscript now lost but whose contents in Froben's works have recently been described by Professor Bischoff, was clearly written in early Carolingian Salzburg. Besides its important witness to the Irish *Stowe Missal,* [108] the manuscript contained isolated extracts from the *Hibernensis* in two places. One is in a tract without title, [109] and the other is within a tract with the rubric, "Incipit epistola de

---

[100]For manuscripts of this text see Reynolds, "Canon Law Collections," p. 24, n. 53, to which add St. Gall, SB 899, p. 93 (partial text).

[101]Mordek, *Kirchenrecht,* p. 259; and Johanne Autenrieth, "Die kanonistischen Handschriften der Dombibliothek Konstanz," in Autenrieth and Kottje, *Kirchenrechtliche Texte im Bodenseegebiet,* p. 11.

[102]3.179; PL 97:820.

[103]Mordek, *Kirchenrecht,* p. 259.

[104]See Contreni, *Cathedral School of Laon,* p. 62, n. 81; and the forthcoming article by Professor Contreni in *Viator.*

[105]Reynolds, "Canon Law Collections," p. 27.

[106]Reynolds, *Ordinals of Christ,* p. 72, n. 13 (1).

[107]Fol. 133v.

[108]See Bernhard Bischoff, *Salzburger Formelbücher und Briefe aus Tassilonischer und Karolingischer Zeit,* Bayerische Akad. der Wissenschaften, Phil.-Hist. Kl., Sitzungsb. Jhg. 1973, Hft. 4 (Munich, 1973), pp. 51f.

[109]Bischoff, *Salzburger Formelbücher,* pp. 42–44.

apatibus vel de principibus."[110] Included in the snippets drawn from the *Hibernensis* are those from LL. 25 and 37, *De regno* and *De principatu*, whose influence would be felt far into the Middle Ages.[111]

(d)  Fragments of the *Hibernensis* Associated with Sedulius Scottus

One of the most celebrated scholars of the ninth century, Sedulius Scottus, worked in the company of Irish scholars at Liège.[112] In light of his Irish origins it is not surprising to discover that his own works acted as a magnet for other Irish texts, including the *Collectio Hibernensis*. In the twelfth-century manuscript of his *Collectaneum*, Bernkastel-Kues, St. Nikolaus-Hosp., Bibl. der Cus.-Stift. 37 (C 14), there are excerpts from the *Hibernensis* not distantly removed from the *Proverbia grecorum*,[113] fragments of which also appear in the Karlsruhe manuscript of the *Hibernensis*,[114] Sedulius's *Liber de rectoribus*,[115] and in the eleventh-century Norman Anonymous, who also used the *Hibernensis*.[116] Moreover, in another twelfth-century manuscript, Bamberg, SB 127 (B V 24), fol. 106v, there are attached to Sedulius's *Collectaneum in omnes sancti Pauli epistolas* fragments from the *Hibernensis* L. 46.6,29,27.[117] In short, just as we have seen the *Hibernensis* attached to canonistic texts written in locations with long traditions of Irish scholarship, so with the Irishman Sedulius we find *Hibernensis* texts naturally clustering around his work.

(e)  Miscellaneous Isolated Extracts from the *Hibernensis*

As a source of canonical authority the *Hibernensis* was, as we have seen, attractive to the compilers of legal collections because it provided them

---

[110]Bischoff, *Salzburger Formelbücher*, pp. 44–46.

[111]See below, n. 116.

[112]Contreni, *Cathedral School of Laon*, p. 83.

[113]S. Hellmann, *Sedulius Scottus,* Quellen und Untersuchungen zur lateinischen Philologie des Mittelalters 1 (Munich, 1906), pp. 96f.

[114]Hellmann, *Sedulius Scottus*, p. 132.

[115]According to Hellmann, *Sedulius Scottus*, pp. 11, 73, there are ninth-century manuscripts of this text.

[116]See Roger E. Reynolds, "The Unidentified Sources of the Norman Anonymous: C.C.C.C. MS. 415," *Transactions of the Cambridge Bibliographical Society* 5, 2 (1970), 123; and Roger E. Reynolds, "Liturgical Scholarship at the Time of the Investiture Controversy: Past Research and Future Opportunities," *Harvard Theological Review* 71 (1978), 121–123.

[117]I am grateful to Professor Bischoff for having pointed out this instance of the use of the *Hibernensis*.

with an abundance of patristic and scriptural texts not found in the standard collections of papal and conciliar canons. But more than that, these texts were arranged in the *Hibernensis* in a convenient systematic fashion. Hence, it is not surprising to find that the *Hibernensis* quickly became a sourcebook for scholars working in a variety of extracanonical disciplines. A careful search through the hundreds of florilegial tracts compiled in the Carolingian period[118] and the biblical exegetical texts written by Irish scholars or those working in their tradition[119] would undoubtedly turn up an abundance of such borrowings from the *Hibernensis*. But here it is necessary only to cite a few such isolated instances in several Carolingian florilegia and exegetical manuscripts to illustrate the point.

(i) Florilegia. Professor Bischoff has very kindly drawn my attention to an extraordinary example of a Carolingian florilegium into which texts from the *Hibernensis* have been liberally sprinkled. The manuscript in which it is found, Munich, Clm 6433, fols. 2r–24v, was written in Anglo-Saxon minuscule in the late eighth century at Freising.[120] Among the authors cited in addition to those of the books of the Bible are Gaseus or Commodian, Eusebius, Gregory, Sedulius, Cassian, Gregory Nazianzus, Augustine, Isidore, Jerome, Basil, Barnabas, Clement, Virgilius Maro, Pelagius, and Athanasius; and the subjects range from love and hate to the fear of God and watchfulness in prayer. The snippets from the *Hibernensis* include not only those from such popular books as L. 47, *De penitentia*, but also from other less likely books such as LL. 13, 14, and 38.

(ii) Biblical Commentaries. Professor Bischoff in his seminal article, "Wendepunkte in der Geschichte der lateinischen Exegese im Frühmittelalter,"[121] also has drawn attention to the influence of the *Hibernensis* in a variety of Hiberno-Latin biblical commentaries of the late eighth and early ninth century. In the Genesis section of the *Pauca problesmata*

---

[118]See H.-M. Rochais, "Contribution à l'histoire des florilèges ascétiques du haut moyen âge latin," *Revue bénédictine* 63 (1953), 246–291.

[119]See Robert E. McNally, *The Bible in the Early Middle Ages,* Woodstock Papers 4 (Westminster, Md., 1959), p. 71; and Martin McNamara, "A Plea for Hiberno-Latin Biblical Studies," *Irish Theological Quarterly* 39 (1972), 337–353.

[120]*Codices Latini antiquiores: A Paleographical Guide to Latin Manuscripts Prior to the Ninth Century*, ed. E. A. Lowe (Oxford, 1934–), ix, 1283.

[121]*Mittelalterliche Studien: Ausgewählte Aufsätze zur Schriftkunde und Literaturgeschichte,* 1 (Stuttgart, 1966), 205–273 trans. as "Turning-Points in the History of Latin Exegesis in the Early Irish Church: A.D. 650–800," in *Biblical Studies: The Medieval Irish Contribution,* ed. M. McNamara, *Proceedings of the Irish Biblical Association* 1 (Dublin, 1976), 74–160.

*de enigmatibus ex tomis canonicis,* for example, the etymology of the word *bestia* found in the works of the Irish Virgilius Maro[122] seems to have been drawn from the *Hibernensis,* L. 53.1.[123] This same etymology is also found in the Irish Pseudo-Hilarius, *Expositio in vii epistolas canonicas,*[124] recently edited by Professor McNally.[125] In his editions of other Hiberno-Latin exegetical works McNally also called attention to what he saw as the influence of the *Hibernensis,* especially L. 46, *De ratione matrimonii.*[126]

### 5. The *Collectio Sangermanensis* and Its Supplement

One of the most important collections deriving from the *Hibernensis* was not dealt with earlier in this paper[127] because of its special nature as a bridge between canonistic and liturgical texts in the Carolingian period. This derivative is one of several collections designated by canonists as the *Collectio Sangermanensis* because it was first found in a manuscript from the fonds St.-Germain in the Bibliothèque Nationale in Paris. But a significant number of fragments of this collection, many with additional texts, have more recently been found, and hence not only should there be a new edition and study of this derivative collection but perhaps a rechristening to accompany it.[128]

Among the distinctive traits of Hiberno-Latin literature in the eighth and ninth centuries are the use of Irishisms, puns,[129] and glosses explaining the who, when, and where of matters,[130] but none are as obvious

---

[122]Michael Herren, "The Pseudonymous Tradition in Hiberno-Latin: An Introduction," in *Latin Script and Letters: A.D. 400–900. Festschrift Presented to Ludwig Bieler on the Occasion of His 70th birthday,* ed. J.J. O'Meara and B. Naumann (Leiden, 1976), pp. 125f.

[123]Bischoff, "Wendepunkte," p. 233.

[124]Bischoff, "Wendepunkte," p. 267.

[125]Scriptores Hiberniae minores 1:70.

[126]Scriptores Hiberniae minores 1:23, 33, 59, 86, 119.

[127]See above, p. 108.

[128]The other *"Collectiones Sangermanenses"* are in Paris, BN Lat. 12012, 12098, and Wolfenbüttel, Herz.-Aug. Bibl. 212 Gud. [4517] (and the newly found manuscript, Gent, UB 235, studied by L. Waelken and D. Van den Auweele, "La collection de Thérouanne en IX livres à l'abbaye de Saint-Pierre-au-Mont-Blandin: le Codex Gandavensis 235," *Sacris Erudiri* 24 [1980], 115–153). On the problem of the use of the appellation *Collectio Sangermanensis,* see Roger E. Reynolds, "A Florilegium on the Ecclesiastical Grades in Clm 19414: Testimony to Ninth-Century Clerical Instruction," *Harvard Theological Review* 63 (1970), 248, n. 71; and Mordek, *Kirchenrecht,* p. 144, n. 216.

[129]Herren, "Pseudonymous Tradition," p. 122.

[130]Bischoff, "Wendepunkte," p. 218; and Reynolds, *Ordinals of Christ,* p. 93.

as the love of numerology,[131] etymologies, and a question-response or
didactic structure. In the *Collectio Hibernensis* itself questions of all sorts
abound, and many are the canons that contain numbered lists of explanations and etymologies. These distinctive traits in the Irish material made
them perfect vehicles to effect the directives of the Carolingian capitularies
and conciliar canons which stated that both clergy and laymen were to know
and understand the basis of their religious practice. Hence, an Irish tract
with, for example, its questions and answers as to how many verses there are
in the Creed, who wrote each, and what they mean, responded exactly to the
educational program of the Carolingian rulers.

Among the sacraments a priest in the Carolingian realm was specifically
charged with understanding and being able to explain were sacred orders,
baptism, and the Mass,[132] and, of course, the *Collectio Hibernensis* provided
brief descriptions of all of these. Thus, at the very end of the eighth century
these descriptions were combined with the legislative sources of the
*Hibernensis* and cast in didactic form to become what is now called the *Collectio Sangermanensis.*

The longest form of the *Sangermanensis* is in the Paris manuscript, BN
Lat. 12444 (olim Sangerm. 928, Corbie), dealt with earlier as an abridgment
of the *Collectio Hibernensis.*[133] The manuscript was written not in Corbie,
as has often been stated,[134] but probably at Fleury in the late eighth or early
ninth century.[135] The first extensive section deals with the ecclesiastical and
religious hierarchies, the second with the Church and baptism, the third with
the Mass and the ecclesiastical calendar, the fourth with penance, and the
last with matrimony. The greatest proportion of texts consists of modifications of the *Hibernensis*, but they are also supplemented with texts that were
to have very wide broadcast in Carolingian liturgical tracts.

Beyond this long form of the *Sangermanensis* there are what appear to
be[136] several partial manuscripts and manuscripts with isolated excerpta.

---

[131]See, e.g., Robert E. McNally, *Der irische Liber de numeris: Eine Quellenanalyse des
pseudo-isidorischen Liber de numeris* (Diss., Munich, 1957), passim.

[132]On these directives see, e.g., H. Netzer, *L'Introduction de la Messe romaine en France
sous les carolingiens* (Paris, 1910), pp. 40–48; and Keefe, "Baptismal Instruction," pp.
149–152.

[133]See above, pp. 106f.

[134]See, e.g., Rosamond McKitterick, *The Frankish Church and the Carolingian
Reforms, 789–895* (London, 1977), p. 148.

[135]Reynolds, "Florilegium on the Ecclesiastical Grades," p. 248, n. 71.

[136]Mordek, *Kirchenrecht,* pp. 144f., correctly warns that until a full study of the *Sangermanensis* is made, one must reckon with the possibility that what appear to be partial

The longest of the extracts is in a manuscript written in northern France in the last quarter of the ninth century but early taken to St. Emmeram in Regensburg, Munich, Clm 14508, fols. 75r–ca.105v. In this codex there are several sections with canonical material including the *Sangermanensis*, the *Capitula* of Theodulf of Orléans, *Capitula a sacerdotibus preposita*, and the *Collection in 53 Titles*.[137] The canons in our section of the manuscript cover most of the topics found in Paris, BN Lat. 12444, ranging from LL. 1 through 21 according to Nürnberger's description,[138] but there are many omissions and additions of material not found in the Paris manuscript. Also, the sequence of books has been radically altered, and a supplement added containing the ordination rubrics from the *Statuta ecclesiae antiqua*.[139]

The second extensive extract from the *Sangermanensis* is in Cologne, DB 117, fols. 69r–89v (s. IXca. med., France).[140] In this manuscript topics ranging from sacred orders through penance are treated, but again in many instances texts found in the Parisian codex of the *Sangermanensis*, such as the Ordinal of Christ and the *De distantia graduum*, have been omitted.

The third extensive extract from the *Sangermanensis* is in a southern French manuscript from the mid-ninth century, Albi, Bibl. Roch. 38bis, fols. 38v–42r. This codex also contains the *Collectio Vetus Gallica*, again illustrating the close association of the Irish and Frankish collections in ninth-century manuscripts. The extract from the *Sangermanensis* is particularly interesting for two reasons. First, it deals almost exclusively with synods and the ecclesiastical hierarchy. Second, after the word "Explicit," on fol. 42r, there is a supplement in dialogue form dealing with the duties of the presbyter and beginning with the words, "INT. Dic mihi pro quid est presbiter benedictus?" and short discussions of baptism and the Mass. As will be seen, this supplement had an extraordinary diffusion in manuscripts from the ninth century on.

---

manuscripts or excerpta may indeed have provided the sources of the *Sangermanensis* as it appears in Paris, BN Lat. 12444.

[137]Peter Landau, "Kanonistische Aktivität in Regensburg im frühen Mittelalter," *Zwei Jahrtausende Regensburg: Vortragsreihe der Universität Regensburg zum Stadtjubiläum*, ed. D. Albrecht, Schriftenreihe der Universität Regensburg 1 (Regensburg, 1979), pp. 63f., 74; and Mordek, *Kirchenrecht*, p. 172, n. 356.

[138]August J. Nürnberger, "Über eine ungedruckte Kanonensammlung aus dem 8. Jahrhundert," *25. Bericht der wissenschaftlichen Gesellschaft Philomathie in Neisse vom Oktober 1888 bis zum Oktober 1890* (Neisse, 1890), 125–197.

[139]Fol. 104r–v.

[140]Mordek, *Kirchenrecht*, p. 145, n. 223.

There is a fourth extensive extract from the *Sangermanensis* in London, BL Harl. 3034, fols. 1r–10r, that has hitherto not been noted. Although this tenth-century manuscript dates from slightly beyond our period, it is of special interest because its extracts from LL. 12–16 are in the interrogatory form of M (*Magister*) and Δ (*Discipulus*) common to a variety of Irish and Carolingian didactic tracts.

Isolated fragments of the *Sangermanensis* frequently appear also in canonical manuscripts from the ninth century on. One of the manuscripts, Orléans, Bibl. de la Ville 116, has already been mentioned for its texts of the *Penitentiale Martenianum*.[141] But sprinkled into its miscellaneous prayers, liturgical expositions, and homilies is a series of interrogatories, among which are several from the *Sangermanensis*.[142] Another mid-ninth-century codex from Lorsch, Vatican, Pal. Lat. 485, contains many of the same didactic tracts and expositions as the Orléans manuscript, but it also has sections from the *Collectio Dionysio-Hadriana*,[143] penitential material,[144] and the *Capitula* of Theodulf of Orléans.[145] The isolated excerpta from the *Sangermanensis* are placed under the name of Isidore[146] and draw on material from L. 12.[147]

Two canonistic manuscripts written slightly after the ninth century but containing Carolingian canonical material also have isolated excerpts from the *Sangermanensis*. Albi, Bibl. Roch. 38, fols. 126v–127v, an early tenth-century codex from southern France, contains, like Albi 38bis, a great variety of canonistic material including the *Collectio Vetus Gallica*,[148] penitential material, *capitula*, and even parts of the Pseudo-Isidorian forgeries. But this later Albi manuscript includes only a few snippets from the *Sangermanensis*, drawn from the introduction and L. 1. The other canonistic manuscript, Vesoul, Bibl. mun. 73, again contains a mélange of material ranging from penitential canons and episcopal capitularies[149] to liturgical commentary. On fols. 81r–83v there is a short

[141]See above, p. 113.
[142]E.g., fol. 72r (cf. Nürnberger, p. 174) and fol. 84v (cf. Nürnberger, p. 161).
[143]Mordek, *Kirchenrecht*, p. 247.
[144]John T. McNeill and Helena Gamer, *Medieval Handbooks of Penance,* Records of Civilization: Sources and Studies 29 (New York, 1938), p. 449.
[145]PL 81:870.
[146]See PL 81:869.
[147]Fol. 44r (cf. Nürnberger, pp. 161–163).
[148]Mordek, *Kirchenrecht*, pp. 268f.
[149]Fournier, "Notices sur trois collections," pp. 79–92.

section in dialogue form that contains material drawn from the introduction and LL. 1–9 of the *Sangermanensis*.

In discussing the codex Albi 38bis it was noted that there was a supplement on the presbyter's duties, baptism, and the Mass cast in the same dialogue form found in the *Sangermanensis* extract itself. This supplement may or may not originally have been within the corpus of the *Collectio Sangermanensis*, and until there is a new edition and study of the collection and its contents, one cannot be certain. But these supplemental texts are of extraordinary interest for several reasons. First, at least some of them are closely related to Irish texts. For example, the first text has a close parallel in the *Liber de numeris* of the Irishman Virgil of Salzburg:[150]

| [*Sangermanensis* Supplement] | [*Liber de numeris*] |
|---|---|
| INT. Dic mihi pro quid est presbiter benedictus? | |
| R. Ad adnuntiandum verbum divinum et ad tradendum baptismum vel paenitentiam lacrimarum, hostiis offerentem omnipotenti Deo pro salute vivorum et requiem defunctorum.[151] | Quattuor causis ordinantur sacerdotes id est, verbum Dei populis praedicare retinere baptismum in recta fide, penitentiam fideliter omnibus largire, hostias puras pro salute vivorum et reliquis [*sic*] defunctorum omnipotenti Deo semper offerre.[152] |

Second, these texts were widely scattered in both didactic and canonistic manuscripts from the ninth century. And third, the texts were often arranged in different sequences or used in part only.

There are two manuscripts from the ninth century that contain the section of the supplemental text on the presbyter's duties. One, St. Gall, SB 40, p. 304, has the *Joca episcopi ad sacerdotes* consisting of a variety of material on sacred orders and baptism.[153] The other manuscript, Albi, Bibl. Roch. 43 (15) (s. IX4/4, probably southern France) contains the *Collectio Dacheriana* and an *Interrogatio sacerdotalis* beginning with the words, "Dic mihi pro quid es presbiter benedictus?"[154] Again, this section of the manuscript contains much of the same material found in the St. Gall *Joca*, but in a different sequence.

[150]McNally, *Liber de numeris*, p. 83.
[151]Albi, Bibl. Roch. 38bis, fol. 42r.
[152]Munich, Clm 14392, fol. 85r.
[153]s. IX2–3/3, Switzerland: Reynolds, *Ordinals of Christ*, p. 70, n. 6.
[154]Fol. 15v. On the manuscript see Mordek, *Kirchenrecht*, p. 261.

Several codices later than the ninth century also have the *Sangermanensis* supplement with the question on the presbyter's duties, and they all seem to point to a southern European tradition of the text. The earliest is in Barcelona, Bibl. Univ. 228, fols. 134v–39r (s. $X^2$, southern France or northern Italy),[155] a manuscript with material on sacred orders, baptism, and a variety of ninth-century penitentials including Halitgar's penitential and a penitential described as the *Penitentiale Vallicellianum I*.[156] Slightly later is the manuscript, Florence, Bibl. Ricc. 256 (K.III.27), fol. 126v. This codex again has treatises on the sacred orders, baptism, and the Creed in dialogue form, but preceding it are texts from the *Institutio canonicorum* of 816/17.[157] And finally, in the twelfth-century manuscript, El Escorial, RBSL Q.III.10, fol. 127v, there is the *Sangermanensis* supplemental text together with baptismal literature.[158]

At least two additional codices have material from the *Sangermanensis* supplement on baptism, unusual because the pedilavium of the Milanese, Gallican, and Irish rites is included. The elder of the two manuscripts is Laon, Bibl. mun. 288, fol. 37v (s. IX1/3, eastern France, Laon?).[159] The other one, Paris, BN Lat. 13092, fol. 136v (s. XII), is later, but the baptismal text is within a florilegium on the sacraments, parts of which may be very ancient indeed. The text of the Ordinal of Christ in the manuscript, for example, contains the unusual grade of gravedigger, found especially in ancient texts written in Spain, southern France, and northern Italy.[160] Hence, the baptismal text from the *Sangermanensis* supplement with its Milanese-Gallican pedilavium is not unexpected.

### 6. Carolingian *Liturgica*

The *Collectio Sangermanensis* with its canons on the sacraments and the didactic form in which they are stated clearly shows the connection between the Irish collection of canon law and Carolingian liturgical tracts. In this concluding section of this article we shall examine the way in which material in the *Sangermanensis* was modified and used in the abundant Carolingian liturgical *expositiones*. Although material from several sections of the *Sangermanensis* seems to have made its way into a

---

[155]Kottje, *Bussbücher Halitgars*, pp. 15f.
[156]Ibid.
[157]Reynolds, *Ordinals of Christ*, p. 91.
[158]Mordek *Kirchenrecht*, p. 145, n. 224.
[159]Keefe, "Baptismal Instruction," p. 59.
[160]Reynolds, *Ordinals of Christ*, pp. 50f.

variety of these expositions,[161] here we shall concentrate on two categories of expositions, those dealing with the Mass and sacred orders, to see how texts deriving from the *Sangermanensis* and *Hibernensis* were used.

### (a) Mass Commentary

During the Carolingian period a plethora of commentaries on the Mass appeared in response to legislative directives,[162] and one of those most frequently found in manuscripts from the ninth to the thirteenth century carried with it a text from the *Sangermanensis*. The tract itself has been attributed by Hanssens to Amalarius of Metz and is entitled *Ordinis totius missae expositio prior*.[163] In Hanssens's descriptions of the thirty or so codices with the commentary[164] one is struck by two things. First, the manuscripts date from the eleventh century and beyond, probably because the majority contain the *Pontificale Romano-Germanicum* of the late tenth or early eleventh century.[165] Further, one notices that the commentary begins in two different ways. In one form[166] it starts abruptly by describing the introit of the Mass. In the other, however, there are two small prefaces, one entitled *Incipit ordo missae a sancto Petro institutus cum expositione sua*, with the incipit "Missa pro multis causis celebratur"; and the other *Cur cotidie iteratur ista oblatio . . .*, with the incipit "Pro multis causis . . . ."[167] As one reads these short prefaces, which have little to do with the subsequent Mass commentary,[168] he is impressed by what have been described as Irish characteristics—the didactic form, numerology, and simplified descriptions of the how and why of the Mass. Hence, the reader begins to suspect that these two short texts probably were written at least by the late eighth or early ninth century in a milieu with Irish influence. Moreover, one suspects that they perhaps circulated independently before being attached to the Mass commentary.

---

[161]See Keefe, "Baptismal Instruction," pp. 332–338.

[162]See Reynolds, "Liturgical Scholarship," p. 110.

[163]Hanssens, 3:297.

[164]Hanssens, 1:217–220.

[165]Cf. Cyrille Vogel and Reinhard Elze, *Le Pontifical romano-germanique du dixième siècle, Le texte,* 1, Studi e Testi 226 (Vatican, 1963), p. 329. To be added to the list of manuscripts with this tract are Fiecht, SB 113, fols. 32r–36r (s. XII, folios unnumbered but described to me by Dr. Peter Jeffery); Graz, UB 1002, fols. 51r–56r (s. XII); and Vic, Mus. Episcopal Frag. XII (s. XII, kindly brought to my attention by Dr. Jeffery).

[166]E.g., in Munich, Clm 14628, fol. 107v, on which see Hanssens, 3:296f.

[167]Hanssens, 3:297f.

[168]See Adolph Franz, *Die Messe im deutschen Mittelalter: Beiträge zur Geschichte der Liturgie und des religiösen Volkslebens* (Freiburg im. Br., 1902), pp. 408f.

There is now evidence to confirm these suspicions. First, we now know that the texts did circulate independently of the Mass commentary. In two ninth-century manuscripts, one whose provenance is Limoges, Paris, BN Lat. 1248, fols. 24v–25r (s. IXm., northern France)[169] and the other from Monte Cassino, 323, p. 56 (s. IX$^2$, mid-Italy),[170] the two texts stand alone not distantly removed from other Mass commentaries. Just as interesting is their appearance in the tenth-century English manuscript, London, BL Royal 8.C.III, fol. 61r–v,[171] where they are found not far from a version of a text on the seven heavens resembling Virgil of Salzburg's *Liber de numeris.*[172] But the suspicion that there is Irish influence behind the texts is further confirmed when it is discovered that the first text is in the *Collectio Sangermanensis.*[173] In the Paris codex of the *Sangermanensis* and in the Cologne extract, there is the title *Ordo missae a sancto Petro apostolo institutus est. Pro quod causis caelebratur missa?* followed by the incipit "Pro multis causis." But in the Munich manuscript of the *Sangermanensis* extract only the title survives. This suggests that both title and the first text were separable and might partially explain why at least one of Hanssens's codices lacks the title.[174]

The second text on the daily offering of the Mass may have been suggested by one part of the *Sangermanensis,* but much closer is a section from a didactic tract on liturgical and doctrinal matters found in the late ninth- and tenth-century manuscripts, Monza, Bibl. cap. e-14/127, fol. 74r; Montpellier, BEM 387, fol. 55r (s. IX2/3, France); and London, BL Royal 8.C.III, fol. 57r:

| [Mass Exposition Preface] | [Didactic Liturgical Tract] |
|---|---|
| CUR COTIDIE ITERATUR ISTA OBLATIO. . . . Pro multis causis: prima, eo quod peccamus cotidie; secunda, eo quod corpus Christi paenitentibus post | Interr. Q[u]ur cottidie offertur corpus xpi et sanguis in ecclesia quando canimus missam? [Resp.] Idcirco cottidie offertur quia peccamus cottidie. septies enim |

---

[169]On this manuscript see Andrieu, *Ordines Romani,* 1:265–269.

[170]On this manuscript see Maurus Inguanez, *Codicum Casinensium manuscriptorum catalogus,* 2.2 (Monte Cassino, 1934), pp. 161f.

[171]See T. A. M. Bishop, "Notes on Cambridge Manuscripts, Part IV: MSS. Connected with St. Augustine's Canterbury," *Transactions of the Cambridge Bibliographical Society* 2 (1954–1958), 335f. and pl. XIVa.

[172]Fol. 62v, and see McNally, *Liber de numeris,* p. 123 and Munich, Clm 14276, fol. 10r–v. In the London manuscript the incipit for the text is "De septem spatiis celorum Virgilius dixit . . . ."

[173]Reynolds, *Ordinals of Christ,* p. 40, n. 19.

[174]Cf. Nürnberger, p. 176. Also cf. the *Collectio Hibernensis* 2.9, Wasserschleben, pp. 14f.

| | |
|---|---|
| peccata offerre iubeatur, ut salutem per corpus Christi inveniant, atque exeant post paenitentiam; tertia, ut magnum beneficium passionis Domini oblivioni non tradatur; quarta, ut similet diem iudicii in ecclesia, in quo iusti ab iniustis separabuntur.[175] | iustus in die cadit. ne obliuioni passio xpi traderetur. Ipse enim dicit: quotienscumque feceritis in meam commemorationem facietis; uel significat diem iudicii in ecclesia discernentem bonos et malos.[176] |

## (b)   Texts on the Ecclesiastical Hierarchy

Earlier it was noted that two texts on the ecclesiastical hierarchy from the *Hibernensis*, the Ordinal of Christ and *De distantia graduum*, were used in a variety of collections, including the *Sangermanensis*.[177] As an addendum to his article on the influence of the *Hibernensis* Fournier noted that another Ordinal of Christ that Carl Weyman had found in Munich, Clm 6330, seems to have been a modification of the one in the *Hibernensis*, L. 8, c. 1.[178] That particular Ordinal of Christ is, indeed, similar to that in the *Hibernensis* and *Sangermanensis*, but it has been shown since Fournier's article that it is of a distinct type and had an independent tradition of its own.[179] But the Ordinal of Christ in the *Hibernensis*, L. 8, c. 1, was, nonetheless, modified and used in a variety of Carolingian liturgical commentaries.

Even in the late eighth century the Ordinal of Christ in the *Hibernensis* was undergoing significant changes in the collection itself, where both a longer and shorter form can be found in the manuscripts.[180] But perhaps most surprising is the modification of the subdiaconal verse in the *Hibernensis* manuscript, Cologne, DB 210:[181]

[Cologne Ordinal]
De recapitulatione septem graduum. De gradibus in quibus Christus adfuit.
Hostiarius fuit quando aperiebat ostia inferni.

---

[175]Hanssens, 3:297f.

[176]Heinrich Brewer, *Das sogenannte Athanasianische Glaubensbekenntnis ein Werk des heiligen Ambrosius. Nebst zwei Beilagen: I. Über Zeit und Verfasser der sog. Tractatus Origenis und verwandter Schriften; II: Symbolgeschichtliche Dokumente aus einer Handschrift von Monza,* Forschungen zur christlichen Literatur-und Dogmengeschichte 9, 2 (Paderborn, 1909), pp. 188f.

[177]See above, p. 115.

[178]Fournier, "De l'influence," p. 53.

[179]As the Hibernian Chronological type, on which see Reynolds, *Ordinals of Christ*, pp. 58, 72.

[180]Reynolds, *Ordinals of Christ*, p. 62, n. 39.

[181]Ibid.

Exorcista fuit quando eiecit septem demonia de Maria Magdalene.
Lectur [*sic*] fuit quando aperiebat librum Isaiae.
Subdiaconus fuit quando subditus fuit patri matrique.
Diaconus fuit quando lavabit pedes apostolorum.
Presbiter fuit quando accepit panem et benedixit.
Episcopus fuit quando elevavit oculos et benedixit apostolus
[*sic*] suos quando ascendit in celum.[182]

Here Christ is said to have been the subdeacon when he was obedient to his father and mother, an explanation not found in any other medieval Ordinal of Christ yet reported.[183]

Since the Ordinal of Christ in the *Hibernensis* itself was being altered in various manuscripts of the collection, it is not surprising that in Carolingian manuscripts containing *liturgica* the form found in the *Hibernensis* was also being changed. One of the more unusual examples of this is found in a ninth-century codex that may have been written at Laon,[184] but was more likely compiled at Metz,[185] Metz, Bibl. mun. 351:

[Metz Ordinal]
De vii gradibus in quibus Christus fuit ecclesiae traditis.
    i.   Hostiarius fuit quando percussit et apperuit ianua inferni.
    ii.  Exorcista quando eiecit vii demonia de Maria Magdalena.
    iii. Lector quando apperuit librum Iesu Nave.
  iiii. Subdiaconus quando fecit vinum de aqua in Chana Galileae.
    v.  Diaconus quando lavit pedes discipulorum suorum.
   vi.  Sacerdos quando accepit panem ac fregit.
  vii. Episcopus quando levavit manus suas et benedixit panem
       et dedit discipulis ut adponerent turbis.[186]

In the grade of doorkeeper in this Ordinal it has been shown elsewhere that there are traces of the text in the B form of the *Hibernensis* found in Oxford, Bodl. Hatton 42.[187] But just as interesting is the modification of the dominical sanction for the bishop.

Much more unusual than any of the ninth-century Ordinals hitherto brought to light is one in the ninth-century Limoges manuscript, Paris,

[182]Fol. 29r–v.
[183]Cf. Reynolds, *Ordinals of Christ,* pp. 165–191.
[184]Cf. Contreni, *Cathedral School of Laon,* p. 62, n. 81.
[185]Cf. Roger E. Reynolds, "A Visual Epitome of the Eucharistic 'Ordo' from the Era of Charles the Bald: The Ivory Mass Cover of the *Drogo Sacramentary,*" in *Charles the Bald: Court and Kingdom, Papers Based on a Colloquium Held in London in April 1979,* ed. Margaret Gibson and Janet Nelson, British Archeological Reports 120 (Oxford, 1981), p. 266.
[186]Reynolds, *Ordinals of Christ,* pp. 75f.
[187]Reynolds, *Ordinals of Christ,* p. 76.

BN Lat. 1248 (s. IXm., northern France), which also contained the short preface to the Mass commentary mentioned earlier.[188]

[Limoges Ordinal]

INT. Fuit Christus rex et sacerdos? R. Utrumque fuit rex, fuit quia semetipsum regit et nos regimur ab illo. Sacerdos fuit quia semetipsum obtulit Deo in holocaustum.

INT. Fuit Christus hostiarius? Fuit. INT. Ubi? R. Post pasionem [*sic*] suam quando aparuit portas inferni et dixit Tollite portas principes vestras.

INT. Fuit Christus exorcista? R. Fuit. INT. Ubi? R. Quando septem eieccit demon[es] de Maria Magdalene.

INT. Fuit Christus acolitus? R. Fuit. INT. Ubi? R. Quando fidelibus suis predicavit suum evvangelium et dixit Erat lux vere que inluminat omnem hominem venientem in hunc mundum.

INT. Fuit Christus subdiaconus? R. Fuit. INT. Ubi? Quando de aqua vinum fecit in Cana Galileae.

INT. Fuit Christus diaconus? R. Fuit. INT. Ubi? Quando lavit pedes discipulorum suorum et tersit linteo quo erat precintus [*sic*].

. . . .

INT. Fuit Christus presbiter? R. Fuit. INT. Ubi? In cena sua quando fecit pasca iudeorum de agno et postea quum cenatum est, accepit panem in sanctas ac venerabiles manus suas benedixit et fregit et communicavit discipulis suis de suo sancto sacrificio novo.[189]

The similarity between this version and that in the *Hibernensis* is seen in the arrangement of the grades of doorkeeper and exorcist, where the exorcist is placed next to the doorkeeper. But the normal *Hibernensis* arrangement of the remainder of the grades has been completely changed, and both augmented and reduced with the addition of the acolyte and priest-king and the omission of the lector. The appearance of the acolyte here may be the first instance of this in an Ordinal of Christ antedating the tenth century;[190] and Christ as priest-king is unique to the Ordinals of Christ thus far reported.[191] Further, the dominical sanctions for the grades of doorkeeper and presbyter have been substantially changed from the *Hibernensis* text. The phrase "post pasionem suam" is reminiscent of the "ante passionem" placed before the doorkeeper in the Hibernian Chronological Ordinals of Christ.[192] And in the unique dominical

---

[188]See above, p. 126.
[189]Fols. 67v–68v.
[190]Cf. Reynolds, *Ordinals of Christ,* pp. 93f.
[191]Cf. Reynolds, *Ordinals of Christ*, pp. 165-191.
[192]Cf. Reynolds, *Ordinals of Christ*, p. 58.

sanction for the presbyter, who has been tacked on to a long series of interrogatories after the deacon, there may be traces of southern French-
Catalan or Insular influence in the reference to the "sanctas et
venerabiles manus suas."[193]

Not quite as unusual as the Limoges Ordinal of Christ but still related
to the one in the *Hibernensis* is one found in the Fleury liturgico-canoni-
cal manuscript already mentioned:[194]

[Fleury Ordinal]
De septem gradus. Hic sunt septem gradus in quibus Christus
adfuit.
Hostiarius quando in templo.
Lector quando legit librum Isaiae prophete.
Exorcista quando eiecit septem demonia de Maria Magdalenae.
Subdiaconus quando fecit vinum de aqua in Chana Galilaeae.
Diaconus quando lavit pedes discipulorum.
Sacerdos quando obtulit corpus suum in crucae.
Episcopus fuit quando accepit panem et benedixit dedit
discipulis suis et elevatis manibus benedixit eos et post resur-
rectionem suam a montem Oliveti et ferebatur in caelum.[195]

It has elsewhere been pointed out that the dominical sanctions for the
grades of lector through deacon in the Fleury Ordinal are simply those of
the *Hibernensis* and that those for the grades of doorkeeper, *sacerdos*,
and bishop are extremely unusual for ninth-century texts. But just as important is the modification of the arrangement of the lector and exorcist,
which are placed in the Romano-Gallican sequence of orders that was being imposed in the ninth century on most texts describing the ecclesiastical hierarchy.[196]

This same Romano-Gallican sequence of the lector and exorcist in an
Ordinal of Christ is found in the *Collectaneum* attributed to Bede:

["Bede's" Ordinal]
Septem sunt gradus in quibus Christus adfuit.
Ostiarius fuit quando destruxit ostia inferni et ligavit diabolum.
Lector fuit quando aperuit librum Isaiae prophetae in quo in-
venit Spiritus Domini super me, evangelizare pauperibus
misit me.
Exorcista fuit quando eiecit septem demonia de Maria Magdalene.

---

[193]Cf. Reynolds, *Ordinals of Christ*, pp. 50, 85.
[194]See above, pp. 113, 122.
[195]Reynolds, *Ordinals of Christ*, p. 82.
[196]Reynolds, *Ordinals of Christ*, p. 77, n. 28.

Acolythus fuit etc. [*sic*]
Subdiaconus fuit quando lavit pedes discipulorum suorum.
Diaconus fuit quando fecit de aqua vinum.
Presbyter fuit quando fregit panem discipulis suis, dicens Accipite et comedite, hoc est corpus meum.[197]

If this text was indeed written in the early eighth century by Bede — and there are substantial doubts that it was[198] — the appearance of the Romano-Gallican sequence of grades is extremely unusual. But just as strange is the "addition" of the acolyte and the omission of the bishop, a phenomenon common enough in Insular and Continental Ordinals from the eleventh century on, but extremely rare in the eighth and ninth centuries. Also the reversal of the pedilavium and miracle at Cana for the subdeacon and deacon is very unusual.

The Romano-Gallican sequence of the Fleury and "Bede" Ordinals was eventually "canonized" in the

[Hiberno-Gallican Hierarchical Ordinal]
Ordo de septem gradibus in quibus Christus ascendit.

i. Ostiarius fuit quando percutiebat portas inferni.
ii. Lector fuit quando aperuit librum Æsiae prophetae.
iii. Exorcista fuit quando eiecit septem demonia ex Maria Magdalenae.
iiii. Subdiaconus fuit quando fecit vinum de aqua in Chana Galileae.
v. Diaconus fuit quando lavit pedes discipulorum suorum.
vi. Sacerdos fuit quando accepit panem et benedixit.
vii. Episcopus fuit quando aelevavit manus suas et benedixit discipulos suos.[199]

The text, found in many manuscripts from the ninth through the twelfth century,[200] is clearly based on the *Collectio Hibernensis* L. 8, c. 1, but the sequence of the lector and exorcist has been reversed.

Incorporated into two of the most celebrated liturgical commentaries of the first half of the ninth century were verses from the Ordinal of Christ

---

[197]PL 94:555f.

[198]Cf. Eligius Dekkers and Aemilius Gaar, *Clavis patrum latinorum* 2 (= *Sacris Erudiri* 3, 1961) (Steenbrugge, 1961), 250f., nr. 1129.

[199]Reynolds, *Ordinals of Christ,* pp. 76f.

[200]To be added to the list of manuscripts in Reynolds, *Ordinals of Christ,* pp. 76f. n. 27, is Princeton University, Garrett 169, fols. 81v–82r (a manuscript from the eleventh or twelfth century from Admont, kindly brought to my attention by Professor Robert Somerville) containing both a Hiberno-Gallican Hierarchical Ordinal and the *De officiis vii graduum,* on which see below, p. 132. Also, Professor Kottje and Dr. Franz Kerff have generously brought to my attention another ninth-century manuscript which contains the two texts in the same recensions: Prag, Stání knihovna, Tepla Cod. 1, pp. 88–91, on which see Bischoff, *Schreibschulen,* 2:250.

taken from the Hiberno-Gallican version. In the *Disputatio puerorum* attributed to Alcuin verses from this form are pieced together with other material to make up a small text on the ecclesiastical hierarchy.[201] In the much more famous *Liber officialis* of Amalarius, Christ's lection and the pedilavium were used in a description of the ecclesiastical hierarchy in which the grades were arranged in the Romano-Gallican sequence.[202]

The other epitome of the ecclesiastical grades appearing in both the *Hibernensis* and *Sangermanensis* was the little text entitled *De distantia graduum*.[203] By the early ninth century this text was being modified in Carolingian *liturgica* in many of the same ways as the Ordinals of Christ. In a strange form found in the extract from the *Sangermanensis* in Albi, Bibl. Roch. 38bis, for example, the text of the *Hibernensis* form of the *De distantia graduum* has been modified in several sections:

> De distantia graduum. Episcopum decet iudicare et interpretari, consecrare et confirmare, ordinare et offerre.
> Sacerdotem oportet offerre, bene preesse et benedicere.
> Diaconum oportet evangelizare, ad altario [*sic*] ministrare, populo verbum Dei adnuntiare.
> Subdiaconum ministrare aquam altari diacono.
> Exorcistam oportet subicere demones et dicere his qui communicant aquam ministeria effundere.
> Lectorem oportet legere ei qui praedicat et lectiones, bene dicere panes et fructus novos.
> Ostiarium oportet tangere cloccas et aperire ecclesiam et sacrarium et codicem quod praedicatur aut legitur.
> Acolitum oportet cereos accendere et ante evangelium deportare.[204]

Besides several minor alterations in the verses for the *sacerdos* and deacon, the most important change has been the addition of the acolyte, in some respects reminiscent of the addition of the acolyte in the Limoges and perhaps the "Bede" Ordinals of Christ.[205]

Just as the Hiberno-Hispanic Hierarchical version of the Ordinals of Christ in the *Collectio Hibernensis* was being altered by the reversal in sequence of the exorcist and lector, so the *De distantia graduum* was changed in the early ninth century to correspond more nearly to the sequence of grades found in Romano-Gallican ordination rites. Hence,

---

[201] Reynolds, *Ordinals of Christ*, p. 79.
[202] Reynolds, *Ordinals of Christ*, pp. 77f.
[203] See above, p. 115.
[204] Reynolds, *"De officiis vii graduum,"* p. 137.
[205] See above, pp. 129f.

there came into being a proto-pontifical form of the *De distantia graduum* in which the text was rechristened as the *De officiis septem graduum* and the verses arranged from lowest doorkeeper to highest bishop. But most important, the Romano-Gallican sequence of grades was followed.[206]

This same sequence was used, as has been seen, in the ordering of grades in the Alcuinian *Disputatio puerorum*, a liturgical exposition whose manuscript tradition is largely bound up with southeastern Germany.[207] Into this text there was inserted a highly modified fragment of the *De distantia graduum*, "Oportet enim illis [subdiaconibus] apostolum legere, honestare altare, et aquam praeparare in ministerio altaris."[208] This same fragment also appears in the so-called *Collection of Laon*, which, as was earlier seen, contained other extracts from the *Hibernensis*.[209]

## Conclusion

"Naturam expellas furca, tamen usque recurret" is an old adage perhaps better suited to farming than to canon law texts, but in our study we have seen how it might also be applicable to the *Collectio Hibernensis* in the Carolingian period. Despite the promotion by the Carolingian rulers of Roman canonical texts and their apparent disapproval of the Irish, the *Hibernensis* continued to flourish and luxuriate in a variety of contexts both canonical and literary as well as geographical. We have seen, for example, how the collection was quickly modified and disguised in abridgments. Then, useful excerpta were incorporated or hidden within many other collections, including the ancient *Collectio Vetus Gallica*, which seems to have been the quasi-official Frankish systematic collection of the Carolingians, or such newly composed collections as the *Collection of Laon*. Extracts of *Hibernensis* texts dealing with subjects inadequately covered in the "officially" promulgated collections also cropped up in isolated contexts, especially chapters dealing with matrimony and the ecclesiastical hierarchy. As a source of biblical and patristic citations we have seen, moreover, how the *Hibernensis* was used within Carolingian florilegia and biblical commentaries. And finally, we saw how texts from the *Hibernensis* and its derivative, the *Collectio Sangermanensis*, were cast in interrogatory forms to further the Carolingian educational intention to instruct the clergy on sacramental topics ranging from the Mass to sacred orders.

---

[206]Reynolds, "*De officiis vii graduum*," pp. 135f.
[207]See Reynolds, "Canon Law Collections," p. 29.
[208]Reynolds, "*De officiis vii graduum*," p. 139.
[209]Ibid. See above, p. 112.

By examining the origins of the manuscripts of the *Collectio Hibernensis* and its derivatives according to geographical distribution, it has also been found that in the late eighth and ninth century the collection flourished especially in those localities and areas with long Celtic traditions or where the "officially" promulgated Roman texts seem to have been poorly represented in the manuscripts. Hence, St. Gall, Reichenau, Brittany and southeastern Germany with their long Celtic traditions and western and southern France with their relative paucity of manuscripts of the *Collectio Dionysio-Hadriana* all seem to have been areas where texts of the *Hibernensis* were copied and used. Even in northern France, where one might have expected the *Hibernensis* to have disappeared entirely, manuscripts of it under a variety of guises just enumerated were made. But perhaps the most surprising flowering of the *Hibernensis* took place in a geographical region over which the Carolingians claimed domination but which has not been noted here thus far because the only extant manuscripts date to the tenth century and beyond. Fournier in his "De l'influence de la collection irlandaise" and in his later article, "Un groupe de recueils canoniques italiens des $X^e$ et $XI^e$ siècles,"[210] dealt with these texts, all from central and southern Italy, but did not dwell on the fact that they were probably based on Carolingian models of the *Hibernensis* that seem to have circulated widely in those areas. These texts that Fournier studied are in the collection of Rome, Bibl. Vallicelliana T. XVIII, famous for its recension of the B Form of the *Hibernensis,*[211] the *Collection in Nine Books* of the Beneventan codex, Vatican, Vat. Lat. 1349,[212] the *Collection in Five Books,*[213] and their nearly dozen derivatives.[214] Beyond these collections that Fournier treated as *Hibernensis* derivatives are several found more recently, such as the *Collection of Rieti*, written in Beneventan script,[215] and the *Multiloquiorum of Farfa.*[216] But most important are five additional Italian manuscripts with extracts from the *Hibernensis* itself. One of these,

[210]*Mémoires de l'Académie des Inscriptions et Belles-Lettres* 40 (1916), 95–212.

[211]For the date of this codex see E. A. Loew, *The Beneventan Script, a History of the South Italian Minuscule*, 2nd ed. Virginia Brown *II Hand List of Beneventan MSS.*, Sussidi eruditi 34 (Rome, 1980), p. 131.

[212]For the date of this manuscript see Loew-Brown, *Beneventan Script*, p. 145.

[213]A partial edition of this collection may be found in Mario Fornasari, *Collectio canonum in V libris: Libri I-III*, Corpus christianorum, Cont. med. 6 (Turnhout, 1970).

[214]See Fournier, "Un groupe," pp. 190–208.

[215]On this collection see Reynolds, "Basil," p. 526.

[216]On this collection see Roger E. Reynolds, "The 'Isidorian' *Epistula ad Leudefredum*: An Early Medieval Epitome of the Clerical Duties," *Mediaeval Studies* 41 (1979), 306.

Vatican, Vat. Ottob. 6, is a tenth-century manuscript from Nonantola with miscellaneous texts drawn from the *Hibernensis* from beginning to end.[217] The second, Vatican, Vat. Lat. 4162, has *Hibernensis* texts on the higher grades of the ecclesiastical hierarchy.[218] The third and fourth manuscripts, Florence BML VII sin. 1, and Calci 11 Archivio della Certosa, are Italian manuscripts of Burchard's *Decretum* to which extracts from the *Hibernensis* LL. 11–18 have been added.[219] The fifth codex, the early eleventh-century manuscript of the collection of Vatican, Archivio San Pietro H 58, with its extracts from the *Hibernensis*, LL. 1–10, cheek by jowl on "Sedulius in Carmen Alpha," is most surprising because it seems to have been written in Rome itself.[220] In the geographical area and in the city itself, then, where the Carolingians would have expected the Romanity of the ancient canonical collections to have obliterated traces of other collections, the leavening influence of the Irish collections of canons continued to be felt long after Charlemagne and his contemporaries.

[217]See Roger E. Reynolds, "Excerpta from the *Collectio Hibernensis* in Three Vatican Manuscripts," *Bulletin of Medieval Canon Law*, n.s. 5 (1975), 2f.

[218]Reynolds, "Excerpta," pp. 3f.

[219]Gérard Fransen, "Manuscrits des collections canoniques," *Bulletin of Medieval Canon Law*, n.s. 6 (1976), 67; and cf. Hubert Mordek, "Handschriftenforschungen in Italien," *QFIAB* 51 (1972), 637, 646.

[220]Reynolds, "Excerpta," pp. 4–9; and Kottje, *Bussbücher Halitgars*, pp. 65–69. For Professor Bischoff's dating of this manuscript, see Damien Sicard, *La Liturgie de la mort dans l'église latine des origines à la réforme carolingienne,* Liturgiewissenschaftliche Quellen und Forschungen 63 (Münster/W., 1978), pp. xiv, 115, n. 33.

# Pseudo-Dionysius, Gregory of Nyssa, and Maximus the Confessor in the Works of John Scottus Eriugena

Edouard Jeauneau

## Introduction

The man about whom I am going to speak today is probably one of the most prominent and puzzling figures in the intellectual history of the early Middle Ages.[1] Born in Ireland, John Scottus spent his entire literary career on the Continent (850–877 ca.). His earlier background was certainly Irish: his script, if we trust the most recent studies,[2] his attitude towards the Bible and his esteem for the "Book of Nature" are all undoubtedly Irish. On the other hand, John was a son of Carolingian culture. But we must say more. This Irishman is for us a witness to the high degree of learning attained by the movement begun by Charlemagne and his court, a movement generally referred to as a renaissance. Although the relevance of the term for this period has been challenged by historians, I think it practical to use it. It is, however, not out of place to stress differences between the cultural achievement of the time of

---

[1] For a general view of John Scottus and his works, see Maïeul Cappuyns, *Jean Scot Erigène, sa vie, son oeuvre, sa pensée* (Louvain-Paris, 1933), and Edouard Jeauneau, *Jean Scot, Homélie sur le prologue de Jean*, Sources chrétiennes 151 (Paris, 1969), 1–50. For a bibliography, see Mary Brennan, "A Bibliography of Publications in the Field of Eriugenian Studies, 1800–1975," *Studi medievali*, ser. 3, 18 (1977), 401–447.

[2] Terence A. M. Bishop, "Autographa of John the Scot," in *Jean Scot Erigène et l'histoire de la philosophie*, ed. René Roques (Paris, 1977), pp. 89–94; Bernhard Bischoff, "Irische Schreiber im Karolingerreich," ibid., pp. 47–58; Jean Vezin, "A propos des manuscrits de Jean Scot . . . ," ibid., pp. 95–99.

Charlemagne and that of the time of Charles the Bald. It would not be in-
appropriate to say that if the reign of Charlemagne was the springtime of
the Carolingian renaissance, the reign of Charles the Bald was its
glorious summer. Nor did this summer lack one of the most striking
features of that later renaissance, the renaissance of the fifteenth century, that is to say, the revival of the study of Greek.[3] In this, we have
one of the chief differences between the cultural inclinations of the court
of Charlemagne and that of Charles the Bald. If under Charlemagne
Latin letters were restored, under the patronage of Charles the Bald,
Greek patristic literature found readers and translators. Of course, at the
court of Charlemagne there was some interest in the Greek. Imperial ac-
clamations, for instance, were sometimes sung in Greek. There were contacts between the two language groups from time to time. In 781, when
the Byzantine empress Irene arranged for her son Constantine to marry
Rothrud, a daughter of Charlemagne, she sent the eunuch Eliseus to the
West, in order to teach the young Frankish princess how to write and
speak Greek. Charlemagne himself, we are told, attempted to learn
Greek. But this was a timid beginning in comparison with the study of
Greek which was to follow. Aided by the patronage of Charles the Bald,
the study of Greek can be found in those schools in contact with his
court, such as the Abbey of St. Denis, the Cathedral of Laon and the
monastery of St. Médard of Soissons. The most outstanding scholar of
Greek, working under Charles the Bald, was John Scottus Eriugena.[4]
Yet, the Greek texts available to him were not those of classical authors,
but rather those of the New Testament and the patristic period. We must
not imagine that the "sacred nectar of the Greeks,"[5] from which John
drew, came from the works of Homer, Plato or Aristotle. Access to
classical Greek was denied him. Apart from some books of the Holy
Scripture, he could only read in Greek the writings of the Greek Fathers,
such as the complete works of the Pseudo-Dionysius and a few works of
Maximus the Confessor, Gregory of Nyssa, Epiphanius of Salamis and,
perhaps, Basil of Caesarea. Hence, we shall concentrate on three of these

---

[3]Bernhard Bischoff, "Das griechische Element in der abendländischen Bildung des Mittelalters," *Mittelalterliche Studien* 2 (Stuttgart, 1967), 246–275; Roberto Weiss, *Medieval
and Humanist Greek* (Padua, 1977); Walter Berschin, *Griechisch-lateinisches Mittelalter:
Von Hieronymus zu Nikolaus von Kues* (Munich-Bern, 1980).

[4]Gabriel Théry, "Scot Erigène traducteur de Denys," *Archivum Latinitatis Medii Aevi* 6
(1931), 185–278; Edouard Jeauneau, "Jean Scot Erigène et le grec," *Archivum Latinitatis
Medii Aevi* 41 (1979), 5–50.

[5]John Scottus, *Carmina* 7.1.1; MGH Poet. 3:547; PL 122:1029a.

Greek Fathers whom John Scottus translated, namely, Pseudo-Dionysius, Gregory of Nyssa and Maximus the Confessor.

The importance and, indeed, the originality of John Scottus lay in the
fact that he was, at once, a translator and a thinker, a philologist and a
philosopher. He was a thinker who, seeking to invigorate his thought by
recourse to Greek sources, became a translator. My intention here is to
examine this particular and, perhaps, unique aspect of Eriugena's position in the history of Western philosophy. John of Salisbury and Thomas
Aquinas, for instance, were eager to use new translations of Greek texts,
but these were made for them by others. John Scottus found in the act of
translating a new impulse for his thought. Neither his philosophical
vocabulary nor his world view would have been what they were, had he
not had to translate works as difficult as those of Dionysius and Maximus the Confessor. He admitted that Latin texts would have sent him to
sleep, had not king Charles awakened him and urged him to consider
"the pure and abundant Greek sources."[6] Certainly, the Irish scholar
needed little encouragement to carry out the king's wishes, since he was
already favorably disposed towards Greek learning. According to him,
Greek was both clearer (*manifestius*) and more adequate (*expressius*)
than Latin.[7] The adverb which combines both ideas, *significantius*, was
also used by St. Jerome when comparing Greek to Latin.[8] John obviously felt much sympathy for the Greek Fathers "who saw things with
greater insight [*acutius considerantes*] and expressed their thought with
greater precision [*expressiusque significantes*]."[9] In studying John Scottus's approach to the Greek Fathers, we are not dealing with philological
problems alone, nor are we acting as mere antiquarians. Rather, it is the
mystery inherent in the philosopher's act of creation which we are faced
with, and which forms the proper object of our enquiry; yes, a mystery,
because of the disparity between the elements employed and the
remarkable result achieved, that is to say, between Greek texts painfully
and often poorly translated and a sophisticated set of philosophical
speculations inspired by them. I should now like to consider two questions:
First, how did John Scottus become acquainted with Dionysius, Maximus

---

[6]John Scottus, *Epistola dedicatoria translationi Dionysii praefixa*, MGH Epp. 6:158,
36–159, 2; PL 122:1031c.
[7]John Scottus, *Expositiones in Hierarchiam caelestem* 9.199–203; CCM 31:139; PL 122:213a.
[8]See my article, "Jean Scot Erigène et le grec," p. 9, n. 18.
[9]John Scottus, *Periphyseon* 5.35; PL 122:955a.

the Confessor and Gregory of Nyssa? And secondly, how much and how deeply was he influenced by them?

*I*

*How did John Scottus become acquainted with Dionysius, Maximus the Confessor and Gregory of Nyssa?*

It seems unquestionable that the first of the Greek Fathers whom John Scottus had to translate was Dionysius. The works of this mysterious author reached the Frankish court in 827. That year, in Compiègne, ambassadors of the Byzantine emperor, Michael the Stammerer, presented Louis the Pious with a codex (now Paris, Bibliothèque Nationale, Grec 437) containing the works of the Pseudo-Areopagite. The book was solemnly transferred to the Abbey of St. Denis on the 8th of October 827, that is to say, on the eve of the feast of Saint Denys, patron saint of the Royal Abbey. Soon after its arrival at St. Denis, the abbot Hilduin translated this text or, as is more likely, had it translated.[10] But nothing is more quickly outdated than a translation, so that within thirty years there was need for a new one. Charles the Bald asked John Scottus to translate anew the works of Dionysius. This was a difficult task, because, as John himself tells us, he was, at that time, but an apprentice and a raw recruit in his knowledge of the Greek language: "rudes admodum tyrones elladicarum gymnasiarum."[11]

Yet, his translation was not entirely successful. A contemporary, Anastasius, the librarian of the Holy See, wrote a letter to Charles the Bald, in which, speaking of Eriugena's rendering, he said: "It is astonishing that this barbarian who lives at the frontier of the civilized world . . . could achieve this translation."[12] This condescending statement was followed by an even more critical comment. According to Anastasius, the Eriugenian translation needed itself to be translated: "quem interpretaturus susceperat adhuc redderet interpretandum."[13] In order to compensate for the obscurity of the translation, Anastasius sent to Charles the Bald a copy in which the Latin text was accompanied, in

[10]Gabriel Théry, *Etudes dionysiennes: Hilduin traducteur de Denys*, vols. 1 and 2 (Paris, 1932 and 1937).
[11]John Scottus, *Epistola*, MGH Epp. 6:159, 3–4; PL 122:1031c.
[12]Anastasius, *Epistola ad Karolum regem*, MGH Epp. 7:431, 18–21; PL 122:1027–1028.
[13]Anastasius, *Epistola*, MGH Epp. 7:432, 8–9; PL 122:1027–1028.

the margins, not only by his own emendations, but also by glosses of Maximus the Confessor, translated by himself.[14] Presumably, Charles the Bald showed both the letter of Anastasius and the copy of Dionysius to John Scottus. Imagine that you were in John Scottus's place. You receive an extremely critical appraisal of your work, accompanied by corrections and scholia. Would you not desire to become more familiar with the man whose scholia had proved so helpful and had clarified so many difficult passages of Dionysius? Most likely, this is just what John Scottus felt: he wanted to get hold of the works of Maximus. The first work which he was able to obtain was the *Ambigua ad Iohannem*. He soon realized that the task of translating such a work was a bolder and still more audacious undertaking than that of translating Dionysius. But he also knew that Maximus, however obscure himself, was able to illuminate many of the obscurities in Dionysius. He says: "Perhaps, I would not have faced so dark a gloom, had I not noticed that, very often, the blessed Maximus quotes the most obscure sentences of the divine theologian Dionysius the Areopagite. He explains them so clearly that I could not doubt that Divine Mercy . . . had arranged everything in order that the passages which, in the writings of the blessed Dionysius, seemed to me the most difficult, almost unfathomable and ungraspable, had their meaning laid bare thanks to the explanations of the most wise Maximus."[15] Thus, for John Scottus, there was, between Dionysius and Maximus, a kind of providential continuity. His great admiration for Dionysius led him to Maximus. Among the works of Maximus, he translated the *Ambigua ad Iohannem* and the *Quaestiones ad Thalassium*.[16]

If Dionysius led him to Maximus, Maximus seems to have led him to Gregory of Nyssa. The *Ambigua ad Iohannem* is a set of difficulties (ἄπορα, ἀπορίαι), taken from the works of Gregory of Nazianzus. But, for some reason, John Scottus thought that Gregory of Nazianzus (also called

---

[14]In the copy sent by Anastasius, the text of Dionysius was accompanied by two sets of *scholia:* one by Maximus, the other by John of Scythopolis. Anastasius himself carefully distinguished the *scholia* of Maximus from those of John of Scythopolis: MGH Epp. 7:432, 9–22; PL 122:1027–1028. Unfortunately, the marks added by Anastasius are no longer to be found in our manuscripts. Hence the problem arises of the authenticity of the *Scholia Maximi*: Hans Urs von Balthasar, *Kosmische Liturgie*, 2nd ed. (Einsiedeln, 1961), pp. 644–672.

[15]John Scottus, *Epistola dedicatoria translationi Maximi praefixa*, MGH Epp. 6:162, 6–14; PL 122:1195a–b.

[16]An edition of the *Quaestiones ad Thalassium* with the translation by John Scottus is being prepared by Carl Laga and Carlos Steel for the Corpus christianorum, Seria graeca; the first volume (*Quaestiones* 1–55) came out in 1980. For the same series, Raphael Bracke and I have in hand an edition of the *Ambigua ad Iohannem*.

the Theologian) and Gregory of Nyssa were one and the same man. This
confusion could have arisen from the *Historia tripartita* of Cassiodorus.[17]
Having noticed that Maximus held Gregory the Theologian in high
esteem, John, naturally, sought to read and to translate one of his works.
How he came across a Greek manuscript of the Περὶ κατασκευῆς
ἀνθρώπου (*De hominis opificio*) of Gregory of Nyssa, is hard to say. We
know only that he did, that he translated it, and that he believed that the
author was Gregory the Theologian.

I do not want to bore you with details about the manuscripts of
Eriugena's works; nevertheless, I cannot resist the temptation to share
with you a piece of good news regarding Eriugena's translation of the
Περὶ κατασκευῆς ἀνθρώπου of Gregory of Nyssa, called, according to
John Scottus's terminology, *De imagine*. Until recently, we knew only
one manuscript of this translation: MS Bamberg, Staatsbibliothek
*Patristik* 78 (B.IV.13), from the end of the ninth century, upon which
Dom Cappuyns based his edition of 1965.[18] During a colloquium held at
Cluny in 1972, I had occasion to report on some research I had done on
the twelfth-century catalogue of the library of Cluny. I concluded that in
the abbey of Cluny, in the middle of the twelfth century, there were at
least six manuscripts containing works by John Scottus Eriugena.[19]
Three of them were still extant, but three were lost. Among the lost
manuscripts, one should count the translation of Gregory of Nyssa. Using notes taken by Dom Anselme Le Michel when he visited Cluny in
1644-1645, I was able to give a rough description of this lost manuscript,
in the hope—a very small one, I must confess—that, some day, by
chance, the manuscript might resurface. But I was very skeptical. It so
happened however that, last spring, while I was reading in the Bibliothèque Mazarine in Paris, a friend of mine called me aside and told me that
he had recently seen the Cluniac manuscript of Eriugena's translation.
The owner of the manuscript had offered to sell it to the Bibliothèque
Nationale. But the matter had to be kept secret, until the negotiations
were concluded. At the first opportunity, I hastened to the Bibliothèque

[17]See my article, "La division des sexes chez Grégoire de Nysse et chez Jean Scot
Erigène," in *Eriugena: Studien zu seinen Quellen*, ed. Werner Beierwaltes (Heidelberg,
1980), pp. 33-34.

[18]Maïeul Cappuyns, "Le *De imagine* de Grégoire de Nysse traduit par Jean Scot
Erigène," *Recherches de théologie ancienne et médiévale* 32 (1965), 205-262.

[19]Edouard Jeauneau, "La bibliothèque de Cluny et les oeuvres de l'Erigène," in *Pierre
Abélard, Pierre le Vénérable*, ed. Jean Jolivet and René Louis (Paris, 1975), pp. 703-725.

Nationale and asked for permission to see the manuscript. You can understand how excited I was. The Keepers of the Manuscripts left me alone with the precious book, so that I might enjoy the moment in peace. After a while, they came into the room where I was, to discover my reaction: "Well," I told them, "imagine a theologian who has written a treatise on the beatific vision. One day he dies and goes to heaven, where he enjoys the vision of God. Asked what he was thinking, he replies: It is exactly as I described it." Perhaps, I overstepped the bounds of modesty! In any event, the lost sheep has now returned to the fold. And since, in our society, to be in the fold means to be registered, the lost sheep is now: Paris, Bibliothèque Nationale, nouvelles acquisitions latines, MS 2664.[20] Admittedly, this Cluniac manuscript of the eleventh century will probably not add anything to our knowledge of the text, as edited by Cappuyns.[21] It is, nevertheless, important to note that the presence of such a manuscript in Cluny made a reading of Gregory of Nyssa possible for people who frequented the great abbey.

*II*

*How much and how deeply was John Scottus influenced by Dionysius, Gregory of Nyssa and Maximus the Confessor?*

There are two ways of approaching this question: in terms of the quantity of borrowing, and in terms of the quality of reading. You will perhaps object that a qualitative approach is better and surer than a quantitative one, and that we could dispense with the latter. Nevertheless, quality can be more adequately judged when considered in opposition to quantity. I consider it, therefore, useful to begin with a quantitative estimate of the influence which the three Greek Fathers mentioned above exerted on John Scottus. By a quantitative estimate, I mean the quantity of the Greek patristic texts which John Scottus actually quoted in his major work, the

---

[20]The manuscript was listed as number 1 in the catalogue for a sale at the *Hôtel Drouot* (Paris) on the second and third of December 1901: *Catalogue de livres anciens . . .* (Paris, Librairie Henri Leclerc, 1901), pp. 1–2. For this information, I am indebted to M. l'Abbé Raymond Etaix. Mr. Pierre Gasnault and Mr. François Avril kindly allowed me to examine the manuscript before its official acquisition by the Bibliothèque Nationale.

[21]In the Paris manuscript, Bibl. Nat. n.a.l. 2664, the text of Gregory of Nyssa's *De imagine* is incomplete, ending with the word *succumbere materie* (ed. Cappuyns, p. 245, 5). Moreover, because of the loss of the first folio, it begins with the words *ac firmitas* (ed. Cappuyns, p. 210, 37).

*Periphyseon*. The estimates I am going to offer you are based on the Floss edition of Eriugena's *Periphyseon* (Patrologia Latina, volume 122). But I should warn you that I will not be able to give you exact figures, only a rough approximation which, I hope, will not be too far removed from the truth.[22]

In the Floss edition, the *Periphyseon* itself occupies 589 columns. Of this total, quotations from Maximus the Confessor (*Ambigua ad Iohannem* only) fill 9 columns, those from Dionysius 10, and those from Gregory of Nyssa 15. In other words, the quotations from Maximus represent 1.55% of Eriugena's text, those from Dionysius 1.69%, and those from Gregory of Nyssa 2.66%. The comparison is unquestionably in favor of Gregory of Nyssa. Now, if we compare the percentages of each of these Greek texts quoted in the *Periphyseon*, the predominance of Gregory of Nyssa is still more remarkable: while only 5% of Maximus's *Ambigua ad Iohannem* was used in Eriugena's major work and only 6.5% of Dionysius's *Opera*, as much as 25% of Gregory of Nyssa's *De imagine* was quoted. Just a quarter! If we were to trust the quantitative approach, we should conclude that, of the three Greek Fathers with whom we are dealing, Gregory of Nyssa had the greatest impact on Eriugena's thought. We would, however, be wrong. If John Scottus quotes Gregory of Nyssa at length and on a greater scale than the two others, it is, perhaps, because he did not assimilate his thought as completely as he did that of Dionysius or that of Maximus. In other words, quantitative appraisals do not reveal how deeply John Scottus was influenced by these two Greek Fathers.

In fact, the influence of Dionysius was the formative one for him. What Eriugena learned from Dionysius is well known. To mention two aspects only: apophatic theology, that is, the superiority of negation over affirmation when speaking of God, and the Neoplatonic scheme of descent and ascent, procession and return. What is worth noticing is the manner in which John Scottus attempted to harmonize Augustine and Dionysius.[23]

---

[22]For a general appraisal of the influence exerted by Greek sources on John Scottus see Johannes Dräseke, *Johannes Scotus Erigena und dessen Gewährsmänner in seinem Werke De Divisione Naturae Libri V,* Studien zur Geschichte der Theologie und Kirche 9, 2 (Leipzig, 1902; reprint ed., Aalen, 1972); and Inglis P. Sheldon-Williams, "Eriugena's Greek Sources," in *The Mind of Eriugena*, ed. John J. O'Meara and Ludwig Bieler (Dublin, 1973), pp. 1–15.

[23]On the occasion of three colloquia organized by the Society for the Promotion of Eriugenian Studies (SPES) and held successively in Dublin (1970), Laon (1975), and Freiburg-im-Breisgau (1979), several scholars addressed themselves to Eriugena's use of Augustine. See, in particular, the papers of Goulven Madec, Joseph Moreau, John J. O'Meara, Robert Russell and Brian Stock in the collections already noted: *The Mind of Eriugena, Jean Scot Erigène et*

Both these Christian thinkers certainly belonged to the Neoplatonic tradition, but in different ways and subject to different influences: Augustine is closer to Plotinus and Porphyry, Dionysius closer to Proclus. Modern scholars are, perhaps, more sensitive to the nuances of thought which distinguish these two schools than was John Scottus. The Irishman, consciously or unconsciously, seems to have ignored the differences in order to stress the common tradition. Yet, nothing is more striking than the contrast between the Augustinian world view, according to which God is intimately united to the human mind — *interior intimo meo*[24] — and the hierarchical scheme of the Dionysian universe in which the Divine Light descends to the inferior orders only through a series of intermediaries.[25] John Scottus does not appear to have been aware of any discrepancy between Augustine and Dionysius on this point. He often quotes Augustine's *De uera religione*: "Between our mind, by which we know the Father, and the Truth, that is to say, the inward light through which we know Him, no creature intervenes."[26] Not only did John Scottus see no contradiction between this solemn affirmation and the hierarchical universe of Dionysius,[27] but he thought that such an affirmation could be supported by Dionysian texts, namely, *Mystic Theology.*[28] Similarly, when dealing with negative theology, John Scottus tends to fuse Augustinian and Dionysian texts, in order to establish his own doctrine. He says: "It is plainer than daylight that the Divine Ignorance is to be understood as nothing else than the incomprehensible and infinite Divine Knowledge. For what the Holy Fathers, I mean Augustine and Dionysius, say with total truth of God — Augustine says that He is better known by not knowing, Dionysius that His ignorance is true wisdom — should, in my opinion, be understood not only of the intellects which reverently and earnestly seek Him, but also of Himself."[29] In this passage, it is easy to distinguish the quotation of

---

*l'histoire de la philosophie* and *Eriugena: Studien zu seinen Quellen.* See also Goulven Madec, "Le dossier augustinien du *Periphyseon* de Jean Scot (livres 1-2)," *Recherches augustiniennes* 25 (1980), 241-264.

[24]Augustine, *Confessions* 3.6; CSEL 33:53, 10; PL 32:688.

[25]René Roques, *L'univers dionysien: Structure hiérarchique du monde selon le Pseudo-Denys* (Paris, 1954). For Proclus and Pseudo-Dionysius, see Henri D. Saffrey, "Nouveaux liens objectifs entre le Pseudo-Denys et Proclus," *Revue des sciences philosophiques et théologiques* 63 (1979), 3-16.

[26]Augustine, *De uera religione* 55 (113), lines 122-125; CCL 32:259; PL 34:172.

[27]John Scottus, *Expositiones in Hierarchiam caelestem* 4.404-412; CCM 31:75 (ed. J. Barbet).

[28]PG 3:997b6-1000a3; PL 122:1173a2-11. Cf. John Scottus, *Periphyseon* 4.5; PL 122:759c.

[29]*Periphyseon* 2.29; PL 122:597c-d; translation adapted from Inglis P. Sheldon-Williams, vol. 2 (Dublin, 1972), p. 163.

Augustine's *De ordine*[30] from that of Dionysius's *Epistle I*.[31] But, in another passage, taken from Eriugena's Commentary on St. John's Gospel,[32] the quotations are so intricately interwoven that it is almost impossible for the reader, unless aided by footnotes,[33] to distinguish the borrowings made from the two authors. John Scottus was the first, as far as I know, to blend Dionysian and Augustinian teachings in this way, becoming, therefore, the founder of a new kind of Neoplatonism, typically medieval.[34]

When we turn to Gregory of Nyssa, we discover that John Scottus also considered him in the light of his reading of Augustine. In the *Periphyseon*, Gregory of Nyssa is regarded as an equal of Augustine: "We know," Eriugena says, "that after the blessed Apostles, no one has enjoyed greater authority among the Greeks, in explaining Holy Scripture, than Gregory the Theologian [= Gregory of Nazianzus = Gregory of Nyssa], no one has enjoyed greater authority among the Latins than Augustine."[35] For those who know how highly Augustine was held in the esteem of the Latin world, this statement is the supreme compliment which could be paid by a Latin writer to a Greek Father. John Scottus was, however, not unaware of differences between these two giants of Christian exegesis. When dealing with the question of a terrestrial paradise, he noticed that Augustine and Gregory held opposite views. Augustine had taught that, at a determined time and in a determined place, there was a real terrestrial paradise. John Scottus disagreed with this opinion. For him, there was no time, no history at all before the Fall. Because it is the principle of History, if I may allow myself the expression, the Fall cannot be a part of History. Everything which the Bible relates as having happened before the Fall has, therefore, to be interpreted allegorically and not historically. In explaining the narrative of man's creation in such a way, John Scottus was conscious that he was unfaithful to the traditional exegesis of Genesis, authoritatively expressed by Augustine. In such a cause, a powerful ally was needed. Eriugena

---

[30]Augustine, *De ordine* 2.26.44; PL 32:1015.

[31]Pseudo-Dionysius, *Epistle I*; PG 3:1065a13–15; PL 122:1177b.

[32]PL 122:302b10–14.

[33]*Jean Scot, Commentaire sur l'évangile de Jean*, Sources chrétiennes 180 (Paris, 1972), p. 126, nn. 19–21.

[34]Joseph Koch, "Augustinischer und dionysischer Neuplatonismus und das Mittelalter," *Kant-Studien* 48 (1956–1957), 117–133. Stephen Gersh, *From Iamblichus to Eriugena: An Investigation of the Prehistory and Evolution of the Pseudo-Dionysian Tradition* (Leiden, 1978).

[35]*Periphyseon* 4.14; PL 122:804c-d.

found this ally in Gregory of Nyssa. In this instance, however, his purpose was not to convince his readers that Gregory of Nyssa was teaching the same doctrine as Augustine, but rather the contrary. Just as he had been inclined to overrate the consensus of Augustine and Dionysius, so now he was inclined to exaggerate the discrepancy between Augustine and Gregory of Nyssa. From Gregory, he borrowed many important philosophical themes, including: the concept of matter as a confluence of invisible realities, speculation about the division of the sexes, the theory of man as an image of God, the notion of *epectasis*. This last term, adapted from the Pauline ἐπεκτεινόμενος (Phil. 3.13), epitomizes a crucial theme in Gregory of Nyssa: a spiritual effort, the soul's straining towards the divine; a movement which requires us, however far we have reached already, to press ever onwards to a higher degree of love and of knowledge.[36]

But among the three Greek Fathers with whom we are dealing, the one who exerted the strongest influence on John Scottus was probably Maximus the Confessor. Yet, the influence of Dionysius was of the first importance: he it was who awakened John Scottus and kept him from dropping off over his Latin texts. But it is Maximus who, eventually, finished the work begun by Dionysius. The Dionysius whom John Scottus read was a Dionysius revised and corrected by Maximus.[37] In the preface to his translation of Maximus's *Ambigua ad Iohannem*, John Scottus spelt out the principal teachings for which he was indebted to Maximus.[38] These were generally points of doctrine which Maximus shared with Dionysius. But, in fact, he discovered in Maximus much more than that. Maximus introduced him to an original method of exegesis which had no equivalent in the Latin world. On the other hand, the philosophical vocabulary of Maximus was richer than that of Dionysius, more eclectic, drawing on an Aristotelian tradition as well as on a Platonic one. The theological problems dear to Maximus were soon dear to John Scottus, above all, the strong dyophysite doctrine, in whose defense Maximus had had to die in exile. The stress which Eriugena put upon correlating the mystery of God's becoming man (ἐνανθρώπησις) with the mystery of

---

[36]Jean Daniélou, *Platonisme et théologie mystique: Essai sur la doctrine spirituelle de saint Grégoire de Nysse* (Paris, 1944), pp. 309–327. Placide Deseille, "Epectase," *Dictionnaire de spiritualité*, 4:785–788.

[37]On the thought of Maximus himself, see *Maximus Confessor: Actes du Symposium sur Maxime le Confesseur, Fribourg, 2–5 septembre 1980*, ed. Felix Heinzer and Christoph von Schönborn (Fribourg, Switzerland, 1982).

[38]MGH Epp. 6:161–162; PL 122:1193d–1196c.

man's becoming God (θέωσις) goes back to Maximus. From Maximus John Scottus also drew the doctrine that we can know only that God is (*quia est*), not what He is (*quid sit*).[39]

However deeply Maximus influenced John Scottus, he was still not the highest authority for him; nor was any other Father of the Church. If there was one supreme authority he recognized, it was not that of a human book, but the authority of the Divine Book, the Bible. I would like to illustrate this by reading the prayer with which Eriugena ends his great work, the *Periphyseon*. I shall use a translation made by Professor John J. O'Meara, with a few minor changes.[40]

> O Lord Jesus, I ask of you no other reward, no other happiness, no other delight than to understand, purely and without any error of false speculation, your words which were inspired by your Holy Spirit. This is the sum of bliss for me and the end of perfect contemplation: for even the purest rational soul will find nothing beyond this, since there is nothing beyond this. As you are sought nowhere else more suitably than in your words, so you are found nowhere else more clearly than in them. There you live, and there you bring those who seek and love you; there you prepare for your elect spiritual banquets of true knowledge. And coming, you minister to them.
>
> And what, O Lord, is that coming of yours but an ascent through the infinite steps of your contemplation? — for you always come to the intellects of those who seek and find you. You are sought by them always, and are found always, and are always not found. You are found indeed in your theophanies,[41] in which in many different ways, as though in certain mirrors,[42] you encounter the minds of those who understand you in the way in which you allow yourself to be understood — not what you are, but what you are not, and that you are. But you are not found in your superessence, by which you surpass and excel all intellect wishing and ascending to comprehend you. You give to your followers your presence in an ineffable manner of appearing; you pass from them in the incomprehensible height and infinity of your being.

---

[39]See Sources chrétiennes 180, p. 128, n. 3.

[40]*Periphyseon* 5.38; PL 122:1010b12-d9. See John J. O'Meara, *Eriugena* (Dublin, 1969), pp. 60-61.

[41]For the notion of theophany, see Joaquín M. Alonso, "Teofanía y visión beata en Escoto Erigena," *Revista Española de Teologia* (Madrid) 10 (1950), 361-389, and 11 (1951), 255-281; Tullio Gregory, "Note sulla dottrina delle *teofanie* in Giovanni Scoto Eriugena," *Studi medievali*, ser. 3, 4 (1963), 75-91; Edouard Jeauneau, "Quisquiliae e Mazarinaeo Codice 561 depromptae," *Recherches de théologie ancienne et médiévale* 45 (1978), 123-124.

[42]1 Cor. 13.12.

It would be better to finish on this note, instead of breaking the rhythm of this passage with a pedantic comment. I have, nevertheless, to point out that, under this marvelous piece of poetry, some important philosophical and theological themes lie hidden. There is a play on words which no translation can express perfectly. The whole prayer is a meditation—in French, we would say *une élévation*—based on St. Luke 12.37, where we read:

> Blessed are those servants whom the master finds awake when
> he comes; truly, I say to you, he will gird himself and have
> them sit at table, and he will come and serve them.

"He will come and serve them." In Latin: "Et *transiens* ministrabit illis." The term which unlocks the cryptic meaning of Eriugena's passage is the verb *transire*. Five times in his prayer, not by accident, we find either *transitus* or *transire*.[43] The exegetical use of *transitus* points to Tyconius, whose *Regulae* were transmitted to the Middle Ages through Augustine.[44] The themes of negative theology, in the prayer, derive from Dionysius and Maximus. The desire to press ever onwards, to ascend through ever higher degrees of contemplation, takes us back to Gregory of Nyssa's *epectasis*. So, in this solemn moment, when John Scottus so passionately praises Holy Scripture, he shows clearly that he approached sacred texts with faith and devotion, to be sure, but also with a mind carefully prepared by an intense study of the liberal arts and by a sedulous reading of the Fathers. His desire was to be counted among those servants whom the Master finds awake when He comes for His spiritual banquet. The Greek authors, whom Charles the Bald encouraged him to translate, must have helped him to keep vigil.[45]

---

[43]"And coming, you minister to them": *illic transiens ministras eis* (PL 122:1010c9)—"that coming of yours": *iste . . . transitus tuus* (c10)—"you always come": *semper . . . transitum facis* (c13)—"you surpass and excel": *transis et exuperas* (d5)—"you pass from them": *transis ab eis* (d8).

[44]Edouard Jeauneau, *Quatre thèmes érigéniens* (Montreal-Paris, 1978), pp. 84–87.

[45]Dr. Paul Dutton very generously gave his time to revising the English of this paper. Miss Mary Brennan and Dr. Denis O'Brien kindly read a subsequent draft.

# The Problem of Speaking about God in John Scottus Eriugena

## Dominic J. O'Meara

Ubi affirmatio impropria, negatio uera[1]

In his great philosophical-theological dialogue, the *De diuisione naturae* (or *Periphyseon*, the more correct title),[2] John Scottus Eriugena presents us with two personages, a Master and Pupil, embarking together on an extraordinary quest. Their quest is for a truth (*inuestigatio ueritatis*) which is nothing less than knowledge of God and of the universe as a creation of God. In scale of conception and in sheer length, the *Periphyseon* matches this ambition, which is but natural and fundamental to the human condition in that the knowledge sought by the Master and Pupil is the happiness possessed by man before the Fall and promised him on his return to God. Eriugena sees the communal search by his Master and Pupil as a small part of, and modest contribution to, the history of the efforts of those before and after him already trying in this life to recover the lost knowledge.[3]

The Master and Pupil conduct their *inuestigatio ueritatis* by way of a long sequence of problems that they try to solve. The sequence is by no

---

[1]Alan of Lille, *Liber in distinctionibus dictionum theologicalium*, PL 210:687b.

[2]Abbreviated henceforth as *Per.* I will refer to the column and section numbers (and line numbers where appropriate) of the text in PL 122, quoting, for *Per.* 1, from the text and translation published by Inglis P. Sheldon-Williams, *Iohannis Scotti Eriugenae Periphyseon (De Diuisione Naturae) Liber primus* (Dublin, 1968). Extensive translations from *Per.* can be found in Myra L. Uhlfelder and Jean A. Potter, *John the Scot, Periphyseon: On the Division of Nature* (Indianapolis, 1976).

[3]For further details, see my article "L'Investigation et les investigateurs dans le *De divisione naturae* de Jean Scot Erigène," in *Jean Scot Erigène et l'histoire de la philosophie*, ed. René Roques (Paris, 1977), pp. 225–233.

means straightforward: some problems seem merely to be provoked by others, digressions rather than central issues, but in fact, like strands in a rope, they arise out of, overlap and lead back repeatedly to a set of major themes which serve to structure the work as a whole.[4] The major themes are introduced right at the beginning of the *Periphyseon* and have already been partially indicated. The knowledge sought by Master and Pupil is of God and his creation. This implies a distinction between creat*ing* and creat*ed* to which the Master gives full logical expression by combining the distinguished terms in all possible ways: what creates and is not created (God as beginning or source); what is created and creates (the "primordial causes"); what is created and does not create (creation in space and time); what does not create and is not created (God as end or final goal). Eriugena's well-known fourfold division reflects only in part a distinction between God and creation, since the first and last divisions both refer to the same object, namely, God; they reflect a difference in *our* ways of looking at God, and not a difference in God himself. The collapsing distinction between first and fourth divisions allows, however, for expression of the cyclic rhythm of the progression of creation from God and of its return to him, and thereby furnishes a metaphysically appropriate sequence to the subjects (God and creation) to be investigated by Master and Pupil in the *Periphyseon*: God as source (Book I); the primordial causes (Books II–III); spatio-temporal creation (Books III–IV); God as goal (Book V).[5]

Another major theme that appears in the opening pages of the *Periphyseon* is a distinction, among objects of inquiry, between what can be grasped by the senses and by intellect and what transcends the senses and intellect. This distinction is fundamental for Eriugena. The difference between *esse* and *non esse* is for him primarily a difference between what we can comprehend and what we can not. The objective basis of this distinction can be brought out if we refer to the difference between a manifestation (or appearance) and that which manifests itself

---

[4]"Conuoluuntur enim quaestiones inquirendo ueritatem": Eriugena, *Annotationes in Martianum*, ed. Cora E. Lutz (Cambridge, Mass., 1939), p. 88, 19–20. It must be admitted that the digressions can become so long—anticipating later discussions, recapitulating earlier ones—that the rope can become considerably entangled. Edouard Jeauneau, in his edition of Eriugena, *Homélie sur le Prologue de Jean* (Paris, 1969), p. 45, describes the composition of the *Per.* as a "trajectoire hélicoîdale." I have simplified the description of the general structure of the *Per.* in this paragraph.

[5]For a fuller discussion of what is said here and in the following paragraph, see my article "The Concept of *Natura* in John Scottus Eriugena," *Vivarium* 19 (1981), 126–145.

but is not the manifestation. Included in the class of "what is not," i.e., what transcends our grasp, is much of the subject matter of the *Periphyseon*: God, the primordial causes and even the essences of spatio-temporal objects. This fact means that in their very approach to their subject matter, the Master and Pupil will be confronted with a difficult and persistent problem: how can we go about thinking and talking about what is beyond our comprehension?

In this essay I would like to examine the way in which the Master and Pupil approach their inquiry into God as creator in Book I of the *Periphyseon*, in particular the way in which they think that anything can be said about what transcends human grasp. Almost all of Book I is concerned with this problem. The Master and Pupil find that very many things are said of God in Scripture and in the Church Fathers, and yet that these same texts also stress the inaccessibility and ineffability of the divine. As well as attempting to find some coherence in this long and, on the face of it, contradictory history of discourse about God, Eriugena must also satisfy us, his readers, that he himself can, with consistency, both say that nothing can be said of God, and at the same time make claims about God (including of course the claim that "nothing can be said of God").[6] By examining this question of consistency of claims, I hope to be able to point to an answer in Eriugena to the underlying issue, namely, the problem of how anything can be said about what transcends our grasp.

*I*

The problem of how anything can be said about God is approached in *Periphyseon* Book I mainly in the context of a discussion of the question as to whether or not all of the ten Aristotelian categories can be predicated of God.[7] The Master expresses dissatisfaction with the state of the question[8] and then proceeds to set forth the ways in which the

---

[6]The problem is succinctly stated by Anselm, *Monologion*, chapters 64 and 65. Cf. Augustine, *De doctrina christiana* 1.6.6: "Ac per hoc ne ineffabilis quidem dicendum est deus, quia et hoc cum dicitur aliquid dicitur" (quoted by Goulven Madec, "Le dossier augustinien du *Periphyseon* de Jean Scot (livres 1–2)," *Recherches augustiniennes* 15 [1980], 247).

[7]This question arises out of the more specific issue of the applicability of the category of relation to God, which itself arises out of discussion of the first division (God as creator) as trinity.

[8]"De hoc negotio nescio quis breuiter atque aperte potest dicere" (458a). The subject had been discussed, for example, by Augustine (see below, n. 34), Boethius (*De Trinitate* 4), and Alcuin (see below, n. 34). Eriugena was familiar with Augustine's treatment, which

categories may or may not be predicated of God. These ways are determined in function of Eriugena's interpretation of the two sorts of discourse about God that he found in the Pseudo-Dionysius, namely, affirmative (*kataphatic*) and negative (*apophatic*) theology.[9] It has been noted that, in contrast to Hilduin, his predecessor in translating the Pseudo-Dionysius, Eriugena fully realized the opposition between Dionysian *kataphatic* and *apophatic* theology.[10] This opposition Eriugena could find clearly emphasized in Maximus the Confessor, who also claimed, following the Pseudo-Dionysius, that the two theologies could be harmonized.[11] I would like to explore here, however, another background to Eriugena's interpretation of the character, opposition and eventual reconciliation of Dionysian *kataphatic* and *apophatic* theology, a background available to him primarily in *Latin* sources. In this section of the essay I will compare Eriugena's understanding of the nature and opposition of *kataphatic* and *apophatic* theology with the Aristotelian theory of affirmative and negative propositions.[12] In the next section (II) I will compare Eriugena's reconciliation of the two theologies with ideas to be found in Augustine, Martianus Capella and Alcuin. This in turn will lead in the final section (III) to an answer to the issue which is the topic of the essay.

Since a full-scale precise study of Eriugena's knowledge and use of the different available sources in Latin for Aristotelian logic remains to be done, it is not always possible at present to be certain about which particular logical texts underlie the Master's arguments in *Periphyseon* I.

---

he could with reason regard as neither brief nor very clear, and probably with Alcuin's, which, if brief, is not much clearer! The reasons for the Master's dissatisfaction will be brought out in section II below.

[9] On the Master's application of the categories to God in accordance with *kataphatic* and *apophatic* theology, see now J. F. Courtine, "La dimension spatiotemporelle dans la problématique catégoriale du *Du divisione naturae* de Jean Scot Erigène," *Les Etudes philosophiques* (1980), pp. 343–367.

[10] René Roques, *Libres sentiers vers L'érgènisme* (Rome, 1975), pp. 120–122. This book brings together some major articles published previously, and includes useful indices.

[11] Maximus, *Ambigua*, PG 91:1288c (discussed below, n. 47). An important text in this regard in the Pseudo-Dionysius is *Mystical Theology* 1.2; PG 3:1000b = PL 122:1173b7–13 in Eriugena's translation. I have not been able to see M. Wallace, "Affirmation and Negation in the Theology of St. Maximus the Confessor" (thesis, Rome, 1960).

[12] I am developing here an approach used by Werner Beierwaltes, "Das Problem des Absoluten Selbstbewusstseins bei Johannes Scotus Eriugena," in *Platonismus in der Philosophie des Mittelalters,* ed. Werner Beierwaltes (Darmstadt, 1969), pp. 488ff. (article originally published in *Philosophisches Jahrbuch* 73 (1965–1966), 264–284).

The *Categoriae decem*, a summary of Aristotle's *Categories* given currency and attributed to Augustine by Alcuin, is certainly being used, as is another text, Martianus Capella's summary of Aristotelian logic in Book IV of his *De nuptiis Philologiae et Mercurii*, a work much studied in Eriugena's day. Other sources should probably be added to this list, perhaps Boethius's translations of Porphyry's *Isagoge* and of Aristotle's *Categories* and *De interpretatione* (and perhaps even his commentaries on Aristotle's texts), but this matter has yet to be investigated thoroughly.[13] In what follows then I will attempt merely to bring out the general Aristotelian background to Eriugena's interpretation of Dionysian *kataphatic* and *apophatic* theology, without claiming at every point to have identified Eriugena's precise source.

Let us begin by looking at the way in which the Master in *Periphyseon* I understands *kataphatic* and *apophatic* theology.

> The one, that is ἀποφατική, denies that the Divine Essence or Substance is any one of the things that are, that is, of the things which can be discussed or understood; but the other, καταφατική, predicates of it all the things that are, and for that reason is called affirmative.[14]

This interpretation of *kataphatic* and *apophatic* theology appears to be based on a phrase in the Pseudo-Dionysius in which there is no explicit mention of κατάφασις and ἀπόφασις.[15] What is significant, however,

[13]For lists of early Medieval Latin sources for Aristotelian logic, see G. Schrimpf, "Wertung und Rezeption antiker Logik im Karolingerreich," *Logik, Ethik, Theorie der Geisteswissenschaften,* 11. Deutscher Kongress für Philosophie (1975) (Hamburg, 1977), pp. 451–452 (discussion also on pp. 452–453 of Alcuin's role); J. Marenbon, "John Scottus and the 'Categoriae Decem,'" in *Eriugena: Studien zu seinen Quellen*, ed. Werner Beierwaltes (Heidelberg, 1980), pp. 117–119. There is, for example, some disagreement about whether or not Eriugena was familiar with Boethius's translation of the *De interpretatione*: Jean Isaac, *Le Peri Hermeneias en Occident de Boèce à Saint Thomas* (Paris, 1953), p. 41, does not believe that he knew this text at first hand, but Isaac does not appear to have looked beyond Eriugena's two rather formulaic references to the *De interpretatione (Annotationes*, p. 93, 7–9; *Per.* 597c); Lutz, the editor of Eriugena's *Annotationes* (p. xxiii), thinks that he did know the Aristotelian text.

[14]"Vna quidem, id est ΑΠΟΦΑΤΙΚΗ, diuinam essentiam seu substantiam esse aliquid eorum quae sunt, id est quae dici aut intelligi possunt, negat; altera uero, ΚΑΤΑΦΑΤΙΚΗ, omnia quae sunt de ea praedicat et ideo affirmatiua dicitur" (*Per.* 458a13–b2). The same definition reappears in Eriugena's *Expositiones in Hierarchiam caelestem*, ed. Jeanne Barbet (Turnhout, 1975), 2, lines 517–524.

[15]*On Divine Names* 5.8, PG 3:824b4–6, which Eriugena translates as follows (PL 122:1150b8–9): "Proinde et omnia de eo et simul praedicantur, et nihil est existentium" (Eriugena's Greek MS has ὄντων, not πάντων as in the text in PG; see Gabriel Théry, *Etudes dionysiennes*, 2 [Paris, 1937], 242, n. 7).

is that Eriugena selects a Dionysian phrase which points to a particular context for the understanding of *kataphatic* and *apophatic* theology: the two theologies are in fact being assimilated to affirmative and negative propositions in Aristotelian logic. This may be seen more clearly if the above quotation is compared to Aristotle's definition of affirmative and negative propositions in the *De interpretatione* (in Boethius's translation):

> A simple statement [proposition] is speech signifying of it, that it is or is not something . . . . Affirmation is indeed saying something of something, whereas negation is denying something of something.[16]

There are indeed terminological indications of Eriugena's assimilation of Dionysian *kataphatic* and *apophatic* theology to Aristotelian affirmative and negative propositions. As well as using *affirmatio* and *negatio* to translate κατάφασις and ἀπόφασις in the Pseudo-Dionysius, he also consistently uses Cicero's terms *intentio* and *depulsio* which he found in Martianus Capella's discussion of affirmative and negative propositions.[17]

In Aristotle's *Categories* (chap. 10), affirmations and negations form one of four types of opposites. The three other types of opposites are mentioned by the Master shortly after his explanation of *kataphatic* and *apophatic* theology: relatives (*per relationem*), contraries (*per contrarietatem*) and privations (*per privationem*).[18] It appears that the fourth type of opposition, affirmation and negation, is not mentioned here[19]

---

[16]"Est autem simplex enuntiatio uox significatiua de eo quod est aliquid uel non est. . . . Adfirmatio uero est enuntiatio alicuius de aliquo, negatio uero enuntiatio alicuius ab aliquo" (Boethius, *Versio libri perihermenias* 5-6, ed. C. Meiser [Leipzig, 1877], p. 6, 9-13).

[17]See Martianus Capella, *De nuptiis* 4.399, ed. Adolph Dick and Jean Preaux (addenda) (Stuttgart, 1978), p. 193, 2-4; Eriugena, *Annotationes*, p. 101, 27ff.; Eriugena's translation of Pseudo-Dionysius *Mystical Theology* 1.2, PL 122:1173b11; *Per.* 461b2-5 (Sheldon-Williams, in his note ad. loc., pp. 230-231, misses the source in Martianus and thus has to come up with a tortuous explanation for the appearance of Cicero's term here). See also Théry, *Etudes*, p. 435 s.v. ἀπόφασις and p. 462 s.v.v. κατάφασις, καταφάσκω, and Roques, *Libres sentiers*, p. 121. Eriugena's assimilation of Dionysian *kataphatic* and *apophatic* theology to affirmative and negative propositions in Aristotelian logic may account for the curious fact that, in his Preface to his translation of the Pseudo-Dionysius, he refers to *kataphatic* and *apophatic* theology as the two parts of *logic*: "Vnde et in duas maximas logicae disciplinae diuitur partes, kataphaticam plane et apophaticam" (PL 122:1036a2-3; ed. Ernst L. Dümmler, MGH Epp. 6 Karolini aevi 4, p. 161, 21-23).

[18]*Per.* 458d-459a. See Martianus, *De nuptiis,* pp. 180, 3-184, 11 (similar texts can be found in the Pseudo-Augustine *Categoriae decem*, in Boethius's commentary on Aristotle's *Categories* and in Alcuin's *De dialectica*, for example).

[19]But it is found in MS P: "per negationem, ut est non est" (see Sheldon-Williams's app. crit. on p. 76 for lines 3-6).

because it is not relevant to the immediate context which has to do with the nonexistence of realities (not propositions) opposite to God.

However, some lines further on the opposition between affirmation and negation assumes central importance for the Master and Pupil. Before examining their treatment of this subject, I would like to return to Aristotle's *De interpretatione*. Having defined affirmative and negative propositions, Aristotle then deals with the opposition and contradiction between them. Contradiction is in fact the opposition between affirmation and negation.[20] By showing that there is no true opposition between an affirmation and a negation, apparent contradiction can be removed. Similarly, some pages after defining *kataphatic* and *apophatic* theology, the Master points to an apparent opposition between them,[21] which he then argues is not a true opposition and thus that there is no contradiction between affirmations and negations of God:

> For when you have reached the point of view of perfect reasoning you will see clearly enough that these two which seem to be the contraries of one another are in no way mutually opposed when they are applied to the Divine Nature . . . . For instance: καταφατική says: 'It is Truth'; ἀποφατική contradicts: 'It is not Truth.' Here there appears some kind of contradiction, but a closer investigation reveals that there is no conflict.[22]

In Aristotelian theory, a true contradiction between an affirmation and a negation is found when the same subject and the same predicate are involved in both propositions and when the terms are used without ambiguity.[23] In such a case the affirmation and negation cannot both be true. Eriugena shows his awareness of this principle later on in the *Periphyseon*:

> For contradictory propositions concerning the same subject . . . cannot both be true at the same time, or both false at the same time.[24]

[20]"Et sit hoc contradictio, adfirmatio et negatio oppositae" (Boethius's *Versio* 6, p. 6, 20–21).

[21]"Nonne uides haec duo, affirmationem uidelicet et negationem, sibi inuicem opposita esse?" (461b8–10).

[22]"Nam cum ad perfectae ratiocinationis contuitum perueneris, satis clarum considerabis haec duo quae uidentur inter se esse contraria nullo modo sibimet opponi dum circa diuinam naturam uersantur, sed per omnia in omnibus sibi inuicem consentiunt; et ut hoc apertius fiat paucis utamur exemplis. Verbi gratia: ΚΑΤΑΦΑΤΙΚΗ dicit: Veritas est; ΑΠΟΦΑΤΙΚΗ contradicit: Veritas non est. Hic uidetur quaedam forma contradictionis, sed dum intentius inspicitur nulla controuersia reperitur" (461b12–c6).

[23]See Boethius *Versio* 6, p. 6, 21–22; this is of course a rather bald summary of Aristotle's position and needs further qualification.

[24]"Non enim aut simul uera possunt esse, aut simul falsa contradictoria proloquia de subiecto eodem, siue uniuersaliter sint, siue particulariter" (*Per.* 4.756d7–757a1; this text is discussed

Equally, if an affirmation and a negation concern different subjects and/or different predicates, then they are not contradictory. Since, for Eriugena, the same subject must be referred to in affirmations and negations of God, we might expect that resolving the contradiction between them would involve exploiting differences in predicates as they are affirmed or denied of God. For example, "truth" when affirmed of God might not be identical in meaning with "truth" as denied of God. However, Eriugena resolves the contradiction between affirmations and negations of God, not by finding differences in the apparently identical *predicates* used, but by distinguishing between two different *kinds of predication*, namely, "proper" and what might be called "possible" predication:

> For that which says: 'It is Truth,' does not properly affirm that the Divine Substance is Truth, but that it can be called by such a name . . . . On the other hand, that which says: 'It is not Truth,' . . . does not deny that it is, but [denies] that it can properly be called Truth or properly be Truth.[25]

This text calls for some comment. Firstly, Eriugena's use of a distinction between "proper" and "possible" predication (*vocari proprie, vocari posse*), as a method for resolving apparent contradiction between propositions, is without equivalent in Aristotle. What then inspired this distinction, and why did he prefer it to a distinction between predicates as they are affirmed or denied of God? Secondly, to remove contradiction between affirmations and negations of God, Eriugena needed only to show that the claims made by them are not in true opposition, but are merely different.[26] However, the above passage suggests that Eriugena's reconciliation of *kataphatic* and *apophatic* predications tends in fact to reduce them to

---

briefly by Stephen Gersh, "Omnipresence in Eriugena: Some Reflections on Augustino-Maximian Elements in *Periphyseon*," *Eriugena. Studien*, pp. 64–65). Although Eriugena uses Martianus's term *proloquium* rather than Boethius's term *enuntiatio* for the Aristotelian πρότασις (proposition), here and elsewhere (see Edouard Jeauneau's edition of Eriugena's *Commentaire sur l'Evangile de Jean* [Paris, 1972], p. 100, n. 4), it is not apparent how he could derive his relatively refined (but not entirely correct) formulation of the Aristotelian principle of non-contradiction (see also his *Annot.*, p. 100, 31–33) from Martianus's summary or from the *Categoriae decem*. (On this principle, see Boethius's *Versio*, Chapter 7.) Even in his *Annot.* he seems to know more about Aristotelian logic than can be found in Martianus.

[25]"Nam quae dicit: Veritas est, non affirmat proprie diuinam substantiam ueritatem esse sed tali nomine . . . uocari posse . . . . Ea uero quae dicit: Veritas non est, . . . non eam negat esse, sed ueritatem nec uocari proprie nec esse" (461c–d).

[26]For a distinction between different and contradictory propositions see Boethius's *Versio* 7, p. 8, 8–10; Eriugena, *Per.* 4.756d–757a.

unity. Far from being contradictory, to affirm and to deny $X$ of God is in fact to say the same thing of God, namely that he can be, but is not properly said to be $X$:

> So the one says: 'It can be called this,' but does not say: 'It properly is this'; the other says: 'It is not this although it can be called after this.'[27]

In other words, there are not two different sorts of discourse about God, but really only one. What then prompted Eriugena to reduce Dionysian *kataphatic* and *apophatic* theology to unity?[28] Finally, I would like to note that an answer appears already to be at hand to the question I raised at the beginning about consistency of claims, since to reconcile *kataphatic* and *apophatic* propositions about God is to show that the claim "$X$ can be said of God" is consistent with the claim "nothing can be said of God." To be satisfied that this is so, however, we must know more about the reconciliation in question and more in particular about the distinction between "proper" and "possible" predication on which the reconciliation is based. For this purpose it will be useful to leave the *Periphyseon* temporarily and examine a work written some ten years earlier, i.e., in 850/851, in which Eriugena first showed his speculative abilities, the *De diuina praedestinatione*.

## II

The *De praedestinatione* is an important work for the study of the evolution of Eriugena's ideas. In respect both to the primarily Latin sources which it uses and to the positions it takes on certain issues, the *De praedestinatione* contrasts with the *Periphyseon* where much more use is

---

[27]"Vna igitur dicit: Hoc uocari potest, sed non dicit: Hoc proprie est; altera dicit: Hoc non est, quamuis ex hoc appelari potest" (461d4–7).

[28]In the following section I hope to suggest answers to these questions. With Eriugena's account of *kataphatic* and *apophatic* theology contrast Pseudo-Dionysius's own very different understanding of them, as presented, for example, by René Roques, *Structures théologiques de la Gnose à Richard de Saint-Victor* (Paris, 1962), pp. 140ff., 165ff. For Maximus's unification (but on different principles) of *kataphatic* and *apophatic* theology, see below, n. 47. One might think that if Eriugena here tends to unify the two theologies, he cannot maintain also the Dionysian principle of the superiority of *apophatic* to *kataphatic* theology (see, for instance, *Per.* 757d–758a). But for Eriugena, it is really the superiority of "proper" to "possible" predication that is in question, and insofar as he finds both modes of predication contained in both theologies, then superiority (of "proper" to "possible" predication) and unity (of *kataphatic* with *apophatic* theology) can be reconciled.

made of Greek sources (Pseudo-Dionysius, Maximus the Confessor, Gregory of Nyssa) and where discussion of the same issues is conducted on a more comprehensive and sophisticated level.[29] The problem of speaking about God is one such issue, since in Chapter 9 of the *De praedestinatione* Eriugena considers, echoing terminology in Augustine, "Whether it is properly [*proprie*] or improperly [*abusiue*] that God is said to have foreknown and predestined in Scripture and in the holy Fathers."[30] He meets this problem with the help of ideas he found in various Latin authors, Augustine, Martianus Capella and probably Alcuin. We can thus compare Eriugena's treatment of the problem of divine predication in the *De praedestinatione* with the Latin sources he uses there, contrasting then the position in the *De praedestinatione* with that

[29]We cannot simply compare the *De praedestinatione*, as an early work witnessing to an exclusively Latin culture, to the *Periphyseon,* as a later work reflecting the impact of Eriugena's study of Greek authors. As Professor Goulven Madec, the editor of the *De praed.,* has pointed out to me, the extent to which Eriugena was already familiar with Greek literature in the *De praed.* has yet to be determined. For signs of Greek learning, see Madec's edition (Turnhout, 1978), p. 6 (ad l.19–27), and pp. 111–112 (and app.); Hans Liebeschütz, in *The Cambridge History of Later Greek and Early Medieval Philosophy,* ed. Arthur H. Armstrong (Cambridge, 1967), pp. 584–585. I would like to add the following comparison between *De praed.* 9.12–14: "omnia paene siue nominum siue uerbum aliarumque orationis partium signa proprie de deo dici non posse" and *Per.* 456a3–5: "Ait enim [Dionysius]: Nulla uerborum seu nominum, seu quacunque articulatae uocis significatione summa omnium . . . essentia potest significari." Could we have here a quotation from the Pseudo-Dionysius in the *De praed.*? The matter is not simplified by the fact that the text in *Per.* 456a (see also 522c) does not appear to be a quotation, strictly speaking (see Sheldon-Williams's app. ad loc.; yet, following the edition in PL, he prints the text as if it were a true quotation). It seems to be an elaboration on Pseudo-Dionysius's idea that there is no *nomen* or *uerbum* for God (see Hilduin's and Eriugena's translation of ὄνομα and λόγος in *On Divine Names* 13.3 [PG 3:981a9] = PL 122:1170d1–2, quoted in *Per.* 510d1: "neque nomen eius est neque uerbum"). Yet this still leaves open the possibility that the sentence in *De praed.* 9.12–14 betrays a reading of the Pseudo-Dionysius. On the other hand, it seems implausible to suppose that Eriugena had completely mastered, say, the Pseudo-Dionysius and Maximus by 850, concealing this behind a show of Latin erudition more appropriate to the polemical context in which the *De praed.* was written. It is reasonable to assume that between 850 and the 860s Eriugena did in fact acquire the profound knowledge of Greek texts manifested in the *Per.* and that his knowledge of such texts (including perhaps the Pseudo-Dionysius) in 850 was rather rudimentary. Yet it might have been enough—a reading, for example, of the above Dionysian text, even if only in Hilduin's translation—to set the tone of his treatment in the *De praed.* 9.

[30]"Vtrum proprie an abusiue in sacris litteris et sanctae scripturae et sanctorum patrum dicatur deus praesciise uel praedestinasse" (*De praed.* 9.6–8); cf. Augustine, *De Trinitate* 7.5.10: "Vnde manifestum est deum abusiue substantiam uocari ut nomine usitatiore intelligatur essentia, quod uere ac proprie dicitur . . ." (referred to by G. Anders, *Darstellung und Kritik der Ansicht von Joh. Scotus Eriugena, dass die Kategorien nicht auf Gott anwendbar seien,* Inaugural-Dissertation, Jena [Sorau, 1877], p. 10, n. 16).

reached a decade later, in the 860s, in the *Periphyseon*.[31] This should yield a clearer view of the origins and structure of Eriugena's final position on the question in the *Periphyseon*.

At the beginning of *De praedestinatione* Chapter 9, Eriugena adopts as a general rule Augustine's statement that "nothing is worthily [*digne*] said of God."[32] He puts considerable emphasis on this inadequacy of human discourse about God, assimilating the inadequacy to an impropriety of human language about God, as can be seen from his expansion of the Augustinian statement:

> Almost [*paene*] all of the signs of nouns and verbs and the other parts of speech cannot properly [*proprie*] be said of God.[33]

The "almost" is probably not intended to have much weight, nor is the *propria* in a later sentence where some words for God are described as *quasi propria* (line 27), since the chapter is on the whole clear about the impropriety of human language about God. Among the (improper) predicates said of God are the *quasi propria*, which take what is best in human nature and refer it to the highest which is God, and words which are described as *aliena (hoc est translata)*, predicates said of God on the basis of similarity, contrariety and difference between creatures and God (lines 25–37). Thus prescience and predestination are transferred (*translatiue*) predications based on the spatio-temporal world and are therefore improper (*abusiue*) predications of God (lines 139–142).

Apart from the idea of an impropriety of human language of God, Eriugena could also find in Augustine and in Alcuin's summary of Augustine[34] a discussion of the applicability of the Aristotelian categories to God, in which a distinction was suggested between those categories said

---

[31]For comparisons between *De praed.* 9 and *Per.* 1, see already Maïeul Cappuyns, *Jean Scot Erigène* (Paris, 1933), pp. 317–321; Mario Dal Pra, *Scoto Eriugena*, 2nd ed. (Milan, 1951), pp. 116–122; René Roques, *Libres sentiers*, pp. 90–95; Bernard McGinn, "Negative Theology in John the Scot," *Studia patristica* 13, ed. E. Livingstone, Texte und Untersuchungen 116 (Berlin, 1975), pp. 233–237.

[32]"Nihil digne de deo dicitur" (9.12); for Augustine see Madec's app. ad loc.

[33]9.12–14 (Latin text quoted above, n. 29). Eriugena's shift from the inadequacy to the impropriety of language about God seems reasonable; it is less clear how Augustine can assert inadequacy and yet describe certain terms as properly predicated of God (see *De Trin.* 7.5.10, quoted in part above, n. 30).

[34]Augustine, *De Trin.* 5 (especially 5.8.9); 7.5.10; Alcuin, *De fide sanctae et indiuiduae Trinitatis* 1.15, PL 101:22c–24b, referred to by Maures Jacquin, "Le Neo-platonisme de Jean Scot," *Revue des sciences philosophiques et théologiques* 1 (1907), 683 (see Madec's app. p. 57 ad *De praed.* 9.36–38, and the next note below for Alcuin's dependence on Augustine). It seems improbable that Eriugena was not acquainted with Alcuin's text.

*proprie, translate* (or *translatiue*) and *relatiue* of God. In Augustine *essentia* (rather than the category of substance) and the category of making (*facere*) are said properly of God, whereas Alcuin accepts substance, as well as making, as said properly of God (but he adds: "If however anything can properly be said of him by human tongue").[35] Some words, those in the category of relation (*ad aliquid*), are said *relatiue* of God, and other categories, such as time and place, are predicated of God *translate* or *translatiue* on the basis of similarity, *per similitudines*. In Chapter 9 of the *De praedestinatione*, however, Eriugena is clear in his mind about the impropriety of predications of God. What counts as a proper predicate for Augustine and Alcuin can at best be *quasi proprium* for him. The somewhat anomalous class of predicates said *relatiue* is not retained, falling we must assume into the remaining class of predicates, which Eriugena keeps, namely, transferred (*translata*) predicates. Finally, this last class of predicates, which in Augustine and Alcuin are transferred to God from creatures on the basis of similarity, receives a more elaborate explanation in Eriugena: he identifies these transferred predicates with the *aliena uerba* described in Martianus Capella as applied outside their normal use not only on the basis of similarity but also on that of contrariety and difference.[36]

If Eriugena's account of predication of God in Chapter 9 of the *De praedestinatione* is in some respects more systematic and technical than the treatments of the subject in Augustine and Alcuin, it is nonetheless not entirely satisfactory. In particular, the class of *quasi propria* predicates retains, rather than dissipates, the tension in Augustine and Alcuin between, on the one hand, indications of the inadequacy and impropriety of human language about God, and, on the other hand, claims made for certain predicates as said properly of God.[37] In the *Periphyseon*, however, the impropriety of human language about God is stated much more insistently—Eriugena quotes the Pseudo-Dionysius as quite emphatic on this[38]—and the class of *quasi propria* predicates disappears

---

[35]"Si tamen de illo proprie aliquid dici ore hominis potest" (23a14–15, a phrase taken from Augustine, *De Trin.* 5.10.11).

[36]Martianus, *De nuptiis* 4.360, p. 165, 6ff. (referred to by Madec app. ad *De praed.* 9.36–38).

[37]Roques, *Libres sentiers*, p. 92, n. 2, thinks that Eriugena's position in the *De praed.* is a compromise related to the polemical context of the work and that in fact Eriugena is already *very* clear in the *De praed.* about the impropriety of language about God. Cf. McGinn, "Negative Theology," p. 234.

[38]*Per.* 456a (quoted and discussed above, n. 29); see Roques, *Libres sentiers*, p. 92.

(as did before the class of predicates said *relatiue*)[39] into the class of predicates which *can* be said of God, i.e., those transferred (*translatiue*) from creatures to God.[40]

There are other significant improvements to be noted in the account in *Periphyseon* Book I as contrasted with the position in *De praedestinatione* Chapter 9. The clarification of the general principle that nothing is properly predicated of God, but is only predicated *translatiue*, is emphasized in the Master's interpretation of Dionysian *kataphatic* and *apophatic* theology as concerning respectively what I have called above "possible" (i.e., transferred) and proper predication, or rather as each containing both kinds of predication, whose harmony is preserved by observing the distinction between them. Embodied now in *kataphatic* and *apophatic* theology, proper and transferred ("possible") predication provide the basis on which a full systematic answer can be given in the *Periphyseon* to the question, which was that of Augustine and Alcuin, of the applicability of the ten Aristotelian categories to God.

Finally, and perhaps most important of all, the nature of "possible" or transferred predication emerges more clearly in *Periphyseon* Book I. In the *De praedestinatione* Eriugena suggested, following Martianus Capella, that predicates could be used in a transferred sense of God on the basis of similarity, contrariety and difference between creatures and God. The Master in *Periphyseon* I develops this theory as follows:

> But not unreasonably, as we have often said, all things that are,
> from the highest to the lowest, can be spoken of him by a kind of
> similitude or dissimilitude or by contrariety or by opposition.[41]

"Dissimilitude" seems to be a Dionysian replacement for Martianus's "difference." "Opposition" is new, suggested perhaps by the Aristotelian

---

[39]However, the apparently different status of the category of relation causes difficulty in *Per.* 464cff. (note *relatiue* at 464c14).

[40]See Dal Pra, *Scoto*, p. 116. (In *Per.* 1 Eriugena tends to substitute for *translatiue* the more Hellenic equivalent *per metaphoram*.) *Nomina quasi propria* attempt another appearance in *Per.* 460c12–13 (see Cappuyns, *Jean Scot Erigène*, p. 328), this time as possibly applying to Dionysian "superlative" predicates, which are then shown, however, as belonging to *kataphatic* and especially *apophatic* predication. Hence, to the extent that they affirm something, they are improper. It has been pointed out that Eriugena exaggerates in *Per.* 463b in claiming that Augustine says that the categories are quite powerless where God is concerned (Madec, "Dossier," p. 247).

[41]"Non autem irrationabiliter, ut saepe diximus, omnia quae a summo usque deorsum sunt de eo dici possunt quadam similitudine aut dissimilitudine aut contrarietate aut oppositione" (510d).

distinction between opposites and contraries.[42] But what is especially
noteworthy is what the Master next says:

> Since he [God] is the source of all things which can be
> predicated of him.[43]

The causal relationship between God and creation is then the basis for all
"possible" or transferred predications of God. This idea Eriugena found
most clearly indicated in the Pseudo-Dionysius, if we can judge by the
Dionysian language used by the Master when he states immediately after
the first passage quoted above (p. 155):

> For that which is the cause can reasonably be expressed in
> terms of the things that are caused.[44]

This rule applies to predications in virtue of similarity as well as
predications in virtue of dissimilarity, contrariety and opposition: $X$ can
be predicated of God, not because it is like God, but because God is its
cause, the cause of things like him, as well as the cause of things
dissimilar to him or contrary. The causal relation between God and creation gives a metaphysical foundation and a unity to human discourse
about God: there can be no proper predications of God, only transferred
predications, and the latter all ultimately share the same character, being
based on creation as the creation of God.[45]

The main features of proper and "possible" or transferred predication
thus emerge. Proper predication presumably involves predicating of
something a word which, by human convention or otherwise,[46] signifies
it. Transferred predication involves taking this word and applying it to
God on the basis of the fact that the thing it signifies is a creation of God.
Since God transcends thought and language, there are no words properly
signifying God. But we can use for God words properly signifying

---

[42]See, for example, Martianus, *De nuptiis* 4.384, p. 180, 5-6.

[43]"Quoniam ab ipso omnia sunt quae de eo praedicari possunt" (510d4-5).

[44]"Rationabiliter enim per causitiua causale potest significari" (*Per.* 458b5-6; see also
468c, 480b). *Causatiua* is Eriugena's translation of αἰτατά in some very similar passages in
the Pseudo-Dionysius's *On Divine Names*; see his translation in PL 122:1117a-b: "ex omnibus causatiuis laudandum . . . ipsi omnium causalem theosophi multiuoce ex omnibus
causatiuis laudant"; see also 1124a-b. The idea of a causal relation as the basis of transferred predication is suggested, but not developed, in *De praed.* 9.32-35.

[45]This, I believe, is the important reason for Eriugena's unification of *kataphatic* and
*apophatic* theology (see above, p. 159). On the causal basis of divine predication see further
Werner Beierwaltes, "Negati Affirmatio: Welt als Metapher," *Philosophisches Jahrbuch* 83
(1976), 237ff.

[46]On this question, see Roques, *Libres sentiers*, p. 91.

creatures in virtue of the creatures' status as a creation of God. A parallel situation is found on the level of thought: we can only know God as he manifests himself in creation. As creation manifests the hidden God to us, so our speech, in manifesting creatures, can also manifest God.[47]

## III

I would like to conclude with a few short comments about Eriugena's position in *Periphyseon* Book I as it relates to the questions which I raised at the beginning of the essay. It seems indeed that Eriugena can claim to be consistent in denying that anything can be said about God while at the same time saying many things about God. Far from being in conflict, the denial that anything can be predicated of God refers to what can *properly* be predicated of him, whereas affirmations about God work on a different level: they have to do with what can be predicated of God in a "transferred" way. Indeed negations and affirmations about God are

---

[47] I have argued in this and in the preceding section that Eriugena understood the nature, opposition and contradiction of Dionysian *kataphatic* and *apophatic* theology in the light of the Aristotelian theory of affirmative and negative propositions (as this theory was available to him primarily in Latin sources) and that he resolved the contradiction by means of a distinction between proper and transferred predication which again he found in Latin sources, although the metaphysical basis he gave to transferred predication was derived from the Pseudo-Dionysius himself. However, in his Preface to his translation of Maximus (PL 122:1196a, ed. Dümmler, p. 162, 27–31), Eriugena says that it was *Maximus* who helped him see how Dionysian *kataphatic* and *apophatic* theology, "cum inter se oppositae ualdeque contrariae uideantur, ad unum tamen consensum perueniunt ut . . . utrunque in utraque contineatur." Eriugena is referring no doubt to Maximus *Ambigua*, PG 91:1288c (English translation by Sheldon-Williams in *The Cambridge History*, p. 493) = 477–478 of R. Flambard's edition of Eriugena's translation (*Jean Scot Erigène traducteur de Maxime le Confesseur*, handwritten Ecole Nationale des Chartes thesis, Paris, Archives Nationales AB XXVIII 100). The Maximus passage in Flambard's edition has not less than three relatively long glosses marking its importance and explaining it (one gloss shows knowledge of the original Greek text of Maximus). Although Maximus does indeed unify *kataphatic* and *apophatic* theology (ἐνοῦνται, *adunantur* in Eriugena's translation), blending them into each other as does Eriugena, this is done by means of a different distinction, namely that between statements about the *quia* and the *quid* of God: both *kataphatic* and *apophatic* theology do not say *what* God is; *kataphatic* theology only says *that* God is. Thus, although Eriugena's resolution of the contradiction of the two theologies follows Maximus in unifying them, the unification is accomplished on different principles, and in this respect at least, his actual practice does not agree with his claim in his Preface to Maximus. (This is not to say that Maximus's distinction between *quia* and *quid* statements is not of importance to Eriugena.) Eriugena's next claim in his Preface, namely that Maximus showed him how *kataphatic* and *apophatic* theology apply not only to God but also to creatures, appears to refer to *Ambigua*, PG 91:1240c–1241a and is the background to Eriugena's second mode of *esse* and *non esse* in *Per.* 1.443d–444c.

"contained" in each other, since to say that $X$ can be predicated *translatiue* of God is to recognize that it cannot be predicated *proprie* of him, and since, presumably, to deny that $X$ is predicated *proprie* of God is to raise the possibility of predicating it *translatiue*. The basis of predications of God also emerges from the reconciliation of affirmations and negations: discourse about God is made possible by, and grounded on, the causal relation of creation to God: God makes himself manifest to us in creation and it is by thinking and talking about creation that we can think and talk about God.[48]

At this point serious questions arise which I would like to indicate briefly here. Perhaps answers to them can be found in, or at least for, Eriugena. Such answers might also show the limits of his account, as a philosophical explanation, of human discourse about God.

1. One would like to know more about what could be called the semantic structure of transferred predications: when a word is used of God and outside of its proper context, what meaning does it then have, and in virtue of what does it have this meaning?

2. Related to this is an issue concerning the epistemological status of the claims made in transferred predications. Eriugena indicates that such predications need not be false, but neither are they true: they appear to occupy an intermediary region between truth and falsehood, the "probable."[49] But if they are not true, why should we believe them, and why are they not false? To the extent that the Master's discourse about God in *Periphyseon* I is composed of affirmations or transferred predications (and should we not say that after all negations are also transferred predications about God?), it has the character of a "likely tale" whose claims to our assent are not clear.

3. There are also problems connected with negative predications. Supposing Eriugena were to ask himself: "On what basis do I claim that nothing

---

[48]Eriugena returns to his theory of *kataphatic* and *apophatic* predication in his *Expositiones*, ed. Barbet, 2, lines 514ff. and 1185–1216. On the relation of *kataphasis* and *apophasis* to theophany, see also Beierwaltes, "Negati affirmatio," pp. 241ff. The Eriugenian position on predication of God is also that (to some degree) of Anselm (*Monologion* 65: language about God is not *proprie* but *per aliquam . . . similitudinem*) and is standard in the "School of Chartres" (language about God is not *proprie* but *translatiue* or *transsumptiue*; for references, see G. R. Evans, "Alan of Lille's *Distinctiones* and the Problem of Theological Language," *Sacris Erudiri* 24 [1980], 67–86, who discusses in particular Alan of Lille's novel attempt to reverse the orthodoxy: the application of words to God is, on the contrary, their *proper* use; theological language sets the standard for normal usage, and not vice versa).

[49]See *Per.* 522b (note *verius*), 757c–758a, 458a–b, 463c, 509a, 511c–512a, 518c.

can be properly said of God?" his answer, I believe, would have to begin with creation and then be developed by means of the causal relation between creation and God. How this could be done, however, is unclear. He must infer from creation that God is very different from creation and thus not a proper subject of predicates signifying creatures. But I wonder if the "theophanic" or manifestatory way in which God is known through creation does not in fact block his making such an inference. If God is known as manifested in creation, he is known as the *same* as, not as *different* from, creation. In fact "his manifestation hides him"[50] in his difference from creation. Perhaps the theophanic model of the causal relation between creation and God should be abandoned and another causal model adopted which would better permit of inferences from creation to God — one thinks of the physical and metaphysical systems of causality exploited later in the thirteenth century. And yet perhaps Eriugena has a way of explaining theophany that makes such inferences possible.[51]

[50]Jean Trouillard's phrase, "Erigène et la théophanie créatrice," in *The Mind of Eriugena*, ed. John J. O'Meara and Ludwig Bieler (Dublin, 1973), p. 98.

[51]For suggestive hints in this direction, see R. L. Silonis, "Sentido y valor del conocimiento de Dios en Escoto Erigena," *Pensiamento* 23 (1967), 131–165; Donald F. Duclow, "Pseudo-Dionysius, John Scotus Eriugena, Nicholas of Cusa: An Approach to the Hermeneutic of the Divine Names," *International Philosophical Quarterly* 12 (1972), 264–272 (on the causal structure of theophany); Bernard McGinn, "The Negative Element in the Anthropology of John the Scot," *Jean Scot Erigène et l'histoire*, pp. 322–323 (on the richness of man's *quia* knowledge of God, for which see also Thomas Tomasic, "Negative Theology and Subjectivity: An Approach to the Tradition of the Pseudo-Dionysius," *International Philosophical Quarterly* 9 [1969], 410–412). I would like to thank Professor Madec for helpful comments on ideas presented in this essay.

# Carolingian Baptismal Expositions:
## A Handlist of Tracts and Manuscripts
### Susan A. Keefe

A number of important publications in recent years have made us aware of an enormous corpus of literature from the late eighth and ninth centuries, which until now has been largely untouched.[1] This scholarship has changed several assumptions of the past. Not only are we finding that numerous manuscripts are extant from this era with, as yet, unidentified, unpublished material, but also we are gaining a revised impression about the value of certain genres of literature not previously given careful examination and analysis.

One literary genre of the greatest interest to Carolingian manuscript compilers was the liturgical exposition. Among works of this nature, an astonishingly large number of tracts concerned with the subject of baptism still abound in the extant early medieval manuscripts. Some of the tracts have been edited in scattered publications reaching back to the eighteenth century, but most of them have received no critical commentary. There are

---

[1]To name only a few: Hubert Mordek, *Kirchenrecht und Reform im Frankenreich: Die Collectio Vetus Gallica, Die älteste systematische Kanonenssammlung des fränkischen Gallien: Studien und Edition,* Beiträge zur Geschichte und Quellenkunde des Mittelalters, 1 (Berlin–New York, 1975); Raymund Kottje, *Die Bussbücher Halitgars von Cambrai und des Hrabanus Maurus,* Beiträge zur Geschichte und Quellenkunde des Mittelalters, 8 (Berlin–New York, 1980); Roger E. Reynolds, *The Ordinals of Christ from Their Origin to the Twelfth Century*, Beiträge zur Geschichte und Quellenkunde des Mittelalters, 7 (Berlin–New York, 1978); and articles by Peter Brommer, "Capitula Episcoporum," *Zeitschrift für Kirchengeschichte* 91 (1980), 207–236; Pierre Salmon, "Livrets de prières de l'époque carolingienne," *Revue bénédictine* 86 (1976), 218–234; and Jean-Paul Bouhot, "Explications du rituel baptismal à l'époque carolingienne," *Revue des études augustiniennes* 24 (1978), 278–301.

numerous baptismal treatises that have not been published, and now many more manuscripts of the edited texts have been identified. These tracts, in spite of the importance given to Christian initiation during the Carolingian period, have never been the object of a comprehensive study. I wish to offer here the beginnings of such a project.[2]

  One reason the baptismal literature has been neglected is because it consists largely of anonymous works that did not capture the attention of editors who in the past were more interested in the works of celebrated authors. Because so many of the manuscripts before the work of Bernhard Bischoff could not be pinpointed to the Carolingian period or to a place of origin, anonymous works had little value. Another reason why the tracts have not been studied is because, by their nature, they are not an obvious source of information for historians or even for liturgists or theologians. The tracts are not liturgical texts *per se*, but are commentaries on the rite. Nor do the texts deal primarily with the theology of the sacrament. Rather, they are explanations of the ceremonies of baptism on a very elementary level. A final rationale why the Carolingian baptismal literature has been largely ignored has been the feeling that the tracts, along with many other liturgical commentaries, were unoriginal and repetitive.

Even granting the legitimacy of these reasons, it is nevertheless very surprising that the baptismal literature has not received more attention. The importance of baptism in the Carolingian world has been recognized in the great architectural, political, legislative, and educational programs of that period. When Leidrad, archbishop of Lyon, began his explanation of baptism with the story of the creation of the world, in whose birth out of the watery abyss he saw the first prefiguration of the Christian sacrament,[3] he captured the importance that the sacrament of baptism played in the Carolingian era in bringing harmony out of chaos.

Let us imagine for a moment the Latin West in the year 800, a few years before Leidrad composed his baptismal treatise. By that date Charlemagne ruled a vast empire, but large parts had submitted to Frankish domination and Christianity in little more than name. Christianity for a great number of recently conquered peoples was a new phenomenon. St. Boniface, it

---

[2] I am currently preparing my doctoral dissertation, "Baptismal Instruction in the Carolingian Period: The MS Evidence" (University of Toronto, 1981) for publication. I would greatly appreciate hearing about further manuscripts containing Carolingian baptismal instruction that I fail to mention here.
  [3] PL 99:855.

must be remembered, had suffered martyrdom while baptizing pagans within the lifetime of Charlemagne. The rite of baptism, comprising the entire initiation process for a Christian from catechetical preparation to reception of the Eucharist as a full member of the Church, put its stamp on every individual not only as a part of the Church, but as a member of society. It was often the only thing that distinguished the peoples of the newly conquered borders of the Carolingian empire from the pagan tribes.

There is another way that baptism, as a rite, was the cornerstone of Carolingian society. In its preparatory stages, whether for adult catechumens or sponsors of infant candidates, baptism was an opportunity for education. In 812, near the end of his reign, Charlemagne composed an extraordinary letter to his archbishops demanding that each report to him exactly how they and their suffragan bishops taught the rite of baptism to the priests and the people commissioned to them.[4] What had stirred the emperor to concern himself in the minutiae of baptismal instruction in his realm? If we can judge by Charlemagne's correspondence, it was no shallow interest. After receiving the replies of the metropolitans, he sent praises to one and criticism to another with a request for a fuller explanation of one ceremony of the rite.[5]

Baptism, then, was inseparable from the chief preoccupations of the Carolingian world, and it is in this context that the following list of texts and manuscripts is presented.

Below is an inventory of Carolingian expositions of baptism and their manuscripts currently known to me. The primary aim of the inventory is to identify the manuscripts in order that a systematic study can in future be made of the numerous tracts explaining the meaning and ceremonies of Christian initiation for priests in the Frankish realm in the late eighth and ninth centuries.

Regarding these texts, the need for a study of the Carolingian baptismal literature and of its importance as a means of measuring the nature and extent of religious education in that period has been recognized in the last decade.[6] Previous assumptions that the tracts, composed largely

---

[4]Jean Michel Hanssens, ed., *Amalarii episcopi opera liturgica omnia*, 1, Studi e Testi 138 (Vatican, 1948), pp. 235f.

[5]The letters were sent to Archbishop Leidrad of Lyon (cf. Leidrad's remarks in a second letter to Charlemagne, PL 99:873) and to Archbishop Amalarius of Trier (ed. by Jean Michel Hanssens, op. cit., p. 251).

[6]Cf. Elisabeth Dahlhaus-Berg, *Nova Antiquitas et Antiqua Novitas* (Cologne, 1975), p. 100, and Jean-Paul Bouhot, op. cit., pp. 278f.

of excerpts from Alcuin, Isidore, and earlier Church authorities, have little
to offer, must be laid aside. When the tracts are studied comparatively, a
quite different impression of the baptismal literature emerges. In fact,
there is a surprising variety of interpretation illustrated in the Carolingian
compilers' selection, rearrangement, partial omission, substitution,
rephrasing, and supplementation of their most common sources.
Together, the numerous commentaries from this era, when properly
analyzed, will permit us to fill a gap in our knowledge of the development of baptismal theology regarding the popular understanding of the
sacrament in the early Middle Ages.

Regarding the manuscripts themselves, far from all of those in which
the tracts are to be found have been adequately described as to their contents, age, or area of origin. For assistance in identifying some Carolingian tracts and dating and locating their manuscripts I am indebted to
a number of scholars currently working in this field, especially Pro-
fessors Bischoff and Roger Reynolds.[7] It is important to analyze carefully the manuscripts with the texts for two reasons. First, they reveal to
some degree the context in which the baptismal tracts were written. For
example, the repeated connection in the earliest manuscripts between the
tracts and legislative material indicates that the interest in baptism was a
result of clerical educational reforms. The tracts are found within or
beside — to name some of the most common contexts — canonical collections, episcopal capitularies and acts of Carolingian councils, penitential
material, liturgical commentaries on the Mass and dedication of a
church, expositions of the Lord's Prayer, the creeds, and clerical orders,
and *interrogationes sacerdotalis*. It becomes clear that they were meant
as *instructiones* and are an important witness to a remarkable effort to
raise the intellectual level of the clergy and, through them, the people.
Sometimes the tracts are striking evidence of problems of conversion

[7] I also wish to thank the Deutscher Akademischer Austauschdienst for a scholarship
which permitted me to spend ten months viewing manuscripts in Germany. I owe special
gratitude to the staffs of the Handschriftenabteilung of the Bayerische Staatsbibliothek in
Munich, of the Staatliche Bibliothek in Bamberg, and of the Deutsche Staatsbibliothek in
Berlin for making their manuscripts available to me. Second, I wish to acknowledge the in-
valuable aid of the Hill Monastic Manuscript Library at St. John's University, Collegeville,
Minnesota, where I was able to examine a number of the manuscripts on film and make use
of its incipit file, as well as the most generous assistance of its staff in facilitating the
research of manuscripts while I was there and by mail. Finally, I am indebted to the
California Institute of Technology for providing me with a Mellon Foundation postdoc-
toral grant to teach and to continue my current work on Carolingian tracts.

from pagan observances, and of local divergencies in the understanding, teaching, and celebration of baptism. Second, because of the variety among the expositions, as critical a knowledge as possible of the date and place of origin of the manuscripts is important. This information may tell us where and when anonymous tracts containing unique or unusual baptismal instruction were written, and where and for how long they were copied.

The following inventory is in two parts, consisting of a list of the texts or tracts, and then an alphabetical list of the manuscripts. In the inventory of texts the reader will first find the tracts grouped into fifteen categories. This arrangement deserves some explanation. The difficulty of categorizing the tracts in a meaningful way for the reader may already be apparent, given their often anonymous and repetitive nature. While some of their composers are known, such as Alcuin, Amalarius of Metz, and Theodulf of Orléans, most are not. It is unlikely that any of the manuscripts of the anonymous compositions are the originals, so that their date and area of origin does not necessarily reveal who was responsible for these tracts. Moreover, the texts cannot easily or profitably be listed alphabetically by incipit, because of the great similarity of so many of the incipits, because each manuscript of the text may offer substantial variations, and finally because the texts often have two incipits — one version bearing an epistolary preface, another version omitting this, or even adding a foreign preface. One option would be to list the texts chronologically within the Carolingian period, or at least to group them before or after certain reform councils or influential figures, such as Charlemagne or Rabanus Maurus, but often the date of the tracts cannot be made precise. Another option would be to group the texts under one of five or six major models to which their descriptions of the baptismal ceremonies tend to conform, such as the "Alcuinian *ordo* of baptism," the "Isidorian *ordo*," the "Roman *ordo*," or the "Gallicanized *ordo*." The difficulty here, however, is that in some texts the sequence of ceremonies in the model is altered, or no single model is discernible. Hence, the most interesting and informative arrangement of the texts would seem to be a generally geographical one grouping them according to their probable common areas of origin. Despite what can only be a tentative classification at this stage, an attempt to show the affinity of different tracts with different geographical areas is a beginning to an appreciation of the significance of the variety among them.

An important fact must be kept in mind in order to understand the arrangement of the texts below. This is that the Carolingian compilers borrowed and re-edited the tracts composed by their contemporaries. One reason they did this relates to what gave rise to the great number of baptismal tracts in the first place. Undeniably, the greatest impetus for the multiplication of expositions on baptism in the early ninth century was Charlemagne's questionnaire of 812 to his metropolitans on baptism. The questionnaire was probably issued in preparation for the five great regional reform councils of 813 called by Charlemagne, at which he wished the bishops to legislate on clerical reform and liturgical unity regarding the teaching and celebration of baptism.[8] Charlemagne's inquiry asked the prelates "how you and your suffragans teach and instruct the priests of God and the people commissioned to you on the sacrament of baptism,"[9] and then posed a series of questions pertaining to the individual ceremonies of the baptismal rite. In the archdiocese of Sens it is documented that Archbishop Magnus wrote to at least one of his suffragans, Theodulf of Orléans, and asked him to respond to the questionnaire of Charlemagne. Theodulf did so, addressing his exposition on the ceremonies of baptism to Magnus. Magnus used parts of Theodulf's long treatise in composing his own much briefer response to Charlemagne. What has not been noted before is the similarity of Magnus's treatise to three other anonymous tracts besides Theodulf's. Two of these are unquestionably by bishops. It appears, in fact, that Magnus composed his response after polling, not just Theodulf, but all the bishops of his archdiocese. He sent them copies of the imperial questionnaire and urged them to respond to the questions, as Charlemagne wished. Magnus, after compiling the responses from around his archdiocese, addressed Charlemagne thus: "Most glorious emperor, we your servants, that is Magnus and my colleagues, the rest of the bishops, though unworthy, in the diocese of Sens, have presumed to make known to your highness . . ."[10]

Such a polling of suffragans by archbishops was probably not confined to Sens. A number of cases of evident borrowing between texts have emerged. This, also, was due to the copying of the metropolitans' responses by local bishops. As an expression of Charlemagne's interest in clerical reform and

---

[8] This famous document is cited *passim* in works on Charlemagne and the Carolingian Renaissance, mostly as a witness to Charlemagne's interest in liturgical reform and because of the responses of the archbishops which the questionnaire generated. It has not been generally appreciated in connection with the Reform Synods of 813, nor with the diocesan legislation on baptism that was issued after the regional synods, but see Elisabeth Dahlhaus-Berg, op. cit., pp. 165f.

[9] ". . . qualiter tu et suffraganei tui doceatis et instruatis sacerdotes Dei et plebem vobis commissam de baptismi sacramento" (ed. Jean Michel Hanssens, op. cit., p. 235).

[10] "Gloriosissime imperator, innotescere magnitudini vestrae praesumpsimus nos servi vestri, Magnus scilicet et ceteri compares mei, licet indigni episcopi ad Senonicam diocesim pertinentes . . ." (PL 102:981).

liturgical unity, the imperial questionnaire gave rise to diocesan legislation on baptism. This, in turn, led to the copying of the archbishops' tracts for the instruction of parish priests on the sacrament. For example, the response by Archbishop Leidrad of Lyon to Charlemagne's questionnaire became a model for local priests: a manuscript from southern Gaul contains an anonymous baptismal tract, which consists simply of excerpts from the chapters of Leidrad's work. What is most interesting, however, is that while Leidrad described the ceremonies of baptism according to the Roman rite for Charlemagne, the anonymous compiler rearranged the order of ceremonies and omitted a few so that his version describes the Gallicanized *ordo* of baptism.

These examples from Sens and Lyon indicate why the tracts have been arranged according to a geographical scheme, despite its sometimes problematic nature. Several factors determined the fifteen divisions in the following inventory. Some texts of known author, date, and place of composition can be assigned to specific ecclesiastical provinces. Of the anonymous texts, some can be grouped under these specific ecclesiastical provinces while others must be classed under a more general region, or, in a few cases, must be placed in the final category of texts of uncertain origin, depending on the place of origin of their earliest manuscripts, the similarity of their contents with other texts, and the relationship between their manuscripts and other codices with kindred texts.

Within these tentative divisions, then, each tract is identified by: (1) a number ("TEXT 1"),[11] for easier cross reference from the index of manuscripts; (2) composer, if known; (3) a brief description of the TEXT; (4) incipit and explicit; (5) manuscript(s); and (6) most recent edition (if one exists) as well as any older edition using a manuscript not employed in the most recent edition.

There are a few explanations to be made regarding these modes of identification. In the "brief descriptions," it is sometimes noted that one TEXT is similar to another or that two TEXTS share identical passages. These passages are not quotations from the popular sources such as Isidore and Alcuin, which are constantly repeated in all the Carolingian baptismal expositions, but passages that are not ostensibly citations, and that are found only in these two tracts among all the tracts in the inventory.

The incipits and explicits are somewhat lengthy. I have tried to provide what is helpful to distinguish one TEXT from another, at times even

---

[11] I will use the word "TEXT" in capital letters when referring to one or more of the sixty-one tracts identified in this inventory.

supplying "samples" consisting of distinct phrases within the TEXT. This complex procedure is required by the nature of the baptismal instructions, which vary in length from as much as seventeen columns in the Migne edition to as little as ten lines, but typically run about two printed pages, and which are one of three basic types. First, the vast majority are explanations of the rite, or individual ceremonies constituting baptism, from the initial making of the catechumen to the final episcopal chrismation and reception of the Eucharist after immersion in the font. These tracts are usually divided into chapters or titles for each successive ceremony. Second, some of the tracts do not describe the entire rite, but are limited to one or a few topics, such as "de baptismo," or "de catechumeno." Usually the explanation of any topic includes the definition of the word in question (such as "catechumenus," "competens," "scrutinium," or "exorcismus"), a statement as to why the ceremony is done, and a scriptural precedent. Finally, a very small percentage of the tracts are glosses on the words of the prayers spoken in the rite of baptism. Another explanation needed to understand the nature of the incipits and explicits is that a number of the tracts were originally letters or synodal addresses. Later they were recopied, shorn of their epistolary prefaces and conclusions, for use as instructions in clerical handbooks. For this reason, the same TEXT may begin or conclude quite differently in different manuscripts.

I have footnoted only the major variations offered by each manuscript of each TEXT, such as omission of preface, different title, abridgment, or incompletion (due to loss of folios).

For the incipits and explicits I have followed the orthography of the manuscript if there is only one witness to the TEXT. For TEXTS with more than one manuscript, if there are orthographical variations the quotation is edited. "E" for "ae," "i" for "y," "t" for "c," "n" for "m," insertion of "h" and "p," and other common variations I have copied without "(sic)," as well as the many spellings of "catechumenus." I have expanded almost all abbreviations and have supplied punctuation. Italics are used to show what are designated as titles in the MSS, or for what seem to be titles, even when they are not distinguished by size or lettering from the rest of the script. Finally, I have included in parentheses in the incipits and explicits legitimate alternate or additional words found in one or more MSS of the TEXT. In the more significant cases, these are elaborated on in a footnote or the manuscript with the alternate reading is identified in the parentheses.

The sixty-one tracts are found in 132 MSS. Twenty-nine of the tracts have only one MS witness and sixty-six of the MSS contain more than one tract. A common occurrence in the MSS is a selection of tracts strung together to form a "block" of baptismal instruction. To save space and a fair amount of repetition (because of the MSS with multiple expositions of baptism), the MSS have been assigned sigla. In the inventory, the MSS under each TEXT are listed by sigla in the order of their age, from oldest to most recent. More precise dates ("s. IX 3/4") precede a general date ("s. IX") within any century. Fourteen of the sixty-one TEXTS are not represented in a ninth-century MS, but they are very probably Carolingian not only because of their position among other Carolingian literature in their MSS, but also because of their form and content. The second part of the inventory, the alphabetical listing of the MSS, is the key to the sigla where the MSS are identified, and their date and place of origin (if determined) are given. As far as possible, for the MSS prior to the eleventh century their date and place of origin have been supplied by Professor Bischoff, through personal correspondence or in one of his publications; or, in some cases, from other paleographers and scholars working most recently with the MSS. Sometimes the date or location is controversial. I note my source of information (a name alone in parentheses means I have received the information orally or in a letter) only for the MSS dating prior to the eleventh century. Also under each MS are listed the TEXTS found in it and the folios on which they occur. I have not yet examined all the MSS, as question marks for the folios of some of the TEXTS indicate.

Finally, regarding the editions, the title, date, and place of publication are given in full once; subsequent references to them are abbreviated.

As an appendix to this article I have included an alphabetical list of incipits of Carolingian baptismal expositions. The difficulties with such a list as a means of identifying with security any given tract with one of the TEXTS of the inventory have been discussed. Because of the often great similarity of titles or first lines of the baptismal instructions, the reader, for example, may know of a text having the same incipit as a TEXT in the inventory, but which in fact develops quite differently. Caution given, the list has possible value and could contribute to the unraveling of the still unidentified contents of many medieval manuscripts.

The plan of this file of incipits is to offer several incipits for each TEXT, if necessary. That is, the entries are drawn from the individual MSS dealt with in the inventory, and every variant incipit of every TEXT is listed. If there is a title preceding the TEXT in any MS, this is treated as the first words of the incipit, although it is distinguished by capital letters. I have opted to do this because what seems to be treated as a title in one MS is clearly treated as the incipit in another. Also Roman numerals beginning a TEXT, such as "I. Cap.," are treated as the first letter of the incipit (filed under the letter equivalent "i"). I have corrected the orthography of the incipits, in order to avoid listing as separate entries every different spelling of an incipit of a single TEXT. Regarding the TEXTS that are in epistolary form, the salutation or preface is treated as the incipit. I never try to guess what the incipit would be if the letter was shorn of its preface; such an anonymous form is only listed as an entry if it actually exists in a MS.

Following each incipit is the TEXT it identifies, in order that the reader may refer back to the inventory of TEXTS for more of the incipit, for the explicit, and for alternate incipits of the TEXT given in the notes. The MSS in which the incipit is found are given in parentheses (not necessarily all the known MSS of the TEXT). If there are no MSS listed after the TEXT number, it simply means that in all the MSS of this TEXT there is some sort of title preceding its incipit (as given in the inventory description of the TEXT)—which title is listed as a separate entry. Obviously, the list is provisional in nature, because I have not seen all the MSS that reportedly contain abridged forms of TEXTS and probably have different incipits.

## INVENTORY OF TEXTS

### I. North Italian/Swiss Baptismal Instruction
### (Milan Area to Bodensee Area)

*TEXT 1*

Composer:    Anonymous
Description:  A florilegium citing Isidore, John the Deacon, Gregory, Celestine, Augustine, Ambrose, Cyprian, and Scripture on baptism and the ceremonies of the rite, in twenty-two chapters. This TEXT was used by Odilbert, archbishop of Milan, in 812, as his response to Charlemagne's questionnaire (TEXT 14).[1]

Incipit: "Ite," inquit Iesus discipulis suis, "docete omnes gentes, baptizantes eos in nomine Patris et Filii et Spiritus Sancti...

Explicit: ...*XXII. De pedum nuditate. Iohannes.* Hi etiam nudis pedibus iubentur incedere, ut depositis morticinis et carnalibus indumentis cognoscant se illius vitae iter arripere, in qua nihil asperum, nihil potest inveniri nocivum. Finit feliciter.

MSS: S4,[2] S1,[3] Spl,[2] Vi5,[2] B2,[4] M,[5] P7, V1,[5] Mul,[2] Mull[6]

Edition: Friedrich Wiegand, *Erzbischof Odilbert von Mailand über die Taufe* (Leipzig, 1899), pp. 27–37, using: Spl and Mull.

*TEXT 1*

[1]Spl is the only known MS with a letter of Odilbert, archbishop of Milan, to Charlemagne as a preface to TEXT 1 (ff. 139r–140v). Odilbert used the TEXT in the year 812 to respond to Charlemagne's inquiry (TEXT 14) without altering it, because S4, written ca. 800, contains TEXT 1 in exactly the same form as in Spl. TEXT 1 was probably composed before the ninth century, because S4 has orthographical errors that might be explained if its copyist had a model in Insular script. For example, "De regula fidei" appears in S4 as "De fecu fidi." The abbreviation "fecu" is probably due to the Insular "r" that looks like the continental "f," and the Insular "g" that looks like the continental "c."

[2]Title: *"(Spl: I.) De baptismi (Vi5: babtismi) praecepto in evangelio."*

[3]Title: *"De baptismi sacramento diverse incipiunt narraciones sanctorumque testimito (sic) quae evangelium prodit."*

[4]Only excerpts from the TEXT, according to Michel Andrieu, *Les Ordines Romani du Haut Moyen Age,* 1 (Louvain, 1931), p. 86.

[5]An abridged version of the third through twenty-second chapters of the TEXT, beginning: *"Cap. II. De sacramento baptismi quid sit in verbo et aqua.* Quid enim est aliud baptismum, nisi quia culpa mergitur . . ." M and V1 are directly related. They have a similar collection of TEXTS, and other liturgical material is the same (see R. E. Reynolds in *Bulletin of Medieval Canon Law,* n.s. 5 [1975], 4, n. 21).

[6]The TEXT is in question-response form. The title and incipit are: *"De baptismi. Interrogatio.* Ubi est baptismi preceptum? Resp. Ubi Dominus discipulis suis ait: 'Ite, docete . . .'" The TEXT is interrupted by the insertion of the first part of TEXT 6, the rest of which follows TEXT 1 in this MS.

*TEXT 2*

Composer: Anonymous

Description: A florilegium related to TEXT 1, and citing in addition Jerome, Bede, and Leo.

Title: *De baptismi officio ac misticis sensibus eorumque auctoribus nominatim designatis et de ordine venientium ad fidem eiusdemque mysterii*

Incipit: De catechumenis. Ysidori in Libro officiorum. Catechumeni sunt qui primum de gentilitate veniunt. . .

Explicit: . . . Tunc enim donum plene sanctificavit et esse filii Dei possunt, si sacramento utroque nascentur, cum scriptum est: "Nisi quis renatus fuerit ex aqua et Spiritu Sancto non potest introire in regnum Dei. Abrenunciet, abalienat vel avertat; avertit, excludit. (*add.* Explicit.)

MSS:         P5, No,[1] Z1(?),[2] Mo,[3] R

Edition:     Dom Ambrogio Maria Amelli, in *Spicilegium Casinense complectens analecta sacra et profana,*[1] (Monte Cassino, 1888), pp. 337–341, using: No.

*TEXT 2*

[1]Title and incipit: "*Incipit de baptismi officio.* A (sic) misticis sensibus eorum qui (sic) auctoribus nominatis (sic) designatis . . ."

[2]I have not yet seen Z1. Jean-Paul Bouhot in *Revue des études augustiniennes* 24 (1978), 283, says it contains the form of the TEXT edited by Amelli, and Jean Michel Hanssens, *Amalarii episcopi opera liturgica omnia*, 1, Studi e Testi 138 (Vatican, 1948), p. 96, says the text on ff. 55r–59v in Z1 is the same as in P5 and R.

[3]The final citation of the TEXT is Cyprian, whose words conclude with Jn. 3.5, ". . . potest introire in regnum Dei." According to Annalisa Belloni, *Catalogo de la Biblioteca Capitolare di Monza* (Padua, 1974), p. 89, this is the explicit in Mo. Clearly, the final sentence, "Abrenunciet . . . excludit.", which follows the citation from Cyprian in the other MSS, does not belong to the original TEXT 2. It may be a remnant of a second instruction glossing words from the prayers of the baptismal rite.

*TEXT 3*

Composer:    Anonymous

Description: A florilegium related to TEXTS 1 and 2, divided into five sections, each with numbered chapters, including a final section on penitents.

Title:       *De baptismi officio ac misticis sensibus eorumque auctoribus nominatim designatis et de ordine venientium ad fidem eiusdemque mysterii*

Incipit:     [I.] Isidorus. Primus gradus est catechumenorum, ii competentium, iii baptizatorum. II. Idem. Catechumeni sunt qui primum de gentilitate veniunt. . .

Samples:     III. De abrenuntiatione. Duae sunt namque pactiones credentium. . . IIII. De abrenuntiatione vel confessione parvulorum. Isidorus. . . V. De catechesi. Item. . .VI. De exsufflatione et exorcismo. Caelestinus Papa. . .VII. De salis acceptione. Item. . .I. De competentibus. Isidorus. . .

Explicit:    I. De penitentibus. Ezechiel. . .Hieronymus. Simulque considerandum qualem impium et peccatorem suscipiat penitentem. . .et ego omnium iniquitatum eius quas operatus est obliviscor.

MSS:        Es1,[1] V4, Mi2, Mu9,[2] Z2, P9

Edition:    André Wilmart, *Analecta Reginensia*, Studi e Testi 59 (Vatican, 1933), pp. 157–166,[3] using: Esl, V4, and P9.

---

*TEXT 3*

[1]The TEXT is incomplete, ending in the middle of the penultimate chapter (in Wilmart's edition, p. 165, line 47).

[2]The title precedes TEXT 43, which precedes this TEXT. Another title and the incipit of the TEXT is this MS are: "*De caticuminis Esidorus (sic) dixit. Primus gradus est caticuminorum conpetentium in* (sic, not "iii") *baptizatorum* . . ."

[3]Wilmart's edition adds TEXT 10 at the end, which he did not distinguish as a separate instruction from TEXT 3. There are three MS witnesses to TEXT 3 not followed by TEXT 10, which Wilmart did not know (Mi2, Mu9, and Z2).

---

*TEXT 4*

Composer:    Anonymous

Description:  A florilegium related to TEXTS 1, 2, and 3.

Title:       *De ordine ad fidem venientium quorum primus gradus est catechumenorum, secundus competentium, tertius baptizatorum. De catechumenis. Isidorus.*

Incipit:     Catechumeni sunt qui primum de gentilitate veniunt. . .

Samples:   . . .varios idolorum. De exsufflatione. Caelestinus Papa. Cum sive parvulis sive iuvenes ad regenerationis veniunt sacramentum. . .Iohannes Chrysostomus de eadem re. . . De exorcismo. Isidorus. . .De salis acceptione. Isidorus. . . De competentibus. Post catechumenorum. . .De symbolo. Symbolum autem quem idem competentes accipiunt. . .De scrutinio. Iohannes ut supra. . .

Explicit:     . . .De impositione manus episcopi. . .Non tamen frontem ex eodem oleo signare quod solis debetur episcopis cum tradunt Spiritum Sanctum paraclitum, sed cerebrum. Finit Deo gratias. Amen.

MSS:        M, V1, P6[1]

Edition:    None.

---

*TEXT 4*

[1]The TEXT is given as chapters XLIIII–LXIII of a larger ecclesiastical compendium. (Chapter XLIIII begins with the title.) The explicit lacks the final words, "sed cerebrum. Finit Deo gratias. Amen."

## TEXT 5

Composer:      Anonymous
Description:   A commentary on the baptismal ceremonies in eleven
               chapters corresponding to the series of questions posed by
               Charlemagne (TEXT 14), in question-response form. In
               all of its MSS it is preceded by TEXT 1.
Title:         *Cap. I. Cur catechumenus infans efficitur*
Incipit:       Catechumenus ideo primo (primum) efficitur infans ut au-
               diens a sacerdote doctrinam fidei credat. . .
Explicit:      . . . Ita nec sine corporis et sanguinis sacramento perven-
               itur ad vitam aeternam sicut et Dominus in evangelio dicit:
               "Nisi manducaveritis. . . non habebitis vitam in vobis."
MSS:           Spl, B2,[1], M,[1] P7,[2] Vl,[3] Mul, Mull[4]
Edition:       None.

TEXT 5
[1]Title: *"Cur catechumenus infans efficitur. Cap. I."*
[2]The title is omitted, although there are blank spaces where all the titles in this MS remain
to be filled in.
[3]Title: *"Cur catechuminum infans fiat. I."*
[4]Title and incipit: *"Recapitulatio.* Cur cathecuminus infans efficitur? Resp.
Cathecuminus ideo primo efficitur infans. . ."

## TEXT 6

Composer:      Anonymous
Description:   A florilegium consisting of extracts from Isidore,
               Augustine, Ambrose, and one anonymous author on the
               baptism and post-baptism ceremonies. In all of its MSS it
               is adjacent to TEXT 1.
Title:         *Incipit de regula fidei. Ysidorus.*
Incipit:       Post apostolorum symbolum haec est certissima fides
               quam doctores nostri tradiderunt, ut profiteamur Patrem
               et Filium et Spiritum Sanctum unius esse (Spl adds: essen-
               tiae) eiusdemque potestatis. . .
Explicit:      . . . Alibi idem. Valde valde (sic) necesse est ut eius cor-
               poris et sanguinis sacramenta sumantur quatenus ad vitam
               aeternam valeant (S4: valeat) pervenire.
MSS:           S4, Spl,[1] B2, Mul,[2] Mull[2]
Edition:       None.

*TEXT 6*

[1]Title: "*Ysidorus. De regula fidei.*"
[2]Explicit: "Idem valde necesse est. . . pervenire." The title in Mull lacks "de."

*TEXT 7*

| | |
|---|---|
| Composer: | Anonymous |
| Description: | A brief explanation of the stages of becoming a Christian through baptism. |
| Incipit: | Dispositis nonnullis Differentiarum sententiis, deinceps sacramentorum aecclesiasticorum distinctio subiciatur. Quid ergo inter caticuminum et competentem vel Christianum distinguitur. . . |
| Explicit: | . . .Caticuminus tantum inunctus est et nondum tamen lotus est. |
| MS: | Spl |
| Edition: | Friedrich Wiegand, *Erzbischof Odilbert*, p. 21, using: Spl. |

*TEXT 8*

| | |
|---|---|
| Composer: | Anonymous |
| Description: | An extract from Isidore consisting of his two chapters on baptism and chrism in *De ecclesiasticis officiis* (2.25–26). In all its MSS it precedes TEXT 1. |
| Title: | *Incipit de baptismo et omni eius ordine iuxta indaginem catholicorum. Cap. I.* |
| Incipit: | Baptismi sacramentum si prima repetens ab origine pandam baptizavit Moyses in nube et (M adds: in) mari. . . |
| Explicit: | . . .Ergo quia genus sacerdotale et regale sumus, ideo post lavacrum unguimus ut Christi nomine censeamur. |
| MSS: | B2(?),[1] M,[2] Vl,[2] Mul,[3] Mull[4] |
| Edition: | None using the above MSS. (The chapters from Isidore are printed in PL 83:820–824.) |

*TEXT 8*

[1]I have not seen B2, but according to the description of Michel Andrieu, *Les Ordines*, 1:86, the text on f. 125v–? is similar to TEXT 8 of Mull and VI.

[2]In M and Vl the second chapter on chrism is labeled "*Cap. I.*" (see TEXT 1, note 5). The first chapter on baptism is divided into seven smaller chapters, labelled "Cap. I"–"Cap. VII."

[3]Title: "*De baptismo.*"

[4]In this MS the two chapters from Isidore are cast in question-response form. Incipit and questions: "Incipit liber iii de officio et ordine baptisterii ex autenticis libris prudenter collectus. *Interrogatio.* Ubi primum inchoavit baptismi sacramentum? Resp. Baptismi

sacramentum si prima repetens. . .Interr. Quod sunt genera baptismi? Resp. Tria. . .Interr. Quid est baptismum? Resp. Baptismum enim aqua est. . . Interr. Quis (sic) est fons? Resp. Fons autem origo. . .Interr. Quod sunt pactiones credentium? Resp. Due sunt. . .*De crisma*. *Interr*. Quis primum xrisme unguentum composuitur? Resp. Xrisme unguentum Moyses. . ."

## II. Baptismal Instruction from the Ecclesiastical Province of Tours and Western France

*Text 9*

Composer:     Alcuin? (Abbot of Tours, 796–804)

Description:  A brief instruction on the entire *ordo* (liturgical pro-
              cedure) of baptism, in its earliest form part of two letters
              written by Alcuin ca. 798 to a priest Oduin and to monks
              in Septimania.[1]

Incipit:      Primo paganus catechumenus fit accedens ad baptismum
              ut renuntiet maligno spiritui et omnibus eius damnosis
              pompis. Exsufflatur etiam ut fugato diabolo Christo Deo
              nostro paretur introitus. . .

Explicit:     . . .Novissime per inpositionem manus a summo sacer-
              dote septiformis gratiae Spiritum accipit, ut roboretur per
              Spiritum Sanctum ad praedicandum aliis, qui fuit in bap-
              tismo per gratiam vitae donatus aeternae.

MSS:[2]       *Vi3, *Mu4, *P18,[3] *Tr2, *Col,[4] *Mu12,[3] (*?)P4,[5]
              *Mu13,[4;3] *Au,[4] *S1,[6] S3,[7] Sp1,[8] *V5,[9] Vi5,[8] Mi2,[10] S5,[11]
              *S5,[3] B2,[8] *Br2, Ei,[11] *Ei,[4;3] M,[8] Mu5,[11] V1,[11] V1,[8]
              Mu1,[8] Mu11,[8] Be,[12] *P8, *P17[3;13] S6,[14] Mi1,[14] and an
              unidentified MS used by Ioannes Cordesius (Jean des Cor-
              des) in his edition, *Opuscula et epistolae Hincmari Remen-
              sis archiepiscopi accesserunt Nicolai PP I et aliorum
              eiusdem coevi quaedam epistolae et scripta Ioannes Cor-
              desius, ecclesiae lemouicensis presbyter et canonicus ex
              MSS codicibus nunc primum evulgavit* (Paris, 1615) betw.
              pp. 664–685; reprinted in PL 105:791f.[15]

Edition:      Ernst Dümmler, ed., MGH Epp. 4, Epistolae Karolini
              aevi 2 (Berlin, 1895), pp. 202f., edits the TEXT in its form
              within the letter of Alcuin to the priest Oduin. Preceding
              the incipit of TEXT 9 is: "Albinus magister filio carissimo
              Oduino presbitero (Mu4: "Illi" written over "Oduino
              presbitero"), salutem. Et quia divina. . .quod a sanctis
              patribus institutum est in illo officio." He uses: Br2, Mu4,

Mu11 (without preface), Mu12, P18, S5 (pp. 145f), and Tr2 (incomplete after first third of the TEXT).

On pp. 214f., he edits the TEXT in its form within the letter of Alcuin to monks in Septimania. Preceding the incipit of TEXT 9 here is: "Religiosae in Christo conversationis vestrae per illum electum pontificem laudabilem audiens sollicitudinem magno me esse gaudio delibutum fateor. . .statutum esse neminem dubitare fas esse arbitramur." He uses: P8, Sl, V5, and Vi3.

*TEXT 9*

[1]The succinct description of the entire *ordo* of baptism, beginning "Primo paganus catechumenus fit," was by far the most popular model for the Carolingian composers of baptismal instructions. The work is known earliest in two letters of Alcuin. One letter was addressed, ca. 798, to a certain priest "Oduin"; the other was written to monks in Septimania. Whether Alcuin first composed "Primo paganus," or only incorporated it into his letters (see note 9 below), Carolingians attributed it to him. According to the MS evidence, however, the copying of "Primo paganus" as an anonymous work to instruct priests on the rite of baptism does not antedate the time of Charlemagne's inquiry on baptism to his metropolitans in 812. Of the twenty-nine MSS known to me, the four earliest, probably dating before 812 (Vi3, Mu4, P18, Tr2), contain "Primo paganus" in the letters of Alcuin, in the context of other letters and works of Alcuin; slightly later ninth-century MSS contain the TEXT outside of Alcuin's letters and surrounded by other baptismal tracts. Still other ninth-century MSS retain the epistolary form of TEXT 9, but its context is other baptismal tracts, not a collection of Alcuin's works. (I have placed an asterisk before the MSS in which TEXT 9 appears within the letter to Oduin or to the monks in Septimania, and see edition.) In fact, the popularity of "Primo paganus" as an instruction for priests or as a model for fuller instructions was the result of Charlemagne's baptismal inquiry of 812. In the letter he sent to his metropolitans (TEXT 14) Alcuin's description was the model used for inquiring specifically about the ordered series of ceremonies involved in baptism. When Carolingian compilers heeded the demand for clerical handbooks brought on by the repetition of clerical reform legislation instigated by Charlemagne, they used Alcuin's description, officially sanctioned because of Charlemagne's use of it, to provide instructions on baptism. Many simply copied "Primo paganus" without change, as the following MSS indicate. Others, however, rearranged, supplemented, and in other ways intentionally altered their model. Among our sixty-one TEXTS are twelve such variations of "Primo paganus."

[2]The *De divinis officiis* of Pseudo-Alcuin, perhaps an early tenth-century compilation (PL 101:1217f.) also contains TEXT 9 entire and unaltered. The MSS of this work (currently under investigation by Roger E. Reynolds) are not given here.

[3]Title: "(*Item.*) *De sacramento baptismatis.*"

[4]The TEXT is in the form of the letter of Alcuin to the priest Oduin. It is not used in Dümmler's edition. Alcuin's name is omitted in Au, beginning: "Filio carissimo Adoino (sic) presbitero, salutem. . ."

[5]There are substantial variations from the edited form of TEXT 9 in orthography, sentence structure, and omission of phrases. One phrase is in what may be Tironian notes. The beginning of the TEXT on f. 1r is not discernible except for a few words (it has been written over), but the amount of space indicates it probably had the epistolary preface of Alcuin to Oduin.

[6]Incomplete; the last words at the bottom of p. 355 are: ". . .Et recte homo qui ad imaginem Sanctae Trinitatis"//. (A different hand on p. 356 contains a brief *ordo* of baptism.)

⁷In the form of fifteen capitula and immediately preceding other capitula (of Charlemagne) in the MS. Incipit: "I. Primitus paganus catezuminus fit. . ."

⁸Title: (*Item.*) *Ratio de sacro baptismi (baptismatis)*." Mull adds: "*Recapitulatio*." and its incipit (only) is in interrogatory form: ("Interrogatio." in margin) "Cur primo paganus cathecuminus fit accedens ad baptismum? Resp. Ut renunciet. . ."

⁹The TEXT is contained within the letter of Alcuin to monks in Septimania, but it and a paragraph preceding and following it on baptism are set off from the rest of the letter with the title (f. 79v): "*Expositio de baptisterio*." Two ninth-century MSS of the letter of Alcuin to monks in Septimania do not contain TEXT 9 or the whole section on baptism that is set off with the distinct title in V5 (London, BL Royal 8. E. XV and St. Gall, SB 271). It is thus possible that TEXT 9 did not originate with this letter.

¹⁰Title and incipit: "*In Dei nomine pauca de misteriis et officiis sacri baptismatis sicut a sanctis patribus traditum est incipiunt.* In illo officio primo paganus caticuminus fit. . ."

¹¹Title and incipit: "*De mysteriis sacri baptismatis.* In illo officio primum paganus catechumenus fit. . ."

¹²Title: "*De sacro baptismo*."

¹³P17 is an apograph of P18.

¹⁴Incipit: "In illo officio primus (sic) paganus. . ."

¹⁵Title and incipit: "*Item. Traditio baptisterii.* Primo paganus, postea catechumenus, fit, accedens. . ." The title applies to TEXT 9 and an additional paragraph that also follows the TEXT in Alcuin's letter to monks in Septimania (incipit and explicit in this MS: "Videtis quam fideliter seu rationabiliter. . .quos a suis diversos intelligit doctrinis."). Regarding the identification of this MS, Jean Devisse, *Hincmar archevêque de Reims 845–882* (Geneva, 1976), 1:15, n. 38, says only that Jean des Cordes was lent the MSS he used by Jacques-Auguste De Thou (1553–1617).


## TEXT 10

| | |
|---|---|
| Composer: | Anonymous |
| Description: | An instruction on the entire *ordo* of baptism composed of excerpts from Isidore and others and concluding with TEXT 9. |
| Incipit: | Cur infans caticuminus (sic, all MSS) efficitur et quid sit caticuminus? Caticumini sunt qui primum de gentilitate veniunt, habentes voluntatem credendi in Christo, et quia primum exortationis praeceptum est in lege: "Audi, Israel. . . |
| Sample: | Exsufflantur etiam caticumini, ut maligno flatu fugato, divino flatu (sic), id est Spiritui Sancto, paretur introitus. Exorcizantur autem hi primum. Deinde salem accipiunt et unguuntur. . . |
| Explicit: | . . .qui fuit in baptismo per eiusdem gratiam vita (sic) donatus aeterna (sic). |
| MSS: | Au?,¹ V4, P9 |
| Edition: | André Wilmart, *Analecta*, pp. 166–170, using: V4 and P9. |

*TEXT 10*

[1]The MS is incomplete. At the end of its last folio, following TEXT 9, is this fragment, possibly of TEXT 10: "Cur infans caticuminus efficitur et quis [est] caticuminus? Caticumini sunt qui pri[mum]"//.

*TEXT 11*

| | |
|---|---|
| Composer: | Anonymous |
| Description: | Glosses on words selected from the prayers of the baptismal rite. |
| Incipit: | Baptizo te: hoc est (H: id est) intingo te. Electus: a Deo coronatus. Catechumenus: hoc est instructus (Au: institutus). . . |
| Explicit: | . . .Et quando dicit, 'Credis et in Spiritum Sanctum?': hoc est (H, Bl: id est) in personam Spiritus Sancti. |
| MSS: | Au,[1] P5,[1];[2] Mc1,[3] E,[4] B1,[4] Lo2,[4] Mc2,[4] Mu5,[4] Vi2,[5] W2,[5] W1,[4] Vi7,[5];[6] Ft, H,[4] T |
| Editions: | Cyrille Vogel and Reinhard Elze, eds., *Le Pontifical Romano-Germanique du dixième siècle*, 2, Studi e Testi 227 (Vatican, 1963), p. 172, using: Bl, E, Mc2, and Vi2. Martin Gerbert, ed., *Monumenta veteris liturgia Alemannicae*, 2 (St. Blasien, 1779), p. 210, using: Vi7. |

*TEXT 11*

[1]Explicit: ". . .Et quando dicis, 'Credis et in Spiritum Sanctum, sanctam ecclesiam catholicam, remissionem peccatorum, carnis resurrectionem?" hoc est in persona (sic) Spiritus Sancti. (P5: *Explicit*.)"

[2]Title (nearly effaced): "*De illa verba Greca quae vertuntur in Latina quae sunt in illo baptisterio.*"

[3]Title: "*De illa verba Greca quod vertunt in Latina baptisteri.*"

[4]Title: "*De verbis Graecis baptisterii quomodo vertantur in Latinum.*" The TEXT was included under this title in the tenth-century *Pontificale Romano-Germanicum (PRG).* The title is abbreviated in B1: "*De verbis Grecis baptisterii.*"

[5]Title and incipit: "*Ordo de verbis Grecis baptisterii quomodo vertantur in Latinum.* Baptizo te: hoc est unguo (Vi7: intinguo) te. . .*"

[6]Explicit: ". . .Et quando dicis, 'et in Spiritum Sanctum,' hoc est in persona Spiritus Sancti."

*TEXT 12*

| | |
|---|---|
| Composer: | Anonymous |
| Description: | An instruction on the *ordo* of baptism in question-response form incorporating all of TEXT 9 and other sources. In the earliest and in most MSS it is preceded by TEXT 11. |
| Incipit: | Item querendum est quid sit scrutinium. Scrutinium a scrutando dictum est (dicitur), quia ante baptismum fidem |

|  |  |
|---|---|
|  | catechumeni scrutari oportet. Item querendum est catechumenus quid sit. . . |
| Explicit: | . . .Item cur primum ministri et non pontifex super catechumenum manus imponunt? Ideo ut novissimae. . .per baptismi gratiam vitae donatus aeternae. |
| MSS: | P5,[1],[5] Mc1,[1] E,[1] B1,[1] B3,[2] Lo2,[6] Mc2,[1] Mu5,[1] Vi2,[1];[7] W2,[1] W1,[1] Vi7,[1];[7] B4,[3] Ft,[1];[8] H,[1] Lb,[2] Sf,[2] T[1],[4] |
| Editions: | Cyrille Vogel and Reinhard Elze, eds., *Le Pontifical*, 2:173–175, using: B1, E, Mc2, and Vi2. |
|  | Martin Gerbert, ed., *Monumenta*, 2:210f., using: Vi7. |

*TEXT 12*

[1]The TEXT immediately follows TEXT 11. Both TEXTS were incorporated into the *PRG*.

[2]The TEXT is not joined to TEXT 11. It is contained in a ceremonial describing the ecclesiastical offices, which consists largely of extracts from the *Liber officialis* of Amalarius and the *De divinis officiis* of Pseudo-Alcuin. Title and incipit: *"De scrutinio (B3: XXVIII. Descriptio scrutinii)*. Scrutinium a scrutando dicitur, quia ante baptismum. . ."

[3]Title and incipit: *"De verbis grecis baptisterii.* Quid sit scrutinium. . ."

[4]The last paragraph of the TEXT, describing the episcopal confirmation, is omitted. Explicit: ". . .ut illius capitis sit membrum, qui pro eo passus est et resurrexit."

[5]Title and incipit: *"Interrogatio.* Quaerendum namque est, quid sit scrutinium? Resp. Scrutinium ad (sic) scrutandum dictum. . ." Explicit: ". . .qui fuit ad (sic) baptismum gratiam vite donatus. *Explicit.*"

[6]This MS is mutilated at the end and thus contains only the first twenty words of the TEXT.

[7]The first two sentences are inverted, beginning: "Scrutinium a scrutando dictum est. . ."

[8]Incipit: "Querendum est quid sit scrutinium. . ."

*TEXT 13*

|  |  |
|---|---|
| Composer: | Anonymous |
| Description: | Excerpts from Isidore (*Origines* 6.19.43–51) on baptism and chrism. |
| Title: | *De baptismo* |
| Incipit: | Baptismum Graecae, Latine tinctio interpretatur. Quae (sic) idcirco tinctio dicitur quia ibi homo Spiritu gratia (sic) in melius inmutatur et longe aliud quam erat efficitur, dicente Domino ad apostolos: "Ite, docete omnes gentes. . ." |
| Sample: | *Xrysma* Graecae, Latine unctio nominatur ex cuius nomine et Christus dicitur. . . |
| Explicit: | . . .ita per unctionem sanctificatio Spiritus adhibetur. |
| MS: | Or |
| Edition: | None. |

## III. The Baptismal Questionnaire from Aachen

*TEXT 14*

Composer: Charlemagne (d. 814)

Description: A questionnaire, ca. 812, known in forms addressed to Archbishops Amalarius and Odilbert and to "N," in which they are asked how they and their suffragans teach baptism to their priests and the people commissioned to them. The series of questions posed on the ceremonies of the rite is inspired by TEXT 9.

Salutation: In nomine Patris et Filii et Spiritus Sancti, Karolus serenissimus augustus a Deo coronatus magnus pacificus imperator Romanum gubernans imperium, qui et per misericordiam Dei rex Francorum et Langobardorum, Amalario (Odilberto) (N) venerabili episcopo (archiepiscopo) (*add.* aeternam) in Domino salutem (Ar: salutem in Domino aeterno).

Preface: Saepius tecum, immo et cum ceteris collegis tuis familiare conloquium de utilitate sanctae Dei ecclesiae haere voluissemus. . .

Commentary: Nosse itaque per tua scripta aut per te ipsum volumus qualiter tu et suffraganei tui doceatis et instruatis sacerdotes Dei et plebem vobis commissam de baptismi sacramento. . .

Explicit: . . . Vel cur corpore et sanguine Dominico confirmatur? Haec omnia subtili indagine per scripta nobis, sicut diximus, nuntiare satage, vel, si ita teneas et praedices, aut si in hoc quod praedicas, te ipsum custodias. Bene vale et ora pro nobis.

MSS: V3,[1] Sp1,[2] Z1,[3] Co2,[1] P7,[2] Ar,[3] Vi1,[4] Zw,[4] unidentified MS[2] (see editions)

Editions: Dom Jean Mabillon, ed., *Vetera analecta,* 1 (Paris, 1723), pp. 21f. (2nd ed., 1733, pp. 75f.), using: an unidentified codex from Metz received through a Benedictine of the Congrégation de St.-Vanne in Verdun (sur-Meuse); repr. in PL 98:933f.

Jean Michel Hanssens, ed., *Amalarii episcopi opera liturgica omnia,* 1, Studi e Testi 138 (Vatican, 1948), pp. 235f., using: Ar, Spl, Vi1, and Z1.

*TEXT 14*

[1]The TEXT is in the form of a capitulary issued probably by Waltcaud, bishop of Liège
[810–831] (ed. Albert Werminghoff, *Neues Archiv* 27 [1902], 578–580). Waltcaud modifies
the TEXT to address his priests; he rearranges the order of questions and omits two of
them. Title in V3: "*Item alia capitula sacerdotibus.*" Incipit and explicit in V3 and Co2: "I.
De ordine baptisterii qualiter unusquisque presbiter scit vel (et) intellegit vel qualiter primo
infans catechumenus efficitur. . .vel cur corpore et sanguine Domini confirmatur."
Perhaps this variant form should be classified as a separate text under division X below
(from the archiepiscopal province of Cologne).

[2]The TEXT is addressed to Odilbert (archbishop of Milan): ". . .Odilberto venerabili archiepiscopo. . ."

[3]The TEXT is addressed to Amalarius (of Metz and archbishop of Trier): ". . .Amalario
(Ar: Amalchero) venerabili episcopo. . ." In Ar the title is: "*Incipit interrogatio Karoli
serenissimi augusti ad Amalherum (sic) episcopum.*" In Z1 the title is: "*Interrogacio Karoli
imperatoris.*" In Ar the last two sentences are omitted, explicit: ". . .vel cur corpore et
sanguine Dominico confirmetur."

[4]The TEXT is part of a collection of form letters of Udalric of Bamberg (s. XI), addressed to "N." The incipit is: "Karolus serenissimus augustus a Deo coronatus Romanum gubernans imperium, qui et per misericordiam Dei rex Francorum et Langobardorum, N venerabili archiepiscopo in Domino salutem."

## IV. Baptismal Instruction from the Archiepiscopal Province of Sens (including Chartres, Auxerre, Troyes, Orléans, Paris, Meaux, Nevers)

*TEXT 15*

| | |
|---|---|
| Composer: | Magnus, archbishop of Sens (801–818) |
| Description: | The corporate response of the bishops of Sens to Charlemagne's baptismal questionnaire (TEXT 14), addressed to Charlemagne and explaining the ceremonies according to his series of questions. |
| Preface: | Gloriosissime imperator, innotescere magnitudini vestrae praesumpsimus nos servi vestri, Magnus scilicet et ceteri compares mei. . . |
| Commentary: | Baptismum Graece, Latine tinctio interpretatur, quia ibi homo Spiritu gratiae in melius mutatur. Et propterea infans ter mergitur in sacro fonte. . . |
| Explicit: | . . .corpore Domini pascatur et sanguine eius potetur, ut in corpore Christi traditus, et ille in Christo maneat, et Christus in eo. |
| Alter. In.: | De baptismo. Baptisma Graecum (An adds: nomen) est, quod in Latinam linguam conversum tinctio sive lavacrum interpretatur, quod ibidem infans, vel etiam cuiuscumque aetatis homo, per gratiam Spiritus Sancti renovatur in melius. Item. Idcirco mergitur infans tribus vicibus. . . |

Alter. Ex.: (A final clause begins: A parvulo enim recens nato usque ad decrepitum senem). . .Sicut ergo acceptatur baptismus, quem non potuit amittere qui ab unitate discesserat: sic acceptandus est baptismus, quem dedit ille qui sacramentum dandi cum discederet non amisit (An: amiserat).

MSS: An,[1] P10,[1] P19, P21,[1] unidentified MS (see editions)

Editions: Dom Edmund Martène, ed., *De antiquis ecclesiae ritibus libri quatuor,* 1, 1st ed. (Rouen, 1700), pp. 158–161, using: An; 2nd ed. (Antwerp, 1736), coll. 169–171, using: An and P19 (2nd ed. repr. in PL 102:981–984).

Jacques Sirmond, ed., *Antirrheticus II de canone Arausicano adversus Petri Aureli. . .*(Paris, 1634), pp. 56f., cites a fragment of the letter of Magnus in a MS from Corbie unknown today (according to Jean-Paul Bouhot in *Revue des études augustiniennes* 24 [1978], 287).

*TEXT 15*
[1]The preface of the letter is omitted. The TEXT has the alternative incipit and explicit, containing a final clause not in P19.

## TEXT 16

Composer: Theodulf, bishop of Orléans (ca. 798–818)

Description: An indirect response to Charlemagne's inquiry (TEXT 14) in (originally?) eighteen chapters addressed to Archbishop Magnus. Eight passages are found identically in Magnus's response (TEXT 15).

Preface: Reverentissimo atque charissimo fratri Magno (Iohanni) episcopo Theodulfus salutem. Praeceptum tuum, vir venerabilis Magne (Iohannes), peregi, et si non solerti efficacia. . .

Commentary: *I. Cur infans catechumenus efficitur.* Quod modo infantes catechumeni efficiuntur antiquus mos servatur. Quicunque enim ad apostolos credentes adveniebant, instruebantur et docebantur. . .

Explicit: . . .ubi satietur in bonis desiderium eius, et cum Propheta dicere possit: "Ego autem cum iustitia apparebo in conspectu tuo, satiabor cum manifestabitur gloria tua."

Alter. Ex.:  (A final clause begins: Ecce, vir venerabilis, quod pru-
             denter iussisti, humiliter implevi). . .dummodo
             apostolica auctoritate omnia sunt (sint) probanda, et quae
             bona sunt retinenda. (P13, A12: *Explicit*. Lo1: Finit.)

MSS:         Tr1,[1] Mp1,[2] V2,[2] V6,[3] A12,[4] Lg,[1] Mu10,[5] P13,[2] Lo1,[6]
             Mu6,[7] R,[8] Bn,[9] Ca,[10] P2,[11] P14,[1] Mu14,[5] Ox,[6] F1,[12]
             Le[13]P11, unidentified MS[2] (see edition)

Edition:     Jacques Sirmond, ed., *Theodulfi Aurelianensis episcopi
             opera* (Paris, 1646), pp. 28–60, using: Mp1, Lg, V2, and
             an unidentified codex from Verdun (one of the above
             MSS?); repr. in PL 105:223–240.

*TEXT 16*

[1]The letter is addressed to "Iohanni episcopo" in place of "Magno episcopo." (In Tr1 "Iohannes" in the second sentence of the preface has been corrected [contemporary hand?] in the margin to "Magne.") Tr1 has the additional final clause with the alternative explicit. Lg and its copy, P14, do not have the additional final clause. Tr1, Lg, and P14 list the titles of the eighteen chapters after the preface; they are not repeated at the beginning of each chapter of the commentary.

[2]The letter is addressed to Bishop Magnus and includes a final paragraph ending with the alternative explicit. In P13 the eighteen chapter titles are listed before the commentary and each is repeated before its chapter.

[3]Preface is omitted. Title: *"Incipiunt capitula."* The titles of the eighteen chapters are listed in the beginning and not repeated before the chapters of the commentary.

[4]Preface is omitted. Title: *"Incipiunt capitula cur infans cathecuminus efficitur."* The TEXT is in fifteen chapters, whose titles are listed first, beginning: "I. Quid sit cathecuminus? II. Quur exsufflatur?. . ."Each is repeated before the chapters of the commentary. It has the alternate explicit.

[5]The preface is substituted with an entirely foreign prologue: "(Mu14 only: Incipit prologus super sequentem libellum.) Sicut enim de Domino nostro Iesu Christo in actionibus apostolorum scriptum est quod post passionem. . .mortifera humani generis peccata.", after which is our TEXT, with the eighteen chapter titles listed first: *"Incipiunt capitula.* (I.) Quur (cur) infans catechumenus efficitur. . ." It does not contain the final clause, "Ecce, vir venerabilis. . ." Mu14 is a direct copy of Mu10.

[6]Incipit: "Reverentissimo atque charissimo fratri. Peregi, et si non sollerti efficacia. . ." After the preface the eighteen chapter titles are listed first and not repeated before each chapter: *"Incipiunt capitula.* I. Quur infans catechumenus efficitur. II. Quid sit catechumenus. . ." Lo1 has the alternate explicit. Ox is incomplete, ending in the middle of chapter XIII with: ". . .Dominus fuisse legitur, praeteritur"// (PL 105:232d).

[7]Preface is omitted. Title: *"Incipit capitula de baptismo."* The eighteen chapter titles are listed before the commentary begins and each is repeated before its chapter. The TEXT is incomplete after the first words of the last chapter due to loss of a folio or folios.

[8]An extracted form, according to Dom Germain Morin in *Revue bénédictine* 14 (1897), 482.

[9]The TEXT is in a form reworked by Ademar of Chabannes (d. 1034). He substitutes his own preface and conclusion, condenses the chapters to fifteen, divides them into four separate sermons, and adds material of his own.

[10]Preface is omitted. Title and incipit: *"De baptismo. I. Quur infans catecuminus efficitur.* Quod modo infantes caticumini efficiuntur. . ." The TEXT is incomplete, containing only the first thirteen chapters.

¹¹Preface is omitted. Title and incipit: *"Questiones de ordine baptismi.* Quia infantes catecumini efficiuntur antiquus mos servatur. . ."* The TEXT consists only of excerpts from each of the eighteen chapters, explicit: ". . .'Ego autem cum iusticia apparebo' et reliqua."

¹²Preface is omitted and there is a false title: *"Liber sancti Hieronymi de Christianitate. . ."* (rest of title illegible). This MS has the alternative explicit.

¹³The TEXT is incomplete, breaking off at the same point as Ox (see note 6).

## TEXT 17

| | |
|---|---|
| Composer: | Anonymous |
| Description: | An explanation of the ceremonies of baptism corresponding to Charlemagne's series of questions (TEXT 14). Five passages are found identically in Magnus's response (TEXT 15). |
| Title: | *Item alia expositio de eadem re. Querendum nobis est cur ille qui ad baptismi gratiam venit prius caticuminus efficitur* |
| Incipit: | Ideo primus (sic) cathicuminus efficitur qui baptizandus est ut non rudis nec neofitus suscipiat corpus et sanguinem Domini. . . |
| Explicit: | . . .in baptismo tribuitur, remittitur peccata animae. Unde et Apostolus dicit: "Cor creditur ad iustitiam, ore autem confessio fit ad salutem." |
| MS: | Tr1 |
| Edition: | None. |

## TEXT 18

| | |
|---|---|
| Composer: | Anonymous |
| Description: | A capitulary from a diocesan synod inspired by Charlemagne's questionnaire (TEXT 14), giving instruction on baptism. It is incomplete, breaking off after Cap. IV. Four passages are found identically in Magnus's response (TEXT 15). |
| Preface: | Haec sunt causae quas domnus imperator augustus nobis ad utilitatem semper sanctae ecclesiae per sacram suam mandavit epistolam. |
| Commentary: | Cap. I. Quomodo vel qualiter unusquisque Dei sacerdos plebem sibi a Deo commissam insinuat, praedicat, atque gubernat? Resp. Nos igitur populum nobis commissum iuxta nostram exigui intellectus scientiam praedicamus et ammonemus sicut sancti iam nobis patres per illorum reliquerunt exempla, Augustinus, Cyprianus, Hieronymus, |

|                |                                                                                                                                                                                                                                                                          |
|----------------|--------------------------------------------------------------------------------------------------------------------------------------------------------------------------------------------------------------------------------------------------------------------------|
|                | Ambrosius, Gregorius, Ephraim, Cassianus, Cassiodorus, caeterique. . .                                                                                                                                                                                                    |
| Break-off:     | . . .IV. Cap. De scrutinio ecclesiastico, cur scrutinium fit, et quo tempore, et quid est scrutinium? Resp. Scrutinium a scrutando dicitur, quia tunc scrutandi sunt catechumeni si rectam iam noviter fidem symboli eis traditam firmiter tenent//.                       |
| MS:            | unidentified (see edition)                                                                                                                                                                                                                                                |
| Edition:       | Etienne Baluze, ed., *Capitularia regum Francorum,* 2 (Paris, 1677), coll. 1402f.; the MS used is not identified (repr. in PL 98:939f.)                                                                                                                                    |

*TEXT 19*

|                |                                                                                                                                                                                                                                                                          |
|----------------|--------------------------------------------------------------------------------------------------------------------------------------------------------------------------------------------------------------------------------------------------------------------------|
| Composer:      | Anonymous                                                                                                                                                                                                                                                                 |
| Description:   | A commentary on the *ordo* of baptism in question-response form based on TEXT 9 and including a final clause which follows TEXT 9 in the letter of Alcuin to monks in Septimania. Six passages are found identically in Magnus's response (TEXT 15).                        |
| Incipit:       | Primitus namque interrogandi sunt, quid est baptismum vel qua dicitur lingua? Resp. De baptismi autem mysterio nos ita intellegimus, quod baptismum Graece, Latine tinctio interpretatur. . .                                                                              |
| Sample:        | Interr. Cur abrenuntio (sic, Vd) dicitur? Resp. Abrenuntiatio dicitur abominatio sive detestatio quia ante baptismum unusquisque propter originalia peccata servus est peccati. Et ideo abrenuntiat diabulo, qui est servus peccati, et omnibus operibus eius, et omnibus pompis eius, id sunt viciis, ut dominatione (sic) illius spernatur. . . |
| Explicit:      | (Final clause begins: Videtis quam fideliter, rationabiliter, et prudenter haec omnia tradita sunt). . .nec clavis regni caelestis abiciat, quos a suis deviasse intellegis doctrinis. |
| MSS:           | Vd,[1] Mo[2]                                                                                                                                                                                                                                                              |
| Edition:       | Dom Germain Morin, "Textes relatifs au symbole et à la vie chrétienne," *Revue bénédictine* 22 (1905), 513f., using: Vd.                                                                                                                                                   |

*TEXT 19*

[1]Title: "*De baptismum (sic) et de caticuminum (sic).*"

[2]The TEXT is incomplete, ending with: ". . .tunc sacro crismate caput"// (f. 30 has been erased).

*TEXT 20*

| | |
|---|---|
| Composer: | Anonymous |
| Description: | A brief Isidorian compilation in question-response form on the definition of baptism, the trinitarian formula, and the use of water (*Origines* 6.19.43–49), included in a canon law collection.[1] |
| Title: | (*X.*) *De baptismo. (Mu9: Interrogatio.)* |
| Incipit: | Baptismum in qua lingua dicitur? Resp. Grecum nomen est et interpretatur tinctio. . . |
| Sample: | Interr. Cur per aquam fit baptismum? Resp. Haec ratio est. Voluit enim Dominus. . . |
| Explicit: | . . .ut in eis caro et anima delictis inquinata mundetur. |
| MSS: | P15, Mu9 |
| Edition: | None. |

*TEXT 20*

[1]Called the *Collectio Sangermanensis* after the MS Paris, BN lat. 12444 (P15), whose provenance is St. Germain-des-Prés. Mu9 contains a fragment of the *Collectio Sangermanensis*.

*TEXT 21*

| | |
|---|---|
| Composer: | Anonymous |
| Description: | A brief Isidorian compilation in question-response form on the prefigurations, effect, and minister of baptism (*De ecclesiasticis officiis* 2.25) included in a canon law collection (see TEXT 20, note 1). |
| Title: | *De baptismo. Isidorus in libro secundo De officiis dixit in cap. XXIIII* |
| Incipit: | Primus (sic) Moyses baptizavit in mare et in nube. . . |
| Samples: | Interr. Quae sunt peccata quae remittuntur per baptismum? Resp. Peccata Adae. . .Interr. Cur non purgatur poena mortis per baptismum. . . |
| Explicit: | . . .in ultimo langore ne pereat sine baptismo. |
| MS: | P15 |
| Edition: | None. |

*TEXT 22*

Composer: Anonymous

Description:  A series of extracts from Isidore on the catechumen (*Origines* 7.14.7 and *De eccl. off.* 2.21) included in a canon law collection (see TEXT 20, note 1).

Title:  *De caticuminis. XII.*

Incipit:  Caticuminus dictus pro eo quod adhuc doctrinam fidei audivit, nec tamen adhuc baptismum recepit. Nam catechumenus auditor interpretatur. *Isidorus in Libro officiorum.* . .

Explicit:  . . .Sal caticuminis a patribus institutum est ut eius gusto condimentum sapientie percipiant neque desinant a sapore Christi.

MS:  P15

Edition:  None.

## V. Baptismal Instruction from the Archiepiscopal Province of Trier (including Metz, Toul, Verdun)

*TEXT 23*

Composer:  Amalarius of Metz (archbishop of Trier, 809–814)

Description:  A letter addressed to Charlemagne in response to his inquiry (TEXT 14), commenting on the baptismal ceremonies in their Roman liturgical sequence.

Salutation:  Gloriosissimo et excellentissimo augusto a Deo coronato Karolo serenissimo, vita salusque perpetua.

Preface:  Domine mi, Christianissime imperator, misistis ad servulum vestrum inquisitiones secundum vestram misericordiam de sacro baptismate. . .

Commentary:  (I.) De catechumeno. Scimus enim, excellentissime imperator, omnes homines sub iugo peccati teneri. . .

Explicit:  . . .deinde dilectio, "quia caritas operit multitudinem peccatorum."

MSS:  V6, Fr,[1] P10,[2] S5, Z1,[3] An,[4] Mu7,[5] Sp2,[6] P21,[7] Ei,[8] St,[9] Ar[10]

Editions:  Henricus Canisius, ed., *Antiquae Lectiones, seu antiqua monumenta ad historiam mediae aetatis illustrandam,* 6 (Ingolstadt, 1604), pp. ?, using: St.

Jean Michel Hanssens, ed., *Amalarii,* 1:236–251, using: Ei, Mu7, P21, S5, Sp2, V6, and Z1.

*TEXT 23*

[1]The last chapter and half of the penultimate chapter are missing due to loss of the last folio or folios of the MS, ending: ". . .Non ait sepulturam"// (in Hanssens's edition, p. 248, line 14).

[2]The last half of the TEXT is lacking due to mutilation of the MS, ending: ". . .et dicimus eis: 'Effeta in odorem suavitatis' "// (in Hanssens's edition, p. 244, line 10). Probably note 4 applies to this MS, which has the same block of baptismal tracts as An and P21.

[3]Title: "*Responsio Amalarii episcopi.*"

[4] The preface is lacking, beginning: "Scimus enim omnes homines sub iugo peccati teneri. . ." There are variations from the edited form in the chapter divisions.

[5]Preface is omitted and the order of the first three chapters is rearranged, TEXT beginning: "*De symbolo.* Simbulum autem sic, 'Credo in Deum. . .'"

[6]The last half of the final clause is lacking; f. 38v ends: ". . .me ipsum custodiam, ita respondeo"// (in Hanssens's edition, p. 250, line 20). F. 39r is blank.

[7]The TEXT begins like An (note 4). Also, the first section of the final clause where Amalarius directly addresses Charlemagne ("Dixistis, serenissime auguste. . .vera caelestia petere.") is omitted.

[8]Title: "*Idem de baptismo ad Karolum augustum.*"

[9]Omits name of its author, Amalarius. Canisius (see editions) thought it was written by Alcuin.

[10]Title: *Responsio Amalheri (sic) episcopi ad Karolum imperatorem.* The last chapter is omitted, ending: ". . .quae per unum hominem intravit in mundum, Christiano adiutorio liberetur." (in Hanssens's edition, p. 249, line 3).

*TEXT 24*

| | |
|---|---|
| Composer: | Anonymous |
| Description: | Glosses on words selected from the prayers of the rite of baptism, similar to TEXT 43. |
| Title: | *Incipit exposicio super signaculum et baptismum* |
| Incipit: | Respicere: videre vel considerare. Ad rudimenta: ac documenta. Caecitatem: ignoranciam cordis. . . |
| Explicit: | . . .Procul: longe. Hinc: de isto. Latendo: abscondendo. Subripiat: subveniat. |
| MS: | Vd |
| Edition: | None. |

## VI. Baptismal Instruction from the Archiepiscopal Province of Lyon (including Autun, Langres, Mâcon, Chalon-s-S)

*TEXT 25*

| | |
|---|---|
| Composer: | Leidrad, archbishop of Lyon (798–814?) |

Description:   An instruction on the Roman *ordo* of baptism addressed
              to Charlemagne in response to his questionnaire (TEXT
              14), in eleven chapters.
Salutation:   Domino Christianissimo et gloriosissimo Carolo im-
              peratori, felicissimo, augusto.
Preface:      Praecipere nobis dignati estis, ut aut per nostra scripta aut
              per nos ipsos cognoscatis, qualiter nos et suffraganei
              nostri doceamus. . .
Commentary:   *Cap. I. De significationibus sacri baptismatis.* Igitur rudis
              mundus, necdum sole rutilante, nec pallente luna. . .
Explicit:     . . .ad cuius fastigium in sempiterna gloria participan-
              dum, vos, ut pote charissimum membrum eius, perducere
              dignetur, transferendo de regno ad regnum, "Rex regum
              et Dominus dominantium."
MSS:          P12,[1] P3,[2] Ba2,[3] unidentified MS (see edition)
Edition:      Dom Jean Mabillon, ed., *Vetera analecta,* 3.1, pp.
              778–784, using: P3, P12, and an unidentified codex from
              the Benedictine abbey of St. André-lez-Avignon in
              Villeneuve lès-Avignon (repr. in PL 99:853–872).

*TEXT 25*
    [1]Title: *"Responsio Leidradi archiepiscopi"*. The salutation is omitted, beginning: "Pre-
cipere nobis. . ."
    [2]Includes only the preface and first seven chapters, up to: ". . .sine Spiritu Sancto
nullatenus sanctificetur."// (PL 99:864d), according to Philippe Lauer, *Bibliothèque Nationale: Catalogue général des manuscrits latins*, 1 (Paris, 1939), pp. 359f.
    [3]The TEXT has many interpolations and variations, according to F[rancisco] X[avier]
Miquel Rosell, *Inventario General de Manuscritos de la Biblioteca Universitaria de
Barcelona*, 1 (Madrid, 1958), p. 294.

*TEXT 26*

Composer:     Anonymous
Description:   An instruction on the ceremonies of baptism introduced
              by one question, in the context of an *interrogatio sacer-
              dotalis*. It consists entirely of extracts from Leidrad
              (TEXT 25).
Incipit:      Qualiter catizizas infantem qui baptizandus est? Primus
              (sic) doceo ut credat, id est instruo fidem. Hoc est
              caticumanum (sic), id est instructum. . .
Explicit:     . . .Dum chrisma cocuntur, Spiritus Sanctus (sic) in-
              lustrentur gratia et confirmentur.

Edition: None.

## *TEXT 27*

Composer: Anonymous
Description: A supplemented form of TEXT 9, including a long passage on the renunciation of Satan, his works, and pomp.[1]
Incipit: Primitus enim paganus catechumenus fit, id est, audiens; scilicet ut unum agnoscens Dominum (An: Deum), relinquat errores varios idolorum. . .
Sample: Abrenuntio, id est recuso vel contradico operibus Sathanae qui omnium malorum princeps est: haec sunt superbia, invidia, homicidium, adulterium, falsum testimonium, luxuria, idolorum servitus, avaritia. . .
Explicit: . . .ut roboretur per Spiritum Sanctum ad praedicandum aliis, qui fuit in baptismo per gratiam vitae donatus aeternae.
MSS: P10, An, P21
Edition: Dom Edmund Martène, ed., *De antiquis ecclesiae ritibus*, 1, 2nd ed., coll. 172f., using: An.

*TEXT 27*
[1]After receiving Leidrad's response (TEXT 25), Charlemagne asked for more on the renunciation and Leidrad wrote him a long separate treatise on the renunciation of Satan and the vices (PL 99:873–884). This work may have had some repercussions in the archiepiscopal province of Lyon.

## *TEXT 28*

Composer: Anonymous
Description: A letter addressed to Charlemagne in response to his inquiry (TEXT 14), with chapters corresponding to his questions, but incomplete after Cap. V. The preface is almost entirely a copy of Leidrad's preface (TEXT 25). It is possible that TEXT 29 is the completion of this TEXT.
Preface: O serenissime adque piissime aguste (sic), praecepit nobis dignitas vestra aut per vestra scriptura (sic) aut per nos ipsos cognoscatis qualiter nos et suffragane (sic) nostri doceamus. . .
Commentary: Cur caticuminis (sic) efficitur? Caticuminis (sic) ideo efficitur quia non potest accedere ad gratiam Christi, id est ad baptismi sacramentum, antequam instruatur a sacerdote. . .

Explicit:            . . .De conpedibus (sic). Conpetentes autem sunt quia
                     (sic) iam post doctrinam fidei. . .indicium quo instructi
                     agnoscant quales ad gratiam Christi exibere debeant.
MSS:                 Or, P1
Edition:             Jean Michel Hanssens, "Deux documents carolingiens sur
                     le baptême," *Ephemerides liturgicae* 41 (1927), 81f.,
                     using: Or.

*TEXT 29*

Composer:            Anonymous
Description:         Perhaps the completion of TEXT 28; it consists of three
                     sections: on the profession of faith (an abridgment of the
                     *expositio symboli* of Leidrad); on the renunciation of
                     Satan, his works and pomp; and on baptism, (a variation
                     of TEXT 9 with a passage found identically in Leidrad
                     [TEXT 25]).
Incipit:             *De credulitate.* Post apostolicum certissima fides quam
                     magistri eclesiarum (sic) crediderunt, hec scilicet, ut pro-
                     fiteamur Patrem et Filium. . .
Samples:             *De abrenuntione* (sic). Abrenuntio, id est dispicio, derelin-
                     quo, sive contradico Satane. . .*De baptismo.* Babtismum
                     (sic) Grece, Latine tunctio (sic) interpretatur. . .Ut in-
                     vocatio Sancte Trinitatis ad nihilum videatur adnullari.
                     Primo infans caticuminus fit accedens ad baptismum. .
                     .Tangunttur (sic) ut venturi ad baptismum ab omni malo
                     et turpi verbo aures suas inpollutas custodia (sic). . .
Explicit:            . . .qui fuit in baptismo vite donator (sic) eterne.
MS:                  Or
Edition:             None.

VII. Baptismal Instruction from the Archiepiscopal Province of Reims
(including Soissons, Châlons-s-M, Noyon, Arras, Cambrai, Tournai,
     Senlis, Beauvais, Amiens, Térouanne-Boulogne, Laon)

*TEXT 30*

Composer:            Jesse, bishop of Amiens (799–814)
Description:         Jesse's address to the priests of his diocese on baptism; an
                     instruction, partly in question-response form, on the

Roman liturgical sequence of the rite, including a long extract from *Ordo Romanus* XI.[1]

Preface: Sacris sacerdotibus et in Christo omnibus diocesi nostrae
digne militantibus, Iesse humilis episcopus in Domino
salutem. Quoniam quidem dubitor me loqui vobis. . .

Commentary: De catechumeno primum dicendum est, quia ipse primus
efficitur in (*add.* eo) ordine. Interrogatio. Catechumenus
cur dicitur, et in qua lingua dicitur, et quo tempore vel
(*add.* quo) ordine efficitur si necessitas non invenerit. . .

Explicit: . . .Ideoque qui vult venire, accedat, credat, vivat Deo:
(*add.* de) Deo incorporetur, ut vivificetur.

MSS: F2,[2] S2,[3] V3,[4] P17,[2] unidentified MS (see edition)

Edition: Ioannes Cordesius, ed., *Opuscula*, pp. 664-685; the MS
used is not identified (repr. in PL 105:781-791).[5]

---

*TEXT 30*

[1]Michel Andrieu, *Les Ordines Romani du Haut Moyen Age*, 2 (Louvain, 1948), pp.
417-437 (#1-69, beg.).

[2]P17 is a direct copy of P18, of which a *membrum disiectum* is F2.

[3]Lacks preface; the first sentence of the commentary is treated as the title.

[4]Title: *Iterum incipi (sic) expositio de conpetenti*. The name "Iesse" in the preface is
replaced with "Ille."

[5]Part of the contents of the unidentified MS used by Cordesius are reproduced in PL
105:781-796 under the name of Jesse. Jesse's commentary, in fact, only extends to column
791. It is followed by other baptismal tracts that are joined together in Cordesius's MS to
form a collection of baptismal instruction. Following TEXT 30 are TEXTS 9 and 31.

*TEXT 31*

Composer: Anonymous

Description: Glosses on entire prayers selected from the rite of baptism. Part of TEXT 48 is contained in this TEXT.

Title: *Orationes et preces super electus Dei ad catticuminum
(sic) fatiendum*

Incipit: 'Omnipotens sempiterne Deus Pater Domini nostri Iesu
Christi': omnipotens dititur quia omnia post (sic) facere.
Ecce addedisti omnipotentem et veratiter addedesti. . .

Explicit: . . .id est, et ego te unguo de oleo qui te sanitatem
spiritalem facit in Christo Iesu Domino nostro in vitam
aeternam. Amen.

MS: L

Edition: None.

*TEXT 32*

Composer:      Angilmodus, bishop of Soissons (862–864/5)
Description:   An instruction addressed prob. ca. 861, when Angilmodus
               was a priest at Corbie, to Bishop Odo of Beauvais, consisting
               of a florilegium of citations from many authorities, but es-
               pecially John the Deacon (s. VI), Isidore, and Scripture.
Dedication:    Domino, sacrae religiones (sic) non minus merito quam
               dignitate conspicuo, Odoni, episcoporum sanctissimo,
               Angilmo de (sic), vestrorum infimus. . . .
Preface:       Ea, quae in ecclesiasticis officiis, antiquo religiosorum
               tradita decreto, vel privato servantur more vel publico. . .
Commentary: Mihi nunc propositum est primi ordinis, id est cathecum-
               inorum sive competentium, causam, defloratis indeque
               (sic) occurrerint patrum sententiis, vel proprio vel eorum
               pingere stilo. Catechumeni igitur sunt qui primum de gen-
               tilitate veniunt. . .
Explicit:      . . . sed iam rimosam revehamus ab aequore cymbam, in-
               currat scopulos ne vagabunda feros. Amen.
MS:            Bal
Edition:       Friedrich Stegmüller, "Bischof Angilmodus über die Taufe,"
               *Römische Quartalschrift* 52 (1957), 15–32, using: Bal.

VIII. Baptismal Instruction from Aquileia

*TEXT 33*

Composer:      Maxentius, archbishop of Aquileia (811–ca. 826)
Description:   A response to Charlemagne's inquiries on the ceremonies
               of baptism addressed to the emperor. The exposition of
               the creed is identical with that in TEXT 57.
Dedication:    Piissimo ac Christianissimo gloriosoque principi a Deo
               coronato et conservato pacifico victori ac triumphatori
               serenissimo et perpetuo augusto domno Karolo magno
               imperatori atque Romanum gubernati (sic) imperium,
               Maxentius, exiguus servorum Domini servus, sanctae
               catholicae Aquilegensis aecclesiae humilis episcopus, in
               Domino aeternam salutem. . .
Preface:       De eo vero, quod nosse cupitis, qualiter nos et suffraganei
               nostri doceamus. . .

Commentary: Cum sive parvoli sive iuvenes ad regenerationis veniunt sacramentum, non prius fonte (sic) vitae adeunt quam catecumini efficiantur. . .

Sample: Symbolum autem plurimus ex causis appellatum est. . .Hic Dei Patris et Filii una et aequalis pronuntiatur potestas, hic unigenitus Dei de Maria virgine et Spiritu Sancto secundum carnem natus ostenditur. Hic eiusdem crucifixio. . .

Explicit: . . .Pax Dei quae exuperat omnem sensum, custodiat corda vestra et intelligentias vestras in Christo Iesu Domino nostro, qui cum Patre et Spiritu Sancto vivit et regnat Deus per omnia saecula saeculorum. Amen.

MS: Mu8

Edition: Joseph Michael Heer, *Ein karolingischer Missionskate-chismus* (Freiburg-i.-Br., 1911), pp. 90–95, using: Mu8.


## IX. Baptismal Instruction from the Archiepiscopal Province of Salzburg (including Passau, Regensburg, Freising, Brixen)

### TEXT 34

Composer: Anonymous (Arno, archbishop of Salzburg? [d. 821])

Description: An instruction on the catechumenate extracted from a letter of Alcuin (with minor variations), and on the *ordo* of baptism, consisting of a florilegium of sentences from Alcuin, Isidore, and earlier authorities.

Title: *Ordo vel brevis explanatio de caticizandis rudibus*

Incipit: Primo ergo in caticizandis rudibus apostolicum oportet intueri sermonem quem dixit. . .

Sample: Niceta in libro primo ad competentes. Instructiones igitur necessarias ad fidem currentibus opus est explorare. . .

Explicit: . . .et sit perfectus filius Dei in operibus misericordiae sicut Pater noster caelestis perfectus est.

MS: Vi6

Edition: None.[1]

---

*TEXT 34*

[1] Jean-Paul Bouhot in *Recherches augustiniennes* 15 (1980), 205, 208f., used this MS to edit TEXT 36, a variation of this TEXT.

## TEXT 35

| | |
|---|---|
| Composer: | Anonymous |
| Description: | A florilegium; this TEXT is an abbreviated form of TEXT 34. |
| Title: | *Ordo de catezizandis rudibus vel quid sint singula quae ceruntur* (sic, Mu3) |
| Incipit: | Primo ergo in catezizandis rudibus apostolicum oportet intueri sermonem. . . |
| Sample: | (not in TEXT 34) Postea vero dicendum est breviter qualiter ipsum symbolum intellegere valeat, sicut et sanctae Dei ecclesiae tractaverunt doctores, beatus scilicet Athanasius, Hilarius, Niceta, Hieronimus, Ambrosius, Augustinus, Gennadius, Fulgentius, Isidorus, et ceteri. . . |
| Explicit: | . . .in operibus misericordiae sicut Pater noster caelestis perfectus est. |
| MSS: | Mu3 and Mu2[1] |
| Editions: | A[ndrew] E[wbank] Burn, "Neue Texte zur Geschichte des apostolischen Symbols," *Zeitschrift für Kirchengeschichte* 25 (1904), 149–154, using: Mu3 and Mu2. |
| | (Partial edition by Rosamond McKitterick, *The Frankish Church and the Carolingian Reforms 789–895* [London, 1977], p. 213, using: Mu3.) |

TEXT 35

[1]Mu2 is a direct copy of Mu3. Originally Mu3 contained only the first part of TEXT 35, up to "Niceta in libro primo ad competentes," written in a hand from Freising in the period of its Bishop Hitto (811/12–836). Ff. 136r, line 3–141v was added to the original MS a little while later (Bernhard Bischoff, *Die südostdeutschen Schreibschulen und Bibliotheken in der Karolingerzeit*, 1 [Wiesbaden, 1960], p. 107). Thus it is possible that the first part of TEXT 35 was originally a separate baptismal tract and not just an incomplete form of TEXT 35.

## TEXT 36

| | |
|---|---|
| Composer: | Anonymous |
| Description: | A lengthy instruction on the entire initiation process, including: the necessity of catechesis; the ceremonies of the catechumen; and baptism. All of TEXT 34 and long excerpts from Augustine's *De caticizandis rudibus* are incorporated into the TEXT. |

Title: *Ordo de catecizandis rudibus vel quid sint singula quae geruntur in sacramento baptismatis: ex diversis sanctorum dictis patrum excerpta testimonia*

Incipit: Primo ergo in catecizandis rudibus apostolicum oportet intueri sermonem. . .

Sample: (first section not in TEXT 34) Non unus autem atque idem in omnibus catecizandis rudibus doctrinae ordo observandus est. . .laetissimum nobis ad exordiendum sermonem aditum praebet. Niceta in libro primo. . .

Explicit: . . .in operibus misericordiae sicut Pater noster caelestis perfectus est.

MS: Ro

Edition: Jean-Paul Bouhot, "Alcuin et le 'De caticizandis rudibus' de saint Augustin," *Recherches augustiniennes* 15 (1980), 205–230.

## TEXT 37

Composer: Anonymous

Description: An extract from Isidore consisting of his three chapters on the catechumen, competent, and creed (*De eccl. off.* 2.21–23).

Title: *De caticuminis*

Incipit: Caticumini sunt qui primum de gentilitate veniunt habentes voluntatem credendi in Christum. . .

Samples: Caticuminus id est audiens nominetur, scilicet ut unum agnoscens Dominum, relinquat errores varios idolorum. Puto autem. . .regno caelorum aptus esse non potest. *De conpetentibus.* Post caticuminos secundus conpetentium gradus est. . .ad gratiam Christi exhibere se debeant. *De symbolo.* Symbolum autem quem (sic) idem conpetentes accipiunt. . .

Explicit: . . .et olim a Propheta predictum: "Quoniam verbum breviatum faciet Dominus super terram."

MS: Mu8

Edition: Bernard Pez, ed., *Thesaurus anecdotorum novissimus. . . (*Augsburg, 1721–1729), 2.2, coll. 12–15, using: Mu8.

## TEXT 38

Composer: Anonymous

Description: A supplemented form of TEXT 9.

Incipit:        A paganis quis vel a gentilitate veniens fit caticuminis (sic) habens voluntatem credendi in Deum, hic a sacerdote instruitur, quomodo credere debeat, et exortationis praeceptum accipit, qualem se ad fidei regulam et ad cultum Dei vivi debeat exhibere. . .

Explicit:       . . .qui fuerunt in baptismo per gratiam vite donati eterne.
MS:             Mu8
Edition:        Joseph Michael Heer, *Missionskatechismus*, pp. 97–101, following edition of Pez, using: Mu8.

## TEXT 39

Composer:       Anonymous
Description:    A brief instruction on the definition of baptism and the effect of water and chrism, compiled from Isidore, in the context of an *interrogatio sacerdotalis*.
Incipit:        (*add.* Interrogatio.) Baptismum quid est? (*add.* Resp.) Baptismum Graece, tinctio Latine (Mp2: Latine tinctio) interpretatur. . .
Sample:         (*add.* Interr.) Quid per baptismum et per chrismatis unctionem, (*add.* et) per manus impositionem, efficitur? (*add.* Resp.) In baptismo peccatorum remissio. . .
Explicit:       . . .Manus (W3: Manorum) vero impositio inde fit, ut per benedictionem (*add.* advocatus) invitetur Spiritus Sanctus.
MSS:            W3, Mp2, Mo, Lo1
Edition:        Heinrich Brewer, *Das sogennante Athanasianische Glaubensbekenntnis* (Paderborn, 1909), p. 188, using: Mo.

## TEXT 40

Composer:       Anonymous
Description:    Variation of TEXT 9 in question-response form, in the context of an *interrogatio sacerdotalis* which is identical in all three MSS (no other material in the three MSS is common to all).
Incipit:        (Interrogatio.) Quot et quibus modis constat officium baptismatis et quid prius agere debet ille qui baptizat? Resp. Salvator noster in evangelio hoc insinuat dicendo: "Ite, docete. . .
Explicit:       . . .qui fuit in baptismo per gratiam vitae donatus aeternae.

MSS: Mp2, Mo, Lo1
Edition: Heinrich Brewer, *Glaubensbekenntnis*, p. 189, using: Mo.

## X. Baptismal Instruction from the Archiepiscopal Province of Cologne (including Liège, Utrecht, Münster, Osnabrück, Minden, Bremen)

### TEXT 41

Composer: Anonymous (Archbishop Hildebald of Cologne [785–819]?)

Description: A letter addressed to Charlemagne in response to his inquiry (TEXT 14), using TEXT 9, entire, and other sources. It includes a phrase in OHG. In one MS it is attributed to Amalarius.

Preface: Domino meo Karolo serenissimo imperatori augusto a Deo coronato magno et pacifico regi Francorum et Langobardorum ac patricio Romanorum. Gratias etenim agimus Deo omnipotenti, qui tantam sapientiam cordi vestro inspirare dignitus est. . .

Commentary: Primitus enim paganus catechumenus fit. Catechumenus enim dicitur imbutus vel instructus (instructus vel imbutus dicitur), accedens ad baptismum, ut renuntiet maligno spiritui et omnibus dampnosis eius et pompis. Pompas autem nos dicimus: 'siniulgep ardosinen vvillon'. . .

Explicit: . . .hos anathematizat catholica et apostolica ecclesia. (Finit, amen.)

MSS: W4, Mu15,[1] Br1,[2] Br3[2]

Edition: Jean Michel Hanssens, *Amalarii*, 3:269–271, using: Br1, Br3, Mu15, and W4.

---

*TEXT 41*

[1]This MS falsely attributes the TEXT to Amalarius, bishop of Trier; on a superior line in a different hand it states: "Ammolarius Trenerenssis (sic) episcopus." Dom Germain Morin (*Revue bénédictine* 13 [1896], 294), Jean Michel Hanssens (*Amalarii*, 1:215), and Norbert Kruse (*Die kölner volksprachige Überlieferung des 9. Jahrhunderts* [Bonn, 1976], pp. 89–132) agree the TEXT could not have been written by Amalarius and suggest either Hildebald of Cologne, Riculf of Mainz, or Arno of Salzburg as the archbishop who was responding to Charlemagne's inquiry. Kruse, through a study of the orthography of the phrase in OHG, says the TEXT was written in the Cologne area and for this reason believes it was composed by Archbishop Hildebald of Cologne.

[2]Br3 is an apograph of Br1. The TEXT is incomplete in these MSS, containing only the first third (in Hanssens's edition, to p. 270, line 21).

XI. Baptismal Instruction from the Archiepiscopal Province of Mainz
(including Paderborn, Verden, Hildesheim, Halberstadt, Würzburg,
Eichstätt, Augsburg, Constance, Basel, Strasbourg, Speyer, Worms)

## TEXT 42

| | |
|---|---|
| Composer: | Anonymous |
| Description: | An instruction on the ceremonies of baptism in fifteen chapters based on Isidore and TEXT 9, partly in question-response form. It has the same title as TEXTS 2, 3, and 43 (some MSS). |
| Title: | *De baptismi officio ac misticis sensibus eorumque auctoribus nominatim designatis et de ordine venientium ad fidem eiusdemque misterii* |
| Incipit: | [I.] Primus gradus est caticuminorum, nam caticuminus Grece, Latine dicitur auditor. Caticuminus dictus est pro eo quod adhuc Sancte Trinitatis fidem audit et discit, necdum tamen baptismum recepit. . . |
| Sample: | IIII. Cur caticuminus accipit salem. . .in Propheta: "Aperi os tuum et ego adimplebo illud." Et rursum secundum Marcum: "Et solutum est vinculum lingue eius". . . |
| Explicit: | . . .ad praedicandum aliis quod ille fuit in baptismo per gratiam vitae donatus aeterne. |
| MS: | V3 |
| Edition: | Carlo De Clercq, "Ordines unctionis infirmi IXe et Xe siècle," *Ephemerides liturgicae* 44 (1930), 120–122, using: V3. |

## TEXT 43

| | |
|---|---|
| Composer: | Anonymous |
| Description: | Glosses on words selected from the prayers of the baptismal rite, similar to TEXT 24. |
| Incipit: | 'Oratio': quasi oris ratio, eo quod ex ore et ratione procedit. 'Super electos': id est advocatos qui de gentilitate ad Christi fidem veniunt. . . |
| Explicit: | . . .'Chrismate salutis': id est unctione salvationis. 'Amen': confirmatio est verbi. |
| MSS: | Me, Mu9,[1] Z2, Lo1,[1] P16,[1];[2] unidentified MS[3] (see edition) |
| Edition: | None of the complete TEXT. A partial edition exists from an unidentified MS used by Ioannes Cordesius in his *Opuscula*, between pp. 664–685, repr. in PL 105:792f. |

TEXT 43
[1]Title: same as in TEXTS 2, 3, and 42.

[2]P16 has several substantial variations from the other MSS of the TEXT.
[3]Title: *"Item de baptismo officioque eius auctoribus nominatim venientium ad fidem."* This MS contains only the first half of the TEXT, explicit: ". . .id est, ad comparationem falsorum."

## TEXT 44

| | |
|---|---|
| Composer: | Anonymous |
| Description: | An instruction on the ceremonies of baptism consisting of extracts from the *De clericorum institutione* 1.25–31 of Rabanus Maurus, abbot of Fulda and archbishop of Mainz. The order of ceremonies corresponds to the *ordo* of baptism incorporated into the *PRG* compiled at Mainz, ca. 950. |
| Incipit: | Sunt autem sacramenta ecclesiae baptismum (baptisma) et chrisma, corpus et sanguis. . . |
| Sample: | (De catechizandi ordine.) Catechizandi enim ordo hic est. Primo interrogatur pagnus si abrenunciet diabolo. . . |
| Explicit: | . . .Nec panis nisi aqua mixtum et confectum offeratur, ne(?) tali oblatione caput membris se iunctum esse significetur. |
| MSS: | Sp1, W4,[1] Mu15[1] |
| Edition: | None. |

### TEXT 44
[1]Title: *"De sacramentis ecclesiae."* Mu15 contains only the first half of the TEXT, ending: ". . .Ungitur inter scapulas ut undique muniatur et ad bona opera per gratiam Dei roboretur."

## TEXT 45

| | |
|---|---|
| Composer: | Anonymous |
| Description: | (same description as TEXT 44) |
| Title: | (In right margin:) *De baptistatis*(?) *sacramento* |
| Incipit: | Baptisma(?) Grece, tinctio interpretatur Latine. Et iccirco (sic) tinctio dicitur quia ibi homo Spiritu gratie in melius mutatur. . . |
| Explicit: | . . .nam Dominus noster Spiritum Sanctum et semel dedit in terra consistens et semel in celo residens. |
| MS: | Cb |
| Edition: | None. |

## TEXT 46

| | |
|---|---|
| Composer: | Anonymous |

Description:    (same description as TEXT 44)
Incipit:        Primum sacramentum est quod Grece dicitur baptismum,
                Latine autem tinctio, cuius mysterium sub Trinitatis invoca-
                tione, id est Patris et Filii et Spiritus Sancti, completur. . .
Explicit:       . . .nomen Christi coram regibus et potestatibus audaciter
                et libere predicet et portet.
MS:             P20
Edition:        None.

*TEXT 47*

Composer:       Anonymous
Description:    An instruction on the Gallicanized *ordo* of baptism (as
                represented in the *PRG* compiled at Mainz) in question-
                response form in the context of an *interrogatio sacer-
                dotalis*. The TEXT is partly identical to TEXT 48.
Title:          *De cathecuminis et baptismi ordine* (*LV.* in right margin)
Incipit:        Cathecuminus quare dicitur? Resp. Cathecismos (sic) Grece,
                doctrina dicitur sive instructio. Unde cathecuminus dicitur
                instructus sive audiens. Catecizatus similiter eruditus. . .
Samples:        Interr. Conpetentes quare dicuntur? Resp. Quia iam post
                doctrinam fidei, post continentiam vitae, ad gratiam
                Christi percipiendam festinant toto amore et desiderio. In-
                terr. Cur signatur catheminus (sic) a sacerdote. . .Interr.
                Cur ei ostenditur symbolum. . .Interr. Cur exsufflatur?
                Resp. Ut ab eo saeva potestas per pium sacerdotis
                ministerium Spiritui Sancto cedat. . .
Explicit:       . . .ita per hanc unctionem sanctificatio Spiritus
                adhibetur ad gloriam. Per Dominum.
MS:             Tr3
Edition:        None.

*TEXT 48*

Composer:       Anonymous
Description:    (same description as TEXT 47, from which this composer
                borrowed a number of passages.)
Incipit:        Interrogatio. Catecuminus quare dicitur? Resp. Ca-
                tecismos (sic) Grece, doctrina dicitur sive instructio. . .
Samples:        Interr. Baptismum quid est? Resp. Grece baptisma dicitur.
                . .Interr. Quid est quod baptizandis primo abrenuntiacio

proponitur? Resp. Abrenuntiare est abnegare. . .Interr.
Symbolum quid est. . .Interr. Quid est quod baptizandis
a sacerdotibus insufflantur? Resp. Ut ab eis inmundi
demones et aerii spiritus flatu divino, id est opere Sancti
Spiritus, expellantur. . .

Explicit: . . .et tamquam rex atque sacerdos mitra spirituali et
diademate redimitur atria Christi pasticeps (sic) eius effec-
tus penetret.
MS: Vi4
Edition: None.

## XII. Baptismal Instructions from Southern France/Northern Italy

*TEXT 49*

Composer: Anonymous
Description: A brief inquiry on why and how the priest baptizes in the
context of a larger *interrogatio sacerdotalis.*
Incipit: (Interrogatio.) Pro (Propter) quid baptizas? Resp. Pro
(Propter) omnia peccata quae committuntur in mundum,
tamquam (que) ex Adam generaliter (originaliter) trax-
imus (*add.* quam) et ante baptismum nos ipsi com-
missimus (in nobis ipsis gerimus). . .
Sample: Interr. Quomodo baptizas? Resp. In nomine Sanctae
Trinitatis trinam facio mersionem in conca fontis. . .
Explicit: . . ."Nisi manducaveritis carnem Filii hominis et biberitis
eius sanguinem, non habebitis vitam aeternam in vobis."
MSS: L,[1] A11, S1,[2] A13,[3] Ba2, F3,[4] P16,[1] Es2
Editions: Adolf Franz, *Die Messe im deutschen Mittelalter* Freiburg-i.-Br., 1902), p. 343, n. 1, using: S1 (but see note 2 to
this TEXT).

---

*TEXT 49*

[1]L and P16 contain only the first question and response of the TEXT, as follows: "(P16:
Interr.) Propter (L: Pro) quid baptizas? (P16: Resp.) Propter (L: Pro) omnia peccata que
committuntur (L: cummituntur) in mundo (L: mondum) que ex Adam originaliter traximus
(L: trasimus) et que utte (sic, P16) (L: et qui ante) baptismum in nobis ipsis gerimus. Et
secundum, quia (L: hoc que) Christus sanctificavit aquas in suum baptismum ut lavaret
omnia peccata cum crisma et Spiritu Sancto (L: crismate Spiritus Sancti)." All the other
MSS contain the TEXT in the context of an *interrogatio sacerdotalis* that varies in length
and content in each MS, but often begins with, and always precedes our TEXT with: "Dic
mihi, pro quid est presbyter benedictus (Sl: ordinatus)? Resp. Ad adnuntiandum verbum
divinum et ad tradendum baptismum vel. . ."

²The form of the TEXT edited by Adolf Franz with this MS has substantial variations from the form of the TEXT in all its other MSS.

³Incipit: "Interr. Dic mihi pro quid baptizas? Pro omnia peccata que conmituntur in mundum ex Adam originaliter. Quod et ante baptissimum (sic) nos ipsi conmisimus. . ."

⁴Incipit: "Interr. Resp. (sic) Quid baptizas? Resp. Pro omnibus(?) peccatis que commituntur in mundo tamquam ex Adam originaliter transfigimur. . ."

## TEXT 50

| | |
|---|---|
| Composer: | Anonymous |
| Description: | An instruction on the baptismal *ordo* consisting of seventeen questions and responses. |
| Incipit: | Interrogatio. Quare nomina eorum qui catechizandi sunt ab acolito describuntur? Responsio. Ut scilicet impleatur et in eis illud quod scriptum est: "Inperfectum meum viderunt oculi mei. . . |
| Sample: | Interrogatio. Quare post descriptionem nominum signantur catechumeni? Responsio. Videlicet ut possint dicere: "Signatum est super nos lumen vultus tui, Domine". . . |
| Explicit: | . . .Unde ipse huius rei perfectionem demonstrans ait: "Qui manducet carnem meam et bibit sanguinem meum, in me manet et ego in eum." |
| MSS: | Ba2, Vc, Es2 |
| Edition: | André Wilmart, "Une catéchèse baptismale du IXe siècle," *Revue bénédictine* 57 (1947), 196–200, using: Vc. |

### XIII. Further Baptismal Instructions of French (?) Origin, Inspired by Charlemagne's Questionnaire

## TEXT 51

| | |
|---|---|
| Composer: | Anonymous |
| Description: | An instruction on the baptismal ceremonies corresponding to the questions posed by Charlemagne (TEXT 14), but incomplete. It includes an *expositio symboli* similar to TEXT 52. |
| Title: | *Item de baptismo* |
| Incipit: | Cur primo infans capacuminus (sic) effici[a?]tur vel qui (sic) sit caticuminus? Caticuminus dictus per (sic) eo quod adhuc doctrinam fidei audiat. . . |
| Sample: | Expositio smboli (sic). VIIII. Credo in Deum Patrem omnipotentem. Deus enim sic Deus semper est, ita semper et |

omnipotens quia ego (sic) semper Pater fuit in Filio cuius Pater est. Omnipotens vero ideo dicit quia omnia potest cuiusque nihil inposibile est. . .

Explicit:  '. . .ad dextris eius ut adversaretur ei et dixit Dominus ad Satanum, incre//(end folio)

MS:  P4

Edition:  None.

## TEXT 52

Composer:  Anonymous

Description:  Variation of TEXT 9 in question-response form supplemented with Isidore and other sources, preceded by Charlemagne's questions (with variations).

Title:  *Interrogatio* [ ? ]

Incipit:  Quid sit caticuminus, vel quare sit infans baptizatus, vel quare trina mersio sit in baptismo, aut quare ponitur sal in ore, aut cur de sputo tanguntur ei nares et aures, aut quid sit effeta, aut quare unguntur ei scapule et pectus oleo, vel quare post baptisma albis induitur vestimentis, aut quid sit credere in Deum Patrem omnipotentem, quomodo credat et in Iesum Filium eius, quomo (sic) et in Spiritum Sanctum, quomodo sanctam ecclesiam, aut quid sit sanctorum communio, vel carnis resurrectio, aut quare postea accipit manus inposicionem a summo sacerdote, omnia quantum possumus intimare curamus.
Prima necessitas est ut paganus caticuminus sit. . .

Explicit:  . . .qui fuerint in baptismo per gratiam vita (sic) donatur (sic) aeterna (sic)

MS:  Vs

Edition:  None.

## TEXT 53

Composer:  Anonymous

Description:  An instruction in the form of a letter to Charlemagne in response to his questionnaire (TEXT 14), based on TEXT 9. There are a few passages identical with TEXT 54.

Preface:  Haec est epistola quam ad aures domni imperatoris direximus. Placuit vestrae incomparabili prudentiae, mi domine, gloriosissime imperator et princeps populi Christiani, a me

servorum Dei infimo percuntari de sacrosancti baptismatis mysterio, quomodo illud intelligentes, eos doceamus
qui nobis commissi esse videntur. . .

Commentary: Legimus, quippe, velut nobis orthodoxi fidei catholicae
cultores scriptum reliquerunt, quod infans priusquam
salutaris ablutione lavacri peccatorum suorum purga-
tionem adipiscatur, catechuminus fit, id est audiens,
sive instructus. . .

Explicit:      . . .qui fuit in baptismo per gratiam vitae donatus aeternae.

MS:            unidentified (see edition)

Edition:       Edmund Martène and Ursin Durand, eds., *Thesaurus
novus anecdotorum*. . .(Paris, 1717) 1, coll. 15–17; the
MS used is not identified. Repr.: Ernst Dümmler, MGH
Epp. 4:535–537 and PL 98:938f.

## *TEXT 54*

Composer:      Anonymous

Description:   A variation of TEXT 9 in question-response form, including topics on *opera, pompa*, and *aures*. There are a
few passages identical with TEXT 53.

Incipit:       Interrogatio. Quur paganus caticuminus fit vel quid sit
caticuminus? Resp. Caticuminus Graecae, Latinae
auditor interpretatur. . .

Samples:       Opera diaboli manifesta sunt quae Apostolus opera carnis
nominavit, quae sunt fornicationes, inmundiciae, in-
pudicitiae, luxoriae (sic). Pompe eius sunt idolorum servitus cetereque vane et mortifere delectationes que
mergunt hominem in interitum. Quam qui in talibus usque
in finem vitae perseverant, regnum Dei non consequentur. . .Aures vero ideo tanguntur ut in hoc sermone
aperiantur et fidei auditus ingrediatur in novum hominem
et repellatur auditus malus et suggestio inimici. Effeta,
hoc est sterelis vel sine aliquo boni operis fructu. . .

Explicit:      . . .qui fuit in baptismo per gratiam vitae aeternae donatus.

MS:            Or

Edition:       None.

## *TEXT 55*

Composer:      Anonymous

Description: A variation of TEXT 9 in question-response form.
Title: (Vi5:) *Incipiunt questiones de rudimentis caticuminorum vel eorum qui ad gratiam baptismi divina inspirante clementia vocandi sunt. Interrogatio.*
Incipit: (Vi5:) Primum quero a te quare caticuminus vocetur et qua lingua dicatur? Responsio. Greca. Interr. Latine quid interpretatur? Resp. Audiens vel auditor. Primo enim paganus caticuminus fit accedens ad baptismum ut renuntiet maligno spiritui et omnibus pompis eius. (Vi5 and P16:) Interr. Quare in faciem illius a sacerdote insufflatur (P16: exsufflatur)?. . .
Explicit: (Vi5:) . . ."Accipite Spiritum Sanctum. Quorum remiseritis peccata, remittuntur eis," et ut roborentur per Spiritum Sanctum, qui fuerunt in baptismo vitae donati aeternae. (P16:) . . .Resp. Ut per inpositionem manus septiformis gratiae Spiritum accipiunt et ut roborentur per eundem Spiritum ad praedicandum aliis qui fuerunt in baptismo per gratiam vitae donantae (sic) eternae.
MSS: Vi5, P16[1]
Edition: None.

---

*TEXT 55*
[1]The TEXT in this MS has been used to make up part of a larger baptismal instruction. The first fifteen lines of f. 137r are badly mutilated, but it is evident that the TEXT is lacking the first two questions and responses. It begins: "Interr. Quare in faciem illius a sacerdote exsufflatur. . ." There are also a number of variations, mostly abridgments, of the form of the TEXT in Vi5. Following the explicit of P16 are two discernible further questions on baptism: "Interr. Quibus temporibus facis scrutinium vel quantis? Resp. Ita tamen agendum est ut a primo scrutinio quod incipit tercia ebdomada. . .Interr. Quo tempore facis publica baptiste"// (end f. 137r).

## XIV. Baptismal Instruction from Spain

*TEXT 56*

Composer: Beatus, monk of Liébana (d. ca. 798)
Description: An explanation of the grades of baptism, partly from Isidore, incorporated into Beatus's commentary on the Apocalypse (Bk.II, Prologue).
Incipit: Catechumenus dictus pro eo quod adhuc doctrinam fidei audit. . .

| | |
|---|---|
| Sample: | Quum aliquis iam paganus ad fidem venit, quum instruitur ut credat, caticuminus dicitur. Quum recte crediderit et baptizari se postulat, competens nominatur. Quum vero in aqua baptismi tinguitur, fidelis dicitur. Quum vero crismatur a crisma, id est unctione, dicitur Christianus. . . |
| Explicit: | . . .quod solis debetur episcopis, quum tradunt Spiritum Sanctum. |
| MSS: | The MSS are the numerous ones used by Sanders in his edition (see below). None contains any other baptismal instruction. |
| Edition: | Henry Arthur Sanders, ed., *Beati in Apocalipsin libri duodecim* (Rome, 1930), pp. 123–125. |

## XV. Baptismal Instructions of Problematic Place of Origin

### TEXT 57

| | |
|---|---|
| Composer: | Anonymous |
| Description: | Questions and responses on baptism alone, based on Isidore. |
| Title: | *Item alie interrogationes. I Cap. Interrogatur.* |
| Incipit: | Quid est baptismum vel quare dicitur? Resp. Baptismum est per gratiam Spiritus Sancti in melius inmutatio (sic), id est de peccatis ad indulgentiam. . . |
| Samples: | II. Cap. Interrogatur, cur tribus vicibus mergitur? Resp. Idem propter nomen Sanctae Trinitatis et propter ternum testimonium. . . III. Cap. Interrogatur, cur per aquam gratia Patris et Filii et Spiritus Sancti datur in baptismo? Resp. Quia, dicente Domino per Moisen: "In principio Spiritus Sanctus ferebatur super aquas". . . |
| Explicit: | (indiscernible) |
| MS: | P16[1] |
| Edition: | None. |

*TEXT 57*

[1]The mutilation of f. 137r makes it impossible to discern the end of this TEXT (see TEXT 55, note 1). Ff. 135v–137r consist of a collection of baptismal instructions; some are complete texts, some are fragments.

### TEXT 58

| | |
|---|---|
| Composer: | Anonymous |

Description: An instruction on the entire *ordo* of baptism, based extensively on Isidore.[1]

Incipit: Caticuminus Grece, Latine auditor interpraetatur. Caticuminus: instructus sive audiens. . .

Samples: Cathizizare: docere vel castigare, sicut Apostolus dicit:
"Communicet autem is, qui se cathezizat verbo. . .
Scrutinium dictum a scrutando. Scrutare est inquirere,
cognoscere, prospicere, providere, explorare, scrutare, prore
(sic), meditare, speculare, rimare, indicare vel investigare, in-
dagare, erudire, invenire. . .

Explicit: . . .quia Sanctus in ea manens Spiritus eundem sacramentorum latenter operatur.

MS: W4

Edition: None.

*TEXT 58*
[1]This TEXT contain an *expositio symboli* identical with that found in Maxentius of
Aquileia (TEXT 33). It also contains a shorter passage on catechesis found identically in
Jesse of Amiens (TEXT 30).

*TEXT 59*

Composer: Anonymous

Description: TEXT 9 with glosses. The first sentence is similar to TEXT 27.

Incipit: Primus (sic) paganus caticuminus fit, id est audiens, unum
agnoscens Deum, accedens ad pabtismum (sic) ut renuntiat
(sic) maligno spiritui. . .

Explicit: . . .vitae donatus aeternae. Videtis quam fideliter et renun-
tialiter et prudenter haec omnia tradita sunt observanda.

MS: W4

Edition: None.

*TEXT 60*

Composer: Anonymous

Description: A brief explanation of the definition and trinitarian form
of baptism excerpted from Isidore.

Title: *De baptismo*[1]

Incipit: Baptismum Graece, Latine tinctio interpretatur. Quod idcirco tinctio dicitur, quia ibi homo Spiritu gratiae in
melius mutatur. . .

Sample:        Baptizatus in nomine Patris et Filii et Spiritus Sancti; sicut
               in tribus testibus stat omne verbum. . .
Explicit:      . . .super aquam etiam in principio ferebatur Spiri-
               tus Sanctus.
MSS:           V3, S5, Ei, V1, S6,[2] Mi1[2]
Editions:      Aloisius Knöpfler, ed., *Walafridi Strabonis liber de exor-
               diis et incrementis*. . .(Munich, 1899), p. 104, using: S6.
               Martin Gerbert, ed., *Monumenta*, 2:292f., using: Ei.

*TEXT 60*
   [1]The TEXT is one chapter, entitled *"De baptismo,"* of a commentary on the Church, its
ministers, the faithful, and baptism, consisting of excerpts from Isidore. The whole is entitled: *"In Dei nomine pauca ex eruditorum virorum voluminibus excerpta incipiunt de
catholica ecclesia et eius ministris et de baptismatis officio."*
   [2]The title is applied to a chapter preceding the TEXT, beginning: "Orthodoxus Graece,
recte credens. . .," and ending: ". . .Laicus Graece, Latine popularis dicitur."

*TEXT 61*

Composer:      Anonymous
Description:   An instruction on the ten kinds of baptism in the Old and
               New Testaments, and on the use of water and chrism,
               partly consisting of excerpts from Isidore.
Incipit:       Baptismum Graece, Latine tinctio interpretatur. . .
Sample:        Sunt quoque in Veteri et Novo Testamento X genera bap-
               tismi: I, cum in mundi exordio Spiritus Dei superferebatur
               super aquas. II, cum in diluvio totius mundi peccata
               deleta sunt. . .X, cum iudicio per Spiritum et ignem sanc-
               ti baptizabuntur. . .
Explicit:      . . .Ac per hoc cum Dominus a mortuis resurrexisset, non
               terrestrium, sed aquatilium animalium carnem comedit,
               [id] est piscis assi partem et favum mellis.
MS:            Br2
Edition:       Ernst Dümmler, ed., MGH Epp. 4:203, note, using: Br2.


## LIST OF MANUSCRIPTS CITED IN THE INVENTORY

A11    Albi, Bibl. Rocheg. 38 bis, IX ca. med., prob. so. Fr. (Hubert
       Mordek, *Kirchenrecht und Reform im Frankenreich* [Berlin–
       New York, 1975], pp. 269-271); f. 42r. TEXT 49.

A12 Albi, Bibl. Rocheg. 42, s. IX ex., prob. so. Fr. (André Wilmart in Archives d'histoire doctrinale et littéraire du Moyen Age 3 [Paris, 1928], p. 286); ff. 7r–21v, TEXT 16.

A13 Albi, Bibl. Rocheg. 43, s. IX 4/4, prob. so. Fr. (Mordek, p. 261); ff. 15v–16r, TEXT 49; ff. 19v–22v, TEXT 26.

An Angers, Bibl. mun. 277, s. IX 3/4, Angers? (Jean-Paul Bouhot in *Recherches augustiniennes* 15 [1980], 189); ff. 65r–69r, TEXT 15; ff. 69r–71r, TEXT 27; ff. 74v–82r, TEXT 23.

Ar Arras, Bibl. mun. 685, s. XII; ff. 130r–v, TEXT 14; ff. 130v–134v, TEXT 23.

Au Autun, Bibl. mun. 184 (G. III), s. IX 2/3, west. Fr. (not Tours) (Bischoff); ff. 135r–v, TEXT 11; ff. 135v–136v, TEXT 9; f. 136v, TEXT 10?

B1 Bamberg, Staatl. Bibl. Lit. 53, s. XI, Bamberg; ff. 148r–?, TEXT 11; betw. 148r–149v, TEXT 12.

B2 Bamberg, Staatl. Bibl. Lit. 131, s. IX 4/4 or IX/X (Bischoff), so. Ger (Peter Brommer in *Zeitschrift für Kirchengeschichte* 91 [1980], 223); ff. 125v–?, TEXT 8?; ff. ?–138v, TEXT 1; ff. 138v–140v, TEXT 6; ff. 140v–144v, TEXT 5; ff. 144v–145v, TEXT 9.

B3 Bamberg, Staatl. Bibl. Lit. 133, s. XI; ff. 69v–70v, TEXT 12.

B4 Bamberg, Staatl. Bibl. Lit. 140, s. XII; ff. 172r–?, TEXT 12.

Ba1 Barcelona, Arch. de la Corona 64, s. X in. (Friedrich Stegmüller in *Römische Quartalschrift* 52 [1957], 13); s. XI (Reynolds); ff. 93v–97r, TEXT 32.

Ba2 Barcelona, Bibl. Univ. 228, s. X 2/2, so.-east. Fr. or no. It. (Raymund Kottje, *Die Bussbücher Halitgars von Cambrai und des Hrabanus Maurus* [Berlin-New York, 1980], p. 15); s. XI (Mordek, p. 131, n. 154); ff. 106r–109v, TEXT 50; betw. ff. 134v–139r, TEXT 49; ff. 141r–158r, TEXT 25.

Bn Berlin, Deut. Staatsbibl. Phill. 1664 [93], s. XI, Limoges; ff. 64v–83v, TEXT 16.

Be Bern, Burgerbibl. AA90, fragment 3, ff. 1r–6v, s. XII, Fr.?; f. 4r, TEXT 9.

Br1 Brussels, Bibl. Roy. 6828–6869, s. XVII; f. 96r (p. 185), TEXT 41.

Br2 Brussels, Bibl. Roy. 9581–9595, s. X (Ernst Dümmler, MGH Epp. 4, Epistolae Karolini aevi 2, p. 202); ff. 1–50, s. IX 3/3, no. Fr. (Bischoff); ff. 54v–55r, TEXT 9; ff. 55r–v, TEXT 61.

Br3 Brussels, Bibl. Roy. 17349–17360, s. XVIII; f. 8r, TEXT 41.

Ca      Cambrai, Bibl. mun. 413, s. XI; appx. ff. 92r–98r, TEXT 16.

Cb      Cambridge, Pembroke Coll. Lib. 111, s. XII/XIII; ff. 92r–93r, TEXT 45.

Co1     Cologne, Dombibl. CXV, s. IX 1/3, Cologne (Bischoff); ff. 224v–225r, TEXT 9.

Co2     Cologne, Dombibl. CXX, s. X 1/2 (Mordek, p. 226, n. 56); ff. 126r–?, TEXT 14.

E       Eichstätt, Bischöfl. Ordinariatsarch. 1, 1071–3 (with later additions); ff. 150v–?, TEXT 11; betw. ff. 150v–151v, TEXT 12.

Ei      Einsiedeln, SB 110, s. XI in. (Bischoff); betw. pp. 87–93, TEXT 60 and TEXT 9; pp. 140–142, TEXT 9; pp. 142–159, TEXT 23.

Es1     El Escorial, Real Bibl. de S. Lor. L. III. 8, s. IX (ca.856–860) (Pierre Salmon in *Revue bénédictine* 86 [1976], 226) Tours? (André Wilmart, *Analecta Reginensia* [Vatican, 1933], p. 153); ff. 25r–29v, TEXT 3.

Es2     El Escorial, Real Bibl. de S. Lor. Q. III. 10, s. XII ex; ff. 126r–127r TEXT 50; f. 127v, TEXT 49.

FT      Fiecht, SB 113, s. XII; f. [36v], TEXT 11; ff. [36v–37r], TEXT 12.

F1      Florence, Bibl. Med. Laurenz. Aedil. 214, s. XII/XIII; appx. ff. 42r–59r, TEXT 16.

F2      Florence, Bibl. Med. Laurenz. Ashb. App. 1923, s. IX in., Corbie (Bischoff); ff. 1r–13r, TEXT 30.

F3      Florence, Bibl. Riccard. 256, s. X/XI (Roger E. Reynolds, *The Ordinals of Christ from Their Origin to the Twelfth Century* [Berlin–New York, 1978], p. 71, n. 9, #12); f. 126r, TEXT 49.

Fr      Freiburg i. Br., Universitätsbibl. 8, s. IX 2/2, east. Fr. (Bischoff); ff. 136r–138v, TEXT 23.

H       Heiligenkreuz, SB 153, s. XII; f. 68v, TEXT 11; ff. 68v–69v, TEXT 12.

Lb      Lambach, SB XXVII, s. XII; ff. 16v–17v, TEXT 12.

L       Laon, Bibl. mun. 288, s. IX 1/3, east. Fr. (Laon not certain) (Bischoff); ff. 28v–38r, TEXT 31; f. 37v., TEXT 49.

Le      Leiden, Bibl. der Rijksuniv. B.P.L. 169, s. XV; ff. 106r–112v, TEXT 16.

Lg      Leningrad, Gos. Publ. Bib. im M.E. Saltykova–Sčedrina Q. V. I. no. 34, prob. s. IX ex., no.-east. Fr. (Bischoff); ff. 8v–21v, TEXT 16.

Lo1     London, BL Roy. Man. 8. C. III, s. X 2/2 (Reynolds), Canterbury (T[erence] A[lan] M[artyn] Bishop in *Transactions of the Cambridge Bibliographical Society* 2 [1957], 334f.); ff.

26r–50v, TEXT 16; ff. 50v/51r–53r, TEXT 43; ff. 56–57r, TEXT 39; ff. 57r–58v, TEXT 40.

Lo2    London, BL Add. 17004, s. XI, Ger.; p. 494, TEXT 11 and TEXT 12.

M    Mantua, Bibl. Com. 331, s. XI, Polirone; ff. 31r–32v, TEXT 8; ff. 32v–34v, TEXT 1; ff. 34v–35v, TEXT 5; ff. 35v–36r, TEXT 9; ff. 36r–38r, TEXT 4.

Me    Merseburg, Bibl. Domcap. 58, ff. 2r–21v, 820–840, Fulda (Bischoff); ff. 19v–21v, TEXT 43.

Mi1    Milan, Bibl. Ambros. H. 48 sup., s. XIII; f. 154r, TEXT 60; ff. 154r–v, TEXT 9.

Mi2    Milan, Bibl. Ambros. L. 28 sup., s. XI 3/3, prob. no. It. (Bischoff); ff. 54v–64v, TEXT 3; ff. 64v–66v, TEXT 9.

Mc1    Monte Cassino, Arch. dell'Abb. 323, s. IX 2/2, cent. It. (Bischoff); pp. 57–?, TEXT 11; betw. pp. 57–61, TEXT 12.

Mc2    Monte Cassino, Arch. dell'Abb. 451, s. XI, Monte Cassino; ff. 170r–?, TEXT 11; betw. ff. 170r–171r, TEXT 12.

Mp1    Montpellier, Ecole de Méd. 310, s. XI 2/3, west. Fr. (Bischoff); ff. ? (The first text of the MS), TEXT 16.

Mp2    Montpellier, Ecole de Méd. 387, ff. 1r–60v, s. IX 2/3, Fr. (Bischoff); f. 54v, TEXT 39; ff. 55r–57r, TEXT 40.

Mo    Monza, Bibl. Capit. e-14/127, s. IX–X (Bischoff), no. It. (Annalisa Belloni, *Catalogo de la Biblioteca Capitolare di Monza* [Padua, 1974], p. 88); f. 29v (s. X/XI), TEXT 19; ff. 30v–36v, TEXT 2; betw. ff. 70v–74r, TEXT 39; ff. ?–74r, TEXT 40

Mu1    Munich, Bayer. Staatsbibl. Clm 5127, s. XI & XII; ff. 79v–83r, TEXT 8; ff. 83r–89r, TEXT 1; ff. 89r–90r, TEXT 6; ff. 90r–92v, TEXT 5; ff. 93r–v, TEXT 9.

Mu2    Bayer. Staatsbibl. Clm 6324, s. IX 3-4/4, prob. Freising area (Bischoff); ff. 98v–106v, TEXT 35 (apograph of Clm 6325).

Mu3    Bayer. Staatsbibl. Clm 6325, s. IX 1/3, Freising (Bischoff); ff. 134v–142r, TEXT 35.

Mu4    Bayer. Staatsbibl. Clm 6407, ca. 800, Verona (Bischoff); f. 105r, TEXT 9.

Mu5    Bayer. Staatsbibl. Clm 6425, s. XI, Freising; ff. 56r–57r, TEXT 9; ff. 57r–58r, TEXT 11; ff. 58r–60v, TEXT 12.

Mu6    Bayer. Staatsbibl. Clm 12673, s. X, Salzburg? (Kottje, p. 40); ff. 74r–95v, TEXT 16.

Mu7    Bayer. Staatsbibl. Clm 13581, s. IX, west. Fr. mostly (Bischoff); ff. 244v–251v, TEXT 23.

Mu8  Bayer. Staatsbibl. Clm 14410, s. IX 1/3, no. It. or Bavaria (Bischoff); ff. 97v–99v, TEXT 33; ff. 99v–101v, TEXT 37; ff. 101v–102v, TEXT 38.

Mu9  Bayer. Staatsbibl. Clm 14508, ff. 64r–146r, s. IX 3/4, no.-east. Fr. (Bischoff); ff. 84v–85r, TEXT 20; ff. 119r–121r, TEXT 43; ff. 121v–125v, TEXT 3.

Mu10  Bayer. Staatsbibl. Clm 14532, s. IX ex., no.-east. Fr. or Lotharingia (Kottje, p. 41); ff. 3r–25r, TEXT 16.

Mu11  Bayer. Staatsbibl. Clm 14581, ff. 1–163, s. XI/XII, Regensburg; ff. 97r–100v, TEXT 8; ff. 100r–102r, line 16 & 103v, line12–105r, line 9, TEXT 1; ff. 102v, line 17–103r & 105r, line 10–105v,TEXT 6; ff. 105v–107v, TEXT 5; ff. 107v–108r, TEXT 9.

Mu12  Bayer. Staatsbibl. Clm 14727, ff. 53–170, s. IX 1/3, Regensburg (Bischoff); ff. 127v–129r, TEXT 9.

Mu13  Bayer. Staatsbibl. Clm 14760, ff. 39r–115r, ca. 817–847, Regensburg (Bischoff); ff. 111r–113r, TEXT 9.

Mu14  Bayer. Staatsbibl. Clm 17195, s. XII, Schäftlarn? (Kottje, p. 43); ff. 45v–60r, TEXT 16.

Mu15  Bayer. Staatsbibl. Clm 21568, s. XII; ff. 79r–v, TEXT 41; ff. 79v–80v, TEXT 44.

No  Novara, Bibl. Capit. XXX [66. (catal. no. 15)], s. IX 2/2, prob. no. It. (Mordek, p. 244); ff. 277v–280r, TEXT 2.

Or  Orléans, Bibl. mun. 116 [94], s. IX 3/4, west. Fr. (Mordek, p. 200, n. 525); s. IX (ca. 850) (Salmon, p. 228); ff. 9r–11r, TEXT 29; ff. 20v–21v, TEXT 28; ff. 77v–80r, TEXT 54; ff. 80r/80v–81r, TEXT 13.

Ox  Oxford, Bodl. Lib., Bodl. 398, s. XII & XII; appx. ff. 93r–100r, TEXT 16.

P1  Paris, BN nouv. acq. lat. 2056 (formerly Bibl. de l'Arsenal 1008 [109 H.L.]), pp. 211–213, s. XVII (copy of a Fleury MS written before s. IX 3/4; cf. Henry Martin, *Catalogue des manuscrits de la Bibliothèque de l'Arsenal,* 2 [Paris, 1886], pp. 222–227); pp. 211–213, TEXT 28.

P2  BN lat. 242, ff. 63v–69v, s. XI; ff. 63v–69v, TEXT 16.

P3  BN lat. 1008, s. IX & X, Fr. (Mordek, p. 248); ff. 92v–104r, TEXT 25.

P4  BN lat. 1012, s. IX 1/3 (Brommer, p. 217); ff. 1r–2v, TEXT 9; ff. 2v–8v, TEXT 51.

P5  BN lat. 1248, ff. 5–68, 73–79, 89–116, s. IX med., no. Fr., ff. II, 1–4, 69–72, 80–88, s. XI 1/2, Limoges (Bischoff); ff. 25v–35v, TEXT 2; ff. 78v–79r, TEXT 11; ff. 79r–81v, TEXT 12.

P6 BN lat. 2316, ff. 1-25, s. XII; ff. 13r-15r, TEXT 4.

P7 BN lat. 2389, ff. 1-15, s. XI (Philippe Lauer, *Bibliothèque Nationale: Catalogue général des manuscrits latins* [Paris, 1939-1952], 2:439), ff. 1r-40r, s. XII (Élisabeth Pellegrin, *Revue d'histoire des textes* 8 [1978], 295); ff. 1v-2r, TEXT 14; ff. 2r-5v, TEXT 1; ff. 5v-7r, TEXT 5.

P8 BN lat. 3244, s. XII; betw. ff. 128r-131v, TEXT 9.

P9 BN lat. 5577, s. XI; ff. 155v-?, TEXT 3; ff. ?-162v, TEXT 10.

P10 BN lat. 10741, s. IX 3/3, area of Lyon (Bischoff); ff. 129r-131v, TEXT 15; ff. 131v-133r, TEXT 27; 135v-138v, TEXT 23.

P11 BN lat. 12233, s. XVII; appx. ff. 36r-56r, TEXT 16.

P12 BN lat. 12262, ff. 136-148, s. IX ca. med., Fr. (Bischoff); ff. 136r-143r, TEXT 25.

P13 BN lat. 12279, s. IX ex., no. Fr.? (Bischoff); ff. 127r-131v, TEXT 16.

P14 BN lat. 12315, s. XII 2/2, no.-east. Fr., prob. Corbie (Kottje, p. 55); ff. 68r-75r, TEXT 16.

P15 BN lat. 12444, s. VIII-IX, prob. Fleury (Mordek, p. 258); ff. 37r-v, TEXT 20; ff. 40r-v, TEXT 21; ff. 71r-v, TEXT 22.

P16 BN lat 13092, ff. 131r-137v, s. XI; ff. 135v-136v, TEXT 43; f. 136v, TEXT 49; ff. 136v-137r, TEXT 57; f. 137r, TEXT 55.

P17 BN lat. 13372, s. XII; ff. 91r-103r, TEXT 30; ff. ?, TEXT 9 (apograph of Paris, BN lat. 13373).

P18 BN lat. 13373, s. IX in., Corbie (Bischoff); ff. 93v/94r-95r, TEXT 9.

P19 BN lat. 13655, s. X 1/2 or med. (Bischoff); ff. 1r-4r, TEXT 15.

P20 BN lat. 14993, s. XII & XIII; ff. 98r-99r, TEXT 46.

P21 BN nouv. acq. lat. 450, s. X (Bischoff); ff. 1r-6r, TEXT 15; ff. 6r-12v. TEXT 27; ff. 12v-25v, TEXT 23.

R Rome, Bibl. Naz. Cent. Vitt.-Eman. II Sessor. LII [2096], ff. 104-177, 191-205, s. XI ex It.; ff. 158r-161v, TEXT 2; ff. 196r-?, TEXT 16.

Ro Rouen, Bibl. mun. 469, s. XI,Abbey of Fécamp (Bouhot, p. 195); ff. 121v-135r, TEXT 36.

Sf St. Florian, SB 466, s. XII; ff. 27v-28v, TEXT 12.

S1 St. Gall, SB 40, pp. 301-357, s. IX 2/3 & 3/3, Switz. (Bischoff); p. 304, TEXT 49; pp. 342-348, TEXT 1; p. 355, TEXT 9.

S2 St. Gall, SB 124, ca. 804-820, area of St. Amand (no.-east Fr.) (Bischoff); pp. 310-326, TEXT 30.

S 3 St. Gall, SB 222, pp. 137-139, s. IX 2/3, prob. east, Fr. (Bischoff); pp. 137-139, TEXT 9.

S4     St. Gall, SB 235, ca. 800, St. Gall (Bischoff); pp. 294–298,
       TEXT 1; pp. 298f., TEXT 6.
S5     St. Gall, SB 446, pp. 1–168, s. IX 3/3, St. Gall (Bischoff); p. 83,
       TEXT 60; pp. 83f., TEXT 9; pp. 145f., TEXT 9; pp. 147–159,
       TEXT 23.
S6     St. Gall, SB 777, s. XII; p. 3, TEXT 60 and TEXT 9.
Sp1    St. Paul in Carinthia, SB 5/1, ff. 3–6, 9–56, s. IX 1/3, no. It.,
       rest: s. IX 2/3, Reichenau (Bischoff); f. 137v, TEXT 7; ff.
       138r–v, TEXT 14; ff. 140v–145v, TEXT 1; ff. 146r–147r,
       TEXT 6; ff. 147r–149v, TEXT 5; ff. 149v–150r, TEXT 9; ff.
       154r–156r, TEXT 44.
Sp2    St. Paul in Carinthia, SB 10/1, s. X (Jean Michel Hanssens,
       *Amalarii episcopi opera liturgica omnia*, 1, Studi e Testi 138
       [Vatican, 1948], p. 99); ff. 31v–38v, TEXT 23.
St     Stuttgart, Würt. Landesbibl. HB. VI. 108, s. XI 2/2, so.-west.
       Ger.; ff. 126r–130v, TEXT 23.
T      Tours, Bibl. mun. 136, s. XIII; f. 194r, TEXT 11; ff. 194r–v,
       TEXT 12.
Tr1    Troyes, Bibl. mun. 804, ff. 1–79, ca. s. IX 2/4 (2/3), Loire; ff.
       80–180, ca. s. IX 3/4, Reims (Bischoff); ff. 1v–6v, TEXT 16;
       ff. 6v/7r–8r, TEXT 17.
Tr2    Bibl. mun. 1528, s. IX in., prob. Orléans (Bischoff); f. 98r,
       TEXT 9.
Tr3    Bibl. mun. 1979, s. X/XI, maybe east. Fr.-west. Ger. (Kottje,
       p. 63); ff. 332r–334r, TEXT 47.
V1     Vatican, Bibl. Apost. Vat. lat. 1147 (further copies; Vat. lat. 1146;
       1148; Vienna, ÖNB lat. 914), s. XI; f. 22r, TEXT 60; ff. 22r–
       v, TEXT 9; ff. 69r/69v–70v, TEXT 8; ff. 70v–71v, TEXT 1;
       ff. 71v–72v, TEXT 5; ff. 72v–73r, TEXT 9; ff. 73r–74v,
       TEXT 4.
V2     Bibl. Apost. Vat. Pal. lat. 278, s. IX 2/3, no.-east. Fr.? (Bisch-
       off); ff. 64r–79r, TEXT 16.
V3     Bibl. Apost. Vat. Pal. lat. 485, s. IX ca. med., Lorsch (Mordek,
       p. 225, n. 49); ff. 36v/37r–44v, TEXT 30; ff. 45v–46v, TEXT
       42; f. 48r, TEXT 60; f. 95v, TEXT 14.
V4     Bibl. Apost. Vat. Reg. lat. 69, s. IX 2/2, Tours? (Wilmart, p.
       153); ff. 116r–120r, TEXT 3; ff. 120r–122r, TEXT 10.
V5     Bibl. Apost. Vat. Reg. lat. 272, s. IX ca. med., Reims (Bischoff);
       betw. ff. 79v–81r, TEXT 9.

V6    Bibl. Apost. Vat. Reg. lat. 284, s. IX 2/3, no. half of Fr. (not Fleury) (Bischoff); ff. 1r–23r, TEXT 16; ff. 23v–32v, TEXT 23.

Vc    Vercelli, Bibl. Capit. CXLIII, s. X 2/2, very prob. no. It. (Kottje, 74); ff. 134v–136v, TEXT 50.

Vd    Verdun, Bibl. mun. 27, s. IX 2/3, east. Fr. (Bischoff); ff. 118r–121r, TEXT 19, ff. 121r–122v, TEXT 24.

Vs    Vesoul, Bibl. mun. 73, s. X (Carlo De Clercq, *La législation religieuse franque de Clovis à Charlemagne*, 1 [Paris, 1936], p. 131, n. 2); ff. 53v–57v, TEXT 52.

Vi1   Vienna ÖNB lat. 398, s. XII; f. 13v, TEXT 14.

Vi2   ÖNB lat. 701, s. XI, Mainz; ff. 144v, TEXT 11; ff. 144v–145r, TEXT 12.

Vi3   ÖNB lat. 795, ca. 798, vicin. Salzburg (Bischoff); f. 166r, TEXT 9.

Vi4   ÖNB lat. 806, ff. 51–54, s. XII; ff. 52r–53r, TEXT 48.

Vi5   ÖNB lat. 823, s. IX 2/2, west. Ger. or east. Fr. (Bischoff); ff. 40r–43r, TEXT 1; f. 43v, TEXT 9; ff. 44r–v, TEXT 55.

Vi6   ÖNB lat. 1370, s. IX 1–2/4, Mondsee (Bischoff); ff. 1v–18r, TEXT 34.

Vi7   ÖNB lat. 1817, s. XII 2/2; ff. 57r–?, TEXT 11; betw. ff. 57r–59v, TEXT 12.

W1    Wolfenbüttel, Herz.-Aug. Bibl. Helmst. 141 [164], s. XII 1/2, Ger.; f. 108r, TEXT 11; ff. 108r–v, TEXT 12.

W2    Wolfenbüttel, Herz-Aug. Bibl. Helmst. 493 [530], s. XII in., perh. Anspach; ff. 66r–v, TEXT 11; ff. 66v–67v, TEXT 12.

W3    Wolfenbüttel, Herz.-Aug. Bibl. Helmst. 532 [579], ca. 820, prob. Salzburg (Bischoff); f. 93r, TEXT 39.

W4    Wolfenbüttel, Herz.-Aug. Bibl. Weissenb. 75 [4159], s. X 2/2 (Norbert Kruse, *Die Kölner volkssprachige Überlieferung des 9. Jahrhunderts* [Bonn, 1979], pp. 93f.), s. XI/XII (Jean Michel Hanssens in *Ephemerides liturgicae* 41 [1927], 71); ff. 17v–19r, TEXT 41; ff. 19r–21v, TEXT 44; ff. 102v–103v, TEXT 59; ff. 104r–106v, TEXT 58.

Z1    Zürich, Zentralbibl. Car. C. 102, s. IX 3/3, Switz.–no. It. (Bischoff); ff. 55r–59v, TEXT 2; ff. 69v–70r, TEXT 14; ff. 70r–76v, TEXT 23.

V2    Zentralbibl. Rh. 95, ff. 1–124v, s. IX/X, prob. so.-west. Ger. (Bischoff); pp. 115–131 (ff. 57r–65r), TEXT 3; pp. 131–137 (ff. 65r–68r), TEXT 43.

Zw    Zwettl, SB 283, s. XIII; p. 28, TEXT 14.

## APPENDIX
## LIST OF INCIPITS OF CAROLINGIAN BAPTISMAL EXPOSITIONS

A paganis quis vel a gentilitate veniens fit catechumenus habens voluntatem credendi in Deum, hic a sacerdote instruitur . . . TEXT 38; (Mu8)

Albinus magister filio carissimo Oduino presbitero, salutem. Et quia divina . . . in illo officio. Primo paganus catechumenus fit accedens ad baptismum . . . TEXT 9; (Br2; Co1; Mu4; Tr2)

Baptisma Graece, tinctio interpretatur Latine. Et idcirco tinctio dicitur . . . TEXT 45

Baptismi sacramentum si prima repetens ab origine pandam baptizavit Moyses in nube et mari . . . TEXT 8

Baptismum Graecae, Latine tinctio interpretatur. Quae idcirco tinctio dicitur quia ibi homo Spiritu gratiae in melius inmutatur et longe aliud quam erat efficitur, dicente Domino ad apostolos: 'Ite . . . TEXT 13

Baptismum Graece, Latine tinctio interpretatur. Quod idcirco tinctio dicitur, quia ibi homo Spiritu gratiae in melius mutatur, et longe aliud quam erat efficitur. Baptizatus in nomine Patris . . . TEXT 60

Baptismum Graece, Latine tinctio interpretatur. Quod idcirco tinctio dicitur, quia ibi homo Spiritu gratiae in melius inmutatur, et longe aliud quam erat efficitur. Prius enim foedi eramus . . . TEXT 61; (Br2)

Baptismum in qua lingua dicitur? Responsio. Graecum nomen est et interpretatur tinctio . . . TEXT 20

Baptismum quid est . . . TEXT 39; (W3)

Baptizo te, hoc est (id est) intinguo te. Electus, a Deo coronatus . . . TEXT 11; (Au; Ft; T)

CAP. I. CUR CATECHUMENUS INFANS EFFICITUR. Catechumenus ideo primo (primum) efficitur infans . . . TEXT 5; (Mu1; Sp1)

CAP. II. DE SACRAMENTO BAPTISMI QUID SIT IN VERBO ET AQUA. Quid enim est aliud baptismum nisi quia culpa mergitur . . . TEXT 1; (M; V1)

Catechumeni sunt qui primum de gentilitate veniunt . . . varios idolorum. Puto autem et omnes a Iohanne in penitentiam baptizatos . . . TEXT 37

Catechumeni sunt qui primum de gentilitate veniunt . . . varios idolorum. DE EXSUFFLATIONE. CELESTINI PAPAE. Cum sive parvuli . . . TEXT 4

Catechumenus dictus pro eo quod adhuc doctrinam fidei audit, necdum tamen baptismum recepit. Nam catechumenus Graece, Latine auditor interpretatur. Competens vocatus, quia post instructionem fidei competit . . . TEXT 56

Catechumenus dictus pro eo quod adhuc doctrinam fidei audivit, nec tamen adhuc baptismum recepit. Nam catechumenus auditor interpretatur. ISIDORUS IN LIBRO OFFICIORUM . . . TEXT 22

Catechumenus Graece, Latine auditor interpretatur. Catechumenus instructus sive audiens . . . TEXT 58; (W4)

Catechumenus ideo primo efficitur infans ut audiens a sacerdote doctrinam fidei credat . . . TEXT 5; (P7)

Catechuminus quare dicitur? Responsio. Catechismus Graece, doctrina dicitur sive instructio . . . TEXT 47

CUR CATECHUMENUS INFANS EFFICITUR. CAP. I. Catechumenus ideo primo efficitur infans ut audiens a sacerdote doctrinam fidei credat . . . TEXT 5; (B2; M)

CUR CATECHUMENUS INFANS FIAT. I. Catechumenus ideo . . . TEXT 5; (V1)

Cur infans catechumenus efficitur et quid sit catechumenus? Catechumeni sunt qui primum de gentilitate veniunt habentes voluntatem . . . TEXT 10; (Au?; P9; V4)

Cur primo infans catechumenus efficiatur vel qui sit catechumenus? Catechumenus dictus per eo quod adhuc doctrinam fidei audiat . . . TEXT 51

DE BAPTISMATIS SACRAMENTO. Baptisma Graece, tinctio interpretatur Latine. Et idcirco tinctio dicitur . . . TEXT 45; (Cb)

DE BAPTISMI OFFICIO AC MISTICIS SENSIBUS EORUMQUE AUCTORIBUS NOMINATIM DESIGNATIS ET DE ORDINE VENIENTIUM AD FIDEM EIUSDEMQUE MISTERII. [I.] Isidorus. Primus gradus est catechumenorum, ii conpetentium . . . TEXT 3; (Esl; Mi2; P9; V4; Z2)

DE BAPTISMI OFFICIO AC MISTICIS SENSIBUS EORUMQUE AUCTORIBUS NOMINATIM DESIGNATIS ET DE ORDINE VENIENTIUM AD FIDEM EIUSDEMQUE MISTERII. [I.] Primus gradus est catechumenorum, nam catechumenus Graece, Latine dicitur auditor . . . TEXT 42; (V3)

DE BAPTISMI OFFICIO AC MISTICIS SENSIBUS EORUMQUE AUC-
TORIBUS NOMINATIM DESIGNATIS ET DE ORDINE VENIEN-
TIUM AD FIDEM EIUSDEMQUE MISTERII. De catechumenis.
Ysidori in Libro officiorum. Catechumeni sunt . . . TEXT 2; (Mo; P5; R)

DE BAPTISMI OFFICIO AC MYSTICIS SENSIBUS EORUMQUE AUC-
TORIBUS NOMINATIM DESIGNATIS ET DE ORDINE VENIEN-
TIUM AD FIDEM EIUSDEMQUE MISTERII (SUPRA MEMORAVI.
ITEM). 'Oratio': quasi oris ratio . . . TEXT 43; (Lo1; Mu9; P16)

DE BAPTISMI PRAECEPTO IN EVANGELIO. 'Ite', inquit Iesus . . .
TEXT 1; (S4; Sp1; Vi5, Mu1)

DE BAPTISMI SACRAMENTO DIVERSE INCIPIUNT NARRA-
TIONES SANCTORUMQUE TESTIMONIA QUAE EVANGELIUM
PRODIT. 'Ite', inquit Iesus . . . TEXT 1; (S1)

DE BAPTISMI. INTERROGATIO. Ubi est baptismi preceptum? Responsio. Ubi Dominus discipulis suis ait . . . TEXT 1; (Mu11)

DE BAPTISMO ET DE CATECHUMENO. Primitus namque interrogandi sunt . . . TEXT 19 (Vd)

DE BAPTISMO. Baptisma Graecum (nomen) est quod in Latinam
linguam conversum tinctio sive lavacrum interpretatur, quod ibidem infans vel etiam cuiuscumque aetatis . . . TEXT 15; (An; P10; P21)

DE BAPTISMO. Baptismi sacramentum si prima repetens . . . TEXT
8 (Mu1)

DE BAPTISMO. Baptismum Graece, Latine tinctio interpretatur. Quod
idcirco tinctio dicitur, quia ibi homo Spiritu gratiae in melius mutatur, et
longe aliud quam erat efficitur. Baptizatus in nomine Patris . . . TEXT
60; (V3; S5; Ei; V1)

DE BAPTISMO. Baptismum Graecae, Latine tinctio interpretatur.
Quae idcirco tinctio dicitur quia ibi homo Spiritu gratiae in melius in-
mutatur et longe aliud quam erat efficitur, dicente Domino ad apostolos:
'Ite . . . TEXT 13; (Or)

(X.) DE BAPTISMO. (Interrogatio.) Baptismum in qua lingua dicitur?
Responsio. Graecum nomen est et interpretatur tinctio . . . TEXT 20;
(Mu9; P15)

DE BAPTISMO. I. QUUR INFANS CATECHUMENUS EFFICITUR.
Quod modo infantes catechumeni efficiuntur antiquus mos servatur . . .
TEXT 16; (Ca)

DE BAPTISMO. ISIDORUS IN LIBRO SECUNDO DE OFFICIIS DIXIT IN CAP. XXIIII. Primum Moyses baptizavit in mare . . . TEXT 21; (P15)

DE BAPTISMO. Orthodoxus Graece, recte credens vel rectae gloriae Latine . . . TEXT 60; (Mi1; S6)

DE CATECHUMENIS ET BAPTISMI ORDINE. Catechumenus quare dicitur? Responsio. Catechismum Graece, doctrina dicitur sive instructio . . . TEXT 47; (Tr3)

DE CATECHUMENIS ISIDORUS DIXIT. Primus gradus est catechumenorum . . . TEXT 3; (Mu9)

DE CATECHUMENIS. Catechumeni sunt qui primum de gentilitate veniunt . . . varios idolorum. Puto autem et omnes a Iohanne in penitentiam baptizatos . . . TEXT 37; (Mu8)

DE CATECHUMENIS. XII. Catechumenus dictus pro eo quod adhuc doctrinam fidei audivit . . . TEXT 22; (P15)

De catechumenis. Ysidori in Libro officiorum. Catechumeni sunt . . . TEXT 2

De catechumeno primum dicendum est quia ipse primus efficitur in eo ordine. Interrogatio. Catechumenus cur dicitur . . . TEXT 30; (S2)

DE CREDULITATE. Post apostolicam certissima fides quam magistri ecclesiarum crediderunt . . . TEXT 29; (Or)

DE ILLA VERBA GRECA QUAE VERTUNTUR IN LATINE QUAE SUNT IN ILLO BAPTISTERIO. Baptizo te . . . TEXT 11; (P5)

DE ILLA VERBA GRECA QUOD VERTUNT IN LATINA BAPTISTERI. Baptizo te . . . TEXT 11; (Mc1)

DE MYSTERIIS SACRI BAPTISMATIS. In illo officio primum paganus catechumenus fit accedens ad baptismum . . . TEXT 9; (Ei; Mu5; S5; V1)

DE ORDINE AD FIDEM VENIENTIUM QUORUM PRIMUS GRADUS EST CATECHUMENORUM, SECUNDUS CONPETENTIUM, TERTIUS BAPTIZATORUM. DE CATECHUMENIS. ISIDORUS. Catechumeni sunt qui primum de gentilitate veniunt . . . varios idolorum. DE EXSUFFLATIONE. CELESTINI PAPAE . . . TEXT 4; (M; P6; V1)

DE SACRAMENTIS ECCLESIAE. Sunt autem sacramenta ecclesiae

baptismum (baptisma) et chrisma, corpus et sanguis . . . TEXT 44; (Mu15; W4)

DE SACRAMENTO BAPTISMATIS. Albinus magister filio carissimo Oduino presbitero . . . in illo officio. Primo paganus catechumenus fit accedens ad baptismum . . . TEXT 9; (Ei; P17; P18; S5; Mu12; Mu13)

DE SACRO BAPTISMO. Primo paganus catechumenus fit accedens ad baptismum . . . TEXT 9; (Be)

DE SCRUTINIO. Scrutinium a scrutando dicitur . . . TEXT 12; (Sf; Lb)

DE SYMBOLO. Symbolum autem sic, 'Credo in Deum . . . TEXT 23; (Mu7)

DE VERBIS GRAECIS BAPTISTERII QUOMODO VERTANTUR IN LATINUM. Baptizo te, hoc est intingo te. Electus, a Deo coronatus . . . TEXT 11; (B1; E; H; Lo2; Mc2; Mu5; W1)

DE VERBIS GRAECIS BAPTISTERII QUOMODO VERTANTUR IN LATINUM. Item querendum est quid sit scrutinium. Scrutinium a scrutando dictum est . . . TEXT 12; (B4)

Dispositis nonnullis Differentiarum sententiis, deinceps sacramentorum aecclesiasticorum distinctio subiciatur . . . TEXT 7; (Sp1)

Domino Christianissimo et gloriosissimo Carolo imperatori, felicissimo, augusto. Praecipere nobis dignati estis ut aut per nostra scripta aut per nos ipsos cognoscatis . . . TEXT 25; (P3)

Domino meo Karolo serenissimo imperatori augusto a Deo coronato magno et pacifico regi Francorum et Langobardorum ac patricio Romanorum. Gratias etenim agimus . . . Primitus enim paganus catechumenus fit . . . TEXT 41; (Br1; Br3; Mu15; W4)

Domino, sacrae religionis non minus merito quam dignitate conspicuo, Odoni . . . TEXT 32; (Ba1)

Filio carissimo Adoino (Oduino) presbitero, salutem. Et quia divina . . . in illo officio. Primo paganus catechumenus fit accedens ad baptismum . . . TEXT 9; (Au)

Gloriosissime imperator, innotescere magnitudini vestrae praesumpsimus nos servi vestri, Magnus scilicet et ceteri compares mei . . . TEXT 15; (P19)

Gloriosissimo et excellentissimo augusto a Deo coronato Karolo serenissimo; vita salusque perpetua. Domine mi, Christianissime imperator, misistis ad servulum vestrum inquisitiones . . . TEXT 23; (Fr; S5; Sp2; St; V6)

Haec est epistola quam ad aures domni imperatoris direximus . . . TEXT 53 (unid. MS)

Haec sunt causae quas domnus imperator augustus nobis ad utilitatem semper sanctae ecclesiae per sacram suam mandavit epistolam . . . TEXT 18 (unid. MS)

I. De ordine baptisterii qualiter unusquisque presbiter scit . . . TEXT 14; (Co2)

I. Primitus paganus catechumenus fit accedens ad baptismum . . . TEXT 9; (S3)

IDEM DE BAPTISMO AD KAROLUM AUGUSTUM. Gloriosissimo et excellentissimo augusto a Deo coronato Karolo . . . TEXT 23; (Ei)

Ideo primum catechumenus efficitur qui baptizandus est . . . TEXT 17

IN DEI NOMINE PAUCA DE MISTERIIS ET OFFICIIS SACRI BAP-TISMATIS SICUT A SANCTIS PATRIBUS TRADITUM EST INCI-PIUNT. In illo officio primo paganus catechumenus fit accedens ad bap-tismum . . . TEXT 9; (Mi2)

In illo officio primum catechumenus fit accedens ad baptismum . . . TEXT 9; (Mi1; S6)

In nomine Patris et Filii et Spiritus Sancti Karolus serenissimus augustus a Deo coronatus . . . TEXT 14; (Sp1; P7; unid. MS)

INCIPIT DE BAPTISMI OFFICIO. Ac misticis sensibus eorumque auc-toribus nominatim designatis et de ordine venientium ad fidem eiusdem-que misterii. De catechumenis. Ysidori in Libro officiorum. Catechumeni sunt . . . TEXT 2; (No)

INCIPIT DE BAPTISMO ET OMNI EIUS ORDINE IUXTA IN-DAGINEM CATHOLICORUM. CAP. I. Baptismi sacramentum si pri-ma repetens ab origine pandam baptizavit Moyses . . . TEXT 8; (M; V1)

INCIPIT DE REGULA FIDEI. YSIDORUS. Post apostolorum sym-bolum haec est certissima fides quam doctores nostri tradiderunt . . . TEXT 6; (B2; Mu1; S4)

INCIPIT EXPOSITIO SUPER SIGNACULUM ET BAPTISMUM. Respicere, videre vel considerare . . . TEXT 24; (Vd)

INCIPIT INTERROGATIO KAROLI SERENISSIMI AUGUSTI AD AMALHERUM (AMALARIUM) EPISCOPUM. In nomine Patris et Filii . . . TEXT 14; (Ar)

Incipit Liber iii de officio et ordine baptisterii . . . INTERROGATIO. Ubi primum inchoavit baptismi sacramentum? Responsio. Baptismi sacramentum si prima repetens . . . TEXT 8; (Mu11)

INCIPIT REGULA FIDEI. YSIDORUS. Post apostolorum symbolum haec est certissima fides . . . TEXT 6; (Mu11)

INCIPIUNT CAPITULA CUR INFANS CATECHUMENUS EFFICITUR. I. Quid sit catechumenus? II. Quur exsufflatur? . . . TEXT 16; (A12)

INCIPIUNT CAPITULA DE BAPTISMO. I. Cur infans catechumenus efficitur . . . TEXT 16; (Mu6)

INCIPIUNT CAPITULA. I. Cur infans catechumenus efficitur . . . TEXT 16; (Mu10; V6; Mu14)

INCIPIUNT QUESTIONES DE RUDIMENTIS CATECHUMENORUM VEL EORUM QUI AD GRATIAM BAPTISMI DIVINA INSPIRANTE CLEMENTIA VOCANDI SUNT. INTERROGATIO. Primum quero a te quare catechumenus vocetur et qua lingua dicatur? Responsio. Graeca . . . TEXT 55; (Vi5)

INTERROGATIO KAROLI IMPERATORIS. In nomine . . . TEXT 14; (Z1)

INTERROGATIO. Baptismum quid est? (Resp.) Baptismum Graece, tinctio Latine interpretatur et sicut in tribus testibus stat omne verbum . . . TEXT 39; (Lo1; Mo; Mp2)

Interrogatio. Catechumenus quare dicitur? Responsio. Catechismus Graece, doctrina dicitur sive instructio . . . TEXT 48; (Vi4)

Interrogatio. Cur paganus catechumenus fit vel quid sit catechumenus? Responsio. Catechumenus Graecae . . . TEXT 54; (Or)

Interrogatio. Dic mihi, pro quid baptizas? Responsio. Pro omnia peccata que committuntur in mundum . . . TEXT 49; (A13)

Interrogatio. Pro (Propter) quid baptizas? Responsio. Pro (Propter) omnia peccata que committuntur in mundum . . . TEXT 49; (A11; Es2; P16; S1)

INTERROGATIO. Quaerendum namque est, quid sit scrutinium . . . TEXT 12; (P5)

Interrogatio. Quare in faciem illius a sacerdote exsufflatur . . . TEXT 55; (P16)

Interrogatio. Quare nomina eorum qui catechizandi sunt ab acolito describuntur . . . TEXT 50; (Ba2; Es2; Vc)

Interrogatio. Quid baptizas? Responsio. Pro omnibus peccatis que committuntur . . . TEXT 49; (F3)

INTERROGATIO [ ? ]. Quid sit catechumenus, vel quare sit infans baptizatus, vel . . . TEXT 52 (Vs)

Interrogatio. Quot et quibus modis constat officium baptismatis et quid prius agere debet . . . TEXT 40; (Mp2)

ISIDORUS. DE REGULA FIDEI. Post apostolorum symbolum haec est certissima fides . . . TEXT 6; (Sp1)

[I.] Isidorus. Primus gradus est catechumenorum, ii conpetentium . . . TEXT 3

INTERROGATIO. Ubi primum inchoavit baptismi sacramentum . . . TEXT 8; (Mu1)

'Ite', inquit Iesus discipulis suis . . . TEXT 1; (P7)

ITEM ALIA CAPITULA SACERDOTIBUS. I. De ordine baptisterii qualiter unusquisque presbiter scit vel intellegit vel qualiter primo infans caticuminus efficitur . . . TEXT 14; (V3)

ITEM ALIA EXPOSITIO DE EADEM RE. QUERENDUM NOBIS CUR ILLE QUI AD BAPTISMI GRATIAM VENIT PRIUS CATECHUMENUS EFFICITUR. Ideo primum catechumenus efficitur qui baptizandus est ut non rudis nec neofitus . . . TEXT 17; (Tr1)

ITEM ALIE INTERROGATIONES. CAP. I. INTERROGATUR. Quid est baptismum vel quare dicitur? Responsio. Baptismum est per gratiam Spiritus Sancti in melius inmutatur, id est de peccatis ad indulgentiam . . . TEXT 57; (P16)

ITEM DE BAPTISMO OFFICIOQUE EIUS AUCTORIBUS NOMINATIM VENIENTIUM AD FIDEM. 'Oratio': quasi oris ratio . . . TEXT 43; (unid. MS)

ITEM DE BAPTISMO. Cur primo infans catechumenus efficiatur vel qui sit catechumenus? . . . TEXT 51; (P4)

Item querendum est quid sit scrutinium. Scrutinium a scrutando dictum est (dicitur) . . . TEXT 12; (B1; Lo2; E; H; Mc1; Mc2; Mu5; T; W1; W2)

ITEM. RATIO DE SACRO BAPTISMATIS. Primo paganus catechumenus fit accedens ad baptismum . . . TEXT 9; (M; V1; Vi5)

ITEM. TRADITIO BAPTISTERII. Primo paganus, postea catechumenus, fit, accedens ad baptismum . . . TEXT 9; (unid. MS)

ITERUM INCIPIT EXPOSITIO DE COMPETENTIBUS. Sacris sacerdotibus . . . TEXT 30; (V3)

Karolus serenissimus augustus a Deo coronatus . . . TEXT 14; (Vi1; Zw)

LIBER SANCTI HIERONYMI DE CHRISTIANITATE . . . Quomodo infantes catechumeni efficiuntur antiquus mos servatur . . . TEXT 16; (F1)

O serenissime adque piissime auguste, praecepit nobis dignitas vestra aut per vestra scripta aut per nos ipsos cognoscatis qualiter nos et suffraganei nostri doceamus . . . TEXT 28; (Or)

Omnipotens sempiterne Deus Pater Domini nostri Iesu Christi . . . TEXT 31

'Oratio': quasi oris ratio eo quod ex ore et ratione procedit . . . TEXT 43; (Me; Z2)

ORATIONES ET PRECES SUPER ELECTUS DEI AD CATECHUMENUM FACIENDUM. Omnipotens sempiterne Deus Pater Domini nostri Iesu Christi . . . TEXT 31; (L)

ORDO DE CATECHIZANDIS RUDIBUS VEL QUID SINT SINGULA QUAE GERUNTUR. Primo ergo in catechizandis rudibus apostolicum oportet intueri sermonem . . . TEXT 35; (Mu2; Mu3)

ORDO DE CATECHIZANDIS RUDIBUS VEL QUID SINT SINGULA QUAE GERUNTUR IN SACRAMENTO BAPTISMATIS: EX DIVERSIS SANCTORUM DICTUS PATRUM EXCERPTA TESTIMONIA. Prima ergo in catechizandis rudibus . . . TEXT 36; (Ro)

ORDO DE VERBIS GRECIS BAPTISTERII QUOMODO VERTANTUR IN LATINUM. Baptizo te, . . . TEXT 11; (Vi2; Vi7; W2)

ORDO VEL BREVIS EXPLANATIO DE CATECHIZANDIS RUDIBUS. Primo ergo in catechizandis rudibus apostolicum oportet intueri sermonem . . . TEXT 34; (Vi6)

Piissimo ac Christianissimo gloriosoque principi a Deo coronato et conservato pacifico victori ac triumphatori serenissimo et perpetuo augusto domno Karolo magno imperatori atque Romanum gubernanti imperium, Maxentius . . . TEXT 33; (Mu8)

Post apostolicam certissima fides quam magistri ecclesiarum crediderunt . . . ex Patre et Filio procedentem. Filium a Patre nascendo . . . TEXT 29

Post apostolorum symbolum haec est certissima fides quam doctores nostri tradiderunt . . . ex Patre et Filio procedentem. ITEM IN OMELIIS SANCTI AUGUSTINI . . . TEXT 6

Primitus enim paganus catechumenus fit, id est audiens; scilicet ut unum agnoscens Dominum, relinquat errores varios idolorum . . . TEXT 27; (An; P10; P21)

Primitus namque interrogandi sunt, quid est baptismum vel qua dicitur lingua? Responsio. De baptismi autem misterio nos ita intellegimus . . . TEXT 19; (Mo)

Primo ergo in catechizandis rudibus apostolicum oportet intueri sermonem . . . Non unus autem atque idem in omnibus catechizandis rudibus doctrinae ordo observandus est . . . TEXT 36

Primo ergo in catechizandis rudibus apostolicum oportet intueri sermonem . . . tractaverunt doctores. Credo in Deum Patrem . . . TEXT 34

Primo ergo in catechizandis rudibus apostolicum oportet intueri sermonem . . . tractaverunt doctores, beatus scilicet Athanasius . . . TEXT 35

Primo paganus catechumenus fit accedens ad baptismum ut renunciet maligno spiritui et omnibus eius damnosis pompis . . . TEXT 9

Primum paganus catechumenus fit, id est audiens, unum agnoscens Deum accedens ad baptismum . . . TEXT 59; (W4)

Primum Moyses baptizavit in mare . . . TEXT 21

Primum quero a te quare catechumenus vocetur et qua lingua dicatur? Responsio. Greca . . . TEXT 55

Primum sacramentum est quod Graece dicitur baptismum . . . TEXT 46; (P20)

[I.] Primus gradus est catechumenorum, nam catechumenus Graece, Latine dicitur auditor . . . TEXT 42

Pro quid baptizas? Pro omnia peccata quae committuntur in mundum . . . TEXT 49; (L)

Qualiter catechizas infantem qui baptizandus est? Primum doceo ut credat, id est instruo fidem . . . TEXT 26; (A13)

Querendum est quid sit scrutinium. Scrutinium a scrutando dictum est . . . TEXT 12; (Ft)

QUESTIONES DE ORDINE BAPTISMI. Quia infantes catechumeni efficiuntur antiquus mos servatur . . . TEXT 16; (P2)

Quid est baptismum vel quare dicitur? Responsio. Baptismum est per gratiam Spiritus Sancti in melius inmutatur, id est de peccatis ad indulgentiam . . . TEXT 57

Quid sit catechumenus, vel quare sit infans baptizatus, vel quare trina mersio sit in baptismo, aut quare ponitur sal in ore . . . TEXT 52

Quot et quibusmodis constat officium baptismatis et quid prius agere debet ille qui baptizat . . . TEXT 40; (Lo1; Mo)

Quur . . . (see "Cur")

RATIO DE SACRO BAPTISMI. Primo paganus catechumenus fit accedens ad baptismum . . . TEXT 9; (B2; Mu1; Sp1)

RECAPITULATIO. Cur catechumenus infans efficitur? . . . TEXT 5; (Mull)

RECAPITULATIO. Cur primo paganus catechumenus fit . . . TEXT 9; (Mull)

Religiosae in Christo conversationis vestrae per illum electum pontificem laudabilem audiens . . . fas esse arbitramur. Primo paganus catechumenus fit accedens ad baptismum . . . TEXT 9; (P8; S1; V5; Vi3)

Respicere, videre vel considerare . . . TEXT 24

RESPONSIO AMALARII EPISCOPI. Gloriosissimo . . . TEXT 23; (Z1)

RESPONSIO AMALHERI (AMALARII) EPISCOPI AD KAROLUM IMPERATOREM. Gloriosissime et excellentissime augusto . . . TEXT 23; (Ar)

RESPONSIO LEIDRADI ARCHIEPISCOPI. Precipere nobis dignati estis ut aut per nostra scripta aut per nos . . . TEXT 25; (P12)

Reverentissimo atque charissimo fratri Iohanni episcopo, Theodulphus, salutem. Preceptum tuum, vir venerabilis . . . TEXT 16; (Lg; P14; Tr1)

Reverentissimo atque charissimo fratri Magno episcopo, Theodulfus, salutem. Praeceptum tuum, vir venerabilis . . . TEXT 16; (Mp1; P13; V2; unid. MS)

Reverentissimo atque charissimo fratri. Peregi, et si non sollerti efficacia plena tamen obedientia . . . TEXT 16; (Lo1; Ox)

Sacris sacerdotibus in Christo omnibus diocesi nostrae digne militantibus, Iesse, humilis episcopus . . . TEXT 30; (F2; P17; unid. MS)

Scimus enim omnes homines sub iugo peccati teneri ab ipso articulo nativitatis . . . TEXT 23; (An; P10; P21)

Scrutinium a scrutando dictum est . . . TEXT 12; (Vi2; Vi7)

Sicut enim de Domino nostro Iesu Christo in actionibus apostolorum scriptum est quod post passionem . . . TEXT 16; (Mu10; Mu14)

Sunt autem sacramenta ecclesiae baptismum . . . TEXT 44; (Sp1)

XXVIII. DESCRIPTIO SCRUTINII. Scrutinium a scrutando . . . TEXT 12; (B3)

YSIDORUS . . . (see "Isidorus")

# List of Contributors

Donald A. Bullough, Professor of Medieval History at the University of St. Andrews, Scotland, is probably best known for his monograph *The Age of Charlemagne* which has passed through several editions and has been translated into French, German, and Italian. He is one of the editors of *The Study of Medieval Records: Essays in Honour of Kathleen Major* (1971) and has contributed to many journals. Among them are *Deutsches Archiv, English Historical Review, Le Moyen Age,* Papers of the British School at Rome, *Past and Present,* and the Settimane di studio del Centro Italiano di Studi sull' Alto Medioevo.

John J. Contreni, Professor of History at Purdue University, published in 1978 *The Cathedral School of Laon from 850 to 930: Its Manuscripts and Masters.* He has also translated Pierre Riché's *Education and Culture in the Barbarian West from the Sixth through the Eighth Century* (1978). The Carolingian revival of studies is the theme of several among his many articles which were published in the *Catalogus translationum et commentariorium, Le Moyen Age, Speculum, Studi medievali, Revue bénédictine,* and in essay collections such as *Jean Scot Erigène* (ed. R. Roques, 1977), *Die Bedeutung der Iren für Mission und Kultur im frühmittelalterlichen Europa* (in press); *Insular Latin Studies: Latin Texts and Manuscripts of the British Isles, 550–1066* (ed. W. Herren, 1981); and *Renaissances before the Renaissance: The Cultural Revivals of Late Antiquity and the Middle Ages* (ed. W. Treadgold, 1982).

The Rev. Edouard Jeauneau is Directeur de Recherche at the Centre National de la Recherche Scientifique, Paris, and Senior Fellow of the Pontifical Institute of Mediaeval Studies in Toronto. Among his publications are *La Philosophie médiévale,* a third edition of which was published in 1975 and which was translated into many languages, including Portuguese, Spanish, Arabic, and Japanese. *Guillaume de Conches, 1080–ca. 1150: Glosae super Platonem* (1965) and *Entretiens sur la renaissance du douzième siècle* (1965), as well as *Lectio philosophorum, recherches sur l'Ecole de Chartres* (1973), are among his writings dealing with the intellectual life of the twelfth century. His most recent publications as well as his current research focus on John Scottus Eriugena: *Joannes Scotus Eriugena, Commentaire sur l'évangile de Jean* (1972); *Homélie sur le prologue de Jean, Vox spiritualis aquilae* (1969); *Quatre thèmes érigéniens* (1978).

Susan A. Keefe is a Mellon Fellow at the California Institute of Technology where she teaches in the Humanities Division. She completed her undergraduate studies in Classics and History under Edward Peters, at the University of Pennsylvania, where she was elected to Phi Beta Kappa. Her doctoral work was done at the Centre for Medieval Studies at the University of Toronto, where she studied with Roger Reynolds, Edouard Jeauneau, Leonard Boyle, and Peter Brown, and where she won a Mary Beatty Fellowship and a Deutscher Akademischer Austauschdienst Scholarship.

Dominic J. O'Meara, Associate Professor in the School of Philosophy at the Catholic University of America, concentrated his research on Plotinus, witness his monograph, *Structures hiérarchiques dans la pensée de Plotin,* which he published in 1975, as well as several articles. Among them are contributions to *Mnemosyne, Phronesis,* and *Dionysius,* as well as to *The Rediscovery of Gnosticism,* edited by B. Layton (1980). Professor O'Meara is the editor of two essay volumes, *Studies in Aristotle* (1981) and *Neoplatonism and Christian Thought* (1981). Eriugena was also the subject of two of D. J. O'Meara's earlier publications: "L'Investigation et les investigateurs dans le *De divisione naturae* de Jean Scot Erigène," in *Jean Scot Erigène,* edited by R. Roques (1977), and "The Concept of *Natura* in John Scottus Eriugena," *Vivarium* (1981).

Roger E. Reynolds, Senior Fellow at the Pontifical Institute of Mediaeval Studies, Toronto, is well known for his monograph, *The Ordinals of Christ from their Origins to the Twelfth Century* (1978), and articles that are evidence of his outstanding knowledge of early medieval manuscripts of theological and canonical treatises and compilations. He is a specialist in liturgical studies and has contributed to journals such as *Revue bénédictine, Speculum, Mediaeval Studies, Bulletin of Medieval Canon Law,* and *Studia Gratiana.*

Uta-Renate Blumenthal, the editor of this volume, is Associate Professor of History at the Catholic University of America as well as Director of Early Christian Studies and of the Program in Medieval and Byzantine Studies. Apart from articles, she has published *The Early Councils of Pope Paschal II (1100–1110)* (1978) and *Der Investiturstreit* (1982).

# Index of Names

Abelard, Peter, 64
Adelbert, 67
Ademar of Chabannes, 192 n.
Ælbert, 16, 22, 26
Aethelred, King, 22 n.
Æthildrytha, Queen, 68
Agapitus (pope), 74
Agobard of Lyons, 58
Akeley, T. C., 41 n., 48 n.
Alan of Lille, 151 n., 166 n.
Alcuin, 1–69, 73 n., 74 n., 77, 78, 83,
    84, 85 n., 86 n., 88, 90, 91, 92 n.,
    93 n., 94, 98, 132, 133, 153 n., 154,
    155, 156 n., 158 n., 160, 161–62,
    163, 172, 173, 184, 185 n., 186 n.,
    194, 197 n., 203
Alonso, Joaquín M., 148 n.
Altfrid, 16 n., 18 n.
Amalarius of Metz (archbishop of Trier),
    4, 5, 7, 26, 47 n., 125, 132, 171 n.,
    173, 188 n., 189, 190 n., 196,
    197 n., 207
Ambrose, Saint, 23, 25, 85, 86, 105,
    178, 182
Ambrosius Autpertus, 57 n.
Anastasius (librarian of the Holy See),
    140–41
Anders, G., 160 n.
Andrews, Lancelot, 13
Andrieu, Michel, 41 n., 42 n., 112 n.,
    126 n., 179 n., 183 n.
Angelomus of Luxeuil, 82 n., 84, 87, 88,
    89, 90 n., 93 n., 95
Angilmodus (bishop of Soissons), 202
Anselm, Saint, 13, 153 n., 166 n.
Apuleius, 36
Aristotle, 153, 154, 155, 156–57, 161,
    163, 165 n.
Arno (archbishop of Salzburg), 16 n.,
    20 n., 42–43, 44, 45, 49, 67, 68,
    203, 207 n.
Arnobius the Younger, 56
Athanasius, Saint, 50, 118
Augustine, Saint, 6 n., 9, 17, 19, 23, 27,
    28, 30, 39, 40, 41 n., 42, 44, 52,
    53 n., 56 n., 59, 60, 61, 62, 63, 85,
    86, 88, 90, 91, 97 n., 105, 118,
    144–47, 149, 153 n., 154, 155, 160,
    161–62, 163, 178, 182, 204
Autenrieth, Johanne, 116 n.

Bailey, R. N., 21 n.
Baldo, 24 n., 28, 106
Bardy, Gustave, 98 n.
Barnabas, 118
Barré, H., 13 n., 57 n., 66 n.
Basil of Caesarea, 138
Baturich of Regensburg, 50 n.
Beatus of Liébana, 51 n., 215
Bede, 2, 6, 11, 18 n., 26, 59, 60, 61, 62,
    67–68, 69, 74, 77 n., 81, 82 n., 87,
    88, 130, 131, 179
Beierwaltes, Werner, 154 n., 164 n., 166 n.
Bellator, 86
Belloni, Annalisa, 180 n.
Benedict of Aniane, 24, 26, 27, 29, 47 n.,
    48, 57, 67
Beornred of Sens, 53 n.
Berengaudus of Ferrières, 90 n.
Berschin, Walter, 138 n.
Bieler, Ludwig, 76 n.
Bischoff, Bernhard, 11 n., 13 n., 14 n.,
    15 n., 19 n., 20 n., 24 n., 26 n., 33 n.,
    43 n., 45 n., 47 n., 49 n., 61 n.,
    64 n., 65 n., 67 n., 77 n., 85 n.,
    92 n., 94–95, 96 n., 101, 104 n.,
    106 n., 107 n., 115 n., 116, 117 n.,
    118, 119 n., 131 n., 135 n., 137 n.,
    138 n., 170, 172, 177, 204 n.
Bishop, Edmund, 7 n., 10, 11 n., 12 n., 13
Bishop, T. A. M., 126 n., 137 n.
Blancidius, 24, 26
Boethius, 18, 36, 153 n., 155, 156,
    157 n., 158 n.
Boniface, Saint, 11, 170
Bouhot, Jean-Paul, 44, 45, 169 n.,
    171 n., 180 n.
Bourque, E., 64 n.
Brennan, Mary, 137 n.
Brommer, Peter, 169 n.

Brown, Virginia, 134 n.
Bruckner, A., 61 n.
Brunhölzl, Franz, 75 n., 78 n., 98 n.
Burchard (bishop of Worms), 135
Burn, A. R., 45 n.
Byrhtferth of Ramsey, 8 n., 34

Campbell, J. J., 7 n.
Candidus (pupil of Alcuin), 24, 25, 31, 37
Capelle, B., 8 n., 9
Cappuyns, Maïeul, 94 n., 137 n., 142,
    143, 161 n., 163 n.
Carey, Frederick M., 94 n.
Cassian, 118
Cassiodorus, 18-21, 25, 26, 74, 142
Celestine, 178
Chadwick, N. K., 10 n.
Chalcidius, 26
Charlemagne, 5, 13, 15, 16, 35 n., 39,
    46, 50, 54, 63, 75, 76, 77, 85, 90,
    99, 100, 137-38, 170-71, 173, 174-75,
    178, 182, 185 n., 186 n., 189, 190,
    191, 193, 196, 197 n., 198, 199 n.,
    202, 207, 212, 213
Charles the Bald, 76, 77, 138-39, 140,
    141, 149
Chavasse, A., 52 n.
Christian of Stablo, 84, 87, 92, 95,
    96, 98 n.
Cicero, 28 n., 89, 156
Claudianus Mamertus, 23, 25, 28-30
Claudius of Turin, 80 n., 81, 82 n., 83,
    86 n., 87, 88, 89 n., 91 n., 98 n.
Clement, 118
Coccia, Edmondo, 94 n.
Columbanus, Saint, 103
Constantinescu, Radu, 4 n., 5 n., 6 n.,
    7-8, 9 n., 12 n., 13 n., 18 n.
Contreni, John J., 112 n., 116 n.,
    117 n., 128 n.
Courcelle, P., 29 n.
Courtine, J. F., 154 n.
Cristiani, Marta, 72 n.
Cuthbert, 2
Cyprian, 178, 180 n.
Cyril, 50

Dahlhaus-Berg, Elisabeth, 32 n., 36 n.,
    37 n., 41 n., 45 n., 78 n., 79,
    171 n., 174 n.
Dal Pra, Mario, 161 n., 163 n.
D'Alverny, Marie Thérèse, 73 n.
Daniélou, Jean, 147 n.

Defensor of Ligugé, 85
Delisle, Léopold, 51 n.
Dekkers, Eligius, 131 n.
De Lubac, Henri, 73 n.
Des Cordes, Jean, 186 n.
Deseille, Placide, 147 n.
Deshusses, J., 48 n., 65 n., 66, 67 n.
De Thou, Jacques-Auguste, 186 n.
Devisse, Jean, 186 n.
Dräseke, Johannes, 144 n.
Dructeramnus, Abbot, 81 n., 83 n.
Duchesne, L., 10 n.
Duclow, Donald F., 167 n.
Dümmler, Ernst, 54, 58, 84 n.
Duncan, A. A. M., 10 n.
Dungal of Pavia, 80 n.

Eanbald II, Archbishop, 8
Eddius, 2
Egbert (archbishop of York), 3, 4, 5
Elipand (archbishop of Toledo), 9 n.,
    38 n., 39, 49, 50, 58, 65
Ellard, G., 41 n., 48 n., 64 n., 66 n.
Epiphanius of Salamis, 138
Eric (count of Friuli), 24
Eriugena, John Scottus, 74 n., 76, 80 n.,
    82 n., 83, 94, 97, 137-49, 151-67
Eucherius of Lyon, 79, 85
Eugippius, 85
Euphemius, 93
Eusebius, 118
Evans, G. R., 166 n.

Fastrada, Queen, 13
Faustus of Riez, 56 n.
Felix (bishop of Urgel), 39, 49-56, 58,
    59 n., 65
Férotin, M., 65 n.
Fischer, Bonifatius, 59 n., 60 n., 77 n.,
    78 n., 79 n.
Fleckenstein, J., 47 n.
Florus of Lyons, 82, 87
Fortin, E. L., 29 n.
Fortunatianus, 84
Fournier, Paul, 101, 105 n., 110, 111,
    112 n., 113 n., 115, 122 n., 127, 134
Framegaudus, 13 n.
Fransen, Gérard, 135 n.
Frantzen, Allen J., 102 n., 105
Franz, Adolph, 125 n.
Freculphus (bishop of Lisieux), 81 n.,
    82 n., 84, 87 n., 90
Freeman, Ann, 24 n., 31, 32 n., 33,
    35, 79 n.

Fridugis, 67
Fridurichus (bishop of Utrecht), 93 n.
Frobenius, 58
Fulgentius, 56 n.

Gaar, Aemilius, 131 n.
Gamber, Klaus, 11 n., 67 n.
Gamer, Helena, 122 n.
Ganshof, F. L., 77 n.
Ganz, David, 5 n.
Garnier of Rochefort, 96 n.
Gaseus, 118
Gaskoin, C. J. B., 2 n., 51 n., 55 n.,
    56 n., 63 n.
Gennadius, 27
Gersh, Stephen, 146 n., 157 n.
Gibson, M., 18 n.
Gisla (sister of Charlemagne), 16, 59,
    60, 61, 90–91, 95–96
Glauche, Günter, 72 n.
Godman, Peter, 62 n.
Goetz, Georg, 96 n.
Gottschalk of Orbais, 26 n., 27 n.,
    63, 83
Gregory, Tullio, 148 n.
Gregory I (pope), 14, 48, 60, 65, 85, 88,
    105, 118, 178
Gregory of Nazianzus, 53 n., 105, 118,
    141, 146
Gregory of Nyssa, 138–49, 160
Guarnarius, 27

Hadot, P., 18 n., 63 n.
Hadrian, Pope, 32 n., 35 n., 64, 65
Haimo of Auxerre, 80 n., 83, 96, 98
Halitgar of Cambrai, 100, 124
Hanssens, Jean Michel, 125, 207 n.
Hariulf, 4 n.
Hauck, Albert, 53
Heil, W., 2 n., 49 n., 50 n., 51 n., 52 n.,
    53 n., 55 n., 56 n., 58, 59 n., 63 n.
Heiric of Auxerre, 98 n.
Hellmann, S., 117 n.
Hemmerdinger-Iliadou, D., 12 n.
Herren, Michael, 119 n.
Hesyschius, 88
Hilary, 85
Hildebald (archbishop of Cologne),
    47 n., 207
Hilduin (abbot of Saint-Denis), 84, 140,
    154, 160 n.
Hincmar of Laon, 116
Hincmar of Reims, 77, 83

Hitto (bishop of Freising), 44, 45 n., 204 n.
Hohler, C., 8, 12 n., 64 n.
Hrabanus Maurus. *See* Rabanus Maurus
Hughes, K., 10 n.
Humbertus (bishop of Würzburg), 84,
    86, 93 n.

Ildefonsus (bishop of Toledo), 8, 57 n.
Inguanez, Maurus, 126 n.
Irblich, Eva, 28 n., 47 n.
Irene (Byzantine empress), 138
Isaac, Jean, 155 n.
Isenbert, 24, 51 n.
Isidore of Seville, Saint, 53 n., 74, 79,
    85, 86, 114, 118, 172, 178, 182, 183,
    188, 195, 196, 202, 203, 205, 206,
    213, 216, 217, 218

Jacquin, Maures, 161 n.
Jeauneau, Edouard, 76 n., 77 n., 152 n.
Jeffery, Peter, 123 n.
Jerome, Saint, 17, 18, 42, 55, 77 n., 85,
    88, 90, 91, 92, 96, 105, 118, 139, 179
Jesse (bishop of Amiens), 200, 201 n.,
    217 n.
John of Salisbury, 139
John of Scythopolis, 141 n.
John the Anglo-Saxon (bishop of Salz-
    burg), 106
John the Arch-chanter, 4, 5
John the Deacon, 43, 44 n., 178, 202
Jonas, 2
Jones, L. W., 68 n., 99
Joseph "the Irishman" (pupil of
    Alcuin), 18
Josephus Scottus, 85 n., 86 n., 90 n.,
    91–92, 95
Jungmann, J. A., 18 n., 64 n.
Junilius, 85

Keefe, Susan, 100, 113 n., 120 n., 124 n.
Kelly, J. N. D., 46 n.
Kelly, Joseph F., 92 n.
Kenney, James F., 94 n., 95 n.
Kerff, Franz, 131 n.
Kirchmeyer, J., 12 n.
Koch, Joseph, 146 n.
Kottje, Raymund, 11 n., 100, 103, 104,
    107 n., 124 n., 131 n., 135 n., 169 n.
Kruse, Norbert, 207 n.

Lactantius, 30
Laistner, M. L. W., 73 n., 80 n., 84 n.,
    85 n., 92 n.

Lambot, C., 26 n.
Landau, Peter, 121 n.
Lapidge, Michael, 94 n.
Latchen, 85
Lauer, Philippe, 198 n.
Leclercq, Jean, 73 n., 74 n.
Lehmann, Paul, 76 n.
Leidrad (archbishop of Lyons), 23, 37,
    51 n., 57, 58, 59 n., 170, 171 n.,
    175, 197, 198, 199, 200
Lemarié, J., 6 n.
Le Michel, Anselme, 142
Leo I (pope), 52, 179
Lestocquoy, J., 3 n.
Levison, Wilhelm, 38 n., 85 n.
Liebeschütz, Hans, 160 n.
Lindsay, Wallace M., 96 n.
Liudger (abbot of Werden and bishop of
    Münster), 16, 21, 68 n.
Loew, E. A., 134 n.
Lothair I (king of Germany and Holy Ro-
    man Emperor), 86 n., 89 n., 90, 91 n.
Louis the German, 83 n.
Louis the Pious, 91 n., 99, 140
Löwe, Heinz, 25 n., 44, 45 n.
Lupus of Ferrières, 77 n.
Lutz, Cora E., 155 n.

Maassen, Friedrich, 115
McGinn, Bernard, 161 n., 162 n., 167 n.
McKitterick, Rosamond, 22 n., 45 n.,
    75 n., 85 n., 120 n.
McNally, Robert E., 73 n., 103, 118 n.,
    120 n., 123 n., 126 n.
McNamara, Martine, 118 n.
McNeill, John T., 122 n.
Madec, Goulven, 144 n., 145 n., 153 n.,
    160 n., 163 n., 167 n.
Madoz, J., 56 n.
Magnus (archbishop of Sens), 174, 190,
    191, 192 n., 193, 194
Manitius, Max, 76 n.
Marenbon, J., 18 n., 22 n., 23, 24 n., 25,
    28, 29 n., 36 n., 37 n., 40 n., 155 n.
Martianus Capella, 154, 155, 156, 158 n.,
    160, 162, 163, 164 n.
Martimort, Aimé-Georges, 107 n.
Martinus Hiberniensis, 77, 83, 94
Mathon, M., 25 n.
Maxentius (archbishop of Aquileia),
    202, 217 n.
Maximus the Confessor, 138–49, 154,
    159 n., 160, 165 n.

Mearns, J., 47 n.
Merlette, Bernard, 116
Meyvaert, Paul, 17 n., 31, 32 n., 34 n.,
    36 n., 37 n., 74 n., 78 n., 80 n., 88
Michael the Stammerer (Byzantine em-
    peror), 140
Minio-Paluello, L., 31 n.
Miquel Rosell, F. X., 198 n.
Molin, J.-B., 20 n., 69 n.
Mordek, Hubert, 100, 101, 103, 104,
    106 n., 107 n., 108 n., 109 n., 111,
    112 n., 113, 115, 116 n., 119 n.,
    120 n., 121 n., 122 n., 123 n.,
    124 n., 135 n., 169 n.
Moreau, Joseph, 144 n.
Morin, Germain, 94 n., 192 n., 207 n.

Neff, K., 22 n.
Nestorius, 58
Netzer, H., 120 n.
Nicetas of Remesiana, 44, 45
Noble, Thomas F. X., 75 n., 78 n.
Notker of St. Gall, 5–6, 75, 94 n.
Nürnberger, August J., 110, 121,
    122 n., 126 n.

Odilbert (archbishop of Milan), 178,
    179 n., 189, 190 n.
Odilmannus, 87 n.
Odo (bishop of Beauvais), 202
Oduin, 43, 44, 45, 46, 184, 185 n.
Ohly, F., 61 n.
O'Keefe, Katherine O'Brien, 41 n.
O'Meara, John J., 144 n., 148
Origen, 55
Oswald (Northumbrian king), 3
Otgarius (archbishop of Mainz), 81 n.,
    86 n., 93 n.
Ott, L., 49 n.

Paschasius Radbertus, 74 n., 82 n., 84,
    87, 89, 95
Paterius, 85
Paulinus of Aquileia, 24, 27, 46, 51,
    52 n., 53 n.
Paul the Deacon, 22
Pelagius, 55, 118
Pepin, 77, 99
Perrin, M., 30 n.
Petrus Chrysologus, 52 n.
Plotinus, 145
Polycarp, 13 n.
Porphyry, 145, 155

Proclus, 145
Prudentius, 37, 85 n.
Pseudo-Alcuin, 185 n., 188 n.
Pseudo-Augustine, 79, 156 n.
Pseudo-Dionysius, 138-49, 154, 155-56, 159, 160, 162, 163, 164, 165 n.
Pseudo-Isidore, 116, 122
Pseudo-Melito, 79
Pseudo-Symeon, 34 n.

Rabanus Maurus (abbot of Fulda and archbishop of Mainz), 47 n., 74 n., 75, 81 n., 82, 83, 84, 85 n., 86, 87, 88, 89 n., 90, 91-92, 93, 94 n., 95, 97, 173, 209
Rado, Abbot, 3
Reynolds, Roger E., 169 n., 172, 179 n., 185 n.
Richbod of Trier, 53 n.
Riché, Pierre, 72 n., 73 n., 74 n., 75 n., 92 n., 94 n., 97 n.
Riculf of Mainz, 207 n.
Rochais, H.-M., 118 n.
Roger of Wendover, 34 n.
Roques, René, 145 n., 154 n., 156 n., 159 n., 161 n., 162 n., 164 n.
Rotruda (daughter of Charlemagne), 13, 16, 59, 60, 61, 90-91, 95-96, 138
Rufinus, 12 n.
Russell, Robert, 144 n.

Saffrey, Henri D., 145 n.
Salmon, Pierre, 5 n., 169 n.
Samuel (bishop of Worms), 93 n.
Schaller, D., 18 n., 22 n., 37 n.
Scheffczyk, L., 8 n., 53 n., 56 n., 57 n., 58 n.
Schlieben, R., 21 n.
Schneider, H., 34 n., 47 n.
Schönbach, A. E., 53 n., 59 n., 60 n., 61, 62 n.
Schrimpf, G., 155 n.
Sedulius Scottus, 80 n., 94, 117
Senarius of Ravenna, 43
Sheehy, 101, 102
Sheldon-Williams, Inglis P., 144 n., 156 n., 160 n.
Sicard, Damien, 135 n.
Sieben, H. J., 36, 37, 38 n.
Sigwulf (pupil and companion of Alcuin), 5, 6, 28, 40, 83 n., 84 n.
Silonis, R. L., 167 n.
Smalley, Beryl, 17 n., 73, 74 n.
Somerville, Robert, 131 n.

Spicq, C., 73 n.
Stancliffe, Clare, 94 n.
Stegmüller, Friedrich, 95 n.
Steinmeyer, Elias, 96 n.
Stevens, Wesley, 72 n.
Stock, Brian, 144 n.
Strecker, K., 4 n.
Strunk, O., 6 n.

Theodemirus of Psalmody, Abbot, 81 n., 82 n., 87, 90, 98
Theodulf (bishop of Orléans), 31, 37, 50, 51 n., 78-79, 88, 94, 95, 96, 97, 121, 122, 173, 174, 191
Théry, Gabriel, 138 n., 140 n., 155 n., 156 n.
Thomas Aquinas, Saint, 64, 139
Thompson, David E., 54 n.
Tomasic, Thomas, 167 n.
Trouillard, Jean, 167 n.
Tugwell, S., 7 n.
Tyconius, 149

Udalric of Bamberg, 190 n.
Unterkircher, F., 14 n., 15 n.

Van den Auweele, D., 119 n.
Vezin, Jean, 137 n.
Victorinus, Marius, 18, 63, 84
Virgil, 26
Virgil (abbot-bishop of Salzburg), 106, 119, 123, 126
Vogel, Cyrille, 102 n., 113 n.
Von Balthasar, Hans Urs, 141 n.
Von den Steinen, W., 34 n., 36
Von Hörmann, Walther, 113

Waelken, L., 119 n.
Walahfrid Strabo, 82 n., 86 n., 95
Wallace, M., 154 n.
Wallace-Hadrill, J. M., 35 n.
Wallach, L., 9 n., 25 n., 31, 32, 33, 34 n., 35, 36 n., 37 n., 38, 39 n., 46 n., 55 n., 56 n., 75 n.
Waltcaud (bishop of Liège), 190 n.
Wasserschleben, Hermann, 110, 126 n.
Weiss, Roberto, 138 n.
Weyman, Carl, 127
Wicbod, 85, 98
Wido, Count, 67
Wilfrid, Bishop, 4, 5, 38
Wilmart, André, 18 n., 22 n., 43 n., 44 n., 50 n., 51 n., 68 n., 82 n.
Wormald, F., 47 n.
Wulfad, 94 n.

# Index of Manuscripts

(Note: Since the essay by Susan A. Keefe contains its own list of manuscripts, it has not been indexed.)

Albi, Bibliothèque Rochegude, MS 38: 122
—, MS 38bis: 109, 121, 122, 123, 123 n., 132
—, MS 43 (15): 123
Angers, Bibliothèque municipale, MS 18: 15 n.
—, MS 279: 12 n.

Bamberg, Staatsbibliothek, MS Misc. Patr. 17 (B. II. 10): 4 n.
—, MS Patr. 78 (B. IV. 13): 142
—, MS 127 (B. V. 24): 117
Barcelona, Archivo de la Corona de Aragón, MS Ripoll 105: 109
Barcelona, Biblioteca Universitaria, MS 228: 124
Basel, Universitätsbibliothek, Cod. O II 28: 60 n.
Berlin, Deutsche Staatsbibliothek, MS Diez B. 66: 31 n.
—, Lat. fol. 877: 11 n.
—, MS Phillipps 1651 (Rose no. 24): 41 n.
—, MS Phillipps 1763: 109
Berlin-Dahlem, Stiftung Preuss. Kulturbesitz, MS Hamilton 132: 59 n.
Bernkastel-Kues, St. Nikolaus-Hosp., Bibliothek d. Cusanus-Stiftung, MS 37 (C 14): 117
Brussels, Bibliothèque royale, MS 8654–72: 47 n., 109
Budapest, Országos Széchényi Könyvtár, MS 316: 113

Cambrai, Bibliothèque municipale, MS 679 (619): 104
Cambridge, Corpus Christi College, MS 279: 105, 107, 114
Cambridge, University Library, MS Kk.I.24: 21 n.
Cologne, Dombibliothek, MS 106: 13 n., 15 n., 20 n., 68 n.
—, MS 117: 121
—, MS 210 (Darmst. 2178): 104, 110, 127

Durham, Durham Cathedral, MS B II 33: 19 n., 20 n., 21 n.
Düsseldorf, Heinrich Heine-Institut, MS B.3: 40 n.

Einsiedeln, Stiftsbibliothek, MS 205: 109
El Escorial, MS & I.14: 17 n.
—, MS B.IV.17: 5 n.
—, MS Q.III.10: 124

Fiecht, Stiftsbibliothek, MS 113: 125 n.
Florence, Biblioteca Mediceo-Laurenziana, MS VII sin. 1: 135
—, MS Ashburnham 82 (32) [Cat. 29]: 113
—, MS Calci 11 Archivio della Certosa: 135
Florence, Biblioteca nazionale, MS Ashburnham 54: 13 n.
Florence, Biblioteca Riccardiana, MS 256 (K.III.27): 124
Freiburg, Universitätsbibliothek, MS 8: 116

Gent, Universitätsbibliothek, MS 235: 119 n.
Göttingen, Universitätsbibliothek, MS theol. 99: 26 n.
Graz, Universitätsbibliothek, MS 724: 64 n.
—, MS 1002: 125 n.

Ivrea, Biblioteca capitolare, MS 30: 68 n.
—, MS 106: 7 n.

Karlsruhe, Badische Landesbibliothek, Cod. Aug. XVIII: 47 n., 104
—, Cod. Aug. CXII: 42 n.
—, Cod. Aug. CXXXV: 68 n.

Laon, Bibliothèque municipale, MS 201: 112, 112 n.
—, MS 288: 124

Leningrad, Publichnaya Biblioteka, MS
    Q.v.II.5: 112
London, British Library, MS Add. 37518:
    11 n., 12 n.
—, MS Cott. Tib. A.XV: 33 n.
—, MS Cott. Vesp. A.XIV: 33 n.
—, MS Egerton 1046: 21, 21 n.
—, MS Harl. 208: 16 n.
—, MS Harl. 2965: 14 n.
—, MS Harl. 3034: 122
—, MS Harl. 3060: 12 n.
—, MS Royal 2.A.XX: 46 n.
—, MS Royal 5.E.XIII: 107, 115
—, MS Royal 8.C.III: 126
London, Lambeth Palace Library, MS
    218: 54 n.
Lucca, Biblioteca comunale, MS
    490: 54 n.

Metz, Bibliothèque municipale, MS
    236: 111
—, MS 351: 128
Milan, Biblioteca Ambrosiana, MS F 60
    sup.: 62 n.
—, MS H 150: 54 n.
—, MS I 101 sup.: 47 n.
—, MS O 210 sup.: 17 n.
Montecassino, Biblioteca dell'Abbazia,
    MS 323: 126
Montpellier, Bibliothèque de la Faculté
    de Médecine, MS 387: 126
—, MS 409: 14 n., 15 n.
Monza, Biblioteca capitolare, MS
    e-14/127: 126
Munich, Hauptstaatsarchiv, MS Raritäten-
    Selekt no. 108: 11 n.
Munich, Staatsbibliothek, Clm. 4592:
    106, 108, 110
—, Clm. 6242: 115
—, Clm. 6245: 115
—, Clm. 6324: 45 n.
—, Clm. 6325: 45 n.
—, Clm. 6330: 127
—, Clm. 6407: 24 n., 28 n.
—, Clm. 6433: 118
—, Clm. 6434: 106
—, Clm. 14276: 126 n.
—, Clm. 14392: 123 n.
—, Clm. 14447: 68 n.
—, Clm. 14468: 50 n.
—, Clm. 14508: 121
—, Clm. 14510: 64 n.
—, Clm. 14628: 125 n.

—, Clm. 14727: 43 n.
—, Clm. 14743: 67 n.
—, Clm. 14760: 43 n.
—, Clm. 29410/2: 104

Orléans, Bibliothèque municipale, MS
    116: 113, 122
—, MS 184: 13 n., 14, 14 n., 15 n.,
    107, 113
—, MS 221: 103
Oxford, Bodleian Library, MS Bodl.
    572: 108
—, MS d'Orville 45: 57 n.
—, MS Hatton 42: 103, 107, 128
—, MS Laud. gr. 35: 46 n.

Paris, Bibliothèque de l'Arsenal, MS
    663: 32
Paris, Bibliothèque nationale, MS grec
    437: 140
—, MS lat. 1153: 13 n., 14, 14 n.
—, MS lat. 1248: 126, 129
—, MS lat. 1557: 116
—, MS lat. 1572: 49 n.
—, MS lat. 1804: 41 n.
—, MS lat. 2164: 26 n., 29 n.
—, MS lat. 2316: 111
—, MS lat. 2386: 50 n.
—, MS lat. 2388: 58 n.
—, MS lat. 2390: 27 n., 47 n.
—, MS lat. 2731A: 13 n.
—, MS lat. 2846: 51 n.
—, MS lat. 3182: 104
—, MS lat. 3859: 109
—, MS lat. 5577: 50 n.
—, MS lat. 9430: 66 n.
—, MS lat. 9629: 116
—, MS lat. 10588: 108
—, MS lat. 12012: 119 n.
—, MS lat. 12048: 42 n.
—, MS lat. 12098: 119 n.
—, MS lat. 12154: 18 n.
—, MS lat. 12163: 17 n.
—, MS lat. 12239-41: 19 n.
—, MS lat. 12444: 106, 109 n., 115, 120,
    121, 121 n.
—, MS lat. 13092: 124
—, MS lat. 13373: 43 n.
—, MS lat. 13388: 13 n., 15 n.
—, MS lat. 17296: 6 n.
—, nouvelles acquisitions latines, MS
    1096: 16 n.

—, nouvelles acquisitions latines, MS
2664: 143, 143 n.
Prague, Státní knihovna, Tepla Cod.
1: 131 n.
Princeton, Princeton University, MS
Garrett 169: 20 n., 131 n.

Regensburg, Bischöfliche Zentralbibliothek, Clm. 1: 11 n.
Rheims, Bibliothèque municipale, MS
213: 66 n.
—, MS 385: 50 n., 58 n.
—, MS 438: 68 n.
—, MS 1395: 2 n.
Rome, Biblioteca Vallicelliana, MS
T.XVIII: 134
Rome, Casa dei Padri Maristi, MS A.
II. 1: 24 n., 28 n., 35 n., 36 n., 47 n.
Rouen, Bibliothèque municipale, MS
469 (A.214): 45 n.

Saint Gall, Stiftsbibliothek, MS 40: 123
—, MS 243: 103
—, MS 258: 61 n.
—, MS 675: 109
—, MS 899: 115 n., 116 n.
Stuttgart, Landesbibliothek, MS HB VII
48: 26 n.

Tours, Bibliothèque municipale, MS
184: 66 n.
—, MS 556: 104
Trent, Castel de Buon Consiglio, Cod.
s.n.: 65 n.
Trier, Stadtbibliothek, MS 137/50: 104
Troyes, Bibliothèque municipale, MS
441: 59 n.
—, MS 853: 52 n.
—, MS 1165: 51 n., 54 n.
—, MS 1742: 12, 13 n., 14 n., 15 n., 20 n.

Vatican City, Biblioteca Apostolica
Vaticana, MS Archivio della Basilica
di San Pietro H 58: 135
—, MS Ottob. lat. 6: 135
—, MS Palat. lat. 290: 51 n.
—, MS Palat. lat. 485: 122
—, MS Palat. lat. 973: 115
—, MS Palat. lat. 1719: 24 n., 28 n.
—, MS Reg. lat. 69: 50 n.
—, MS Reg. lat. 192: 52 n.
—, MS Reg. lat. 226: 54 n.
—, MS Reg. lat. 316: 12 n., 41 n.

—, MS Reg. lat. 407: 109, 115
—, MS Reg. lat. 421: 115
—, MS Vat. lat. 650: 47 n.
—, MS Vat. lat. 1349: 134
—, MS Vat. lat. 4162: 135
—, MS Vat. lat. 5756: 18, 18 n.
—, MS Vat. lat. 7207: 24, 24 n., 31, 33 n.
Vesoul, Bibliothèque municipale, MS
73: 122
Vic, Museo Episcopal, Frag. XII: 125 n.
Vienna, Österreichische Nationalbibliothek, MS 424: 115
—, MS 458: 24 n., 28 n.
—, MS 522: 106, 108, 109 n., 110, 111 n.
—, MS 795: 43 n., 49 n., 59 n.
—, MS 808: 20 n., 67 n.
—, MS 966: 24 n., 51 n.
—, MS 997: 62 n.
—, MS 1370: 45 n., 115
—, MS 1861: 35 n., 46, 47 n.
—, MS 2171: 109

Wolfenbüttel, Herzog August Bibliothek,
Cod. Guelf. Gud. 212 (4517): 119 n.
—, Cod. 579 (Helmst. 532): 116
Würzburg, Universitätsbibliothek,
M.p.th.q.31: 105, 110, 111